4/92 $95

D1715670

Stratemeyer
Pseudonyms
and
Series Books

Stratemeyer Pseudonyms and Series Books

An Annotated Checklist of Stratemeyer and Stratemeyer Syndicate Publications

Compiled and Edited
by
Deidre Johnson

GREENWOOD PRESS
WESTPORT, CONNECTICUT • LONDON, ENGLAND

Copyright Acknowledgment

The series listed in this bibliography were created by Edward
Stratemeyer and/or the Stratemeyer Syndicate and all rights to these
series are presently owned by Stratemeyer Syndicate. Stratemeyer
Syndicate gratefully gives its permission to reprint the necessary
annotations.

Library of Congress Cataloging in Publication Data

Johnson, Deidre.
  Stratemeyer pseudonyms and series books.

  Bibliography: p.
  Includes indexes.
  1. Stratemeyer, Edward, 1862-1930—Bibliography.
2. Stratemeyer Syndicate.   3.   Children's stories,
American—Bibliography.   4.   Monographic series—Bibliography.
I. Title.
Z8849.69.J63   [PS3537.T817]   016.813'52   81-23750
ISBN 0-313-22632-6 (lib. bdg.)   AACR2

Library of Congress Catalog Card Number: 81-23750
ISBN: 0-313-22632-6

First published in 1982

Greenwood Press
A division of Congressional Information Service, Inc.
88 Post Road West, Westport, Connecticut 06881

Printed in the United States of America

10 9 8 7 6 5 4 3 2 1

To A.S. and A.S.

CONTENTS

ACKNOWLEDGMENTS

Many people assisted with this bibliography, often by patiently answering numerous questions and volunteering additional information. Dr. John T. Dizer, Jr., supplied much information about Edward Stratemeyer's magazine publications and early books. Julius R. Chenu answered many questions on series books. Edward T. LeBlanc and J. Randolph Cox provided much-needed information on Street & Smith publications. Maurice Owen and Jack Schorr had answers to questions about some hard-to-find series, while Bob Bennett supplied bibliographic information on some of Stratemeyer's Alger serials, and John M. Enright filled in many blank areas about Hardy Boys tie-ins. Special thanks are due to Nancy Axelrad and the Stratemeyer Syndicate for their cooperation and for the information they provided about Stratemeyer Syndicate house names.

Dr. G. B. Cross, Dr. Agnes Perkins, and Dr. Helen Hill provided guidance and encouragement in the early stages of the project, as did Dr. Alethea Helbig, who also sent material on Harriet Adams. Marilyn Brownstein of Greenwood Press answered countless questions and made valuable suggestions about the format. Nancy Whorton Hurd offered moral support throughout the project, as did Pat Pflieger, who also helped with information on the Nugget Library. Special thanks go to my mother, Anita Schlieder, for her help and encouragement.

J. B. Dobkin, University of South Florida Library (Tampa); W. R. DuBois, Northern Illinois University Library; Carolyn W. Field, Free Library of Philadelphia; Janette Fiore, Russel B. Nye Collection, Michigan State University; Gene M. Gressley, American Heritage Center, University of Wyoming; J. Frederic Hanson, University of Missouri Library; Linda Lester, University of Virginia Library; Nathaniel H. Puffer, University of Delaware Library; Karen Rizzo, Cooperative Children's Book Center, Wisconsin; and Wilma R. Slaight, Margaret Clapp Library, Wellesley College, all supplied information about Stratemeyer and Stratemeyer Syndicate holdings. The staff of Wilson Library at the University of Minnesota allowed me to use the OCLC (formerly the Ohio College Library Consortium) system and answered assorted questions. Special thanks are due to Dr. Karen Hoyle and the staff of the Children's Literature Research Collection at the University of Minnesota, where much of the research was accomplished, for their help and patience.

Acknowledgments are also due to several publishers for permission to reprint material from advertisements: Grosset & Dunlap (for Grosset & Dunlap, Barse & Hopkins, Barse & Company, and Cupples & Leon annotations), Condé Nast Publications, Inc. (for Street & Smith material), Doubleday (for Doubleday, Garden City, and George Sully & Company annotations), and William Morrow & Co. (for Lothrop, Lee & Shepard material).

INTRODUCTION: THE PEOPLE BEHIND THE BOOKS

When discussing Edward Stratemeyer and the Stratemeyer Syndicate, it's difficult to avoid "overkill." After all, this is the man and the organization responsible for over thirteen hundred books—fifteen hundred, if dime novels, retitled reprints, and revised editions are included in the count—with sales estimated at 200,000,000 copies, enough books literally to circle the world. This is a writing organization whose works have been translated into fourteen languages; whose American editions have been issued by thirty-eight publishers and illustrated by over one hundred artists; whose series have inspired movies, television series, cartoon shows, comic books, coloring books, gameboards, fan clubs, diaries, calendars, and even a cookbook. In a changing world, the Stratemeyer Syndicate has survived two world wars, a nationwide depression, television and the electronic revolution, two lawsuits, and numerous attacks by librarians and educators. After more than fifty years, new editions in the top Syndicate series still sell over 2,000,000 copies annually, while older editions have become collectors' items. From a $75.00 sale of a magazine serial in 1889 to a six-figure publishing contract in 1979, the history of the series book empire Edward Stratemeyer created can be summed up in one word: success.

The evolution of the Stratemeyer Syndicate has progressed through four stages. The first two, during Edward Stratemeyer's lifetime, could be called the early years and the "golden age." During these years, creativity, variety, and volume provided the impetus needed to launch the Stratemeyer Syndicate and establish it firmly in the series book market. New series were developed annually: from 1912 to 1931, the Syndicate rarely had fewer than twenty-five series in progress at any one time. Every type of series imaginable was offered, from fantasy and science-fiction, to school, career, and travel adventures. If one series failed, another replaced it; if one idea worked, similar series often appeared within the next few years. After Stratemeyer's death in 1930, the Syndicate moved away from this pattern into the next two stages, maintenance and renovation. The juvenile book market was changing, and the number of series—not only by the Stratemeyer Syndicate, but overall—was decreasing. The Syndicate followed the trend, continuing the more popular series, but rarely creating new ones. The number of series dropped, and there was less variety in those remaining. During the "renovation period," some new series, often based on old favorites, were developed. Early volumes in several of the existing series were updated, and new volumes added. Through all four stages, one thing remained constant: the Stratemeyer family's ability to create and maintain successful series.

The Early Years

EDWARD STRATEMEYER

Edward Stratemeyer was born on October 4, 1862, in Elizabeth, New Jersey, a town a few miles south of Newark and roughly fifteen miles west of New York City. His father, Henry Julius Stratemeyer, had emigrated from Germany in 1848, journeying west for the California gold rush of 1849. Several years later, the death of a brother brought Henry to Elizabeth, New Jersey, to help Anna Siegel Stratemeyer, his brother's widow, settle the estate. Henry remained in Elizabeth, later opening a tobacco shop and marrying Anna. They had three children: two sons, Edward and Louis Charles, and a daughter.[1]

Edward attended the public schools in Elizabeth, and after his graduation received private tutoring in literature, composition, and rhetoric[2] before taking a position as a clerk in the tobacco shop, now managed by his half-brother, Maurice.[3] During a slack period in the store, Edward began work on a boys' story, writing the rough draft on sheets of wrapping paper. He submitted the finished manuscript of eighteen thousand words to *Golden Days*, a weekly magazine for boys and girls, published by James Elverson of Philadelphia. The editor responded with a check for $75.00, and "Victor Horton's idea" was serialized in *Golden Days* from November 2 to November 30, 1889.[4]

In 1890 Stratemeyer moved from Elizabeth to Newark, where he opened a stationery store. He acquired a second publisher when Street & Smith, a company specializing in five and ten cent fiction, bought two of his tales about a boy named Match and issued them as dime novels in the Nugget Library in July and August of 1890. Both stories appeared under Stratemeyer's first pseudonym, Ned St. Meyer. *Golden Days* also purchased two Stratemeyer stories, "Captain Bob's secret" and "Alvin Chase's search," serializing the former from April 15 to May 24 under Stratemeyer's name, and the latter from October 11 to December 20 with the pseudonym Ralph Hamilton.[5]

The market for Stratemeyer's stories soon expanded, and the following year Frank Munsey's *Argosy*, a New York weekly for boys, printed "Richard Dare's venture; or, Striking out for himself" and "True to himself; or, Roger Strong's struggle for place." *The Holiday*, another boys' story paper, published "Jack, the inventor; or, The trials and triumphs of a young machinist" the same year, while *Golden Days* serialized "Clearing his name" under Stratemeyer's Ralph Hamilton pseudonym.[6] During this period, Stratemeyer found time not only to write and to manage his stationery store, but also to court Magdalene Baker Van Camp, the daughter of Silas Van Camp, manager for the Fleishmann Yeast Company in Newark, and on March 25, 1891, Edward and Magdalene were married.[7]

The year after his marriage, Stratemeyer sold fourteen dime novels and five magazine stories, more than quadruple his literary output for 1891. Four of the magazine pieces, all boys' success stories, were serialized in Munsey's *Argosy*, two under Stratemeyer's name and two as by Arthur M. Winfield; the fifth story appeared in *Golden Days* with the pseudonym Ralph Hamilton. Street & Smith printed all of the dime novels in three of its series: five in the Nick Carter Library under the pseudonym Nick Carter; five in the New York Five Cent Library with the names Nat Woods, Jim Bowie, Jim Daly, and Tom Ward; and four in the Log Cabin Library with the pseudonym Captain Lew James. As if this were not enough to make 1892 a momentous year, Edward and Magdalene Stratemeyer's first child, Harriet, was born in December.

By this time, Stratemeyer was working regularly for Street & Smith and soon became editor of *Good News*, one of Street & Smith's boys' story papers.[8] As editor, Stratemeyer worked with writers such as James Otis Kaler, who later authored several boys' series and the extremely popular *Toby Tyler*, and Gilbert Patten, who, as Burt L. Standish, wrote the numerous adventures of Frank (and later Dick) Merriwell. Stratemeyer's first encounter with the latter gives some insight into the workings of Street & Smith and the training Stratemeyer acquired there. Patten, who had recently severed his connection with Beadle & Adams, rival publishers, applied to Street & Smith as a possible market for his stories and was sent to Stratemeyer at the *Good News* office. Patten introduced himself and explained that he had written dime novels for Beadle & Adams for some years; after some conversation, Stratemeyer gave him the title of a story and asked him to prepare the opening chapters, commenting that Oliver Optic and Harry Castlemon, both well-known writers, had already tried the title and failed to turn in acceptable material. Patten complied. On returning with the finished chapters, he was dismayed to learn that Stratemeyer was offering only $100 for the story, less than half the price paid by *Argosy*. After some discussion, Stratemeyer raised the price to $150, still considerably less than the $250 Patten had asked, and persuaded him to accept. Although Patten continued to write for Street & Smith, he was never close to Stratemeyer and admitted to being pleased when Arthur Dudley Hall later replaced him as editor of *Good News*.[9] Another writer for Street & Smith, St. George Rathborne, apparently maintained a better relationship with Stratemeyer, for he later worked with the Stratemeyer Syndicate on several series.

In addition to his editorial work, Stratemeyer supplied Street & Smith with four magazine stories and twenty-eight dime novels in 1893. Not surprisingly, the magazine stories all appeared in *Good News*. Three were traditional success and adventure stories published under Stratemeyer's name and the pseudonym Arthur M. Winfield; the fourth, "The electric air and water wizard," published under the pseudonym Emerson Bell, was science fiction, a new area for Stratemeyer. His dime novels again were distributed among three series: eight detective fiction stories in the Nick Carter Library; four tales in the Log Cabin Library written under the pen name Captain Lew James; sixteen stories in the New York Five Cent Library, most of them chronicling the continuing adventures of Gentleman Jack the boxer, Dead Shot Dave, nationwide traveler and gambler, or Jack and Jerry, a pair of hardy bicyclists. Edward Stratemeyer's brother, Louis Charles Stratemeyer, also contributed to the New York Five Cent Library in 1893, writing two "Flip-Up Larry" stories under the pseudonym Louis Tracy and one "Nat Woods" title as by the "author of 'Nat Woods.'"

The year 1894 marked Stratemeyer's entry into hardcover fiction when two of his *Argosy* stories, "Richard Dare's venture" and "Luke Foster's grit," were published by Merriam as the first volumes in the Bound to Succeed and the Ship and Shore series. His work on the dime novel series had stopped, except for occasional titles in the Nick Carter Library, and the bulk of his writing—eight stories—went into *Good News*, which he was still editing. "Reuben Stone's discovery" and "One boy in a thousand," two more stories from *Argosy*, were reprinted in 1895 and added to the Ship and Shore and Bound to Succeed series; at Street & Smith, Stratemeyer wrote seven serials for *Good News* and his last six titles for the Nick Carter Library. Stratemeyer apparently left Street & Smith in 1895, for later that year he began to edit *Young Sports of America* (retitled *Young People of America* on November 3, 1895), a weekly story paper for boys, published in New York by Frank J. Earll.[10] Stratemeyer also provided much of its material: eleven stories from May 1895 to February 1896, embracing a variety of subjects, from the traditional boys' career adventures to outdoor tales focusing on hunting and camping out, along with detective fiction, sports stories, and tales set in the circus and in the theater. Published under his own name and eight pseudonyms, Stratemeyer's stories appeared in almost every issue of *Young Sports of America* for nine months; most of the November and December issues carried three of his serials, all under different names, and one issue actually had five Stratemeyer stories running at the same time.[11]

After editing story papers for three years, Edward Stratemeyer sold his stationery store in Newark and started his own publication, *Bright Days*, in April 1896. *Bright Days*, which began as "A monthly of illustrated stories for boys and girls" and became a weekly on September 5, 1896, was published by the "Bright Days Publishing Co." at 177 William Street in New York, the same address as that of *Young People of America*.[12] Like *Young People of America*, *Bright Days* featured many of Stratemeyer's stories (including reprints of several stories first published in *Young People of America*). Fourteen new tales by Stratemeyer—everything from success stories to school and sports stories—were printed in *Bright Days* in its first year.[13]

Two other story papers also had new stories by Stratemeyer in 1896.[14] In January, *Young People of America* printed Stratemeyer's last tale for that publication, "A New Year's hold-up," as by Albert Lee Ford. "Estella, the little Cuban rebel; or, A war correspondent's sweetheart," published under the pseudonym Edna Winfield, appeared in Street & Smith's *New York Weekly*, a family story paper that relied heavily on romances created by in-house writers and regular contributors.[15]

Bright Days lasted until February 27, 1897. Later that year, twelve of Stratemeyer's serials were reprinted in hardcover editions as the Bound to Win series, published by W. L. Allison. The series marked Stratemeyer's first use of a pseudonym for hardcover fiction: four of the volumes (all containing stories from *Young People of America*) appeared under the name Captain Ralph Bonehill; four (with stories from *Young People of America* and *Good News*) under Arthur M. Winfield; and four (consisting of tales from *Good News*, *Argosy*, and *Bright Days*) under Stratemeyer's name. During this year, Stratemeyer may have been busy working on ideas for new books or preparing the serials for publication in hardcover, for the only proven Stratemeyer story serialized in 1897 was a reprint from *Young People of America*. He may also have spent more time with his family after the birth of his second child, Edna Camilla Stratemeyer.

In 1898, the year the Spanish-American War began, Stratemeyer submitted a manuscript to Lee & Shepard, Boston publishers. These two events might have remained unconnected except for a reader at Lee & Shepard, Commodore George Dewey's May 1 victory at Manila Bay, and the character of Stratemeyer's manuscript—a war adventure. The Lee & Shepard reader remembered Stratemeyer's work and suggested that it be rewritten incorporating Dewey and his triumph. The result, *Under Dewey at Manila; or, The war fortunes of a castaway*, the first volume of the Old Glory series, quickly went through several editions and is often considered Stratemeyer's first truly successful hardcover book.[16] Stratemeyer soon completed a second volume for the series, *A young volunteer in Cuba; or, Fighting for the single star*, and started another historical fiction series, the Minute Boys, for Estes & Lauriat. His only magazine contributions for 1898 were two Western stories published in *Golden Hours* under the name Captain Ralph Bonehill.

Historical fiction for boys proved to be a profitable field, and in 1899 Stratemeyer not only wrote new volumes for the two existing series and finished the Bound to Succeed series (now handled by Lee & Shepard), but also found a new publisher, The Mershon Company, for a third historical fiction series, the Flag of Freedom books. Based on the Spanish-American War, the series was published under the pseudonym Captain Ralph Bonehill, possibly to avoid confusion with Lee & Shepard's Old Glory series. In addition, Stratemeyer completed *An undivided union* by Oliver Optic (William Taylor Adams), the final book in The Blue and the Grey—On Land series, for Lee & Shepard. Adams had died in March 1897, leaving the publishers with only the first chapter and an overall plan for the work.[17]

Ironically, Stratemeyer's greatest contribution in 1899, and the one that would eventually bring him far more fame than any of his earlier books, was a series whose only relation to war was its occasional military school setting. The Rover Boys Series for Young Americans, published under the pseudonym Arthur M. Winfield, followed the adventures of three brothers at school and on vacations. The series progressed for twenty-six years and thirty volumes, taking the boys through school, across the country, and even into business, then introduced the Rover Boys' sons and began their adventures in school and on vacations. Although the Rover Boys ended in 1926, the series remained popular; by 1937 it had sales of almost 2,500,000 copies, placing it third on the list of Grosset & Dunlap's best-selling children's series;[18] ten years later, sales were estimated at almost twice that figure.[19]

By 1900 Stratemeyer was working on several projects. His Optic completion may have suggested an idea for other work, for the year after Horatio Alger, Jr.'s death in July 1899, The Mershon Company announced the publication of a new Alger story, *Out for business*, "one of several volumes left unfinished by Horatio Alger, Jr., at his death and completed by his friend and fellow author Arthur M. Winfield." Three more Alger stories were published in 1900 and 1901, as part of Mershon's Rise in Life series, all listed with Alger as author, but "completed by Arthur M. Winfield." The preface to *Nelson the newsboy*, the fourth volume, dated June 13, 1901, and signed by Arthur M. Winfield, noted that "In its original form Mr. Alger intended this story of New York life for a semi-juvenile drama. But it was not used in that shape . . . [and after Alger's death] this manuscript, with others, was placed in the hands of the present writer, to be made over into such a volume as might have met with the noted author's approval."[20] *Nelson the newsboy* was the last Alger story advertised as "completed by Arthur M. Winfield." In a letter dated November 11, 1901, Alger's sister, O. A. Cheney, wrote Stratemeyer that, since she was unable to find any new

Alger stories to send him, she was returning his $75.00, adding that she would notify him if she discovered any new manuscripts.[21] She may have located additional stories, for seven more Alger titles appeared between 1902 and 1908, five in the Rise in Life series and two as nonseries volumes published by Cupples & Leon. None mention Arthur M. Winfield, though all are thought to be Stratemeyer's work; the extent of Alger's connection with these books is not known.

Although the Rise in Life series centered on the Alger success story, a form Stratemeyer had used for many of his magazine serials, the majority of Stratemeyer's books at the turn of the century were historical fiction. In 1900, the same year the Rise in Life series premiered, two other publishers each advertised a new series by Stratemeyer: the Mexican War series was published by Dana Estes & Co. under the pseudonym Captain Ralph Bonehill, while Lee & Shepard offered the Soldiers of Fortune series, continuing the adventures of the characters from the Old Glory series. (After the Spanish-American War ended, the characters moved to China and later to Japan; by 1904, when the Russo-Japanese War began, they were ready to fight for Japan.)

In 1901 Lee & Shepard acquired two more Stratemeyer series: the American Boys' Biographical Series, which began with the life of William McKinley (and ended, one volume and three years later, with the life of Theodore Roosevelt), and the Colonial series, historical fiction about the experiences of two boy soldiers during the Revolutionary War. Only The Mershon Company, still publishing the Frontier series and the Rover Boys series, and possibly encouraged by the success of the latter, added a nonhistorical series: Arthur M. Winfield's Putnam Hall books, which provided a fictional background for Putnam Hall, the fictitious military academy which the equally fictitious Rover Boys attended.

The Pan-American series, published by Lee & Shepard from 1902 to 1911, introduced a new concept for Stratemeyer's series books—exotic settings and dangers without a military background. In this series, five boys and their tutor toured South America, encountering active volcanos and assorted hazards, but no military campaigns. Street & Smith, Stratemeyer's former employers, also published two short-lived Stratemeyer series in 1902: Silver Lake, under the pseudonym Arthur M. Winfield, and Zero Club, as by Captain Ralph Bonehill. Both series began with stories published in *Good News* under the name Harvey Hicks; neither series reached a second volume.

Another one-volume series, Great American Industries, appeared in 1903, published by Lee & Shepard. More successful was Mershon's Frontier series, fictionalized adventures with Daniel Boone, Lewis and Clark, and, in the final volume, participants in the California gold rush.

Despite his success with series books, Edward Stratemeyer still submitted an occasional story to the boys' story papers. From 1899 to 1901, six new tales, including one Alger completion, appeared in *Golden Hours*;[22] three were later reprinted in hardcover series, and the other three as individual titles. In addition, Stratemeyer's Nick Carter stories were being reissued in the Nick Carter Weekly, often with new titles; indeed, the Nick Carter reprints continued from 1896 until 1927, appearing in the Nick Carter Library, Nick Carter Weekly, Magnet Library, and New Magnet Library.

After 1903, Stratemeyer abandoned historical fiction. The first volume of the Outdoor series, his creation for boys in 1904, sprang from a story serialized in *Popular Magazine* in December 1903 and January 1904 and told of a group of boys who formed a gun club and went camping in winter; the second and final volume, issued in 1905, related the boys' triumphs after forming a baseball team. *The Bobbsey twins; or, Merry days indoors and out*, detailed the "haps and mishaps" of two pairs of twins, ages four and eight. Centered on home and school life, with less dangerous adventures and less threatening characters than Stratemeyer's other series, *The Bobbsey twins* betokened Stratemeyer's first entry into another area—series books for younger children of both sexes.

More adventure series for boys appeared in 1905. Mershon's Deep Sea series, which began with a tale originally published in *Golden Hours*, dealt with the activities of a deep-sea diver, Dave Fearless, while the Dave Porter books, published by Lee & Shepard, continued the trend toward boys' school stories.

In 1905 or 1906, Edward Stratemeyer initiated a new plan—not for a book or a series, but for a new approach to writing and marketing his numerous ideas for books. He established the Stratemeyer Literary Syndicate, headed by himself, with an office in New York City.[23] Here he continued to write all of the books and magazine stories published under his own name and his two most popular pseudonyms, Arthur M. Winfield and Captain Ralph Bonehill. In addition, he developed and plotted new series but did not always do the actual writing. Instead, he hired a number of writers, such as Howard Garis and St. George Rathborne, who "fleshed out" Stratemeyer's detailed chapter-by-chapter outlines, turning a three-page outline into a two hundred-page book.

HOWARD GARIS

Stratemeyer's friend and chief assistant in the Literary Syndicate was Howard Garis, a man whose creativity rivaled Stratemeyer's own. Born in Binghamton, New York, in 1873 and educated in public schools and at the Stevens Institute of Technology, Garis was living in Verona, New Jersey, only a few miles from Stratemeyer's home in Newark, when he began writing for the Syndicate. His background included four published books and several magazine articles, as well as ten years as a reporter for the *Newark Evening News*.[24] A prolific writer, Garis continued to work for the *Evening News* and to turn out over fifty non-Syndicate books on his own during the twenty-five or so years he was associated with Stratemeyer. After leaving the Syndicate, Howard Garis and his wife continued to write juvenile fiction and created several popular series. In his lifetime, Garis wrote approximately fifteen thousand Uncle Wiggily stories, and over one hundred series books under his own name, including the Buddy Books, Curlytops, Daddy series, Dick Hamilton, Happy Home series, Island Boys, Mystery Boys, Rick and Ruddy, Rocket Riders, Smith Boys, Teddy series, Tom Cardiff, Two Wild Cherries, Venture Boys, and Young Reporter series. His first assignment for the Stratemeyer Syndicate was the Motor Boys series, written under the pseudonym Clarence Young; he later worked on the Great Marvel series, Tom Swift, Baseball Joe, Bunny Brown and his Sister Sue, the Six Little Bunkers, and possibly other series as well.[25]

LILLIAN GARIS

Howard Garis was not the only writer—or the only Garis—to work for the Stratemeyer Syndicate in its early years. His wife, Lillian Garis, soon became the Syndicate's first woman writer, working on series for girls and younger children, among them the Bobbsey Twins series, Dorothy Dale, the Motor Girls, and the Outdoor Girls. A year older than her husband, Lillian McNamara Garis had studied at Columbia University before joining the staff of the *Newark Evening News* in 1895. She met Howard Garis when he started on the paper a year later. By then, "Lillian Mack" was working as a reporter and writing the women's page. She left the paper in 1900, when she and Howard were married, but soon after the birth of their son Roger in 1902, Lillian began writing children's books. Like Howard, Lillian had several books to her credit when she was asked to write for the Stratemeyer Syndicate, and, like Howard, she continued to turn out many series books on her own while employed by the Syndicate and afterward.[26] Her non-Syndicate titles were primarily girls' adventure stories, such as the Barbara Hale series, the Connie Loring books, the Girl Scout series, the Judy Jordan series, the Joan books, the Melody Lane Mystery Stories, and the Polly books.

Edward Stratemeyer made two important decisions in 1906. The first was the establishment of the Stratemeyer Literary Syndicate, providing a way to increase his productivity; the second was a reduction in the price of his books, promoting greater sales. After some negotiations with Cupples & Leon, new Stratemeyer series were priced at fifty cents, roughly half the cost of other series books. The Motor Boys, the first series offered at the lower price, proved extremely successful; in twenty-eight years, the twenty-two books in the Motor Boys series ran through thirty-five printings of at least five thousand copies per printing.[27] The price of other series was soon cut to fifty cents, a price tag presumably within the budget of eager readers; the increased sales justified the lower cost.

Although Stratemeyer had established a satisfactory agreement with one publisher, he soon encountered trouble with another. The Mershon Company had been handling many of Stratemeyer's series since 1904, but in 1905 had transferred most of its business to the newly-formed Stitt Publishing Company. Stitt remained in operation only until 1906, and for a short time Mershon resumed publication of some of Stratemeyer's titles, until Chatterton-Peck Company began to issue them in 1906 and 1907. Whether Stratemeyer was unhappy with the rapid changes in publishers, or whether there were other problems is not known, but in October 1907, litigation between Chatterton-Peck Company and Stitt Publishing Company, The Mershon Company, W. L. Mershon, and Edward Stratemeyer began. In January 1908, Chatterton-Peck took an advertisement in *Publishers' Weekly* to notify the trade that it had learned that Stratemeyer was attempting to find new publishers for books currently being handled by Chatterton-Peck, and that Chatterton-Peck claimed "the contract right to the exclusive publication of the books. . . ."[28] Two months later the litigation was settled; the March 7, 1906, issue of *Publishers' Weekly* carried a notice from Chatterton-Peck explaining that Stratemeyer had purchased "all stock and publication rights" for his Frontier series, Deep Sea series, Bobbsey Twins, Rover Boys, Putnam Hall, Railroad series, Rise in Life series, Flag of Freedom series, and for *Jack North's treasure hunt*, *Bob the photographer*, and *Lost in the land of ice*, as well as for some non-Syndicate series (Dorothy Chester, Newspaper series) and titles.[29] Stratemeyer promptly negotiated an agreement with Grosset & Dunlap, who took over the Syndicate titles; Grosset & Dunlap's advertisement announcing the agreement appeared in the same issue of *Publishers' Weekly*.

For the most part, the early years of the Stratemeyer Syndicate produced a continuation of established trends in series books. Some new ideas appeared, but the majority of series emphasized success stories and boys' school and travel adventures. Two career adventure series were published under the pseudonym Allen Chapman in 1906: the Boys of Business (later retitled the Boys of Pluck) contained career success stories similar to Stratemeyer's Bound to Win and Bound to Succeed series, and the Railroad series (Ralph of the Railroad) traced a lad's employment with the railroad, from his days in the roundhouse through his time as an engineer and a train dispatcher. The Boy Hunters, published in 1906 under the pseudonym Captain Ralph Bonehill, was indicative of the outdoor adventure series, chronicling the hunting, trapping, and camping experiences of a group of friends. The Motor Boys, another new series, gave travel adventures a new twist. Focusing on three extremely mobile youths, the series took its name from the many modes of transportation the boys acquired—motorcycles, motor cars, motor boats, and the like; racing competitions and mysteries provided added excitement. Stratemeyer's most original series for 1906 was the Great Marvel books, science-fiction which began with journeys to the North and South Poles in the early volumes and progressed to episodes on the Moon, Saturn, and Mars in later books.

The first volumes of three new boys' series, all similar to established series, were issued in 1907 and 1908. The Lakeport series actually began with retitled reprints of the Outdoor series from 1904; Jack Ranger and the Darewell Chums both continued the pattern of boys' school and travel adventures. The one break from tradition, the Dorothy Dale series, heralded the start of a new line of Syndicate creations—series books for girls. Written under the pen name Margaret Penrose, Dorothy Dale soon proved that girls' series filled with school and home adventures were just as marketable as boys'.

The Webster series was the only new line of books introduced in 1909. Advertisements described the volumes as similar to those of Horatio Alger, Jr., but "thoroughly up-to-date." The Mexican War series, first published in 1900 under the pseudonym Captain Ralph Bonehill, reappeared in 1909 with a new publisher and Stratemeyer's name on the title page.

If 1909 had been a quiet and traditional year, 1910 more than compensated for it. The second girls' series, the Motor Girls, began, again under the pen name Margaret Penrose. Girls were now granted some of the mobility boys enjoyed, as, by car and boat (but never motorcycle) they journeyed through the country discovering their share of adventures. The College Sports series, the first books written under the pseudonym Lester Chadwick, became the first Syndicate series devoted to athletics, while another new pseudonym, Victor Appleton, ushered in what was soon to become the best-selling boys' series—Tom Swift.

ST. GEORGE RATHBORNE

As the number of Syndicate series increased, so did the number of Syndicate writers. St. George Rathborne, who Stratemeyer knew from Street & Smith, was among them. Rathborne, born in Covington, Kentucky, in 1854, had been selling stories to Street & Smith since at least 1878.[30] His stories, ranging from romances to boys' adventures, had been published in at least a dozen story papers, dime novel libraries, and paperback series, under his own name and several pseudonyms. As Graham B. Forbes, he worked on the Syndicate's Boys of Columbia High series; as Captain Quincy Allen, he assisted with volumes in the Outdoor Chums, the only new Syndicate series for 1911.

The Golden Age

The three years from 1912 to 1914 produced a flood of series—twenty-two in all—covering a wide range of topics. A burst of boys' sports series appeared, with Baseball Joe, the Boys of Columbia High, the Fred Fenton Athletic Series, and, for younger readers, Tommy Tiptop. There was even a sports series for girls—The Girls of Central High, published under the pseudonym Gertrude W. Morrison. The Racer Boys, Dave Dashaway, the Speedwell Boys, Tom Fairfield, and the Up and Doing series strengthened the Syndicate's hold on boys' adventure and travel series, while the Pioneer Boys and the Flag and Freedom series (the latter a reprint of the Flag of Freedom and the Frontier series) marked a brief return to historical fiction. Girls' adventure series, a growing field, was represented by the Outdoor Girls, Ruth Fielding, and the Do Something (Janice Day) series; another new series, Amy Bell Marlowe's Books for Girls, offered the female equivalent of the Alger success story. Motion pictures inspired three new career series: the Motion Picture Chums, the Moving Picture Boys, and the Moving Picture Girls. Finally, three new concepts were introduced with the Saddle Boys series; modern Western stories for boys, the University series, set at popular boys' colleges, and the Back to the Soil (Hiram) series, apparently about a farmer in the midwest.

The majority of the Syndicate series were handled by two publishers: Grosset & Dunlap and Cupples & Leon. Interestingly, although Grosset & Dunlap had acquired several popular series after the litigation in 1908, it was another two years before it purchased a new Syndicate series—Tom Swift. Tom proved extremely successful, and Grosset & Dunlap added nine more series from 1911 to 1914. Cupples & Leon, which had issued ten Stratemeyer and Syndicate series from 1905 to 1910, published another two in 1912, and, in 1913, started another six. Two other publishers, Graham & Matlack and Sully & Kleinteich, also advertised Syndicate series between 1912 and 1914. Graham & Matlack concentrated on boys' series, publishing two in 1912, while Sully & Kleinteich offered a wider range with the Do Something, Back to the Soil, and University series, all in 1914. Only one of Stratemeyer's major publishers had moved away from Syndicate series; Lothrop, Lee & Shepard (formerly Lee & Shepard), formerly publishers for almost half of the Stratemeyer series, only acquired three Syndicate series after 1907, although it did issue some reprint volumes.

In late 1914, amid the success of his many series and largely because of it, Stratemeyer became one of the targets of strong criticism by Franklin K. Mathiews, Chief Scout Librarian of the recently incorporated Boy Scouts of America. Mathiews, who had been studying boys' reading habits, found the series books to be in high demand and the classics of children's literature somewhat neglected. After sampling some of the popular literature, he began a crusade. In an article titled "Blowing out the boy's brains" in the

November 1914 issue of *Outlook*, Mathiews attacked "cheap books"—the fifty-cent juveniles; his contention was that these books, containing improbable plots where "insuperable difficulties and crushing circumstances" are readily mastered by larger-than-life heroes, could "by overstimulation, debauch and vitiate" a boy's imagination. According to Mathiews, "the harm done [by reading cheap fiction] is simply incalculable. . . . [A]s some boys read such books, their imaginations are literally 'blown out.'"[31]

Mathiews did not limit his appeal to parents; he also approached Grosset & Dunlap, primary publishers of the fifty-cent juvenile, with suggestions for an inexpensive line of reprints of quality literature (later published as Every Boy's Library) and apparently communicated with a writer, Percy Keese Fitzhugh, who began to create several nonexplosive series for boys.[32] Mathiews also worked with boy scout leaders, librarians, and booksellers, promoting a "Safety first juvenile book week" in November 1915. In an article in *Library Journal* for that month, he encouraged librarians to campaign against cheap fiction by discussing the case against it with newspaper editors, who, Mathiews hoped, would relay the information as news or in editorial columns, reaching the children's parents. In addition, Mathiews suggested the use of book lists, making a thirty-two page pamphlet, "Books boys like best," available in quantities at cost.[33]

While Mathiews's crusade furthered the cause of children's literature, its effects, if any, on the Stratemeyer Syndicate's sales were mild. Although Grosset & Dunlap did not issue any new Syndicate series in 1915 or 1917, and only published one new series, Bunny Brown and his Sister Sue, low-key adventures for younger children, in 1916, it did continue to publish new volumes in many of its existing Syndicate series. Cupples & Leon, possibly influenced by Mathiews's diatribe, advertised only two new series in 1914 and 1915—the White Ribbon Boys and the Y.M.C.A. Boys. The former chronicled the temperance work accomplished by a group of boys; the latter detailed the reformation of a town's youths after a boys' department of the local Y.M.C.A. was organized.[34] Barse & Hopkins, which started publishing Stratemeyer Syndicate series in 1915, avoided the controversy by issuing series written for girls and younger children: the Corner House Girls, the Kneetime Animal Stories, and Bobby Blake. George Sully & Co. (formerly Sully & Kleinteich) sidestepped the issue by bringing out only one Syndicate Series—for girls—the Nan Sherwood books (in 1916). From 1915 to 1917, only two publishers purchased traditional adventure series for boys from the Stratemeyer Syndicate. Joe Strong, a circus boy, and the Rushton boys, with their school activities, were published by Hearst's International Library in 1916; the Motion Picture Comrades, similar to the Moving Picture Boys, was issued a year later by the New York Book Company.

The Stratemeyer Syndicate's movement away from new adventure series for boys continued for the next six years. Although two action and adventure series, the Air Service Boys and Dave Fearless, were released by George

Sully in 1918, the majority of the Syndicate's series were aimed at girls and younger children. The Carolyn books by Ruth Belmore Endicott, Betty Gordon by Ruth Fielding, Billie Bradley by Janet D. Wheeler, and Oriole by Amy Bell Marlowe all sprang up from 1918 to 1920. Four children's series were also developed in this three-year period: the Six Little Bunkers, the Make-Believe series, the Four Little Blossoms, and Sunny Boy. The years 1921 through 1924 brought only a handful of series: the Frank and Andy books, published by Sully in 1921, was the only new series that year, and it was actually retitled reprints of three Racer Boys books; two radio series, the Radio Boys and the Radio Girls, premiered in 1922; 1923 witnessed the advent of Helen Louise Thorndyke and "her" Honey Bunch series for younger girls; and 1924 added the Riddle Club to the list of series for younger children of both sexes.

HARRIET S. ADAMS

Little is known about Edward Stratemeyer's personal life during the years he ran the Stratemeyer Syndicate. He still lived in Newark with his wife and two children. Edna, his younger daughter, appears to have had little connection with the Syndicate. Her older sister, Harriet, had left home about 1910 to attend Wellesley College, graduating in 1914 with a major in English, and courses in music, religion, archaeology, and science.[35] Harriet was interested in writing and submitted articles to the *Boston Globe* during her college years. Although she wanted to work for her father, Stratemeyer did not believe in women working outside the home—at least in Harriet's case—and would not let her write for the Syndicate. A compromise was reached, and Harriet spent part of 1914 and 1915 editing manuscripts and galley proofs for the Syndicate at home, as she was not allowed to work in the office. After her marriage to Russell Vroom Adams, an investment banker, in 1915, she left the Syndicate, again because her father felt she should be concentrating on her home, not outside work.[36]

Stratemeyer's own work habits were regular. He commuted daily to his eighteenth floor office at 24 West 25th Street in Manhattan. There he dictated to a stenographer, detailing plot outlines, writing chapters, editing manuscripts, and communicating with his writers-for-hire—the latter, by letter and appointment, as the writers did not work at the New York office. He is believed to have employed as many as twenty ghost writers at one time.[37] Stratemeyer's activities outside of the Syndicate may have provided him with background for some of his stories. He belonged to the New Jersey Historical Society, the National Geographic Society, the Woodcraft Association, the Author's League, and the Roseville Athletic Association, and he is said to have enjoyed baseball and books on travel.[38]

His interest in travel may have supplied some of the ideas for the Don

Sturdy series, which began in 1925. Set around the adventures of a boy who travels about the world with his uncles, a scientist and a big game hunter, the series moved from episodes in the Sahara Desert to South America, Asia, Alaska, and the North Pole. Also starting in 1925 was the Blythe Girls series, telling the trials and triumphs of three sisters working in New York City, blending career adventures with light romance and mystery. The last entry for 1925 was the Flyaways, a short-lived series taking the Flyaway family into Fairyland for encounters with Goldilocks, Red Riding Hood, and other fairy tale and nursery rhyme characters—an unusual, if not a successful, series.

Another unusual series that was much more popular was Bomba the Jungle Boy, published in 1926. Bomba, a lad not unlike a youthful Tarzan, spent most of the early volumes searching the jungles for his long-lost parents. The X Bar X Boys, a modern Western series, also began in 1926, as did Garry Grayson, a football series. The year's only offering for girls, The Barton Books for Girls, featured mystery and adventure stories, which, according to the advertisements, were written in a style "somewhat of a mixture of that of Louisa M. Alcott and Mrs. L. T. Meade, but thoroughly up-to-date in plot and action."

1926 was also the year that Garden City Publishing Company issued four Stratemeyer series in paperback editions, beginning all four series on January 2 and adding new volumes monthly. Three of the four series started by reprinting some of the Syndicate's earlier publications: the Movie Boys consisted of retitled reprints of the Motion Picture Chums and Moving Picture Boys; the Dave Fearless series started with the first three volumes of the Deep Sea series (already issued by Sully as the Dave Fearless series, but in hardcover editions, in 1918), then added over a dozen new volumes; and Frank Allen, the only series published in hardcover and in paperback, reprinted the Boys of Columbia High books (assigning them new titles), as well as over half-a-dozen new stories. The Nat Ridley Rapid Fire Detective Stories, by Nat Ridley, Jr., was the only one of the four not taken from an existing Syndicate series.

LESLIE McFARLANE

One of the writers who worked on the Dave Fearless series was Leslie McFarlane. A Canadian-born journalist, the twenty-three-year old McFarlane was working for the *Springfield Republican* in Massachusetts when he saw an advertisement in *Editor and Publisher* asking for experienced fiction writers. He answered the ad, placed by Stratemeyer, by mail; Stratemeyer responded by sending two volumes from the Dave Fearless and Nat Ridley series and a letter explaining briefly the operation of the Stratemeyer Syndicate. McFarlane was asked to read the two books, then tell the Stratemeyer Syndicate which series he preferred to work with. From there, the procedure was similar to that encountered by Patten in the office of *Good News* years before: McFarlane received a title and a detailed outline for the book and was requested to submit the first two chapters for approval. If they proved satisfactory, he would be assigned to finish the book. Even the payment of $100 was the same as Stratemeyer's offer to Patten, although this time it was specified in advance.[39]

McFarlane agreed and joined the ranks of Syndicate writers. He was asked to sign a contract giving the Syndicate the rights to all titles he wrote for them; his payment was a flat sum for each book, usually $100 for paperback and $125-$150 for hardcover titles. The contract also contained clauses which required that he not only forego unauthorized use of the Syndicate pseudonyms, but also that he not reveal his connection with, or his work under, any of the Stratemeyer Syndicate house names. McFarlane agreed, breaking his silence fifty years later for his autobiography. During his time with the Syndicate, he contributed to the Dave Fearless series, the Hardy Boys series, and even, for one book, to the X Bar X Boys series.[40]

McFarlane returned to Canada about 1927, dividing his time between writing fiction for Canadian magazines and working on series books for the Syndicate. He left the Stratemeyer Syndicate in 1946 after joining the National Film Board of Canada, and went on to write and direct documentaries for almost ten years, later becoming drama editor for the Canadian Broadcasting Corporation.[41]

In the years before Stratemeyer's death, the Syndicate returned to boys' adventure stories. In 1926, seven series for boys and only one series for girls had been published; in 1927, both of the new series, the Hardy Boys and the Ted Scott Flying Stories, were written for boys. No new series were instituted in 1928, but the following year's creations were again for boys: the Bob Chase Big Game series, Lanky Lawson, and Roy Stover. It was not until 1930 that the Stratemeyer Syndicate issued a new series for girls, the Nancy Drew Mystery Stories, which soon became one of the top series on the market. Along with Nancy Drew, 1930 introduced the Buck and Larry Baseball Stories, the Slim Tyler Air Stories, and the Campfire Girls (retitled reprints of the Radio Girls series).

In May 1930, Edward Stratemeyer contracted lobar pneumonia. He spent a week in bed and died Saturday, May 10, 1930. Services were held at his home at 171 N. 7th Street in Newark on Monday, May 12.[42]

Stratemeyer's publishers were horrified by his death: there were almost thirty series still in progress, and his books had been successful enough to leave the Stratemeyer estate estimated at between half a million and a million dollars. Harriet Stratemeyer Adams, who had spent the years since her marriage writing pieces for Sunday School and for women's clubs, and taking care of her four children, Russell, Jr., Patricia, Camilla, and Edward, discussed the matter with her husband and decided to take over the management of the Syndicate, with the help of her sister Edna, still living in Newark with her mother.[43]

Harriet contacted some of the writers who had worked for her father and made arrangements to continue the series. Her first job was to edit the five manuscripts Stratemeyer had left; soon after, she wrote a Bobbsey Twins title, then began to work on books in other series.[44] At first, the only outward sign of change was the Syndicate's business address: in November 1930, the office was moved to the top of the Hale building at 519 Main Street, in East Orange, New Jersey, so that Mrs. Adams was only fifteen minutes from home.[45]

Three new series appeared in 1931: Doris Force, mystery stories for girls; the Sky Flyers (Randy Starr), another aviation series for boys; and the Jerry Ford Wonder stories, high action and exotic settings in an adventure series for boys. All were issued by Henry Altemus Company, a new publisher for the Syndicate.

WALTER KARIG

Another journalist was contributing to Syndicate series during this period. Walter Karig, a New Yorker six years younger than Mrs. Adams, assisted with volumes in several series including the X Bar X Boys and Doris Force. Before writing for the Syndicate, Karig had served in the foreign legion, been a reporter on the Norfolk *Virginian Pilot*, and worked as editor of the *Elizabeth City Herald* in North Carolina. When he joined the Syndicate, he was employed as a reporter by both the *New York Herald Tribune* and the *Newark Evening News*; he went on to become chief of the Washington bureau of the *Evening News* and later book editor of the *Washington Post and Times-Herald*. In addition to his journalistic career and his work for the Syndicate, Karig authored adventure stories, adult novels, and nonfiction works published under his name and several pseudonyms.[46]

Maintenance Years

The Stratemeyer Syndicate created no new series in 1932 and 1933, but 1934's lineup included two brand-new mystery series for girls—the Dana Girls and the Kay Tracey Mystery Stories. In 1935, the profitable detective fiction format was adapted to appeal to younger children of both sexes, with the Mary and Jerry Mystery Stories. Sadly, 1935 marked the end of the creative period for new series; it would be twelve years before the next series was announced and eighteen years before a truly successful new series appeared. In the interim, many series were discontinued and some of the Syndicate employees, such as Howard and Lillian Garis, stopped writing for the Syndicate. By 1935, the number of publishers advertising new titles in Syndicate series had dropped to two—Grosset & Dunlap and Cupples & Leon.

Although the publishing pattern changed and the number of series decreased, the Stratemeyer Syndicate was still active. In 1935, fourteen series were still in progress, and while the number was reduced by over one-third by 1940, most of the existing series were receiving new volumes annually.[47]

By then, Harriet Adams and Edna Stratemeyer had been managing the Syndicate for ten years, with Mrs. Adams dealing with publishers, plotting new titles, and doing much of the writing, including all of the Nancy Drew and Dana Girls books, while Edna Stratemeyer handled the business at home. In 1942 this arrangement changed, after Edna married Charles Wesley Squier, moved to New York, and became an inactive partner. Mrs. Adams supervised the Syndicate alone then, writing under the pseudonyms Carolyn Keene and Laura Lee Hope, and planning books for the other series. The depression and the paper shortages caused by World War II encouraged Mrs. Adams to limit further the number of series being published, so that by 1945 only five series survived: the Bobbsey Twins (from 1904), Honey Bunch (from 1923), the Hardy Boys (from 1927), Nancy Drew (from 1930), and the Dana Girls (from 1934), all published by Grosset & Dunlap.

ANDREW SVENSON

In 1947 the Stratemeyer Syndicate started a new series, the Mel Martin Baseball Stories, published by Cupples & Leon. Then, in 1948, Andrew Svenson joined the Syndicate as a writer and editor. Born May 8, 1910, in Belleville, New Jersey, the son of Andrew and Laura Svenson, he had attended the University of Pittsburgh, graduating in 1932, the same year he married Marian Stewart. He went to Montclair State Teachers College, planning to become a teacher, but in 1934 took a job on the Newark *Evening News*, working there until 1948. In addition to his work at the Syndicate, he taught writing at Rutgers, in New Brunswick, New Jersey, from 1945 to 1954, and at Upsala College in East Orange, from 1948 to 1954. In 1953, under the pseudonym Jerry West, he began the Syndicate's newest series, the Happy Hollisters, adventure and mystery stories for children.[48]

Renovation Period

In 1954 the Tom Swift, Jr., series began, resurrecting one of the Syndicate's most successful creations, but with second-generation characters, new innovations, and a stronger emphasis on science fiction. Three years later, another favorite series, Honey Bunch, received some alterations when the series was transformed into the Honey Bunch and Norman series, with Norman, Honey Bunch's neighbor, promoted to a more prominent role.

The next few years were busy ones. In 1960 the Bret King Mystery Stories were created, bringing detective fiction to a modern Western setting; in 1962, another new series, Linda Craig, combined mystery, the modern West, and a girl and her horse. The Syndicate also started to rewrite three of its most popular series, The Bobbsey Twins, Nancy Drew, and the Hardy Boys, editing and updating the texts, and, in some cases, altering the plots and changing or deleting peripheral characters. The revisions, a huge project involving almost one hundred titles, continued from the late 1950s into the early 1970s.

Andrew Svenson had become a Syndicate partner in the midst of this activity, in 1961. He was still working on the Happy Hollisters series and once wrote that each book took about six weeks to complete, after the outline was finished. Interested in travel and photography, Svenson generally visited the locations where his stories were set before writing the books.[49] In addition to the Happy Hollister series, he worked on some Hardy Boys and Bret King titles, and, in 1967, he started the Tolliver Adventure Series.

Grosset & Dunlap was still publishing the top five Syndicate series— Nancy Drew, the Hardy Boys, Tom Swift, Jr., the Bobbsey Twins, and the Dana Girls, as well as the Bret King series and the Syndicate's second new series for 1967, Christopher Cool/TEEN Agent. Two other publishers also handled new Syndicate titles: Doubleday, with the Happy Hollisters and Linda Craig series, and World Publishing Company, with the short-lived Tolliver Adventure Series.

NANCY AXELRAD

In early 1975, the full-time staff at the East Orange office consisted of five people: the two partners, Harriet Adams and Andrew Svenson, plus Mrs. Lieselotte Wuenn, Andrew Svenson's assistant; Mrs. Lorraine S. Rickle, Harriet Adams's assistant and office manager; and Ms. Nancy Axelrad, writer and editor.[50] Ms. Axelrad, born in Oxford, Mississippi, in 1944, had joined the Syndicate office staff in 1965, working as an editorial assistant. She graduated from Drew University with a major in religion, and received a Master's degree from Johns Hopkins in 1970.[51] Her work for the Syndicate included some Bobbsey Twins titles, as well as work on other series.[52]

Later that year, the Syndicate's staff was reduced when Andrew Svenson died in Livingston, New Jersey, on August 21, 1975. Before his death, he had worked on the Syndicate's new series for 1975, Wynn and Lonny. The series continued for several volumes after his death, ending in 1978, the year after Nancy Drew Picture Books, the Syndicate's most recent series, premiered.

The Stratemeyer Syndicate acquired a new publisher, followed by a sizeable lawsuit, in 1979. Early in the year, the Stratemeyer Syndicate signed a contract assigning Wanderer Books, Simon & Schuster's juvenile imprint, world literary and licensing rights for new books and revised editions in the Syndicate's most popular series (the Bobbsey Twins, the Dana Girls, the Hardy Boys, and Nancy Drew), as well as the rights to some series currently out of print, in the event they were reprinted. Simon & Schuster planned to issue the series books in a new format, as paperbacks, at a lower price. Information about the terms of the contract was vague: the sale of the rights was somewhere in the "medium six figure range;" the contract was for between six and nine years, with an option to renew, again for between six and nine years.[53]

In May 1979, Grosset & Dunlap filed suit in the United States District Court for the Southern District of New York, charging Simon & Schuster and the Stratemeyer Syndicate with "unfair competition, common law trade mark infringement and common law copyright infringement" and charging Simon & Schuster with "inducing breach of contract and breach of fiduciary obligations" and " 'intentional and wrongful' interference" with economic and contractual relations,[54] because Simon & Schuster would be publishing not only new Nancy Drew, Hardy Boys, and Bobbsey Twins titles, but also older titles in the same series after their copyrights reached the renewal period and reverted back to the Stratemeyer Syndicate. This would affect roughly two dozen Hardy boys books and seventeen Nancy Drew titles within the time period of the Syndicate's contract and renewal option with Wanderer books.[55] The Grosset & Dunlap lawsuit, asking $300,000,000 in punitive damages, was resolved in June 1980; Simon & Schuster and the Stratemeyer Syndicate did not have to pay damages or cease publication of the series. Grosset & Dunlap, however, was allowed to issue the Tom Swift, Jr., series because of a 1951 agreement.[56]

1980 was also noteworthy in that it was Mrs. Adams's fiftieth year managing the Stratemeyer Syndicate. During that time, her activities and achievements made even Nancy Drew, her favorite series book character, look sedentary. She had been (and in some cases, still was) a member of half a dozen organizations: the League of American Pen Women, the Business and Professional Women's Club, the New Jersey Women's Press Club, Zonta, the New York Wellesley Club, and the New Jersey Wellesley Club (she had even helped to found the latter and been its first president). In addition, she had taught Sunday School, founded the magazine for the Maplewood, New Jersey, women's club and acted as chairman of its literature department, served as a Republican county committeewoman, and worked with the Red Cross and the Girl Scouts.[57] In 1978 she was awarded a Certificate of Appreciation from the New Jersey Congress of Parents and Teachers, an Alumnae Achievement Award from Wellesley College (where she had endowed a chair in children's literature), and honorary doctorate degrees from Kean and Upsala Colleges in New Jersey; she had also received two citations (for Nancy Drew books) from the New Jersey Institute of Technology.[58]

A world traveller, Harriet Adams has visited Canada, South America, Europe, Africa, and the Orient, often buying dolls from various locations to add to her collection, a fifty-year hobby. Some changes occurred in her family: one son died in World War II; she was widowed in 1966; and her sister, Edna Squier, passed away in 1974. She is now the mother of three, grandmother of ten, and great-grandmother of two, with a farm in Califon, New Jersey, where she spends many weekends, and a home in Maplewood.

Harriet Adams's work habits have not changed drastically over the years. In the 1960s she worked at the East Orange office from nine to five, five days a week, outlining, editing, and supervising, as well as writing all the titles published under the pseudonym Carolyn Keene. Currently, she tries to spend four to five hours a day writing, but much of the work is done at her home and on her farm.[59] The present-day Syndicate, with an office in Maplewood, New Jersey, consists of four partners: Nancy Axelrad, Lorraine Rickle, Lieselotte Wuenn, and senior partner, Harriet Adams.*

Four Syndicate series are still in progress in 1981: the Bobbsey twins, with seventy-six volumes; the Hardy boys, sixty-six volumes; Nancy Drew, sixty volumes; and Tom Swift, Jr., thirty-six volumes, all with the most recent titles published in paperback by Wanderer Books. Two other series have recently been reissued: Kay Tracey (for the sixth time), by Bantam Books, and Linda Craig, by Wanderer books, both paperback editions.

The books have a new look, and, in most cases, contemporary characters and settings, but all are based on the "Stratemeyer formula"—mystery and action, with a little educational material added. According to the Stratemeyer Syndicate, this is a formula that has been used since 1899 and the Rover Boys, and one which still works today.[60]

Notes

1. "Stratemeyer, Edward," *Dictionary of American biography* 18, ed. Dumas Malone (New York: Charles Scribner's Sons, 1936), p. 125.

2. Ibid.

3. Arthur Prager, "Edward Stratemeyer and his book machine," *Saturday Review*, Oct. 10, 1971, p. 15.

4. Roy B. Van Devier, "Edward Stratemeyer," *Dime Novel Round-Up* 26 (Feb. 15, 1958), p. 10.

*EDITORS NOTE: Harriet S. Adams died on March 27, 1982, after this book was set in type.

5. John T. Dizer, Jr., "Early Stratemeyer writings," *Dime Novel Round-Up*, 50 (June 1981), p. 54. Much of the information about Stratemeyer's early serials and dime novel publications is based on Dr. Dizer's article, which includes information from J. Randolph Cox's research in Street & Smith's files at Syracuse University.

6. A sixth story, "The hermit's protege," as by Ralph Hamilton, was also serialized in *Golden Days* and may have been Stratemeyer's work.

7. "Stratemeyer, Edward," *National cyclopedia of American biography* 32 (New York: James T. White & Company, 1945), p. 168.

8. *Dictionary of American biography* 18, p. 125. Also John T. Dizer, Jr., "Street & Smith Box M58," *Dime Novel Round-Up* 46 (Aug. 1977), pp. 83-84.

9. Gilbert Patten, *Frank Merriwell's "father:" An autobiography by Gilbert Patten*, ed. Harriet Hinsdale (Norman: University of Oklahoma Press, 1964), pp. 162-64.

10. John T. Dizer, Jr., "Serials and boys' books by Edward Stratemeyer," *Dime Novel Round-Up*, 44 (Dec. 1975), p. 127.

11. The December 7, 1895, issue contained the first installment of "A nobody schoolboy," as by Philip A. Alyer; the last installment of "Quarterback Dan, the football champion," under the pseudonym Clarence Young; and parts of "Poor but plucky," as by Albert Lee Ford; "Gun and sled," as by Captain Ralph Bonehill; and "Three ranch boys," by Edward Stratemeyer.

12. Dizer, "Serials and boys' books," p. 127.

13. Three other stories, "Lost in a coal mine," "The stone chest," and "On to Cuba," all published under the pseudonym Ralph Harrington, may also have been Stratemeyer's work, as well as a fourth story, "Malcolm the waterboy," as by D. T. Henty.

14. Two additional stories, published in *Good News* and the *Banner Weekly*, may have been penned by Stratemeyer.

15. Stratemeyer is also thought to have used the Street & Smith house name Julia Edwards for several other romances published in the *New York Weekly* during his years at Street & Smith, but exact titles are not known.

16. Ken Donelson, "Nancy, Tom and assorted friends in the Stratemeyer Syndicate then and now," *Children's Literature*, 7 (1978), p. 19. Also Raymond L. Kilgour, *Lee and Shepard: Publishers for the people* (n.p.: The Shoe String Press, Inc., 1965), p. 275.

17. Kilgour, *Lee and Shepard*, p. 270.

18. George Terry Dunlap, *The fleeting years: A memoir* (New York: privately printed, 1937), p. 193. Four of the five best-selling series were by the Stratemeyer Syndicate: Tom Swift, with 6,566,646 copies; the Bobbsey Twins, with 5,619,129 copies; the Rover Boys, with 2,421,909 copies; and Bunny Brown and his Sister Sue, with 2,153,515 copies.

19. Gordon Allison, "Tom Swift quit inventing in '41; His future secret," *New York Herald Tribune*, April 14, 1946, sec. 2, p. 2.

20. Horatio Alger, Jr., *Nelson the newsboy; or, Afloat in New York*, completed by Arthur M. Winfield (New York: The Mershon Company, 1901), pp. iii-iv. Preface by Arthur M. Winfield.

21. O. A. Cheney, letter dated Nov. 11, 1901. Reprinted in *Newsboy* 19 (Aug. 1980), p. 8.

22. Two other serials published during this time may have been Stratemeyer's work: "Bob Ready, reporter" in *Golden Hours* (1901) and "Footlight Phil" in *Boys of America* (1901-1902).

From 1902 to 1907, *Golden Days* reprinted several of Stratemeyer's stories, as did Street & Smith; three of the Alger stories were also reprinted in magazines. Three new Stratemeyer stories were published in magazines between 1903 and 1907, all under Stratemeyer's name: "Snow Lodge" (1903-1904), "Building the line" (1904), and "In defense of his flag" (1906-1907). The latter was the last story by Stratemeyer that originally appeared as a serial.

23. The Stratemeyer Syndicate is not positive about the date it was founded. In a phone interview on June 9, 1981, Nancy Axelrad gave 1906 as the probable date, adding that it might have been earlier.

24. "Garis, Howard Roger," *Contemporary authors*, ed. Frances Carol Locher (Detroit: Gale Research Co., 1978), 122: 227-29.

25. Roger Garis, *My father was Uncle Wiggily* (New York: McGraw-Hill Book Co., 1966), pp. 69-74, 200-201.

26. Ibid., pp. 34-35, 54-61.

27. "For it was indeed he," *Fortune*, April 1934, pp. 206-208.

28. "The house for juveniles," *Publishers' Weekly*, Jan. 4, 1908, p. 34.

29. "The house for juveniles," *Publishers' Weekly*, March 7, 1908, p. 1102.

30. Albert Johannsen, *The House of Beadle & Adams and its dime and nickel novels: The story of a vanished literature* 2 (Norman: University of Oklahoma Press, 1950), pp. 231-32. Although Johannsen gives "Sure Shot, the hunter chief" as Rathborne's first publication, in the *New York Weekly* "about 1868," Edward T. LeBlanc's bibliographic listing of the *New York Weekly* does not show this story during that time; LeBlanc's earliest entry for Rathborne is "The great mogul" in 1878.

31. Franklin K. Mathiews, "Blowing out the boy's brains," *Boys' Book Collector*, 1, no. 4 (1970), pp. 106-109. Reprinted from *Outlook*, Nov. 18, 1914.

32. Donelson, "Nancy, Tom and assorted friends . . . ," pp. 32-36.

33. Franklin K. Mathiews, "Safety first juvenile book week," *Library Journal* 40 (1915), pp. 791-92.

34. Cupples & Leon did, however, reprint two boys' series in 1917, combining the action-filled Darewell Chums series and the career-oriented Boys of Pluck series to form the Boys' Pocket Library.

35. "Harriet Stratemeyer Adams," *American women writers from colonial times to the present: A critical reference guide*, ed. Lina Mainiero 1 (New York: Ungar Publishing Co., 1975), p. 215.

36. Judy Foreman, "The saga of a mysterious author," *Newsboy* 19, no. 4 (Nov. 1980), pp. 18-19. Reprinted from *The Boston Globe*, July 3, 1980.

37. "For it was indeed he," pp. 203-204.

38. *National cyclopedia of American biography* 32, p. 168. Also "For it was indeed he," p. 204.

39. Leslie McFarlane, *Ghost of the Hardy Boys* (New York: Two Continents, 1976), pp. 1, 9-19.

40. Ibid., pp. 61-63, 72, 181.

41. Ibid., pp. 200-204.

42. "Funeral tonight for E. Stratemeyer," *New York Times*, May 12, 1930, p. 21.

43. Foreman, "Saga of a mysterious author," pp. 18-19.

44. Judy Klemsrud, "100 books—and not a hippie in them," *New York Times*, April 4, 1968, p. 52.

45. Peter A. Soderbergh, "The Stratemeyer strain: Educators and the juvenile series book, 1900-1973," *Journal of Popular Culture*, Spring 1974, p. 868.

46. "Walter Karig," *American novelists of today*, ed. Harry R. Warfel (New York: American Book Company, 1951), pp. 237-38. Also "Karig, Walter, " in *Twentieth Century American Authors*, 1st supplement, ed. Stanley J. Kunitz (New York: H. W. Wilson, 1955), pp. 511-12.

47. The fourteen series for 1935 were Nan Sherwood, the Great Marvel series, Don Sturdy, Bomba the Jungle Boy, Mary and Jerry Mystery Stories, the Bobbsey Twins, Tom Swift, Ted Scott, Honey Bunch, the X Bar X Boys, the Hardy Boys, Nancy Drew, the Dana Girls, and Kay Tracey. The last nine were still in progress in 1940.

48. "Svenson, Andrew E.," *Something about the author* 1, ed. Annie Commire (Detroit: Gale Research, 1971), p. 238-39.

49. Tim O'Herin, letter, *The Mystery and Adventure Series Review*, no. 5 (Summer 1981), n.p.

50. Roger B. May, "Durable heroes: Nancy Drew and kin still surmount scrapes—and critics' slurs," *Wall Street Journal*, Jan. 15, 1975, pp. 1, 17.

51. Nancy Axelrad, phone interview, June 9, 1981.

52. Peggy Herz, *Nancy Drew and the Hardy Boys* (New York: Scholastic Book Services, 1977), p. 16.

53. Daisy Maryles, "Venerable young sleuths find new home," *Publishers' Weekly*, March 5, 1979, p. 18.

54. "Stratemeyer and S & S call Grosset suit frivolous," *Publishers' Weekly*, May 14, 1979, pp. 124, 129.

55. Maryles, "Venerable young sleuths," p. 18.

56. "Swift justice," *Time*, June 30, 1980, p. 71.

57. "Adams, Harriet S(tratemeyer)," *Contemporary authors*, ed. Clare D. Kinsman, 1st revision, 17-20 (Detroit: Gale Research Co., 1976), p. 12.

58. *American women writers*, p. 15.

59. Foreman, "Saga of a mysterious author," p. 19.

60. Herz, *Nancy Drew and the Hardy Boys*, pp. 7-8.

GUIDE TO THE BIBLIOGRAPHY

Organization

The bibliography is arranged alphabetically by pseudonym; entries for each pseudonym are organized by type of work: magazine stories, series publications, and other (nonseries) publications.

MAGAZINE PUBLICATIONS

Magazine publications, arranged alphabetically by story title, include all works from magazines and story papers, but do not include dime novels.

SERIES PUBLICATIONS

Series publications include all books published as part of any series, including dime novels and other publishers' series.*

Series entries are arranged alphabetically by series title; within each series, books are listed chronologically, observing the series order used in advertisements. Each series entry begins with the following block of information about the series:

Volumes:	Total number of titles in the series.
Printed:	Dates show the original publication dates for the series, not reprint dates. If no publication dates are available, this line is omitted.
Publisher:	Original publisher(s) for the series.

---

*The term "publishers' series" in this guide is used to describe a series consisting of books by several authors, often on unrelated subjects, usually reprinted as part of a "catch-all" series. Often, the series have general titles, such as Boys' Own Library or Boys' Liberty series.

Reprint publisher:	Self-explanatory. Listed in chronological order whenever possible.
Illustrator:	Illustrators are for the original publishers' editions, unless otherwise noted. In some cases, information about illustrations is not complete; the absence of an illustrator's name for a volume or volumes in the series about illustrations in reprint editions is included under books published without illustrations. Unsigned illustrations are listed as anonymous. Information about illustrations in reprint editions is included under "Additional information," whenever possible.
Source of annotations:	Some entries are annotated with descriptions from publishers' advertisements or from Library of Congress cataloging in publication data. The source is noted.
Additional information:	This section provides miscellaneous background and supplementary information about some series, as well as charts illustrating changes in the series order and revision schedules for several of the more popular series.
Series description:	Taken from publishers' advertisements.

OTHER PUBLICATIONS

Other publications lists books originally published as individual titles rather than as series books. Books that first appeared as series titles and were later reprinted as individual volumes are not included here unless the reprint edition appeared with a new title. Entries are arranged alphabetically.

Annotations

Changes in title, publisher, year of publication, pseudonym, series title, or series order are noted in annotations for each book. If the title, pseudonym, or other information was not changed, this information is not repeated.

The entry for the first publication of a title lists all reprint editions; entries for reprint editions are annotated only with a cross-reference to the first publication.

Symbols

For purposes of cross-referencing and indexing, entries are numbered consecutively throughout the book; whole numbers are used for magazine stories, series titles '(but not individual volumes in the series), and other (nonseries) publications. Individual titles within a series are indicated by a whole number plus a number after a decimal point showing their position within the series. (For example, *The Bobbsey twins*, the first volume in the Bobbsey Twins series, would be 183S.1: 183S is the entry number for the Bobbsey Twins series, and .1 shows that *The Bobbsey twins* is the first volume.)

In addition to the entry numbers, each reference has one of the following letters, to identify the type of work:

M   denotes a magazine story

S   denotes a series

P   denotes a dime novel series or a publishers' series

N   denotes a nonseries title (a book not issued as part of a series)

Two other symbols are occasionally used for clarification:

Q   (following an entry number) indicates questionable authorship and is used when a title is considered a probable Stratemeyer, but not a proven work.

X   (used only with series book numbers) indicates that the decimal point number of the series book is not the actual volume number. (For example, *The young bridge-tender* by Arthur M. Winfield is the first title by Winfield in the Medal Library; however, the Medal Library was a paperback series of over 300 titles, and *The young bridge-tender* was number 249 in the series. The entry number 337P.1X shows that it is the first book by Winfield in the series, but not the first volume of the series.)

Appendices

Appendices A, B, C, and D summarize information presented in the bibliography: Appendix A lists all Stratemeyer and Stratemeyer Syndicate pseudonyms, with the dates these pseudonyms were used; Appendix B provides a chronological list of Stratemeyer and Stratemeyer Syndicate series, including many reprinted series, but excluding publishers' series, dime novels, and undated reprint series; Appendix C arranges all Stratemeyer and Stratemeyer Syndicate series by publisher and includes some information about the changes in publishing houses; and Appendix D names several writers and the Syndicate series to which they contributed.

Appendices E and F provide additional information about Stratemeyer and series books. Appendix E, a secondary bibliography, is composed of two parts: the first is a list of books and articles containing information about Stratemeyer and the Stratemeyer Syndicate—everything from biographical sketches and bibliographies to analyses of the books; the second part lists primarily bibliographic sources, with some titles discussing dime novels, story papers, or publishing houses. Appendix F notes several libraries with Stratemeyer and Stratemeyer Syndicate holdings and, in most cases, contains a capsule description of the holdings.

Indices

An index to illustrators is included.

References in the magazine, series, and short-title index are to main entries; the index does not include references to annotations that also list these titles, except for title changes mentioned only in annotations (such as those for the revised editions of Bobbsey Twins titles).

Stratemeyer
Pseudonyms
and
Series Books _____

BIBLIOGRAPHY BY PSEUDONYM

Manager Henry Abbott

In 1895 two of Edward Stratemeyer's stories were serialized in Good News, a Street & Smith boys' story paper, under the pseudonym Manager Henry Abbott. Both tales were assigned new titles and pseudonyms and reissued in book form in 1902 by Street & Smith, then reprinted by other publishers. A third tale, tentatively attributed to Stratemeyer, was published in 1901 in another Street & Smith story paper, Boys of America, and was later reprinted as a dime novel. All of the stories dealt with life on the stage.

Until recently, Edward Stratemeyer was also thought to be the author of two other Manager Henry Abbott stories, "Behind the footlights; or, The adventures of Fred Leslie on the stage and off" and "Nimble Nip; or, The call boy of the Olympic Theatre." Research by J. Randolph Cox in Street & Smith's publishing records has shown that "Behind the footlights" was actually the work of J. B. Tracy. While the author of "Nimble Nip" is not known, Stratemeyer seems an unlikely candidate since "Nimble Nip" was taken from no. 5 NUGGET LIBRARY, a dime novel that predates Stratemeyer's earliest work by over a month.

MAGAZINE PUBLICATIONS

001M   "A footlight favorite; or, Born to be an actor." Good News, vol. 10, nos. 257-269, April 6-June 29, 1895.

   Published in book form in 1902 by Street & Smith in the BOYS' OWN LI-
   BRARY as Mark Dale's stage venture; or, Bound to be an actor by Arthur
   M. Winfield (333P.1X), and in 1904 in Street & Smith's paperback MEDAL
   LIBRARY, as no. 279, with the new title and author (337P.3X). It was
   also included in McKay's BOYS' OWN LIBRARY, in 1902, as Mark Dale's
   stage adventure; or, Bound to be an actor, again with Arthur M. Winfield
   listed as author (332P.1X).

002MQ   "Footlight Phil; or, From call boy to star." Boys of America,
nos. 10-15, Dec. 7, 1901-Jan. 11, 1902.

Reprinted as no. 205 in Street & Smith's BRAVE AND BOLD series, Nov. 24, 1906 (004PQ.1X).

003M   "Neka, king of fire; or, A mystery of the variety stage." Good News, vol. 12, nos. 295-307, Dec. 28, 1895-March 21, 1896.

Published in book form in 1902 by Street & Smith in the BOYS' OWN LIBRARY as Neka, the boy conjurer; or, A mystery of the stage by Captain Ralph Bonehill (051P.1X). The new author and title were also used for the next three editions: in 1902, as part of McKay's BOYS' OWN LIBRARY (050P.1X); in 1904, as no. 250 in Street & Smith's paperback MEDAL LIBRARY (059P.2X); and in 1905, as part of Caldwell's FAMOUS BOOKS FOR BOYS (054P.2X).

SERIES PUBLICATIONS

004PQ BRAVE AND BOLD

Volumes: 1*
Printed: 1906*
Publisher: Street & Smith
Additional information: BRAVE AND BOLD was a dime novel series published from December 27, 1902 through March 11, 1911. Many of its stories were from Street & Smith's boys' story papers. Only two of the 429 titles in this series have been attributed to Edward Stratemeyer: the Manager Henry Abbott story, whose authorship is not proven, and "The electric wizard," no. 195, published under the pseudonym Emerson Bell (037P.1X).

004PQ.1X Footlight Phil; or, From callboy to star. No. 205. Nov. 24, 1906.

First published in Boys of America, Dec. 7, 1901-Jan. 11, 1902, as "Footlight Phil; or, From call boy to star" (002MQ).

Harrison Adams

The pseudonym Harrison Adams appeared on one series, the PIONEER BOYS (also called the YOUNG PIONEERS), which was published from 1912 to 1928. There is still some confusion about the author behind this pseudonym: St. George Rathborne took credit for writing the PIONEER BOYS, and his claim is generally undisputed, but the Stratemeyer Syndicate also asserts that it is a Syndicate series. Rathborne and Stratemeyer worked together on several occasions, and Rathborne contributed to at least two Stratemeyer series, the OUTDOOR CHUMS (014S) and the BOYS OF COLUMBIA HIGH (150S). Whether

*   Number of volumes and years published apply only to titles written by Edward Stratemeyer under the pseudonym Manager Henry Abbott.

Edward Stratemeyer provided the plots and editing for the PIONEER BOYS, as he did for so many other Syndicate series, is not known.

SERIES PUBLICATIONS

005SQ PIONEER BOYS (YOUNG PIONEERS)

Volumes: 8
Printed: 1912-1928
Publisher: L. C. Page & Co.
Illustrator: Charles Livingston Bull, vols. 1-2
              H. Richard Boehm, vol. 3
              Walter S. Rogers, vols. 4-6
              Frank T. Merrill, vols. 7-8

005SQ.1   Pioneer boys of the Ohio; or, Clearing the wilderness. (Page, 1912).

005SQ.2   Pioneer boys on the great lakes; or, On the trail of the Iroquois. (Page, 1912).

005SQ.3   Pioneer boys of the Mississippi; or, The homestead in the wilderness. (Page, 1913).

005SQ.4   Pioneer boys of the Missouri; or, In the country of the Sioux. (Page, 1914).

005SQ.5   Pioneer boys of the Yellowstone; or, Lost in the land of wonders. (Page, 1915).

005SQ.6   Pioneer boys of the Columbia; or, In the wilderness of the great Northwest. (Page, 1916).

005SQ.7   Pioneer boys of the Colorado; or, Braving the perils of the Grand Canyon country. (Page, 1926).

005SQ.8   Pioneer boys of Kansas; or, A prairie home in buffalo land. (Page, 1928).

Horatio Alger, Jr.

Eleven of the books attributed to Horatio Alger, Jr., were written either partially or wholly by Edward Stratemeyer. Four volumes are listed as "completed by Arthur M. Winfield," one of Stratemeyer's pseudonyms; others bear only Alger's name on the title page.
     All were issued after Alger's death. Although Edward Stratemeyer explained that he was Alger's literary executor and had finished the manuscripts using Alger's notes, some Alger experts, such as Ralph D. Gardner,

feel the works are written entirely in Stratemeyer's style.
The eleven volumes were first published from 1900 to 1908.

MAGAZINE PUBLICATIONS

006M   "Jerry the backwoods boy; or, The Parkhurst treasure." Comfort
Magazine, Nov. 1906-Oct. 1907.

First published by Mershon in 1904 in the RISE IN LIFE series (011S.5X).

007M   "The young book agent; or, Frank Hardy's road to success."
American Boy, June-Nov. 1906.

First published by Stitt in 1905 in the RISE IN LIFE series (011S.8X).

008M   "Young Captain Jack; or, The son of a soldier." Golden Hours,
nos. 701-710, July 6-Sept. 7, 1901.

Reprinted in Sunshine for Youth, Nov. 1905-Aug. 1906 (009M). Published
in book form by Mershon in 1901 as vol. 3 of its RISE IN LIFE series;
reissued by Stitt and Chatterton-Peck in their RISE IN LIFE series, and
by Grosset & Dunlap as vol. 5 in its RISE IN LIFE series (011S.3).
Also published by Street & Smith in 1919 as no. 89 in the paperback
ALGER SERIES (010P.3X). A reprint of the Mershon edition was published
in 1975 by Aeonian Press, with an introduction by Ralph D. Gardner.
All versions except the ALGER SERIES were listed as "completed by Arthur
M. Winfield."

009M   "Young Captain Jack; or, The son of a soldier." Sunshine for
Youth, vol. 19, no. 10-vol. 20, no. 7, Nov. 1905-Aug. 1906.

First published in Golden Hours, July 6-Sept. 7, 1901 (008M).

SERIES PUBLICATIONS

010P   ALGER SERIES

Volumes: 11*
Printed: 1919*
Publisher: Street & Smith
Source of annotations: Street & Smith advertisements [S&S]
Additional information: The ALGER SERIES, a line of inexpensive paperback
    reprints, began on Nov. 15, 1915, and was issued twice a month until
    Nov. 1, 1920 (no. 123). Publication resumed on a biweekly schedule in
    1926 with no. 124 and continued until no. 202 in 1927. 140 volumes of
    the series were reprinted, again on a biweekly schedule, from Feb. 1928
    through June 1933.

---

* Number of volumes and years published apply only to titles written by
   Edward Stratemeyer under the name Horatio Alger, Jr.

The first eighty-six volumes were by Alger; after that, the series included works by other authors as well, most notably, Edward Stratemeyer and William Taylor Adams (Oliver Optic).

ALGER SERIES AUTHORS

Nos.
1-86   Horatio Alger, Jr.
87-97   Edward Stratemeyer (Stratemeyer Algers)
98-123   Edward Stratemeyer (reprint eds., nos. 102-123)
124-167   William Taylor Adams (Oliver Optic)
168-174   Horatio Alger, Jr. (reprint eds., nos. 98-101)
175-202   Various authors, with emphasis on Roy Franklin (12 titles)

The eleven Stratemeyer Algers were published with only Horatio Alger, Jr., listed as author; the other twenty-six Stratemeyer titles appeared under Stratemeyer's name.

Series description [S&S]: "The following list does not contain all the books that Horatio Alger wrote, but it contains most of them, and certainly the best. Horatio Alger is to boys what Charles Dickens is to grown-ups. His work is just as popular today as it was years ago. The books have a quality, the value of which is beyond computation.

"There are legions of boys of foreign parents who are being helped along the road to true Americanism by reading these books which are so peculiarly American in tone that the reader cannot fail to absorb some of the spirit of fair play and clean living which is so characteristically American.

"In this list will be included certain books by Edward Stratemeyer, Oliver Optic, and other authors who wrote the Alger type of stories, which are equal in interest and wholesomeness with those written by the famous author after which this great line of books for boys is named."

010P.1X   Lost at sea; or, Robert Roscoe's strange cruise. No. 87. June 9, 1919; June 1931.

First published by Mershon in 1904 in the RISE IN LIFE series (011S.6X).

010P.2X   From farm to fortune; or, Nat Nason's strange experience. No. 88. June 23, 1919; June 1931.

First published by Stitt in 1905 in the RISE IN LIFE series (011S.7X).

010P.3X   Young Captain Jack; or, The son of a soldier. No. 89. July 7, 1919; July 1931.

First published in Golden Hours, July 6-Sept. 7, 1901 (008M).

010P.4X   Joe, the hotel boy; or, Winning out by pluck. No. 90. July 21, 1919; July 1931.

First published by Cupples & Leon in 1906 (013N).

010P.5X   Out for business; or, Robert Frost's strange career. No. 91. Aug. 4, 1919; Aug. 1931.

First published by Mershon in 1900 as vol. 1 of the RISE IN LIFE series, with the words "completed by Arthur M. Winfield" on the title page (011S.1).

010P.6X   Falling in with fortune; or, The experiences of a young secretary. No. 92. Aug. 18, 1919; Aug. 1931.

First published by Mershon in 1900 as vol. 2 of the RISE IN LIFE series, with the words "completed by Arthur M. Winfield" on the title page (011S.2).

010P.7X   Nelson the newsboy; or, Afloat in New York. No. 93. Sept. 8, 1919; Sept. 1931.

First published by Mershon in 1901 as vol. 4 of the RISE IN LIFE series, with the words "completed by Arthur M. Winfield" on the title page (011S.4).

010P.8X   Randy of the river; or, The adventures of a young deckhand. No. 94. Sept. 22, 1919; Sept. 1931.

First published by Chatterton-Peck in 1906 in the RISE IN LIFE series (011S.9X).

010P.9X   Jerry the backwoods boy; or, The Parkhurst treasure. No. 95. Oct. 6, 1919; Oct. 1931.

First published by Mershon in 1904 in the RISE IN LIFE series (011S.5X).

010P.10X Ben Logan's triumph; or, The boys of Boxwood Academy. No. 96. Oct. 20, 1919; Oct. 1931.

First published by Cupples & Leon in 1908 (012N).

010P.11X The young book agent; or, Frank Hardy's road to success. No. 97. Nov. 3, 1919; Nov. 1931.

First published by Stitt in 1905 in the RISE IN LIFE series (011S.8X).

011S   RISE IN LIFE

Volumes: 11
Printed: 1900-1912
Publisher: The Mershon Company, vols. 1-6
            Stitt Publishing Company, vols. 7-8
            Chatterton-Peck Company, vol. 9
            Grosset & Dunlap, vols. 10-11
Reprint publisher: Stitt Publishing Company, vols. 1-6
                    Chatterton-Peck Company, vols. 1-8
                    Grosset & Dunlap, vols. 1-9
Source of annotations: Grosset & Dunlap advertisements [G&D]
Additional information: Mershon published the first six titles in the RISE IN LIFE series from 1900-1904. Stitt took over the series in 1905,

adding the seventh and eighth volumes; the series order of Stitt's RISE
IN LIFE series is not known. Chatterton-Peck continued the series in
1906 and also published the ninth volume. Again, the series order is
not known.* The last two volumes were originally published in 1906 and
1908 by Cupples & Leon as individual titles.

Legal problems between Chatterton-Peck, Stitt, Mershon, and Stratemeyer occurred in 1907 and 1908, and on March 7, 1908, a Grosset & Dunlap advertisement in Publishers' Weekly announced that Grosset & Dunlap
had "taken over the publication" of several series, including the nine-
volume RISE IN LIFE series. Four years later, Grosset & Dunlap added
the last two Stratemeyer Algers to the series.

Three of the stories were also serialized in magazines: two were
printed after their initial appearance in book form; the other was first
published as a magazine story. All eleven were also reissued in Street
& Smith's ALGER SERIES (010P).

The first four books (Out for business, Falling in with fortune,
Young Captain Jack, and Nelson the newsboy) were published with the
words "completed by Arthur M. Winfield" on the title page for all
editions except Street & Smith's; the others were not. Though a
Mershon advertisement for the first four volumes mentions Winfield's
contributions, the Grosset & Dunlap advertisements for the eleven-volume
series credit only Horatio Alger, Jr., stating, "These are the stories
last written by this famous author."

011S.1   Out for business; or, Robert Frost's strange career. (Mershon,
1900; Stitt, ca1905; Chatterton-Peck, ca1906; Grosset & Dunlap).**

    Vol. 3 in Grosset & Dunlap's RISE IN LIFE series. Reprinted in 1919
    as no. 91 in Street & Smith's ALGER SERIES, with no mention of the
    Winfield completion (010P.5X).
        [G&D]: "Relates the adventures of a country boy who is compelled
    to leave home and seek his fortune in the great world at large."

011S.2   Falling in with fortune; or, The experiences of a young secretary.
(Mershon, 1900; Stitt, ca1905; Chatterton-Peck, ca1906; Grosset & Dunlap).**

    Vol. 4 in Grosset & Dunlap's RISE IN LIFE series. Reprinted in 1919
    as no. 92 in Street & Smith's ALGER SERIES, with no mention of the
    Winfield completion (010P.6X).
        [G&D]: "This is a companion tale to 'Out for Business,' but com-
    plete in itself, and tells of the further doings of Robert Frost as
    private secretary."

011S.3   Young Captain Jack; or, The son of a soldier. (Mershon, 1901;
Stitt, ca1905; Chatterton-Peck, ca1906; Grosset & Dunlap).**

    Vol. 5 in Grosset & Dunlap's RISE IN LIFE series. First published in
    Golden Hours, July 6-Sept. 7, 1901 (008M).
        [G&D]: "The scene is laid in the South during the Civil War, and
    the hero is a waif who was cast up by the sea and adopted by a rich
    Southern planter."

---

*   When a publisher took over a series, the series order was sometimes al-
     tered, with the new titles listed first: the Stitt ads may have shown
     The young book agent or From farm to fortune as the first volume, while
     Chatterton-Peck's list may have started with Randy of the river.
**   "Completed by Arthur M. Winfield."

011S.4   Nelson the newsboy; or, Afloat in New York. (Mershon, 1901;*
Stitt, ca1905; Chatterton-Peck, ca1906; Grosset & Dunlap).**

> Vol. 6 in Grosset & Dunlap's RISE IN LIFE series. Reprinted in 1919
> as no. 93 in Street & Smith's ALGER SERIES, with no mention of the
> Winfield completion (010P.7X).
>   [G&D]: "Mr. Alger is always at his best in the portrayal of life
> in New York City, and this story is among the best he has given our
> young readers."

011S.5X   Jerry the backwoods boy; or, The Parkhurst treasure. (Mershon,
1904; Stitt, ca1905; Chatterton-Peck, ca1906; Grosset & Dunlap).

> Possibly published at the same time as Lost at sea (011S.6X). Vol. 8
> in Grosset & Dunlap's RISE IN LIFE series. Reprinted in 1919 as no.
> 95 in Street & Smith's ALGER SERIES (010P.9X). Also serialized in
> Comfort Magazine, Nov. 1906-Oct. 1907 (006M).
>   [G&D]: "Depicts life on a farm of New York State. The mystery of
> the treasure will fascinate every boy. Jerry is a character worth
> knowing."

011S.6X   Lost at sea; or, Robert Roscoe's strange cruise. (Mershon, 1904;
Stitt, ca1905; Chatterton-Peck, ca1906; Grosset & Dunlap).

> Possibly published at the same time as Jerry the backwoods boy (011S.5X).
> Vol. 7 in Grosset & Dunlap's RISE IN LIFE series. Reprinted in 1919
> as no. 87 in Street & Smith's ALGER SERIES (010P.1X).
>   [G&D]: "A sea story of uncommon interest. The hero falls in with
> a strange derelict--a ship given over to the wild animals of a menag-
> erie."

011S.7X   From farm to fortune; or, Nat Nason's strange experience. (Stitt,
1905; Chatterton-Peck, ca1906; Grosset & Dunlap).

> Vol. 2 in Grosset & Dunlap's RISE IN LIFE series. Reprinted in 1919
> as no. 88 in Street & Smith's ALGER SERIES (010P.2X).
>   [G&D]: "Nat was a poor country lad. Work on the farm was hard,
> and after a quarrel with his uncle, with whom he resided, he struck
> out for himself."

011S.8X   The young book agent; or, Frank Hardy's road to success. (Stitt,
1905; Chatterton-Peck, ca1906; Grosset & Dunlap).

> Vol. 1 in Grosset & Dunlap's RISE IN LIFE series. Reprinted in 1919
> as no. 97 in Street & Smith's ALGER SERIES (010P.11X). Also serial-
> ized in American Boy, June-Nov. 1906 (007M).
>   [G&D]: "A plain but uncommonly interesting tale of everyday life,
> describing the ups and downs of a boy book-agent."

011S.9X   Randy of the river; or, The adventures of a young deckhand.
(Chatterton-Peck, 1906; Grosset & Dunlap).

---

* Some Mershon ads list the title as Adrift in New York; or, The adventures of a wide awake boy.
** "Completed by Arthur M. Winfield."

Vol. 9 in Grosset & Dunlap's RISE IN LIFE series. Reprinted in 1919 as no. 94 in Street & Smith's ALGER SERIES (010P.8X).
    [G&D]: "Life on a river steamboat is not so romantic as some young people may imagine, but Randy Thompson wanted work and took what was offered."

011S.10   Joe, the hotel boy; or, Winning out by pluck. (Grosset & Dunlap, 1912).

    First published by Cupples & Leon in 1906 (013N).
    [G&D]: "A graphic account of the adventures of a country boy in the city."

011S.11   Ben Logan's triumph; or, The boys of Boxwood Academy. (Grosset & Dunlap, 1912).

    First published by Cupples & Leon in 1908 (012N).
    [G&D]: "The trials and triumphs of a city newsboy in the country."

OTHER PUBLICATIONS

012N   Ben Logan's triumph; or, The boys of Boxwood Academy. (Cupples & Leon, 1908).

    Reprinted as vol. 11 in Grosset & Dunlap's RISE IN LIFE series in 1912 (011S.11), and as no. 96 in Street & Smith's ALGER SERIES in 1919 (010P.10X).

013N   Joe the hotel boy; or, Winning out by pluck. (Cupples & Leon, 1906).

    Reprinted as vol. 10 in Grosset & Dunlap's RISE IN LIFE series in 1912 (011S.10), and as no. 90 in Street & Smith's ALGER SERIES in 1919 (010P.4X).
    [C&L]: "This is one of the last stories penned by that prince of all juvenile writers, Horatio Alger, Jr. It describes the adventures of a youth brought up in the country by an old hermit. When the hermit dies the boy obtains work at a nearby hotel and later on drifts to the city and obtains a position in another hotel."*

Captain Quincy Allen

Captain Quincy Allen, a Stratemeyer Syndicate house name, appeared only on the eight-volume OUTDOOR CHUMS series. St. George Rathborne assisted with this series.

---

* Source of annotation: Cupples & Leon advertisement.

SERIES PUBLICATIONS

014S   OUTDOOR CHUMS

Volumes: 8
Printed: 1911-1916
Publisher: Grosset & Dunlap
Reprint publisher: Goldsmith Publishing Co., vols. 1-8
Illustrator: H. Richard Boehm, vols. 1-5
              N. C. Richards, vol. 6
              Walter S. Rogers, vols. 7-8
Source of annotations: Grosset & Dunlap advertisements [G&D]
Additional information: The Goldsmith editions were not illustrated. There
    may have been Donohue editions of some volumes.
Series description [G&D]: "The outdoor chums are four wide-awake lads,
    sons of wealthy men of a small city located on a lake. The boys love
    outdoor life, and are greatly interested in hunting, fishing, and pic-
    ture taking. They have motor cycles, motor boats, canoes, etc., and
    during their vacations go everywhere and have all sorts of thrilling
    adventures. The stories give full directions for camping out, how to
    fish, how to hunt wild animals and prepare the skins for stuffing, how
    to manage a canoe, how to swim, etc. Full of the spirit of outdoor
    life."

014S.1   The outdoor chums; or, The first tour of the rod, gun and camera
club. (Grosset & Dunlap, 1911; Goldsmith).

014S.2   The outdoor chums on the lake; or, Lively adventures on Wildcat
Island. (Grosset & Dunlap, 1911; Goldsmith).

014S.3   The outdoor chums in the forest; or, Laying the ghost of Oak
Ridge. (Grosset & Dunlap, 1911; Goldsmith).

014S.4   The outdoor chums on the Gulf; or, Rescuing the lost balloonists.
(Grosset & Dunlap, 1911; Goldsmith).

014S.5   The outdoor chums after big game; or, Perilous adventures in the
wilderness. (Grosset & Dunlap, 1911; Goldsmith).

014S.6   The outdoor chums on a houseboat; or, The rivals of the Mississippi. (Grosset & Dunlap, 1913; Goldsmith).

014S.7   The outdoor chums in the big woods; or, The rival hunters of
Lumber Run. (Grosset & Dunlap, 1915; Goldsmith).

014S.8   The outdoor chums at Cabin Point; or, The golden cup mystery.
(Grosset & Dunlap, 1916; Goldsmith).

Philip A. Alyer

Edward Stratemeyer wrote two stories under the pen name Philip A. Alyer. Both were published in boys' story papers between 1895 and 1897. One was later retitled and reprinted in book form, with Roy Rockwood listed as the author.

MAGAZINE PUBLICATIONS

015M   "Among South Sea savages; or, The last cruise of the comet." Bright Days, nos. 28-39, Nov. 28, 1896-Jan. 9, 1897.

016M   "A nobody schoolboy; or, Backbone against the world." Young People of America, nos. 28-39, Dec. 7, 1895-Feb. 22, 1896.

   Published in book form by Mershon in 1900 as A schoolboy's pluck; or, The career of a nobody by Roy Rockwood; reprinted by Chatterton-Peck with the new author and title (239N).

Victor Appleton

From 1910 to 1941, the Stratemeyer Syndicate produced seventy-two stories under the pseudonym Victor Appleton. Seventy of these were originally published by Grosset & Dunlap in four series: TOM SWIFT (1910-1941; 38 vols.), the MOTION PICTURE CHUMS (1913-1916; 7 vols.), the MOVING PICTURE BOYS (1913-1919; 10 vols), and DON STURDY (1925-1935; 15 vols.). Whitman published the remaining two stories as the last volumes of the TOM SWIFT series.
   Victor Appleton also appeared as the author of thirty-one reprint editions: nine TOM SWIFT books, published by Whitman; the seventeen-volume MOVIE BOYS series, by Garden City (retitled paperback editions of the MOTION PICTURE CHUMS and MOVING PICTURE BOYS series); and volumes 11 through 15 of the MOVING PICTURE BOYS series, by Grosset & Dunlap (retitled editions of the first five volumes of the MOTION PICTURE CHUMS series).
   Except for the excerpts published in A superboy, supergirl anthology, all of the stories by Victor Appleton appeared only as series books. All have boys as central characters, either as inventors (TOM SWIFT), world travelers (DON STURDY), filmmakers (MOVING PICTURE BOYS), or owners of a movie theater (MOTION PICTURE CHUMS). All of the series were created by Edward Stratemeyer, though Howard Garis contributed to many of the volumes in the TOM SWIFT series.
   The TOM SWIFT books achieved the most success, with sales estimated at approximately 6,000,000 copies. Indeed, so great was their popularity that in 1954, thirteen years after the publication of the last volume, the Stratemeyer Syndicate resurrected TOM SWIFT and began a new series--TOM SWIFT, JR., by Victor Appleton II.

SERIES PUBLICATIONS

017S   DON STURDY

Volumes: 15
Printed: 1925-1935
Publisher: Grosset & Dunlap
Illustrator: Walter S. Rogers, vols. 1-11
              Nat Falk, vols. 12-15
Source of annotations: Grosset & Dunlap advertisements [G&D]
Series description [G&D]: "Every red-blooded boy will enjoy the thrilling
    adventures of Don Sturdy. In company with his uncles, one a big game
    hunter, the other a noted scientist, he travels far and wide--into the
    jungles of South America, across the Sahara, deep into the African jun-
    gle, up where the Alaskan volcanoes spout, down among the head hunters
    of Borneo and many other places where there is danger and excitement.
    Every boy who has known Tom Swift will at once become the boon companion
    of daring Don Sturdy."

017S.1   Don Sturdy on the desert of mystery; or, Autoing in the land of
caravans. (Grosset & Dunlap, 1925).

    [G&D]: "An engrossing tale of the Sahara Desert, of encounters with
    wild animals and crafty Arabs."

017S.2   Don Sturdy with the big snake hunters; or, Lost in the jungles
of the Amazon. (Grosset & Dunlap, 1925).

    [G&D]: "Don's uncle, the hunter, took an order for some of the biggest
    snakes to be found in South America--to be delivered alive! The filling
    of that order brought keen excitement to the boy."

017S.3   Don Sturdy in the tombs of gold; or, The old Eygptian's great
secret. (Grosset & Dunlap, 1925).

    [G&D]: "A fascinating tale of exploration and adventure in the Valley
    of Kings in Eygpt. Once the whole party became lost in the maze of
    cavelike tombs far underground."

017S.4   Don Sturdy across the North Pole; or, Cast away in the land of
ice. (Grosset & Dunlap, 1925).

    [G&D]; "Don and his uncles joined an expedition bound by air across
    the north pole. A great polar blizzard nearly wrecks the airship."

017S.5   Don Sturdy in the land of volcanoes; or, The trail of the ten
thousand smokes. (Grosset & Dunlap, 1925).

    [G&D]: "An absorbing tale of adventures among the volcanoes of Alaska
    in a territory but recently explored. A story that will make Don dearer
    to his readers than ever."

017S.6   Don Sturdy in the port of lost ships; or, Adrift in the Sargasso
Sea. (Grosset & Dunlap, 1926).

[G&D]: "This story is just full of exciting and fearful experiences on the sea."

017S.7   Don Sturdy among the gorillas; or, Adrift in the great jungle. (Grosset & Dunlap, 1927).

[G&D]: "A thrilling story of adventure in darkest Africa. Don is carried over a mighty waterfall into the heart of gorilla land."

017S.8   Don Sturdy captured by head hunters; or, Adrift in the wilds of Borneo. (Grosset & Dunlap, 1928).

[G&D]: "Don and his party are wrecked in Borneo and have thrilling adventures among the head hunters."

017S.9   Don Sturdy in lion land; or, The strange clearing in the jungle. (Grosset & Dunlap, 1929).

[G&D]: "Don and his uncles organize an expedition to capture some extra large lions alive."

017S.10   Don Sturdy in the land of giants; or, Captives of the savage Patagonians. (Grosset & Dunlap, 1930).

017S.11   Don Sturdy on the ocean bottom; or, The strange cruise of the Phantom. (Grosset & Dunlap, 1931).

017S.12   Don Sturdy in the temples of fear; or, Destined for a strange sacrifice. (Grosset & Dunlap, 1932).

017S.13   Don Sturdy lost in Glacier Bay; or, The mystery of the moving totem poles. (Grosset & Dunlap, 1933).

017S.14   Don Sturdy trapped in the flaming wilderness; or, Unearthing secrets in central Asia. (Grosset & Dunlap, 1934).

017S.15   Don Sturdy with the harpoon hunters; or, The strange cruise of the whaling ship. (Grosset & Dunlap, 1935).

018S   MOTION PICTURE CHUMS

Volumes: 7
Printed: 1913-1916
Publisher: Grosset & Dunlap
Illustrator: Dick Richards, vols. 1-3
              Walter S. Rogers, vols. 4-7
Source of annotations: Grosset & Dunlap advertisements [G&D]
Additional information: The first five volumes of the MOTION PICTURE CHUMS series were retitled and reprinted by Grosset & Dunlap as the last five volumes of the MOVING PICTURE BOYS series (020S). In 1926 the original ten-volume MOVING PICTURE BOYS series and the seven-volume MOTION PICTURE CHUMS series were assigned new titles and combined to form the MOVIE BOYS series (019S). The original plates were used for all editions.

The Stratemeyer Syndicate created several series about motion pictures: the MOTION PICTURE CHUMS, the MOVING PICTURE BOYS, the MOTION PICTURE COMRADES (024S), and the MOVING PICTURE GIRLS (186S). Though the titles are similar, the main characters' occupations are not the same: the MOTION PICTURE CHUMS own a movie theater; the MOVING PICTURE GIRLS are actresses; the MOVING PICTURE BOYS and the MOTION PICTURE COMRADES are filmmakers.

Series description [G&D]: "In these stories we follow the adventures of three boys, who, after purchasing at auction the contents of a moving picture house, open a theater of their own. Their many trials and tribulations, leading up to the final success of their venture, make very entertaining stories."

018S.1   The motion picture chums' first venture; or, Opening a photo playhouse in Fairlands. (Grosset & Dunlap, 1913).

Reprinted by Grosset & Dunlap in 1921 as The moving picture boys' first showhouse; or, Opening up for business in Fairlands, vol. 11 in the MOVING PICTURE BOYS series (020S.11), and by Garden City in 1926 as The movie boys' first showhouse; or, Fighting for a foothold in Fairlands, vol. 11 in the MOVIE BOYS series (019S.11).
[G&D]: "The adventures of Frank, Randy and Pep in running a Motion Picture show. They had trials and tribulations but finally succeed."

018S.2   The motion picture chums at Seaside Park; or, The rival photo theatres of the Boardwalk. (Grosset & Dunlap, 1913).

Reprinted by Grosset & Dunlap in 1921 as The moving picture boys at Seaside Park; or, The rival photo theatres of the Board-walk, vol. 12 in the MOVING PICTURE BOYS series (020S.12), and by Garden City in 1926 as The movie boys at Seaside Park; or, The rival photo houses of the Boardwalk, vol. 12 in the MOVIE BOYS series (019S.12).
[G&D]: "Their success at Fairlands encourages the boys to open their show at Seaside Park, where they have exciting adventures--also a profitable season."

018S.3   The motion picture chums on Broadway; or, The mystery of the missing cash box. (Grosset & Dunlap, 1914).

Reprinted by Grosset & Dunlap in 1921 as The moving picture boys on Broadway; or, The mystery of the missing cash box, vol. 13 in the MOVING PICTURE BOYS series (020S.13), and by Garden City in 1926 as The movie boys on Broadway; or, The mystery of the missing cash box, vol. 13 in the MOVIE BOYS series (019S.13).
[G&D]: "Backed by a rich western friend the chums established a photo playhouse in the great metropolis, where new adventures await them."

018S.4   The motion picture chums' outdoor exhibition; or, The film that solved a mystery. (Grosset & Dunlap, 1914).

Reprinted by Grosset & Dunlap in 1922 as The moving picture boys' outdoor exhibition; or, The film that solved a mystery, vol. 14 in the MOVING PICTURE BOYS series (020S.14), and by Garden City in 1927 as The movie boys' outdoor exhibition; or, The film that solved a mystery, vol. 14 in the MOVIE BOYS series (019S.14).

[G&D]: "This time the playhouse was in a big summer park. How a
film that was shown gave a clew to an important mystery is interestingly
related."

018S.5   The motion picture chums' new idea; or, The first educational
photo playhouse. (Grosset & Dunlap, 1914).

Reprinted by Grosset & Dunlap in 1922 as The moving picture boys' new
idea,* vol. 15 in the MOVING PICTURE BOYS series (020S.15), and by
Garden City in 1927 as The movie boys' new idea; or, Getting the best
of their enemies, vol. 15 of the MOVIE BOYS series (019S.15).
    [G&D]: "In this book the scene is shifted to Boston, and there is
intense rivalry in the establishment of photo playhouses of educational
value."

018S.6   The motion picture chums at the fair; or, The greatest film ever
exhibited. (Grosset & Dunlap, 1915).

Reprinted by Garden City in 1927 as The movie boys at the big fair; or,
The greatest film ever exhibited, vol. 16 of the MOVIE BOYS series
(019S.16).
    [G&D]: "The chums go to San Francisco, where they have some trials
but finally meet with great success."

018S.7   The motion picture chums' war spectacle; or, The film that won
the prize. (Grosset & Dunlap, 1916).

Reprinted by Garden City in 1927 as The movie boys' war spectacle; or,
The film that won the prize, vol. 17 in the MOVIE BOYS series (019S.17).
    [G&D]: "Through being of service to the writer of a great scenario,
the chums are enabled to produce it and win a prize."

019S   MOVIE BOYS

Volumes: 17
Printed: 1926-1927
Publisher: Garden City Publishing Company
Source of annotations: Garden City advertisements [GC]
Additional information: The MOVIE BOYS was a paperback series reprinted
    from the plates of the ten-volume MOVING PICTURE BOYS (020S) and the
    seven-volume MOTION PICTURE CHUMS (018S) series. Except for the covers,
    the MOVIE BOOKS boys were published without illustrations.
        On January 2, 1926, Garden City published paperback editions of the
    first volume of four Stratemeyer Syndicate series: the MOVIE BOYS,
    FRANK ALLEN (151S), NAT RIDLEY (215S), and DAVE FEARLESS (228S). After
    that, all four series were issued monthly: FRANK ALLEN on the 7th of
    each month; DAVE FEARLESS on the 14th; NAT RIDLEY on the 21st; and the
    MOVIE BOYS on the 28th.
Series description [GC]: "Do you want to know how the movies are made?
    Do you want to know how movie showhouses are run? Do you want to know
    all about the perils of taking films of Current Events? If so read
    THE MOVIE BOYS SERIES By Victor Appleton."

---

* Subtitle missing.

019S.1   The movie boys on call; or, Filming the perils of a great city. (Garden City, 1926).

> First published by Grosset & Dunlap in 1913 as The moving picture boys; or, The perils of a great city depicted, vol. 1 in the MOVING PICTURE BOYS series (020S.1).
> [GC]: "Joe and Blake were kept on the jump from morning to night taking pictures of interesting happenings--a man leaping from the Brooklyn Bridge, a big fire, a riot, and numerous other occurrences in and around New York. And more than once the chums got into a tight place. A story full of lively action from the first chapter to the last."

019S.2   The movie boys in the wild west; or, Stirring days among the cowboys and Indians. (Garden City, 1926).

> First published by Grosset & Dunlap in 1913 as The moving picture boys in the west; or, Taking scenes among the cowboys and Indians, vol. 2 of the MOVING PICTURE BOYS series (020S.2).
> [GC]: "An absorbing tale of the great outdoors. How Joe and Blake traveled to the West, how they encountered cowboys and Indians who were friendly and also those who were bitter enemies, and how the movie boys solved a queer mystery, all go to make up a tale no boy will want to miss."

019S.3   The movie boys and the wreckers; or, Facing the perils of the deep. (Garden City, 1926).

> First published by Grosset & Dunlap in 1913 as The moving picture boys on the coast; or, Showing the perils of the deep, vol. 3 of the MOVING PICTURE BOYS series (020S.3).
> [GC]: "From the West the boys go on an assignment to the seacoast and there come face to face with the dreaded wreckers, those who put out false beacons so that a ship with a valuable cargo may be wrecked. It was a time of extreme peril for the movie boys but they proved themselves equal to every emergency."

019S.4   The movie boys in the jungle; or, Lively times among the wild beasts. (Garden City, 1926).

> First published by Grosset & Dunlap in 1913 as The moving picture boys in the jungle; or, Stirring times among the wild animals, vol. 4 of the MOVING PICTURE BOYS series (020S.4).

019S.5   The movie boys in earthquake land; or, Filming pictures amid strange perils. (Garden City, 1926).

> First published by Grosset & Dunlap in 1913 as The moving picture boys in earthquake land; or, Working amid many perils, vol. 5 of the MOVING PICTURE BOYS series (020S.5).

019S.6   The movie boys and the flood; or, Perilous days on the mighty Mississippi. (Garden City, 1926).

> First published by Grosset & Dunlap in 1914 as The moving picture boys and the flood; or, Perilous days on the Mississippi, vol. 6 of the MOVING PICTURE BOYS series (020S.6).

019S.7   The movie boys in peril; or, Strenuous days along the Panama Canal. (Garden City, 1926).

> First published by Grosset & Dunlap in 1915 as The moving picture boys at Panama; or, Stirring adventures along the great canal, vol. 7 of the MOVING PICTURE BOYS series (020S.7).

019S.8   The movie boys under the sea; or, The treasure of the lost ship. (Garden City, 1926).

> First published by Grosset & Dunlap in 1916 as The moving picture boys under the sea; or, The treasure of the lost ship, vol. 8 of the MOVING PICTURE BOYS series (020S.8).

019S.9   The movie boys under fire; or, The search for the stolen film. (Garden City, 1926).

> First published by Grosset & Dunlap in 1918 as The moving picture boys on the war front; or, The hunt for the stolen army film, vol. 9 of the MOVING PICTURE BOYS series (020S.9).

019S.10   The movie boys under Uncle Sam; or, Taking pictures for the army. (Garden City, 1926).

> First published by Grosset & Dunlap in 1919 as The moving picture boys on French battlefields; or, Taking pictures for the U. S. army, vol. 10 of the MOVING PICTURE BOYS series (020S.10).

019S.11   The movie boys' first showhouse; or, Fighting for a foothold in Fairlands. (Garden City, 1926).

> First published by Grosset & Dunlap in 1913 as The motion picture chums' first venture; or, Opening a photo playhouse in Fairlands, vol. 1 of the MOTION PICTURE CHUMS series (018S.1).

019S.12   The movie boys at Seaside Park; or, The rival photo houses of the Boardwalk. (Garden City, 1926).

> First published by Grosset & Dunlap in 1913 as The motion picture chums at Seaside Park; or, The rival photo theatres of the Boardwalk, vol. 2 of the MOTION PICTURE CHUMS series (018S.2).

019S.13   The movie boys on Broadway; or, The mystery of the missing cash box. (Garden City, 1926).

> First published by Grosset & Dunlap in 1913 as The motion picture chums on Broadway; or, The mystery of the missing cash box, vol. 3 of the MOTION PICTURE CHUMS series (018S.3).

019S.14   The movie boys' outdoor exhibition; or, The film that solved a mystery. (Garden City, 1927).

> First published by Grosset & Dunlap in 1914 as The motion picture chums' outdoor exhibition; or, The film that solved a mystery, vol. 4 of the MOTION PICTURE CHUMS series (018S.4).

019S.15   The movie boys' new idea; or, Getting the best of their enemies.
(Garden City, 1927).

   First published by Grosset & Dunlap in 1914 as The motion picture chums'
   new idea; or, The first educational photo playhouse, vol. 5 in the
   MOTION PICTURE CHUMS series (018S.5).

019S.16   The movie boys at the big fair; or, The greatest film ever exhibited. (Garden City, 1927).

   First published by Grosset & Dunlap in 1915 as The motion picture chums
   at the fair; or, The greatest film ever exhibited, vol. 6 in the MOTION
   PICTURE CHUMS series (018S.6).

019S.17   The movie boys' war spectacle; or, The film that won the prize.
(Garden City, 1927).

   First published by Grosset & Dunlap in 1916 as The motion picture chums'
   war spectacle; or, The film that won the prize, vol. 7 in the MOTION
   PICTURE CHUMS series (018S.7).

020S   MOVING PICTURE BOYS

Volumes: 15
Printed: 1913-1922
Publisher: Grosset & Dunlap
Illustrator: Walter S. Rogers, vols. 1-8, 14-15
              R. Emmett Owen, vols. 9-10
              Dick Richards, vols. 11-13
Source of annotations: Grosset & Dunlap advertisements [G&D]
Additional information: The last five volumes of this series first appeared
    in 1913 and 1914 as the first five volumes of the MOTION PICTURE CHUMS
    series (018S); the original plates were used for the reprint editions.
    The MOVING PICTURE BOYS and MOTION PICTURE CHUMS series were retitled
    and reprinted by Garden City in 1926 and 1927 as the paperback MOVIE
    BOYS series (019S).
        There was also a MOVING PICTURE GIRLS series, published by Grosset
    & Dunlap from 1914 to 1916 under the pseudonym Laura Lee Hope (186S).
Series description [G&D]: "Moving pictures and photo plays are famous the
    world over, and in this line of books the reader is given a full de-
    scription of how the films are made--the scenes of little dramas, in-
    doors and out, trick pictures to satisfy the curious, soul-stirring
    pictures of city affairs, life in the Wild West, among the cowboys and
    Indians, thrilling rescues along the seacoast, the daring of picture
    hunters among savage beasts, and the great risks run in picturing con-
    ditions in a land of earthquakes. The volumes teem with adventures and
    will be found exciting from first chapter to last.

020S.1   The moving picture boys; or, The perils of a great city depicted.
(Grosset & Dunlap, 1913).

   Reprinted by Garden City in 1926 as The movie boys on call; or, Filming
   the perils of a great city, vol. 1 in the MOVIE BOYS series (019S.1).

020S.2   The moving picture boys in the west; or, Taking scenes among the cowboys and Indians. (Grosset & Dunlap, 1913).

Reprinted by Garden City in 1926 as The movie boys in the wild west; or, Stirring days among the cowboys and Indians, vol. 2 in the MOVIE BOYS series (019S.2).

020S.3   The moving picture boys on the coast; or, Showing the perils of the deep. (Grosset & Dunlap, 1913).

Reprinted by Garden City in 1926 as The movie boys and the wreckers; or, Facing the perils of the deep, vol. 3 in the MOVIE BOYS series (019S.3).

020S.4   The moving picture boys in the jungle; or, Stirring times among the wild animals. (Grosset & Dunlap, 1913).

Reprinted by Garden City in 1926 as The movie boys in the jungle; or, Lively times among the wild beasts, vol. 4 in the MOVIE BOYS series (019S.4).

020S.5   The moving picture boys in earthquake land; or, Working amid many perils. (Grosset & Dunlap, 1913).

Reprinted by Garden City in 1926 as The movie boys in earthquake land; or, Filming pictures amid strange perils, vol. 5 in the MOVIE BOYS series (019S.5).

020S.6   The moving picture boys and the flood; or, Perilous days on the Mississippi. (Grosset & Dunlap, 1914).

Reprinted by Garden City in 1926 as The movie boys and the flood; or, Perilous days on the mighty Mississippi, vol. 6 in the MOVIE BOYS series (019S.6).

020S.7   The moving picture boys at Panama; or, Stirring adventures along the great canal. (Grosset & Dunlap, 1915).

Reprinted by Garden City in 1926 as The movie boys in peril; or, Strenuous days along the Panama Canal, vol. 7 in the MOVIE BOYS series (019S.7).

020S.8   The moving picture boys under the sea; or, The treasure of the lost ship. (Grosset & Dunlap, 1916).

Reprinted by Garden City in 1926 as The movie boys under the sea; or, The treasure of the lost ship, vol. 8 in the MOVIE BOYS series (019S.8).

020S.9   The moving picture boys on the war front; or, The hunt for the stolen army film. (Grosset & Dunlap, 1918).

Reprinted by Garden City in 1926 as The movie boys under fire; or, The search for the stolen film, vol. 9 in the MOVIE BOYS series (019S.9).

020S.10   The moving picture boys on French battlefields; or, Taking pictures for the U. S. army. (Grosset & Dunlap, 1919).

Reprinted by Garden City in 1926 as The movie boys under Uncle Sam; or, Taking pictures for the army, vol. 10 in the MOVIE BOYS series (019S.10).

020S.11   The moving picture boys' first showhouse; or, Opening up for business in Fairlands. (Grosset & Dunlap, 1921).

First published by Grosset & Dunlap in 1913 as The motion picture chums' first venture; or, Opening a photo playhouse in Fairlands, vol. 1 in the MOTION PICTURE CHUMS series (018S.1).

020S.12   The moving picture boys at Seaside Park; or, The rival photo theatres of the Board-walk. (Grosset & Dunlap, 1921).

First published by Grosset & Dunlap in 1913 as The motion picture chums at Seaside Park; or, The rival photo theatres of the Boardwalk, vol. 2 in the MOTION PICTURE CHUMS series (018S.2).

020S.13   The moving picture boys on Broadway; or, The mystery of the missing cash box. (Grosset & Dunlap, 1921).

First published by Grosset & Dunlap in 1914 as The motion picture chums on Broadway; or, The mystery of the missing cash box, vol. 3 in the MOTION PICTURE CHUMS series (018S.3).

020S.14   The moving picture boys' outdoor exhibition; or, The film that solved a mystery. (Grosset & Dunlap, 1922).

First published by Grosset & Dunlap in 1914 as The motion picture chums' outdoor exhibition; or, The film that solved a mystery, vol. 4 in the MOTION PICTURE CHUMS series (018S.4)

020S.15   The moving picture boys' new idea.* (Grosset & Dunlap, 1922).

First published by Grosset & Dunlap in 1914 as The motion picture chums' new idea; or, The first educational photo playhouse, vol. 5 in the MOTION PICTURE CHUMS series (018S.5).

021S   TOM SWIFT

Volumes: 40
Printed: 1910-1941
Publisher: Grosset & Dunlap, vols. 1-38
          Whitman Publishing Company, vols. 39-40
Reprint publisher: Whitman Publishing Company, vols. 6,** 29-38
Illustrator: R. Mencl, vols. 1-5
          H. Richard Boehm, vols. 6-16
          Walter S. Rogers, vols. 17-20, 24-34
          Nat Falk, vols. 35-38
          H. R. White, vol. 40
Source of annotations: Grosset & Dunlap advertisements [G&D]
Additional information: Edward Stratemeyer first used the name Tom Swift

---

*   Subtitle missing.
**   Possibly a phantom edition.

for the title character in "Shorthand Tom; or, The exploits of a young
reporter, " serialized in <u>Good</u> <u>News</u> in 1894. Although the name was the
same, the character was not: when TOM SWIFT reappeared sixteen years
later, in the first volume of the series, he had a different home, family, and career.*

Edward Stratemeyer created the TOM SWIFT series; Howard Garis as-
sisted with most, if not all, of the first thirty-six volumes. After
Stratemeyer's death, the Syndicate continued the series. Harriet Adams,
Stratemeyer's daughter, wrote the last three volumes.

The first thirty-eight volumes were published by Grosset & Dunlap;
the last two were issued by Whitman in the Better Little Book format
(formerly called Big Little Books). Whitman also reprinted volumes
29 through 38, and may have reprinted volume 6 as well.

The TOM SWIFT series ended in 1941, but the character and ideas
returned in 1954 for the TOM SWIFT, JR., series chronicling the adventures of TOM SWIFT's son. (This was a technique Edward Stratemeyer
had used years before: when the ROVER BOYS matured and married, the
series continued by focusing on their sons [339S]). Although TOM SWIFT
was not a major character in the new series, he did appear regularly
in the books.

Series description [G&D]: "Tom Swift, known to millions of boys of this
generation, is a bright ingenious youth, whose inventions, discoveries
and thrilling adventures carry him to many strange places."

[Another advertisement] [G&D]: "It is the purpose of these spirited
tales to convey in a realistic way the wonderful advances in land and
sea locomotion and to interest the boy of the present in the hope that
he may be a factor in aiding the marvelous development that is coming
in the future."

021S.1   Tom Swift and his motor-cycle; or, Fun and adventure on the road.
(Grosset & Dunlap, 1910).

[G&D]: "Tom longed for a motor cycle and got one unexpectedly."

021S.2   Tom Swift and his motor-boat; or, The rivals of Lake Carlopa.
(Grosset & Dunlap, 1910).

[G&D]: "There are some great races, and a thrilling experience with
an aeronaut."

021S.3   Tom Swift and his airship; or, The stirring cruise of the Red
Cloud. (Grosset & Dunlap, 1910).

[G&D]: "Telling how the airship was built, of a trial trip and a smash-
up in mid-air."

021S.4   Tom Swift and his submarine boat; or, Under the ocean for sunken
treasure. (Grosset & Dunlap, 1910).

[G&D]: "The submarine is stopped by a warship and those on board are
made prisoners, but escape."

* This was not the only time Edward Stratemeyer gave two characters the
same name: Frank Hardy first appeared in <u>The</u> <u>young</u> <u>book</u> <u>agent</u>; <u>or</u>,
<u>Frank</u> <u>Hardy's</u> <u>road</u> <u>to</u> <u>success</u> (011S.8X), twenty-two years before the
creation of the HARDY BOYS (106S).

021S.5   Tom Swift and his electric runabout; or, The speediest car on the road. (Grosset & Dunlap, 1910).

[G&D]: "A runabout is built, and then begins a series of adventures."

021S.6   Tom Swift and his wireless message; or, The castaways of Earthquake Island. (Grosset & Dunlap, 1911; Whitman*).

[G&D]: "A trip to Cape May, a terrific storm and a wreck on a West Indian island. A wireless plant saves them."

021S.7   Tom Swift among the diamond makers; or, The secret of Phantom Mountain. (Grosset & Dunlap, 1911).

[G&D]: "Tom and his friends start out in the 'Red Cloud' to find the diamond makers that they are told are hid in the Rocky Mountains."

021S.8   Tom Swift in the caves of ice; or, The wreck of the airship. (Grosset & Dunlap, 1911).

[G&D]: "Tom and his friends go to Alaska to search for gold in the caves of ice and are almost defeated."

021S.9   Tom Swift and his sky racer; or, The quickest flight on record. (Grosset & Dunlap, 1911.)

[G&D]: "The Humming Bird--a racer of terrific speed--wins a ten thousand dollar prize against other bird-men."

021S.10   Tom Swift and his electric rifle; or, Daring adventures in elephant land. (Grosset & Dunlap, 1911).

[G&D]: "Thrilling adventures in the African jungle with the red pygmies and fine work with the electric rifle."

021S.11   Tom Swift in the city of gold; or, Marvelous adventures underground. (Grosset & Dunlap, 1912).

021S.12   Tom Swift and his air glider; or, Seeking the platinum treasure. (Grosset & Dunlap, 1912).

021S.13   Tom Swift in captivity; or, A daring escape by airship. (Grosset & Dunlap, 1912).

021S.14   Tom Swift and his wizard camera; or, The perils of moving picture taking.** (Grosset & Dunlap, 1912).

021S.15   Tom Swift and his great searchlight; or, On the border for Uncle Sam. (Grosset & Dunlap, 1912).

021S.16   Tom Swift and his giant cannon; or, The longest shots on record. (Grosset & Dunlap, 1913).

---

*   Whitman edition may be a phantom edition.
**   Subtitle also listed as Thrilling adventures while taking moving pictures.

021S.17   Tom Swift and his photo telephone; or, The picture that saved a fortune. (Grosset & Dunlap, 1914).

021S.18   Tom Swift and his aerial warship; or, The naval terror of the seas. (Grosset & Dunlap, 1915).

021S.19   Tom Swift and his big tunnel; or, The hidden city of the Andes. (Grosset & Dunlap, 1916).

021S.20   Tom Swift in the land of wonders; or, The underground search for the idol of gold. (Grosset & Dunlap, 1917).

021S.21   Tom Swift and his war tank; or, Doing his bit for Uncle Sam.* (Grosset & Dunlap, 1918).

021S.22   Tom Swift and his air scout; or, Uncle Sam's mastery of the sky. (Grosset & Dunlap, 1919).

021S.23   Tom Swift and his undersea search; or, The treasure on the floor of the Atlantic. (Grosset & Dunlap, 1920).

021S.24   Tom Swift among the fire fighters; or, Battling with flames from the air. (Grosset & Dunlap, 1921).

021S.25   Tom Swift and his electric locomotive; or, Two miles a minute on the rails. (Grosset & Dunlap, 1922).

021S.26   Tom Swift and his flying boat; or, The castaways of the giant iceberg. (Grosset & Dunlap, 1923).

021S.27   Tom Swift and his great oil gusher; or, The treasure of Goby farm. (Grosset & Dunlap, 1924).

021S.28   Tom Swift and his chest of secrets; or, Tracing the stolen inventions. (Grosset & Dunlap, 1925).

021S.29   Tom Swift and his airline express; or, From ocean to ocean by daylight. (Grosset & Dunlap, 1926; Whitman).

        Listed as vol. 6 in Whitman advertisements.

021S.30   Tom Swift circling the globe; or, The daring cruise of the air monarch. (Grosset & Dunlap, 1927; Whitman).

        Listed as vol. 4 in Whitman advertisements.

021S.31   Tom Swift and his talking pictures; or, The greatest invention on record. (Grosset & Dunlap, 1928; Whitman).

        Listed as vol. 7 in Whitman advertieements.

021S.32   Tom Swift and his house on wheels; or, A trip to the mountain of mystery. (Grosset & Dunlap, 1929; Whitman).

        Listed as vol. 2 in Whitman advertisements.

_____

* Subtitle also listed as Doing his best for Uncle Sam.

021S.33   Tom Swift and his big dirigible; or, Adventures over the forest of fire. (Grosset & Dunlap, 1930; Whitman).

   Listed as vol. 8 in Whitman advertisements.

021S.34   Tom Swift and his sky train; or, Overland through the clouds. (Grosset & Dunlap, 1931; Whitman).

   Listed as vol. 3 in Whitman advertisements.

021S.35   Tom Swift and his giant magnet; or, Bringing up the lost submarine. (Grosset & Dunlap, 1932; Whitman).

   Listed as vol. 9 in Whitman advertisements.

021S.36   Tom Swift and his television detector; or, Trailing the secret plotters. (Grosset & Dunlap, 1933; Whitman).

   Listed as vol. 1 in Whitman advertisements.

021S.37   Tom Swift and his ocean airport; or, Foiling the Haargolanders. (Grosset & Dunlap, 1934; Whitman).

   Listed as vol. 5 in Whitman advertisements.

021S.38   Tom Swift and his planet stone; or, Discovering the secret of another world. (Grosset & Dunlap, 1935; Whitman).

021S.39   Tom Swift and his giant telescope. (Whitman, 1939).*

021S.40   Tom Swift and his magnetic silencer. (Whitman, 1941).*

OTHER PUBLICATIONS

022N   A superboy, supergirl anthology: Selected chapters from the earlier works of Victor Appleton, Franklin W. Dixon, and Carolyn Keene. Edited by Stephen Dunning and Henry B. Maloney. (Scholastic Book Services 1971).

Victor Appleton II

Thirteen years after the publication of the last TOM SWIFT title, the Stratemeyer Syndicate started a new series, TOM SWIFT, JR., with TOM SWIFT son, a space-age inventor, in the starring role. The author of the series was listed as Victor Appleton II, presumably the "son" of the Stratemeyer Syndicate pseudonym Victor Appleton. The real creator of many of the TOM SWIFT, JR., stories was Harriet Adams, daughter of Edward Stratemeyer, the man who developed TOM SWIFT.

---

* A Better Little Book; published without a subtitle.

Grosset & Dunlap, publisher of most of the original TOM SWIFT books, issued the first thirty-three volumes of the TOM SWIFT, JR., series between 1954 and 1971. Several volumes were reprinted in paperback in 1973 and 1977, but no new stories were added until 1981, when Wanderer Books (Simon & Schuster's paperback imprint) published three new titles.

SERIES PUBLICATIONS

023S   TOM SWIFT, JR.

Volumes: 36*
Printed: 1954-
Publisher: Grosset & Dunlap, vols. 1-33
            Simon & Schuster, Wanderer Books, vols. 34X-36X
Reprint publisher: Grosset & Dunlap, Tempo Books, vols. 1-4, 6, 8, 14-17
Illustrator: Graham Kaye, vols. 1-17
              Charles Brey, vols. 18-21
              Edward Moritz, vols. 22-27
              Ray Johnson, vols. 28-32
              Bill Dolwick, vol. 33
              Tony Tallarico, vols. 1-4, 6, 8 (Tempo editions)
Source of annotations: Grosset & Dunlap advertisements [G&D], first series
                        description
                        Grosset & Dunlap, Tempo Books advertisements [G&D],
                        second series description
                        Library of Congress cataloguing in publication data
                        [LC], vols. 1-4, 6, 8, 10-11, 14, 16, 18, 21,
                        23-26, 31-33
Additional information: Grosset & Dunlap originally published the first
    thirty-three volumes of the TOM SWIFT, JR., series in hardcover editions.
    In 1973 Tempo Books printed volumes 14 through 17 as the first four
    titles of the paperback TOM SWIFT, JR., series. Six years later, Tempo
    issued volumes 1 through 4, 6, and 8 in paperback, again numbered as
    the first six books of the series. Finally, in 1981, Wanderer Books
    published three new TOM SWIFT, JR., titles--as volumes 1 through 3 in
    its paperback TOM SWIFT, JR., series.
        The TOM SWIFT, JR., series was created by the Stratemeyer Syndicate.
    Harriet Adams wrote at least twenty of the titles in this series, and
    may have received assistance from William Dougherty (volume 1), John
    Almquist (volumes 2 and 3), Richard Sklar (volume 4), D. L. Lawrence
    (volumes 5 through 7 and 9 through 30), Thomas Mulvey (volume 8), and
    Richard McKenna (volumes 31 through 33).**
        All thirty-six volumes were issued without subtitles.
Series description [G&D]: "These are the famous books about a young scien-
    tist whose amazing inventions promise to be the great achievements of
    the future."
        [G&D]: "Tom Swift--boy genius--outsmarts evil scientists, solves

---

*   As of 1981.
** In A bibliography of hard-cover boys' books (Tampa, Fla.: Data Print,
    1977), Harry K. Hudson lists these six names as the authors of the
    first thirty-three volumes.

confounding mysteries, and builds incredible rocket ships, atomic energy plants, submarines, airplanes, robots, and mind-boggling inventions for the good of mankind!"

023S.1   Tom Swift and his flying lab. (Grosset & Dunlap, 1954; Tempo, 1977).

[LC]: "Tom Swift and his father travel to a South American country in their flying space lab to look for uranium and keep it from falling into the hands of a group of dangerous rebels."

023S.2   Tom Swift and his jetmarine. (Grosset & Dunlap, 1954; Tempo, 1977).

[LC]: "Tom Swift, Jr., and his associates try to unravel the relationship between the dog coins and the mysterious blackouts near Spaniei Island."

023S.3   Tom Swift and his rocket ship. (Grosset & Dunlap, 1954; Tempo, 1977).

[LC]: "Tom Swift, Jr., and his friend, Bud Barclay, enter an international space race hoping to orbit the earth in two hours."

023S.4   Tom Swift and his giant robot. (Grosset & Dunlap, 1954; Tempo, 1977).

[LC]: "Tom Swift, Jr., and his associates hunt the mastermind who is sabotaging a robot which is an integral part of an atomic energy plant."

023S.5   Tom Swift and his atomic earth blaster. (Grosset & Dunlap, 1954).

023S.6   Tom Swift and his outpost in space. (Grosset & Dunlap, 1955; Tempo, 1977).

Tempo edition titled Tom Swift and his sky wheel and listed as vol. 5.

023S.7   Tom Swift and his diving seacopter. (Grosset & Dunlap, 1956).

023S.8   Tom Swift in the caves of nuclear fire. (Grosset & Dunlap, 1956; Tempo, 1977).

Tempo edition listed as vol. 6.
[LC]: "Tom goes to Africa to track down the origin of a mysterious gas."

023S.9   Tom Swift on the phantom satellite. (Grosset & Dunlap, 1957).

023S.10   Tom Swift and his ultrasonic cycloplane. (Grosset & Dunlap, 1957).

[LC]: "Tom finds himself involved in a dangerous adventure trying to track down the origins of a small statue made of a rare and valuable metal."

023S.11   Tom Swift and his deep-sea hydrodome. (Grosset & Dunlap, 1958).

[LC]: "Tom and his father return to an underwater city of gold to do further exploration and discover a new source of helium."

023S.12   Tom Swift in the race to the moon. (Grosset & Dunlap, 1958).

023S.13   Tom Swift and his space solartron. (Grosset & Dunlap, 1958).

023S.14   Tom Swift and his electronic retroscope. (Grosset & Dunlap, 1959; Tempo, 1973).

   Tempo edition titled Tom Swift in the jungle of the Mayas and issued as vol. 1.
      [LC]: "While on an expedition to the Yucatan, Tom Swift discovers records of a space armada that flew to the earth 3000 years ago."

023S.15   Tom Swift and his spectromarine selector. (Grosset & Dunlap, 1960; Tempo, 1973).

   Tempo edition titled Tom Swift and the city of gold and issued as vol. 2.

023S.16   Tom Swift and the cosmic astronauts. (Grosset & Dunlap, 1960; Tempo, 1973).

   Tempo edition issued as vol. 3.
      [LC]: "When his latest invention is stolen, Tom Swift, Jr. and his associates pursue a ruthless scientific pirate."

023S.17   Tom Swift and the visitor from Planet X. (Grosset & Dunlap, 1961; Tempo, 1973).

   Tempo edition issued as vol. 4.

023S.18   Tom Swift and the electronic hydrolung. (Grosset & Dunlap, 1961).

   [LC]: "Tom Swift, Jr. and his friend, Bud Barclay, try to recover a missile, which was mysteriously thrown off course, containing valuable data from Jupiter."

023S.19   Tom Swift and his triphibian atomicar. (Grosset & Dunlap, 1962).

023S.20   Tom Swift and his megascope space prober. (Grosset & Dunlap, 1962).

023S.21   Tom Swift and the asteroid pirates. (Grosset & Dunlap, 1963).

   [LC]: "Tom Swift, Jr. and his friend, Bud Barclay, uncover the plans of space pirates in the lair of the Black Cobra."

023S.22   Tom Swift and his repelatron skyway. (Grosset & Dunlap, 1963).

023S.23   Tom Swift and his aquatomic tracker. (Grosset & Dunlap, 1964).

   [LC]: "Tom Swift, Jr., and his associates use their scientific know-how to recover the valuable contents of a sunken ship."

023S.24   Tom Swift and his 3-D telejector. (Grosset & Dunlap, 1964).

[LC]: "Tom Swift, Jr., and his associates at Swift Enterprises discover
that their invention, the 3-D telejector, is marked for destruction by
group Q."

023S.25   Tom Swift and his polar-ray dynasphere. (Grosset & Dunlap, 1965).

[LC]: "Tom and his friends travel to a small Himalayan country as
guests of the friendly ruler and discover a secret rocket base run by
enemies of the government."

023S.26   Tom Swift and his sonic boom trap. (Grosset & Dunlap, 1965).

[LC]: "When strange blasts of sound engulf several American cities,
Tom's new invention is the only hope of defense."

023S.27   Tom Swift and his subocean geotron. (Grosset & Dunlap, 1966).

023S.28   Tom Swift and the mystery comet. (Grosset & Dunlap, 1966).

023S.29   Tom Swift and the captive planetoid. (Grosset & Dunlap, 1967).

023S.30   Tom Swift and his G-force inverter. (Grosset & Dunlap, 1968).

023S.31   Tom Swift and his Dyna-4 capsule. (Grosset & Dunlap, 1969).

[LC]: "A super submarine especially designed for deep-sea research and
exploration encounters strange green bubbles that feed on manganese
nodules and are capable on [sic] engulfing and destroying large objects.

023S.32   Tom Swift and his cosmotron express. (Grosset & Dunlap, 1970).

[LC]: "Tom Jr. and his friend, Bud Barclay, foil a criminal plot to
conquer the universe."

023S.33   Tom Swift and the galaxy ghosts. (Grosset & Dunlap, 1971).

[LC]: "With the help of his latest invention, a device that can
atomize objects, send them great distances, and reassemble the atoms,
Tom Swift, Jr., and his father locate a frozen mastodon and transport
it to the United States."

023S.34X   Tom Swift: The city in the stars. (Wanderer, 1981).

023S.35X   Tom Swift: Terror on the moons of Jupiter. (Wanderer, 1981).

023S.36X   Tom Swift: The alien probe. (Wanderer, 1981).

Elmer Tracey Barnes

Elmer Tracey Barnes, a Stratemeyer Syndicate house name, was listed as the author of a five-volume series, the MOTION PICTURE COMRADES, first published in 1917.

SERIES PUBLICATIONS

024S   MOTION PICTURE COMRADES

Volumes: 5
Printed: 1917
Publisher: New York Book Co.
Reprint publisher: Saalfield Publishing Company
Illustrator: Lester, vols. 1-5
Additional information: The covers of the books have a hyphenated title:
    MOTION-PICTURE COMRADES; the title pages do not. Some of the Saalfield
    dust jackets give the titles as the MOVING PICTURE BOYS, but the title
    pages still read MOTION PICTURE COMRADES.

024S.1   The motion picture comrades' great venture; or, On the road with
the "big round-top." (New York, 1917; Saalfield).

024S.2   The motion picture comrades in African jungles; or, The camera
boys in wild animal land. (New York, 1917; Saalfield).

    Saalfield edition titled The motion picture comrades through African
    jungles; or, The camera boys in wild animal land.

024S.3   The motion picture comrades along the Orinoco; or, Facing perils
in the tropics. (New York, 1917; Saalfield).

024S.4   The motion picture comrades aboard a submarine; or, Searching for
treasure under the sea. (New York, 1917; Saalfield).

024S.5   The motion picture comrades producing a success; or, Featuring a
sensation. (New York, 1917; Saalfield).

P. T. Barnum, Jr.

In 1895 Edward Stratemeyer wrote one story under the pseudonym P. T. Barnum,
Jr. It was serialized in a boys' story paper, reprinted in another boys'
story paper, this time as by Theodore Barnum, then published in book form
under the pen name Captain Ralph Bonehill.
    Although Stratemeyer did not use the pseudonym P. T. Barnum, Jr.,
again, he did pair the surname Barnum with three other first names over the
next twenty-seven years. Many of the stories produced between 1895 and 1922
under Barnum concerned the circus. P. T. and Theodore Barnum were used on
stories about "Leo, clown and gymnast" and "Carl, the juggler and magician,"
serialized in boys' story papers from 1895 to 1896; Vance Barnum appeared
as author of the JOE STRONG series, about a boy acrobat and magician, in

1916; Richard Barnum was credited with the KNEETIME ANIMAL STORIES, some
of which were about the antics of circus animals, published between 1915
and 1922. The only series published under Barnum that had no relation to
a circus was the FRANK AND ANDY series, a reprint of part of the RACER BOYS
(355S).

MAGAZINE PUBLICATIONS

025M   "Limber Leo, clown and gymnast; or, With the greatest show on
earth." Young Sports of America, nos. 1-5, May 25-June 29, 1895.

    Reprinted in Bright Days, June-Sept. 1896, as "Leo the circus boy; or,
    Life under the great white canvas" by Theodore Barnum (028M). Published
    in book form as Leo the circus boy; or, Life under the great white can-
    vas as by Captain Ralph Bonehill, as vol. 12 in Allison's BOUND TO WIN
    series in 1897 (047S.4X); reprinted with the new author and title as
    vol. 3 of Donohue's YOUNG SPORTSMANS' series, ca1900 (065S.3).

Richard Barnum

The KNEETIME ANIMAL STORIES, the only series written under the pseudonym
Richard Barnum, is one of the only two Stratemeyer Syndicate series that
feature animals rather than humans as the main characters. (The other is
Laura Lee Hope's MAKE BELIEVE series, centering on the adventures of toy
animals [185S].) Prior to 1953 (and the advent of the HAPPY HOLLISTERS
[319S]), the KNEETIME ANIMAL STORIES was also the only Stratemeyer Syndicate
series for younger boys and girls that was published under a male pseudonym.

SERIES PUBLICATIONS

026S   KNEETIME ANIMAL STORIES

Volumes: 17
Printed: 1915-1922
Publisher: Barse & Hopkins
Illustrator: Harriet H. Tooker, vols. 1-3
              Walter S. Rogers, vols. 7-10, 15-16
Source of annotations: Barse & Hopkins advertisements [B&H]
Series description [B&H]: "Amusing stories for children from 4 to 9 years
    old. In all nursery literature animals have played a conspicuous part;
    and the reason is obvious, for nothing entertains a child more than
    the antics of an animal. These stories abound in amusing incidents
    such as children adore and the characters are so full of life, so ap-
    pealing to a child's imagination, that none will be satisfied until
    they have met all of their favorites,--Squinty, Slicko, Mappo, Tum Tum,
    etc."

026S.1   Squinty, the comical pig: His many adventures. (Barse & Hopkins, 1915).

026S.2   Slicko, the jumping squirrel: Her many adventures. (Barse & Hopkins, 1915).

026S.3   Mappo, the merry monkey: His many adventures. (Barse & Hopkins, 1915).

026S.4   Tum Tum, the jolly elephant.* (Barse & Hopkins, 1915).

026S.5   Don, a runaway dog.* (Barse & Hopkins, 1915).

026S.6   Dido, the dancing bear: His many adventures. (Barse & Hopkins, 1916).

026S.7   Blackie, a lost cat: Her many adventures. (Barse & Hopkins, 1916).

026S.8   Flop Ear, the funny rabbit.* (Barse & Hopkins, 1916).

026S.9   Tinkle, the trick pony: His many adventures. (Barse & Hopkins, 1917).

026S.10   Lightfoot, the leaping goat: His many adventures. (Barse & Hopkins, 1917).

026S.11   Chunky, the happy hippo.* (Barse & Hopkins, 1918).

026S.12   Sharp Eyes, the silver fox: His many adventures. (Barse & Hopkins, 1918).

026S.13   Nero, the circus lion: His many adventures. (Barse & Hopkins, 1919).

026S.14   Tamba, the tame tiger.* (Barse & Hopkins, 1919).

026S.15   Toto, the bustling beaver: His many adventures. (Barse & Hopkins, 1920).

026S.16   Shaggo, the mighty buffalo: His many adventures. (Barse & Hopkins, 1921).

026S.17   Winkie, the wily woodchuck.* (Barse & Hopkins, 1922).

Theodore Barnum

Theodore Barnum was listed as the author of two serialized circus stories that were published in boys' story papers in 1896. One was a reprint of P. T. Barnum, Jr.'s story. Edward Stratemeyer wrote both tales.

---

* Subtitle missing; probably His many adventures or Her many adventures.

MAGAZINE PUBLICATIONS

027M   "Carl, the juggler and magician; or, A hundred stage tricks revealed." Bright Days, nos. 8-14, Sept. 19-Oct. 31, 1896.

028M   "Leo, the circus boy; or, Life under the great white canvas."
Bright Days, nos. 3-6, June-Sept. 5, 1896.

    First published as "Limber Leo, clown and gymnast; or, With the
    greatest show on earth" by P. T. Barnum, Jr., in Young Sports of Amer-
    ica, May 25-June 29, 1895 (025M).

Vance Barnum

The Stratemeyer Syndicate house name Vance Barnum was used on two series,
JOE STRONG and FRANK AND ANDY, published by Sully in 1916 and 1921, respectively. The FRANK AND ANDY series consisted of retitled reprints of the
first three RACER BOYS books (355S).

SERIES PUBLICATIONS

029S   FRANK AND ANDY

Volumes: 3
Printed: 1921
Publisher: George Sully & Company
Reprint publisher: Whitman Publishing Company, vols. 1-3
Additional information: Whitman editions were not illustrated.

029S.1   Frank and Andy afloat; or, The cave on the island. (Sully, 1921;
Whitman).

    First published in 1912 by Cupples & Leon as The Racer boys; or, The
    mystery of the wreck by Clarence Young (355S.1).

029S.2   Frank and Andy at boarding school; or, Rivals for many honors.
(Sully, 1921; Whitman).

    First published in 1912 by Cupples & Leon as The Racer boys at boarding
    school; or, Striving for the championship by Clarence Young (355S.2).

029S.3   Frank and Andy in a winter camp; or, The young hunters' strange
discovery. (Sully, 1921; Whitman).

    First published in 1912 by Cupples & Leon as The Racer boys to the res-
    cue; or, Stirring days in a winter camp by Clarence Young (355S.3).

030S   JOE STRONG

Volumes: 7
Printed: 1916
Publisher: George Sully & Company
Reprint publisher: Hearst's International Library Co., vols. 1-7
                    Whitman Publishing Company, vols. 1-7
Illustrator: Walter S. Rogers, vols. 1-7
              Jerome L. Kroeger, vols. 1-7 (Hearst editions)
              Erwin L. Hess, some vols. (Whitman editions)
Source of annotations: George Sully & Company advertisements [GS]
Additional information: Hearst may have been the original publisher,
    rather than Sully: both editions have 1916 copyright dates. The
    Cumulative book index and Harry Hudson's A bibliography of hard-cover
    boys' books list Sully first.
Series description [GS]: "Vance Barnum is a real treasure when it comes
    to telling about how magicians do their weird tricks, how the circus
    acrobats pull off their various stunts, how the "fishman" remains under
    water so long, how the mid-air performers loop the loop and how the
    slack-wire fellow keeps from tumbling. He has been through it all and
    he writes freely for the boys from his vast experience. They are real
    stories bound to hold their audiences breathlessly."

030S.1   Joe Strong, the boy wizard; or, The mysteries of magic exposed.
(Sully, 1916; Hearst, 1916; Whitman).

030S.2   Joe Strong on the trapeze; or, The daring feats of a young circus
performer. (Sully, 1916; Hearst, 1916; Whitman).

030S.3   Joe Strong, the boy fish; or, Marvelous doings in a big tank.
(Sully, 1916; Hearst, 1916; Whitman).

030S.4   Joe Strong on the high wire; or, Motorcycle perils of the air.
(Sully, 1916;* Hearst, 1916; Whitman).

030S.5   Joe Strong and his wings of steel; or, A young acrobat in the
clouds. (Sully, 1916; Hearst, 1916; Whitman).

030S.6   Joe Strong and his box of mystery; or, The ten thousand dollar
prize trick. (Sully, 1916; Hearst, 1916; Whitman).

030S.7   Joe Strong, the boy fire-eater; or, The most dangerous performance
on record. (Sully, 1916; Hearst, 1916; Whitman).

Philip A. Bartlett

The four ROY STOVER books were the only Stratemeyer Syndicate series published under the pseudonym Philip A. Bartlett.

---

*   Sully ads also list the subtitle as A motorcycle of the air.

SERIES PUBLICATIONS

031S   ROY STOVER

Volumes: 4
Printed: 1929-1934
Publisher: Barse & Company, vols. 1-3
            Grosset & Dunlap, vol. 4
Reprint publisher: Grosset & Dunlap, vols. 1-3
Illustrator: John M. Foster, vols. 1-4
Additional information: Barse & Company is listed in Cumulative book index
    1928-1932 as the publisher of the first three volumes; Grosset & Dunlap
    appears as the publisher of all four volumes in Cumulative book index
    1933-1937. No dates for the Grosset & Dunlap editions of the first
    three volumes are given. The books were issued without subtitles; the
    Grosset & Dunlap editions had the same illustrator as the Barse & Com-
    pany editions.

031S.1   The Lakeport bank mystery. (Barse, 1929; Grosset & Dunlap).

031S.2   The mystery of the snowbound express. (Barse, 1929; Grosset &
Dunlap).

031S.3   The Cliff Island mystery. (Barse, 1930; Grosset & Dunlap).

031S.4   The mystery of the circle of fire. (Grosset & Dunlap, 1934).

May Hollis Barton

The Stratemeyer Syndicate house name May Hollis Barton appeared on sixteen
books published by Cupples & Leon between 1926 and 1937: the fifteen volumes of the BARTON BOOKS FOR GIRLS series and one four-in-one reprint edition. Edward Stratemeyer's daughter, Harriet Adams, worked under this
pseudonym in 1931 and 1932.

SERIES PUBLICATIONS

032S   BARTON BOOKS FOR GIRLS

Volumes: 16*
Printed: 1926-1937*
Publisher: Cupples & Leon Company

---

* Number of volumes and dates printed include Favorite stories for girls,
   a four-in-one reprint.

Illustrator: anonymous, vols. 1-2, 4-7, 9
                Walter S. Rogers, vol. 3
                Ernest Townsend, vol. 8
                Russell H. Tandy, vols. 10, 12-14
                Hait [?], vol. 11
Source of annotations: Cupples & Leon advertisements [C&L]
Additional information: The BARTON BOOKS FOR GIRLS do not share a fixed
    set of main characters, nor are they united by a common setting or
    theme. Instead, they are a set of girls' adventure stories that were
    advertised and sold under the series title BARTON BOOKS FOR GIRLS.
    Harriet Adams wrote volumes 13 through 15.
Series description [C&L]: "May Hollis Barton is a new writer for girls who
    is bound to win instant popularity. Her style is somewhat of a mixture
    of that of Louise [sic] M. Alcott and Mrs. L. T. Meade, but thoroughly
    up-to-date in plot and action. Clean tales that all girls will enjoy
    reading."

032S.1   The girl from the country; or, Laura Mayford's city experiences.
(Cupples & Leon, 1926).

    Reprinted in Favorite stories for girls in 1937 (032S.16X).
        [C&L]: "Laura was the oldest of five children and when daddy got
    sick she felt she must do something. She had a chance to try her luck
    in New York, and there the country girl fell in with many unusual ex-
    periences."

032S.2   Three girl chums at Laurel Hall; or, The mystery of the school
by the lake. (Cupples & Leon, 1926).

    [C&L]: "When the three chums arrived at the boarding school they found
    the other students in the grip of a most perplexing mystery. How this
    mystery was solved, and what good times the girls had, both in school
    and on the lake, go to make a story no girl would care to miss."

032S.3   Nell Grayson's ranching days; or, A city girl in the great West.
(Cupples & Leon, 1926).

    [C&L]: "Showing how Nell, when she had a ranch girl visit her in Bos-
    ton, thought her chum very green, but when Nell visited the ranch in
    the great West she found herself confronting many conditions of which
    she was totally ignorant. A stirring outdoor story."

032S.4   Four little women of Roxby; or, The queer old lady who lost her
way. (Cupples & Leon, 1926).

    [C&L]: "Four sisters are keeping house and having trouble to make ends
    meet. One day there wanders in from a stalled express train an old lady
    who cannot remember her identity. The girls take the old lady in, and,
    later, are much astonished to learn who she really is."

032S.5   Plain Jane and pretty Betty; or, The girl who won out. (Cupples
& Leon, 1926).

    [C&L]: "The tale of two girls, one plain but sensible, the other pretty
    but vain. Unexpectedly both find they have to make their way in the
    world. Both have many trials and tribulations. A story of a country
    town and then a city."

032S.6   Little Miss Sunshine; or, The old bachelor's ward. (Cupples &
Leon, 1928).

    [C&L]: "Her guardian Major, an old bachelor, knows nothing about
children."

032S.7   Hazel Hood's strange discovery; or, The old scientist's treasure
box. (Cupples & Leon, 1928).

    Reprinted in Favorite stories for girls in 1937 (032S.16X).
      [C&L]: "Times were hard at the Widow Hood's place and Hazel thought
it her duty to go to work."

032S.8   Two girls and a mystery; or, The old house in the glen. (Cupples
& Leon, 1928).

    Reprinted in Mystery and adventure stories for girls, ca1934 (033N).
      [C&L]: "Bab was quite excited to learn that a distant relative
had died and left her his property."

032S.9   The girls of Lighthouse Island; or, The strange sea chest. (Cupples & Leon, 1929).

032S.10   Kate Martin's problem; or, Facing the wide world. (Cupples &
Leon, 1929).

    Reprinted in Favorite stories for girls in 1937 (032S.16X).

032S.11   The girl in the top flat; or, The daughter of an artist. (Cupples
& Leon, 1930).

032S.12   The search for Peggy Ann; or, A mystery of the flood. (Cupples &
Leon, 1930).

032S.13   Sallie's test of skill; or, Winning the trophy. (Cupples & Leon,
1931).

032S.14   Charlotte Cross and Aunt Deb; or, The queerest trip on record.
(Cupples & Leon, 1931).

    Reprinted in Favorite stories for girls in 1937 (032S.16X).

032S.15   Virginia's venture; or, Strange business at the tea house. (Cupples & Leon, 1932).

032S.16X Favorite stories for girls: Four complete books in one volume:
Kate Martin's problem; Charlotte Cross and Aunt Deb; The girl from the
country; Hazel Hood's strange discovery. (Cupples & Leon, 1937).

    First published as Kate Martin's problem, 1929 (032S.10); Charlotte
Cross and Aunt Deb, 1931 (032S.14); The girl from the country, 1926
(032S.1); Hazel Hood's strange discovery, 1928 (032S.7).

OTHER PUBLICATIONS

033N   Mystery and adventure stories for girls. (Cupples & Leon, ca1934).

     Contains Two girls and a mystery by May Hollis Barton, published in
     1928 (032S.8); Maxie, an adorable girl by Elsie Bell Gardner, published
     in 1932; Betty Gordon at Bramble Farm by Alice B. Emerson, published
     in 1920 (144S.1); Jane Allen of the sub-team by Edith Bancroft, pub-
     lished in 1917. Printed from the original plates.

Charles Amory Beach

Charles Amory Beach was a short-lived, much reprinted Stratemeyer Syndicate
pseudonym. The six AIR SERVICE BOYS books were originally published by
George Sully & Company from 1918 to 1920 and were reprinted by three other
houses.

SERIES PUBLICATIONS

034S   AIR SERVICE BOYS

Volumes: 6
Printed: 1918-1920
Publisher: George Sully & Company
Reprint publisher: Goldsmith Publishing Co., vols. 1, 3, 5-6*
                    Saalfield Publishing Co., vols. 1, 4, 6*
                    World Syndicate Publishing Co., vols. 1-6
Illustrator: Robert Gaston Herbert, vols. 1-3
              Clare Angell, vol. 4
              Walter S. Rogers, vol. 5
              Cress, vol. 6
Source of annotations: George Sully & Company advertisements [GC]
Additional information: The dates and order of volumes 3 and 4 are some-
     times reversed: Air service boys over the Rhine is occasionally listed
     as volume 4, with a publication date of 1919, while Air service boys
     in the big battle becomes volume 3, with a 1918 date. The series order
     here has been taken from Sully advertisements.
          Most of the World editions had plain paper adaptions of the original
     illustrations.
Series description [GC]: "Two chums join the air service in this country
     and then go to France and enter the Lafayette Escadrille. After doing
     their duty to our sister republic they re-enter the American service
     and are put to the most severe tests as airmen. They manage to locate
     a long-range German cannon which is doing terrific damage, and are pres-
     ent at the bombing of the last Hun stronghold. A series by one who

_____
* Possibly other volumes as well.

knows all about army aviation."

034S.1   Air service boys flying for France; or, The young heroes of the Lafayette Escadrille. (Sully, 1918; Goldsmith; Saalfield; World).

034S.2   Air service boys over the enemy's lines; or, The German spy's secret. (Sully, 1918; World).

034S.3   Air service boys over the Rhine; or, Fighting above the clouds. (Sully, 1918; Goldsmith; World).

034S.4   Air service boys in the big battle; or, Silencing the big guns. (Sully, 1919; Saalfield; World).

034S.5   Air service boys flying for victory; or, Bombing the last German stronghold. (Sully, 1919; Goldsmith; World).

034S.6   Air service boys over the Atlantic; or, The longest flight on record. (Sully, 1920; Goldsmith; Saalfield; World).

Emerson Bell

The pseudonym Emerson Bell was originally ascribed to Gilbert Patten, but recent research by J. Randolph Cox among Street & Smith's files indicates that Edward Stratemeyer was the actual author of at least two stories published under the name Emerson Bell.

MAGAZINE PUBLICATIONS

035M   "The electric air and water wizard." Good News, vols. 7-8, nos. 185-190, Nov. 18, 1893-Feb. 3, 1894.

   Reprinted as The electric wizard; or, Through air and water to the pole, no. 198 in the BRAVE AND BOLD series, Oct. 6, 1906 (037P.1X).

036M   "Overhead Steve; or, The wizard of the wires." Good News, vols. 11-12, nos. 289-301, Nov. 16, 1895-Feb. 8, 1896.

SERIES PUBLICATIONS

037P   BRAVE AND BOLD

Volumes: 1*
Printed: 1906*

---
*   Number of volumes and years published apply only to titles written by Edward Stratemeyer under the pseudonym Emerson Bell.

Publisher: Street & Smith
Additional information: See Manager Henry Abbott, BRAVE AND BOLD series
(004PQ).

037P.1X   The electric wizard; or, Through air and water to the pole. No.
198. Oct. 6, 1906.

> First published as "The electric air and water wizard" in Good News,
> Nov. 18, 1893-Feb. 3, 1894 (035M).

Captain Ralph Bonehill

Edward Stratemeyer wrote seven magazine stories and twenty-nine books as
Captain Ralph Bonehill. Eleven of the books had first been serialized in
boys' story papers under seven names: Captain Ralph Bonehill (3), Roy
Rockwood (2), Edward Stratemeyer (2), Manager Henry Abbott (1), Hal Harkaway
(1), and Harvey Hicks (1). Fifteen of the books (the FLAG OF FREEDOM, FRON-
TIER, and MEXICAN WAR series, and Lost in the land of ice) were later reprinted under Stratemeyer's own name in the MEXICAN WAR and ALGER SERIES.
   Unlike many Stratemeyer Syndicate pseudonyms, Captain Ralph Bonehill
was not connected with one particular publishing house. W. L. Allison,
A. S. Barnes & Co., Dana Estes & Co., Mershon, Stitt, Thompson & Thomas,
and A. Wessels were all original publishers of at least one Bonehill title.
Other publishers, such as Chatterton-Peck, Grosset & Dunlap, and Caldwell,
issued reprint editions of several of Bonehill's works.
   Captain Ralph Bonehill was one of the earliest pseudonyms used on
Stratemeyer's books. The majority of the titles written under this name
made their first appearance in book form in one of nine series: BOUND TO
WIN (1897); YOUNG SPORTSMAN'S (1897?-1902?); FLAG OF FREEDOM (1899-1902);
YOUNG HUNTERS (1900?); MEXICAN WAR (1900-1902); ZERO CLUB (1902); FRONTIER
(1903-1906); OUTDOOR (1904-1905); BOY HUNTERS (1906-1910). The seven magazine stories were printed from 1896 to 1899.

MAGAZINE PUBLICATIONS

038M   "Balloon boys; or, Adventures among the clouds." Bright Days,
nos. 12-17, Oct. 17-Nov. 21, 1896.

039M   "Camp and diamond; or, The outing of the young victors." Bright
Days, nos. 4-8, July-Sept. 19, 1896.

040M   "Gun and sled; or, The young hunters of Snowtop Island." Young
People of America, nos. 26-32, Nov. 23, 1895-Jan. 4, 1896.

> Published in book form in 1897 by W. L. Allison as vol. 3 in the BOUND
> TO WIN series (047S.1X), and in the YOUNG HUNTERS series (064S.1).
> Reprinted by Donohue in the YOUNG HUNTERS series (064S.1) and, in 1902,
> in the YOUNG SPORTSMAN'S series (065S.4X).

041M   "May Lillie, princess of the prairie; or, Pawnee Bill's wild ride for life." Golden Hours, nos. 547-555, July 23-Sept. 17, 1898.

042M   "Pawnee Bill, the hero scout of Oklahoma; or, Wild adventures in the wild West. A true life tale of the hero of the plains." Golden Hours, nos. 537-546, May 14-July 16, 1898.

043M   "Single shell Jerry; or, The rival oarsmen of Lakeview." Young People of America, nos. 4-9, June 15-July 27, 1895.

> Published in book form by W. L. Allison in 1897 as The young oarsmen of Lakeview; or, The mystery of Hermit Island, vol. 6 in the BOUND TO WIN series (047S.2X). Also published by Allison and by Donohue as vol. 2 in the YOUNG SPORTSMAN'S series (065S.2), and by Donohue in the BOYS' PRIZE LIBRARY (052P.1X).

044M   "The young bandmaster; or, Solving a mystery of the past." Golden Hours, nos. 576-585, Feb. 11-April 15, 1899.

> Published in book form in 1900 by Mershon as The young bandmaster; or, Concert, stage and battlefield, vol. 4 of the FLAG OF FREEDOM series (056S.4). The new title was used for Grosset & Dunlap's 1912 edition, vol. 6 of the FLAG AND FRONTIER series (055S.6). Reprinted in 1920 by Street & Smith as The young bandmaster; or, Against big odds by Edward Stratemeyer, no. 119 in the ALGER SERIES (289P.22X).

045S   ADVENTURE

Volumes: 2
Publisher: Saalfield Publishing Co.
Illustrations: anonymous, vols. 1-2
Additional information: There may have been other titles in this reprint
    series; a complete list has not been found. Saalfield first issued
    these two titles, written by Edward Stratemeyer, as individual (non-
    series) volumes in 1901 and 1902, and later reprinted them as the two-
    volume BONEHILL series (046S).

045S.1X   Three young ranchmen; or, Daring adventures in the great West. (Saalfield).

> First published as "Three ranch boys; or, The great Winthrop claim" by Edward Stratemeyer in Young People of America, Nov. 30, 1895-Feb. 8, 1896 (281M).

045S.2X   The boy land boomer; or, Dick Arbuckle's adventures in Oklahoma. (Saalfield).

> First published as a non-series title in 1902 by Saalfield (067N).

046S   BONEHILL

Volumes: 2
Publisher: Saalfield Publishing Co.

Source of annotations: Saalfield Publishing Co. advertisements [S]
Additional information: The two volumes were written by Edward Stratemeyer
    and published as non-series titles by Saalfield in 1901 and 1902. They
    also appeared in Saalfield's ADVENTURE series (045S).
Series description [S]: "Stories of western life that are full of adven-
    ture which read as if they happened day before yesterday."

046S.1   The boy land boomer; or, Dick Arbuckle's adventures in Oklahoma.
(Saalfield).

    First published as a non-series title in 1902 (067N).

046S.2   Three young ranchmen; or, Daring adventures in the great West.
(Saalfield).

    First published as "Three ranch boys; or, The great Winthrop claim"
    by Edward Stratemeyer in Young People of America, Nov. 30, 1895–Feb.
    6, 1896 (28iM).

047S   BOUND TO WIN

Volumes: 4*
Printed: 1897
Publisher: W. L. Allison Company
Illustrator: G. B. Dupont, vols. 1X–4X
Additional information: Boys' success and adventure stories written by
    Edward Stratemeyer under his own name and two pseudonyms (Captain Ralph
    Bonehill and Arthur M. Winfield) formed the twelve-volume BOUND TO WIN
    series, published in 1897. Four volumes appeared under each of the
    three names, in the following order:
    1. Bound to be an electrician; or, Franklin Bell's success, by Edward
    Stratemeyer
    2. The schooldays of Fred Harley; or, Rivals for all honors, by Arthur
    M. Winfield
    3. Gun and sled; or, The young hunters of Snow-top Island, by Captain
    Ralph Bonehill
    4. Shorthand Tom; or, The exploits of a young reporter, by Edward
    Stratemeyer
    5. The missing tin box; or, The stolen railroad bonds, by Arthur M.
    Winfield
    6. Young oarsmen of Lakeview; or, The mystery of Hermit Island, by
    Captain Ralph Bonehill
    7. The young auctioneers; or, The polishing of a rolling stone, by
    Edward Stratemeyer
    8. Poor but plucky; or, The mystery of a flood, by Arthur M. Winfield
    9. The rival bicyclists; or, Fun and adventure on the wheel, by Captain
    Ralph Bonehill
    10. Fighting for his own; or, The fortunes of a young artist, by Edward
    Stratemeyer
    11. By pluck, not luck; or, Dan Granbury's struggle to rise, by Arthur
    M. Winfield

---

*   Number of volumes applies only to titles written by Edward Stratemeyer
    under the name Captain Ralph Bonehill.

12. Leo the circus boy; or, Life under the great white canvas, by
Captain Ralph Bonehill
For more information about titles published under the names Edward
Stratemeyer and Arthur M. Winfield, see Edward Stratemeyer, BOUND TO
WIN (292S) and Arthur M. Winfield, BOUND TO WIN (330S).

047S.1X   Gun and sled; or, The young hunters of Snow-top island. (Allison,
1897).

Published as vol. 3. First published in Young People of America, Nov.
23, 1895-Jan. 4, 1896 (040M).

047S.2X   Young oarsmen of Lakeview; or, The mystery of Hermit Island.
(Allison, 1897).

Published as vol. 6. First published in Young People of America,* June
15-July 27, 1895, as "Single shell Jerry; or, The rival oarsmen of Lakeview" (043M).

047S.3X   The rival bicyclists; or, Fun and adventure on the wheel. (Allison, 1897).

Published as vol. 9. First published in Young Sports of America, June
1-July 13, 1895, as "Joe Johnson, the bicycle wonder; or, Riding for
the championship of the world" by Roy Rockwood (218M).

047S.4X   Leo the circus boy; or, Life under the great white canvas. (Allison, 1897).

Published as vol. 12. First published in Young Sports of America, May
25-June 29, 1895, as "Limber Leo, clown and gymnast; or, With the
greatest show on earth" by P. T. Barnum (025M).

048S   BOY HUNTERS

Volumes: 4
Printed: 1906-1910
Publisher: Cupples & Leon Company
Illustrator: Charles Nuttall, vols. 1-3
              G. M. Kaiser, vol. 4
Source of annotations: Cupples & Leon Company advertisements [C&L]
Additional information: Edward Stratemeyer wrote the four books in this
    series.

048S.1   Four boy hunters; or, The outing of the gun club. (Cupples &
Leon, 1906).

[C&L]: "A fine, breezy story of the woods and waters, of adventures
in search of game, and of great times around the campfire, told in
Captain Bonehill's best style. In the book are given full directions
for camping out."

_____

*   Formerly titled Young Sports of America.

048S.2   Guns and snowshoes; or, The winter outing of the young hunters.
(Cupples & Leon, 1907).

 [C&L]: "In this volume the young hunters leave home for a winter outing
on the shores of a small lake. They hunt and trap to their heart's
[sic] content, and have adventures in plenty, all calculated to make
boys 'sit up and take notice.' A good healthy book; one with the odor
of the pine forests and the glare of the welcome campfire in every
chapter."

048S.3   Young hunters of the lake; or, Out with rod and gun. (Cupples &
Leon, 1908).

 [C&L]: "Another tale of woods and waters, with some strong hunting
scenes and a good deal of mystery. The three volumes make a splendid
outdoor series."

048S.4   Out with gun and camera; or, The boy hunters in the mountains.
(Cupples & Leon, 1910).

 [C&L]: "Takes up the new fad of photographing wild animals as well as
shooting them. An escaped circus chimpanzee and an escaped lion add
to the interest of the narrative."

049P   BOYS' LIBERTY

Volumes: 1*
Publisher: M. A. Donohue & Company
Additional information: BOYS' LIBERTY series was an eighteen-volume reprint
 series. Edward Stratemeyer wrote three volumes--two under the name
 Arthur M. Winfield (331P) and one as Captain Ralph Bonehill.

049P.1X   Rival cyclists.** (Donohue).

 Published as vol. 14. First published as "Joe Johnson, the bicycle
wonder; or, Riding for the championship of the world" by Roy Rockwood
in Young Sports of America, June 1-July 13, 1895 (218M).

050P   BOYS' OWN LIBRARY (MCKAY)

Volumes: 2*
Printed: 1902*
Publisher: David McKay
Additional information: McKay's BOYS OWN LIBRARY was a publisher's series
 containing approximately 140 volumes. It was similar to Street &
 Smith's BOYS' OWN LIBRARY and included most, if not all, of the same
 titles. Five books common to both series were written by Edward Strate-
 meyer under the pseudonyms Captain Ralph Bonehill and Arthur M. Winfield

---

* Number of volumes and years published apply only to titles written by
 Edward Stratemeyer under the name Captain Ralph Bonehill.
** Subtitle missing.

(332P; 333P); both series issued the volumes in 1902.

A notice in Publishers' Weekly on February 24, 1906, stated that McKay had purchased Street & Smith's BOYS' OWN LIBRARY, "including 140 volumes and two unpublished titles."

050P.1X   Neka, the boy conjurer; or, A mystery of the stage. (McKay, 1902).

First published as "Neka, king of fire; or, A mystery of the variety stage" by Manager Henry Abbott in Good News, Dec. 28, 1895-March 21, 1896 (003M).

050P.2X   Tour of the Zero Club; or, Adventures amid ice and snow. (McKay, 1902).

First published as "The tour of the Zero Club; or, Perils by ice and snow" by Harvey Hicks in Good News, Dec. 29, 1894-March 23, 1895 (178M).

051P   BOYS' OWN LIBRARY (STREET & SMITH)

Volumes: 2*
Printed: 1902*
Publisher: Street & Smith
Additional information: See Captain Ralph Bonehill, BOYS' OWN LIBRARY
    (MCKAY) (050P).

051P.1X   Neka, the boy conjurer; or, A mystery of the stage. (Street & Smith, 1902).

First published as "Neka, king of fire; or, A mystery of the variety stage" by Manager Henry Abbott in Good News, Dec. 28, 1895-March 21, 1896 (003M).

051P.2X   Tour of the Zero Club; or, Adventures amid ice and snow. (Street & Smith, 1902).

First published as "The tour of the Zero Club; or, Perils by ice and snow" by Harvey Hicks in Good News, Dec. 29, 1894-March 23, 1895 (178M).

052P   BOYS' PRIZE LIBRARY

Volumes: 2*
Publisher: M. A. Donohue & Company
Additional information: The last two books in this twelve-volume reprint
    series were written by Edward Stratemeyer.

052P.1X   Young oarsmen of Lakeview.** (Donohue).

First published in Young Sports of America, June 15-July 27, 1895, as "Single shell Jerry; or, The rival oarsmen of Lakeview" (043M).

---

*   Number of volumes and years published apply only to titles written by
     Edward Stratemeyer under the name Captain Ralph Bonehill.
**   Subtitle missing.

052P.2X   Young hunters in Porto Rico.* (Donohue).

First published either by Allison cal899** or by Donohue in 1900 as
Young hunters in Porto Rico; or, The search for a lost treasure, vol.
2 of the YOUNG HUNTERS series (064S.2).

053P   ENTERPRISE BOOKS

Volumes: 1***
Publisher: Grosset & Dunlap
Source of annotations: Grosset & Dunlap advertisements [G&D]
Additional information: Three of the eight books in this reprint series
    were the work of Edward Stratemeyer under three pseudonyms: Captain
    Ralph Bonehill, Roy Rockwood (230P), and Arthur M. Winfield (335P).
    The eight volumes were, in order:
    1. The crimson banner: A story of college baseball, by William D.
    Moffat
    2. Canoe boys and camp fires, by William Murray Graydon
    3. Andy, the acrobat; or, With the greatest show on earth, by Peter
    T. Harkness
    4. The quest of the silver swan: A tale of ocean adventure, by W.
    Bert Foster
    5. Two boys and a fortune; or, The Tyler will, by Matthew White, Jr.
    6. Bob, the photographer; or, A hero in spite of himself, by Arthur
    M. Winfield
    7. Lost in the land of ice; or, Daring adventures round the South Pole,
    by Captain Ralph Bonehill
    8. Jack North's treasure hunt; or, Daring adventures in South America,#
    by Roy Rockwood
    The order of volumes 7 and 8 is sometimes reversed.
Series description [G&D]: "The episodes are graphic, exciting, realistic--
    the tendency of the tales is to the formation of an honorable and manly
    character. They are unusually interesting, and convey lessons of pluck,
    perserverance, and manly independence."

053P.1X   Lost in the land of ice; or, Daring adventures round the South
Pole. (Grosset & Dunlap).

Published as vol. 7 or 8. First published in Golden Hours, Dec. 1,
1900-Jan. 26, 1901, as "Lost in the land of ice; or, Bob Baxter at the
South Pole" by Roy Rockwood (219M).
[G&D]: "An expedition is fitted out by a rich young man who loves
the ocean, and with him goes the hero of the tale, a lad who has some
knowledge of a treasure ship said to be cast away in the land of ice.
On the way the expedition is stopped by enemies, and the heroes land
among the wild Indians of Patagonia. When the ship approaches the
South Pole it is caught in a huge iceberg, and several of those on
board become truly lost in the land of ice."

*   Subtitle missing.
**   Possibly a phantom title.
*** Number of volumes applies only to titles written by Edward Stratemeyer
     under the pseudonym Captain Ralph Bonehill.
Grosset & Dunlap ads show the subtitle as A story of South American
     adventure.

054P   FAMOUS BOOKS FOR BOYS

Volumes: 2*
Printed: 1905*
Publisher: H. M. Caldwell Company
Additional information: Another publisher's reprint series, FAMOUS BOOKS
    FOR BOYS, included four Stratemeyer titles: two under Captain Ralph
    Bonehill and two by Arthur M. Winfield (336P).

054P.1X   Tour of the Zero Club; or, Adventures amid ice and snow. (Caldwell, 1905).

    First published in Good News, Dec. 29,. 1894-March 23, 1895, as "The
    tour of the Zero Club; or, Perils by ice and snow" by Harvey Hicks
    (178M).

054P.2X   Neka, the boy conjurer; or, A mystery of the stage. (Caldwell,
1905).

    First published in Good News, Dec. 28, 1895-March 21, 1896, as "Neka,
    king of fire; or, A mystery of the variety stage" by Manager Henry
    Abbott (003M).

055S   FLAG AND FRONTIER

Volumes: 9
Printed: 1912
Publisher: Grosset & Dunlap
Illustrator: F, vol. 1
              anonymous, vols. 2, 4-5, 9
              Clare Angell, vol. 3
              W. B. Bridge and Stacy Burch, vols. 6-8
Source of annotations: Grosset & Dunlap advertisements [G&D]
Additional information: This series is a reprint of the three-volume FRON-
    TIER (057S) and the six-volume FLAG OF FREEDOM (056S) series. The
    rights to these series were acquired by Grosset & Dunlap in 1908.
    See Captain Ralph Bonehill, FLAG OF FREEDOM series (056S) and FRONTIER
    series (057S) for further information.
Series description [G&D]: These bracing stories of American life, explo-
    ration and adventure should find a place in every school and home li-
    brary for the enthusiasm they kindle in American heroism and history.
    The historical background is absolutely correct. Every volume complete
    in itself."

055S.1   With Boone on the frontier; or, The pioneer boys of old Kentucky.
(Grosset & Dunlap, 1912).

    First published by Mershon in 1903 as vol. 1 of the FRONTIER series
    (057S.1).
        [G&D]: "Relates the true-to-life adventures of two boys who, in

_____

* Number of volumes and years published apply only to titles written by
   Edward Stratemeyer under the pseudonym Captain Ralph Bonehill.

company with their folks, move westward with Daniel Boone. Contains many thrilling scenes among the Indians and encounters with wild animals."

055S.2   Pioneer boys of the great Northwest; or, With Lewis and Clark across the Rockies. (Grosset & Dunlap, 1912).

First published by Mershon in 1904 as vol. 2 of the FRONTIER series (057S.2).
[G&D]: "A splendid story describing in detail the great expedition formed under the leadership of Lewis and Clark, and telling what was done by the pioneer boys who were first to penetrate the wilderness of the northwest."

055S.3   Pioneer boys of the gold fields; or, The nugget hunters of '49. (Grosset & Dunlap, 1912).

First published by Stitt in 1906 as vol. 3 of the FRONTIER series (057S.3).
[G&D]: "Giving the particulars of the great rush of the gold seekers to California in 1849. In the party making its way across the continent are three boys who become chums and share in no end of adventures."

055S.4   With Custer in the Black Hills; or, A young scout among the Indians. (Grosset & Dunlap, 1912).

First published by Mershon in 1902 as vol. 6 of the FLAG OF FREEDOM series (056S.6).
[G&D]: "Tells of the experiences of a youth who, with his parents, goes to the Black Hills in search of gold. Custer's last battle is well described."

055S.5   Boys of the fort; or, A young captain's pluck. (Grosset & Dunlap, 1912).

First published by Mershon in 1901 as vol. 5 of the FLAG OF FREEDOM series (056S.5).
[G&D]: "This story of stirring doings at one of our well-known forts in the Wild West is of more than ordinary interest. Gives a good insight into army life of to-day."

055S.6   The young bandmaster; or, Concert, stage and battlefield. (Grosset & Dunlap, 1912).

First published in Golden Hours, Feb. 11-April 15, 1899, as "The young bandmaster; or, Solving a mystery of the past" (044M).
[G&D]: "The hero is a youth who becomes a cornetist in an orchestra, and works his way up to the leadership of a brass band. He is carried off to sea and is taken to Cuba, and while there joins a military band which accompanies our soldiers in the attack on Santiago."

055S.7   Off for Hawaii; or, The mystery of a great volcano. (Grosset & Dunlap, 1912).

First published by Mershon in 1899 as vol. 3 in the FLAG OF FREEDOM series (056S.3).

[G&D]: "Several boys start on a tour of the Hawaiian Islands. They have heard that there is a treasure located in the vicinity of Kilauea, the largest active volcano in the world, and go in search of it."

055S.8   A sailor boy with Dewey; or, Afloat in the Philippines. (Grosset & Dunlap, 1912).

First published by Mershon in 1899 as vol. 2 in the FLAG OF FREEDOM series (056S.2).
   [G&D]: "The story of Dewey's victory in Manila Bay as it appeared to a real, live American youth who was in the navy at the time. Many adventures in Manila and in the interior follow."

055S.9   When Santiago fell; or, The war adventures of two chums. (Grosset & Dunlap, 1912).

First published by Mershon in 1899 as vol. 1 in the FLAG OF FREEDOM series (056S.1).
   [G&D]: "Two boys leave New York to join their parents in Cuba. The war between Spain and the Cubans is on, and the boys are detained at Santiago, but escape across the bay at night. Many adventures follow."

056S   FLAG OF FREEDOM

Volumes: 6
Printed: 1899-1902
Publisher: The Mershon Company
Reprint publisher: Chatterton-Peck Company, vols. 1-6
                    Grosset & Dunlap, vols. 1-6
Illustrator: anonymous, vols. 1, 5-6
              W. B. Bridge and Stacy Burch, vols. 2-4
Source of annotations: Grosset & Dunlap advertisements [G&D]
Additional information: Edward Stratemeyer wrote the six volumes in this
   series, which was originally published by Mershon, then reprinted by
   Chatterton-Peck ca1906-1907. After litigation between Mershon, Stitt,
   Chatterton-Peck, and Stratemeyer was settled in 1908, Grosset & Dunlap
   acquired the rights to the FLAG OF FREEDOM series, along with the
   FRONTIER series (057S), and reprinted both series, then combined the
   two and advertised them as the FLAG AND FRONTIER series (055S) in 1912.
   In 1920, the books were reprinted in Street & Smith's ALGER SERIES
   (289P). In the ALGER SERIES, the author was given as Edward Stratemeyer
   and some titles were altered, but the books were issued in the original
   series order; in the Grosset & Dunlap reprintings, the author and title
   remained the same, but the series order was reversed.
      The Chatterton-Peck and Grosset & Dunlap editions had the same
   illustrations as the Mershon editions; the ALGER SERIES was published
   without illustrations.
Series description [G&D]: "A favorite Line of American Stories for America
   Boys."

056S.1   When Santiago fell; or, The war adventures of two chums. (Mershon
1899; Chatterton-Peck, 1905; Grosset & Dunlap, ca1908).

Vol. 6 in Grosset & Dunlap's series. Reprinted in 1912 as vol. 9 in
Grosset & Dunlap's FLAG AND FRONTIER series (055S.9). Also reprinted
in 1920 as no. 116 in Street & Smith's ALGER SERIES as For his country;
or, The adventures of two chums by Edward Stratemeyer (289P.19X).
   [G&D]: "Two boys, an American and his Cuban chum, leave New York
to join their parents in the interior of Cuba. The war between Spain
and the Cubans is on, and the boys are detained at Santiago, but escape
by crossing the bay at night. Many adventures between the lines follow,
and a good pen-picture of General Garcia is given."

056S.2   A sailor boy with Dewey; or, Afloat in the Philippines. (Mershon,
1899; Chatterton-Peck, ca1906; Grosset & Dunlap, ca1908).

Vol. 5 in Grosset & Dunlap's series. Reprinted in 1912 as vol. 8 in
Grosset & Dunlap's FLAG AND FRONTIER series (055S.8). Also reprinted
in 1920 as no. 117 in Street & Smith's ALGER SERIES as Comrades in
peril; or, Afloat on a battleship by Edward Stratemeyer (289P.20X).
   [G&D]: "The story of Dewey's victory in Manila Bay will never grow
old, but here we have it told in a new form--as it appeared to a real,
live American youth who was in the navy at the time. Many adventures
in Manila and in the interior follow, give true-to-life scenes from this
portion of the globe."

056S.3   Off for Hawaii; or, The mystery of a great volcano. (Mershon,
1899; Chatterton-Peck, ca1906; Grosset & Dunlap, ca1908).

Vol. 4 in Grosset & Dunlap's series. Reprinted in 1912 as vol. 7 in
Grosset & Dunlap's FLAG AND FRONTIER series (055S.7). Also reprinted
in 1920 as no. 118 in Street & Smith's ALGER SERIES as The young pearl
hunters; or, In Hawaiian waters by Edward Stratemeyer (289P.21X).
   [G&D]: "Here we have fact and romance cleverly interwoven. Several
boys start on a tour of the Hawaiian Islands. They have heard that
there is a treasure located in the vicinity of Kilauea, the largest
active volcano in the world, and go in search of it. Their numerous
adventures will be followed with much interest."

056S.4   The young bandmaster; or, Concert, stage, and battlefield.
(Mershon, 1900; Chatterton-Peck, ca1906; Grosset & Dunlap, ca1908).

Vol. 3 in Grosset & Dunlap's series. First published in Golden Hours,
Feb. 11-April 15, 1899, as "The young bandmaster; or, Solving a mystery
of the past" (044M).
   [G&D]: "The hero is a youth with a passion for music, who becomes
a cornetist in an orchestra, and works his way up to the leadership of
a brass band. He is carried off to sea and falls in with a secret service cutter bound for Cuba, and while there joins a military band which
accompanies our soldiers in the never-to-be-forgotten attack on Santiago."

056S.5   Boys of the fort; or, A young captain's pluck. (Mershon, 1901;
Chatterton-Peck, ca1906; Grosset & Dunlap, ca1908).

Vol. 2 in Grosset & Dunlap's series. Reprinted in 1912 as vol. 5 in
Grosset & Dunlap's FLAG AND FRONTIER series (055S.5). Also reprinted
in 1920 as no. 120 of Street & Smith's ALGER SERIES as Boys of the fort;
or, True courage wins by Edward Stratemeyer (289P.23X).

[G&D]: "This story of stirring doings at one of our well-known forts in the Wild West is of more than ordinary interest. The young captain had a difficult task to accomplish, but he had been drilled to do his duty, and does it thoroughly. Gives a good insight into army life of to-day."

056S.6   With Custer in the Black Hills; or, A young scout among the Indians. (Mershon, 1902; Chatterton-Peck, ca1906; Grosset & Dunlap, ca1908).

Vol. 1 in Grosset & Dunlap's series. Reprinted as vol. 4 of Grosset & Dunlap's FLAG OF FRONTIER series in 1912 (055S.4). Also reprinted as no. 121 in Street & Smith's ALGER SERIES in 1920 as On fortune's trail; or, The heroes of the Black Hills (289P.24X).
[G&D]: "Tells of the remarkable experiences of a youth who, with his parents, goes to the Black Hills in search of gold. Custer's last battle is well described. A volume every lad fond of Indian stories should possess."

057S   FRONTIER

Volumes: 3
Printed: 1903-1906
Publisher: The Mershon Company, vols. 1-2
            Stitt Publishing Company, vol. 3
Reprint publisher: Stitt Publishing Company, vols. 1-2
                    Chatterton-Peck Company, vols. 1-3
                    Grosset & Dunlap, vols. 1-3
Illustrator: F, vol. 1
              anonymous, vol. 2
              Clare Angell, vol. 3
Source of annotations: Grosset & Dunlap advertisements [G&D]
Additional information: The history of the FRONTIER series is similar to that of the FLAG OF FREEDOM series (056S). It was written by Edward Stratemever and published by Mershon, Stitt, and Chatterton-Peck; in 1908, after litigation between Stratemeyer and several publishers was settled, Grosset & Dunlap published the series, then reprinted it in 1912 as part of the FLAG AND FREEDOM series. In 1920 the books were again reprinted, this time with altered titles and with Stratemeyer as author, in Street & Smith's ALGER SERIES (289P).
     The Grosset & Dunlap, Chatterton-Peck, and Stitt editions had the same illustrations as the original editions; the Street & Smith titles were published without illustrations.

057S.1   With Boone on the frontier; or, The pioneer boys of old Kentucky. (Mershon, 1903; Stitt, ca1905; Chatterton-Peck, ca1906; Grosset & Dunlap, ca1908).

Vol. 3 of Grosset & Dunlap's series. Reprinted in 1912 as vol. 1 of Grosset & Dunlap's FLAG AND FRONTIER series (055S.1). Also reprinted in 1920 as Boys of the wilderness; or, Down in old Kentucky by Edward Stratemeyer, no. 113 of the ALGER SERIES by Street & Smith (289P.16X).
[G&D]: "Relates the true-to-life adventures of two boys who, in company with their folks, move westward with Daniel Boone. Contains many thrilling scenes among the Indians and encounters with wild animals. It is excellently told."

057S.2   Pioneer boys of the great Northwest; or, With Lewis and Clark across the Rockies. (Mershon, 1904; Stitt, 1905; Chatterton-Peck, ca1906; Grosset & Dunlap, ca1908).

> Reprinted in 1912 as vol. 2 of Grosset & Dunlap's FLAG AND FRONTIER series (055S.2). Also reprinted in 1920 as Boys of the great Northwest; or, Across the Rockies by Edward Stratemeyer, no. 114 of Street & Smith's ALGER SERIES (289P.17X).
>   [G&D]: "A splendid story describing in detail the great expedition formed under the leadership of Lewis and Clark, and telling what was done by the pioneer boys who were first to penetrate the wilderness of the northwest and push over the Rocky Mountains. The book possesses a permanent historical value and the story should be known by every bright American boy."

057S.3   Pioneer boys of the gold fields; or, The nugget hunters of '49. (Stitt, 1906; Chatterton-Peck, ca1906; Grosset & Dunlap, ca1908).

> Vol. 1 in Grosset & Dunlap's series. Reprinted in 1912 as vol. 3 of Grosset & Dunlap's FLAG AND FRONTIER series (055S.3). Also reprinted in 1920 as Boys of the gold fields; or, The nugget hunters by Edward Stratemeyer, no. 115 of Street & Smith's ALGER SERIES (289P.18X).
>   [G&D]: "A tale complete in itself, giving the particulars of the great rush of the gold seekers to California in 1849. In the party making its way across the continent are three boys, one from the country, another from the city, and a third just home from a long voyage on a whaling ship. They become chums, and share in no end of adventures."

058P   LAND AND SEA

Volumes: 1*
Publisher: M. A. Donohue & Co.
Additional information: Edward Stratemeyer wrote the first volume of this four-volume publisher's reprint series. The other three volumes were, in order:
2. Blue water rovers, by Victor St. Clare
3. A royal smuggler, by William Dalton
4. A boy Crusoe, by Allen Erie

058P.1   Oscar the naval cadet; or, Under the sea. (Donohue).

> First published as "Holland, the destroyer; or, America against the world" by Hal Harkaway in Golden Hours, Nov. 24, 1900-Jan. 12, 1901 (167M).

059P   MEDAL LIBRARY

Volumes: 2*
Printed: 1904*

---

* Number of volumes and years published apply only to titles written by Edward Stratemeyer under the pseudonym Captain Ralph Bonehill.

Publisher: Street & Smith
Source of annotations: Street & Smith advertisements [S&S]
Additional information: The MEDAL LIBRARY was a paperback reprint series
    published from January 28, 1899 to September 24, 1906, for a total of
    378 issues. All except the first eight were issued weekly. On October
    1, 1906, the series was retitled, and no. 379 appeared as the NEW MEDAL
    LIBRARY. The NEW MEDAL LIBRARY continued until December 7, 1915, and
    ended with no. 858.
        Nos. 241, 249, 250, 269, and 279 (all published in 1904) were
    written by Edward Stratemeyer under the names Captain Ralph Bonehill
    and Arthur M. Winfield (337P).
Series description [S&S]: "Stories for boys must be true to life. If they
    are not, boys will have nothing to do with them. This has been our ex-
    perience with the MEDAL LIBRARY books. In it, we publish all the books
    that other publishers get a dollar for. What do we ask for them? Only
    ten cents!
        "The MEDAL LIBRARY contains stories by Horatio Alger, Jr., Oliver
    Optic, G. A. Henty, Frank H. Converse, James Otis and a hundred others
    who are just as famous. Take our word for it, a boy never bought bet-
    ter reading matter or had a more generous list to select from than what
    we are now offering to you at ten cents per copy in the MEDAL LIBRARY."

059P.1X   The tour of the Zero club; or, Adventures amid ice and snow.
No. 241. Jan. 16, 1904.

    First published as "The tour of the Zero Club; or, Perils by ice and
    snow" by Harvey Hicks in Good News, Dec. 29, 1894-March 23, 1895
    (178M).

059P.2X   Neka, the boy conjurer; or, The mystery of the stage. No. 250.
March 19, 1904.

    First published as "Neka, king of fire; or, A mystery of the variety
    stage" by Manager Henry Abbott in Good News, Dec. 28, 1895-March 21,
    1896 (003M).

060S   MEXICAN WAR

Volumes: 3
Printed: 1900-1902
Publisher: Dana Estes & Co.
Reprint publisher: Lothrop, Lee & Shepard Co., vols. 1-3 (with Edward
                        Stratemeyer as author)
Illustrator: Louis Meynelle, vol. 1
              J. W. Kennedy, vol. 2
              J. J. Mora, vol. 3
Source of annotations: Lothrop, Lee & Shepard Co. advertisements [L,L&S]
Additional information: The Lothrop, Lee & Shepard editions were published
    in 1909 with Stratemeyer listed as author, but with the same series
    title, order, and illustrations (297S). The books were published with-
    out subtitles.

060S.1   For the liberty of Texas. (Estes, 1900; Lothrop, Lee & Shepard,
1909, 1917, 1930).

All Lothrop, Lee & Shepard editions show Edward Stratemeyer as author (297S.1).

[L,L&S]: "Much is told here of Sam Houston, Davy Crockett, Colonel Bowie, and other Texan heroes in connection with the entertaining story of the fortunes of two brothers, Dan and Ralph Radbury. The fall of the Alamo is introduced, and other famous incidents."

060S.2   With Taylor on the Rio Grande.   (Estes, 1901; Lothrop, Lee & Shepard, 1909, 1917, 1930).

All Lothrop, Lee & Shepard editions show Edward Stratemeyer as author (297S.2).

[L,L&S]: "As with each of the series, this is a complete story, but continues the adventures of the patriotic young Radbury brothers. They serve under General Taylor at Palo Alto, Monterey, and Buena Vista and share in the glory of 'Old Rough and Ready.'"

060S.3   Under Scott in Mexico.   (Estes, 1902; Lothrop, Lee & Shepard, 1909, 1917, 1930?).

All Lothrop, Lee & Shepard editions show Edward Stratemeyer as author (297S.3).

[L,L&S]: "In the concluding volume of this valuable historical series Dan and Ralph come under the command of Gen. Winfield Scott and finally bear their part in the triumphant entry of the proud city of Mexico."

061S   OUTDOOR

Volumes: 2
Printed: 1904-1905
Publisher: A. S. Barnes & Co.
Illustrator: Jay Hambidge, vol. 1
              Max Klepper, vol. 2
Source of annotations: Lothrop, Lee & Shepard Co. advertisements [L,L&S]*
Additional information: The two volumes in this series were written by
    Edward Stratemeyer. In 1908 they were retitled and published as the
    first two volumes of Lothrop, Lee & Shepard's six-volume LAKEPORT series,
    with Stratemeyer listed as author (296S).

061S.1   The island camp; or, The young hunters of Lakeport. (Barnes, 1904).

First published as "Snow Lodge" by Edward Stratemeyer in The Popular Magazine, Dec. 1903-Jan. 1904 (280M).
    [L,L&S]: "A bright, breezy, outdoor story, telling how several lads organized a gun club and went camping in the winter time. They had with them a trusty old hunter who revealed to them many of the secrets of Nature as found in the woods. A volume any boy who loves a gun will appreciate."

061S.2   The winning run; or, The baseball boys of Lakeport. (Barnes, 1905).

---

* The Lothrop, Lee & Shepard ads were for the LAKEPORT series (296S).

Reprinted in 1908 by Lothrop, Lee & Shepard as The baseball boys of Lakeport; or, The winning run by Edward Stratemeyer, vol. 2 of the LAKEPORT series (296S.2).

[L,L&S]: "With the coming of summer the boys turned their attention to baseball and organized a club, and played many thrilling games. The rivalry was of the keenest, and the particulars are given of a plot to injure the Lakeport nine and make them lose the most important game of all."

062P   POPULAR AUTHORS

Volumes: 1*
Printed: 1919*
Publisher: Saalfield Publishing Co.
Additional information: The boy land boomer is the only title by Edward Stratemeyer in this reprint series.

062P.1X   The boy land boomer; or, Dick Arbuckle's adventures in Oklahoma. (Saalfield, 1919).

First published as a non-series title in 1902 by Saalfield (067N).

063P   ROUND THE WORLD LIBRARY

Volumes: 2*
Printed: 1927-1931*
Publisher: Street & Smith
Source of annotations: Street & Smith advertisements [S&S]
Additional information: ROUND THE WORLD LIBRARY, a paperback reprint series started in January, 1925, and was usually published twice a month (some months had three issues). The series began with twenty-eight Jack Harkaway stories by Bracebridge Hemyng, followed by fifteen more titles by Hemyng; the next seventy-four were by various authors. After no. 117, the series renumbered and reprinted many of the earlier issues, starting with no. 1 (renumbered no. 118). One of Edward Stratemeyer's books was published in this series as no. 67 and reprinted as no. 180.
Series description [S&S]: "Stories of Jack Harkaway and his companions.
    "'Young man, go West,' that's what Horace Greeley said, and lots of young men took his advice.
    "We say, 'Young man, go East, West, North, or South, in every direction, with the characters in these splendid stories of adventure.
    "First, you are on the road with a showman; second, you are in the jungles among the tigers; next, you are on a football field, and then you are with Robert Lewis Stevenson on a tropical island. There is no end to the vacation that these books will give you, so start right in now to travel."

063P.1X   The tour of the Zero Club.** No. 67. July 1927.

---

*   Number of volumes and years published apply only to titles written by Edward Stratemeyer under the pseudonym Captain Ralph Bonehill.
** Subtitle missing.

First published as "The tour of the Zero Club; or, Perils by ice and snow" by Harvey Hicks in Good News, Dec. 29, 1894-March 23, 1895 (178M).

063P.2X   The tour of the Zero Club.* No. 180. Nov. 1931.

First published as "The tour of the Zero Club; or, Perils by ice and snow" by Harvey Hicks in Good News, Dec. 29, 1894-March 23, 1895 (178M).

064S   YOUNG HUNTERS

Volumes: 2
Printed: 1900?
Publisher: W. L. Allison Company, vols. 1-2**
Reprint publisher: Donohue Bros.,*** vols. 1-2
Additional information: There is some confusion about this series. Allison
    definitely published the first volume in 1897 as part of the BOUND TO
    WIN series, then, presumably, reissued it as volume 1 of the YOUNG HUN-
    TERS series. Allison may have published the second volume in 1899 or
    1900. Shortly after that, Donohue took over many of Allison's Strate-
    meyer titles and printed Young hunters in Porto Rico as the second vol-
    ume of the YOUNG HUNTERS series. According to Dr. John T. Dizer, Jr.,
    Young hunters in Porto Rico is listed in Allison ads and may have been
    published by Allison ca1899, but the book has a 1900 copyright by Dono-
    hue.#
       Edward Stratemeyer wrote both volumes. See also Captain Ralph
    Bonehill, YOUNG SPORTSMAN's series (065S).

064S.1   Gun and sled; or, The young hunters of Snowtop Island. (Allison;
Donohue, ca1900).

First published as "Gun and sled; or, The young hunters of Snowtop
Island" by Captain Ralph Bonehill in Young People of America, Nov. 23,
1895-Jan. 4, 1896 (040M).

064S.2   Young hunters in Porto Rico; or, The search for a lost treasure.
(Allison, ca1899;** Donohue, 1900).

Reprinted by Donohue as part of the YOUNG SPORTSMAN'S series (065S.5X),
and as vol. 12 of Donohue's BOYS' PRIZE LIBRARY (052P.2X).

065S   YOUNG SPORTMAN'S

Volumes: 5
Printed: 1897?-1902?
Publisher: W. L. Allison Company, vols. 1-3
            M. A. Donohue & Company, vols. 4X-5X
Reprint publisher: M. A. Donohue & Company, vols. 1-3

---

*   Subtitle missing.
**   Allison's Young hunters in Porto Rico may be a phantom edition.
***   Later M. A. Donohue & Company.
#   "Serials and boys' books by Edward Stratemeyer," Dime Novel Round-Up
      44, no. 9 (Dec. 1975): 141.

Illustrator: G. B. Dupont, vols. 1-3

Additional information: Allison copyrighted four Captain Ralph Bonehill titles in 1897 and published them in its BOUND TO WIN series (047S). One of these volumes, Gun and Sled, was reissued as the first volume of the YOUNG HUNTERS series (064S); the other three were reprinted by Allison as the YOUNG SPORTSMAN'S series sometime between 1897 and 1900. The three volumes were then reprinted by Donohue, still as the YOUNG SPORTSMAN'S series, sometime between 1900 and 1905--probably in or before 1902, for that was the year Donohue copyrighted Gun and Sled and issued it as part of the YOUNG SPORTSMAN'S series. A fifth volume, Young hunters in Porto Rico (which had appeared earlier as part of the YOUNG HUNTERS books), was also added to the series by Donohue.

 Books in print for 1928 shows five titles in Donohue's YOUNG SPORTSMAN'S series, but does not even mention the YOUNG HUNTERS series, which suggests that the two had merged.

 Edward Stratemeyer wrote all five volumes. The Donohue editions were not illustrated.

065S.1   The rival bicyclists; or, Fun and adventures on the wheel. (Allison; Donohue).

 First published as "Joe Johnson, the bicycle wonder; or, Riding for the championship of the world" by Roy Rockwood in Young Sports of America, June 1-July 13, 1895 (218M).

065S.2   The young oarsmen of Lakeview; or, The mystery of Hermit Island. (Allison; Donohue).

 First published as "Single shell Jerry; or, The rival oarsmen of Lakeview" by Captain Ralph Bonehill in Young People of America,* June 15-July 27, 1895 (043M).

065S.3   Leo the circus boy; or, Life under the great white canvas. (Allison; Donohue).

 First published as "Limber Leo, clown and gymnast; or, With the greates show on earth" by P. T. Barnum, Jr., in Young Sports of America, May 25-June 29, 1895 (025M).

065S.4X   Gun and sled; or, The young hunters of Snow-top Island. (Donohue, 1902).

 First published as "Gun and sled; or, The young hunters of Snowtop Island" by Captain Ralph Bonehill in Young People of America,* Nov. 23, 1895-Jan. 4, 1896 (040M).

065S.5X   Young hunters in Porto Rico; or, The search for a lost treasure. (Donohue).

 First published as vol. 2 of the YOUNG HUNTERS series, either by Alliso ca1899** or by Donohue in 1900 (064S.2).

---

* Formerly Young Sports of America.
** Allison edition may be a phantom edition.

066S   ZERO CLUB

Volumes: 1
Printed: 1902
Publisher: Street & Smith
Additional information: The one-volume ZERO CLUB series was written by
    Edward Stratemeyer.

066S.1   The tour of the Zero Club; or, Adventures amid ice and snow.
(Street & Smith, 1902).

    First published as "The tour of the Zero Club; or, Perils by ice and
    snow" by Harvey Hicks in Good News, Dec. 29, 1894-March 23, 1895 (178M).

OTHER PUBLICATIONS

067N   The boy land boomer; or, Dick Arbuckle's adventures in Oklahoma.
(Saalfield, 1902; Caldwell).

    Saalfield edition illustrated by W. H. Fry. Reprinted by Saalfield
    as part of the ADVENTURE series (045S.2X), the BONEHILL series (046S.1),
    and the POPULAR AUTHORS series (062P.1X). Caldwell edition published
    as a non-series title.

068N   Lost in the land of ice; or, Daring adventures around the South
Pole. (A. Wessels, 1902; Chatterton-Peck, ca1906).

    First published as "Lost in the land of ice; or, Bob Baxter at the
    South Pole" by Roy Rockwood in Golden Hours, Dec. 1, 1900-Jan. 26,
    1901 (219M).

069N   Three young ranchmen; or, Daring adventures in the great West.
(Saalfield, 1901; Caldwell).

    First published as "Three ranch boys; or, The great Winthrop claim"
    by Edward Stratemeyer in Young People of America, Nov. 30, 1895-Feb.
    8, 1896 (281M).

070N   The young naval captain; or, The war of all nations. (Thompson
& Thomas, 1902).

    First published as "Holland, the destroyer; or, America against the
    world" by Hal Harkaway in Golden Hours, Nov. 24, 1900-Jan. 12, 1901
    (167M).

Jim Bowie

Jim Bowie was an early Stratemeyer pseudonym used for eight stories in
Street & Smith's NEW YORK FIVE CENT LIBRARY in 1892 and 1893.

SERIES PUBLICATIONS

071P   NEW YORK FIVE CENT LIBRARY

Volumes: 8*
Printed: 1892-1893*
Publisher: Street & Smith
Additional information: The NEW YORK FIVE CENT LIBRARY was a weekly dime
    novel series that began on August 13, 1892, and continued until November
    2, 1895, for a total of 157 issues. After that, the name was changed
    to the Diamond Dick Library.
        Edward Stratemeyer wrote twenty-one titles in this series, under
    six pseudonyms: Jim Bowie (8 titles), Jim Daly (6** titles [102P]),
    Peter Pad (1 title [208P]), Tom Ward (1 title [315P]), Nat Woods***
    (1 title [349P]), and Zimmy (4 titles [356P]). Stratemeyer's earliest
    contribution was the second volume in the series, on August 20, 1892,
    under the name Peter Pad; his last title was no. 65, as Jim Daly, on
    November 18, 1893. Jim Bowie, Jim Daly, and Zimmy appear to have been
    used only by Stratemeyer; the other names were used by several writers.
        Edward Stratemeyer's brother, Louis Stratemeyer, also wrote three
    books in this series: two as Louis Tracy (nos. 31 and 38) and one as
    Nat Woods*** (no. 58).

071P.1X   Dead shot Dave, the nerviest sport on record; or, The card wizard
of the Mississippi. No. 6. Sept. 17, 1892.

071P.2X   Dead shot Dave in Butte; or, Breaking the green cloth record.
No. 16. Nov. 26, 1892.

071P.3X   Dead shot Dave in Spokane; or, A lone hand and a high stake.
No. 24. Jan. 21, 1893.

071P.4X   Dead shot Dave in Tacoma; or, A fortune at one throw. No. 33.
March 25, 1893.

071P.5X   Dead shot Dave in Denver; or, Foiling the gamblers. No. 45.
June 17, 1893.

071P.6X   Dead shot Dave in Chicago.# No. 53. Aug. 12, 1893.

071P.7X   Dead shot Dave in Omaha; or, The limit of the red and black.
No. 57. Sept. 9, 1893.

071P.8X   Dead shot Dave in Kentucky; or, The blue grass region horse
thieves. No. 62. Oct. 14, 1893.

---

*   Number of volumes and years published apply only to those titles writ-
    ten by Edward Stratemeyer under the name Jim Bowie.
**   One story was published under the name Jim Daley, presumably a mis-
    spelling of "Daly."
*** The story was actually published under the by-line "the author of 'Nat
    Woods.'"
Subtitle missing.

Annie Roe Carr

Annie Roe Carr, a Stratemeyer Syndicate pseudonym, appeared on only one series, the seven-volume NAN SHERWOOD series, published by Sully and World from 1916 to 1937 and reprinted by other publishers.

SERIES PUBLICATIONS

072S   NAN SHERWOOD

Volumes: 7
Printed: 1916-1937
Publisher: George Sully & Company, vols. 1-6*
            World Syndicate Publishing Co., vol. 7
Reprint publisher: World Syndicate Publishing Co., vols. 1-6
                    Goldsmith Publishing Co., vols. 1-5
                    Saalfield Publishing Co., vols. 1-5
Additional information: The sixth volume may have been published without a subtitle, and may only have been published by World. The last volume was published without a subtitle.

072S.1   Nan Sherwood at Pine Camp; or, The old lumberman's secret. (Sully, 1916, 1918; Goldsmith; Saalfield; World).

072S.2   Nan Sherwood at Lakeview Hall; or, The mystery of the haunted boathouse. (Sully, 1916, 1918; Goldsmith; Saalfield; World).

072S.3   Nan Sherwood's winter holidays; or, Rescuing the runaways. (Sully, 1916, 1918; Goldsmith; Saalfield; World).

072S.4   Nan Sherwood at Rose Ranch; or, The old Mexican's treasure. (Sully, 1919; Goldsmith; Saalfield; World).

072S.5   Nan Sherwood at Palm Beach; or, Strange adventures among the orange groves. (Sully, 1921; Goldsmith; Saalfield; World).

072S.6   Nan Sherwood's summer holidays.** (Sully, ca1922;* World, 1937).

072S.7   Nan Sherwood on the Mexican border. (World, 1937).

Captain James Carson

The Stratemeyer Syndicate house name James Carson, or Captain James Carson

---

*   The Sully edition of volume 6 may be a phantom edition.
**   Subtitle missing. This volume may have been published without a subtitle.

(as he was sometimes listed), was credited with only one series, the SADDLE
BOYS, published by Cupples & Leon from 1913 to 1915.

SERIES PUBLICATIONS

073S   SADDLE BOYS

Volumes: 5
Printed: 1913-1915
Publisher: Cupples & Leon Company
Illustrator: Walter S. Rogers, vols. 1-5
Source of annotations: Cupples & Leon Company advertisements [C&L]
Series description [C&L]: "All lads who love life in the open air and a
    good steed, will want to peruse these books. Captain Carson knows his
    subject thoroughly, and his stories are as pleasing as they are in-
    structive."

073S.1   The saddle boys of the Rockies; or, Lost on Thunder Mountain.
(Cupples & Leon, 1913).

    [C&L]: "Telling how the lads started out to solve the mystery of a
    great noise in the mountains--how they got lost--and of the things they
    discovered."

073S.2   The saddle boys in the Grand Canyon; or, The hermit of the cave.
(Cupples & Leon, 1913).

    [C&L]: "A weird and wonderful story of the Grand Canyon of the Colo-
    rado, told in a most absorbing manner. The Saddle Boys are to the front
    in a manner to please all young readers."

073S.3   The saddle boys on the plains; or, After a treasure of gold.
(Cupples & Leon, 1913).

    [C&L]: "In this story the scene is shifted to the great plains of the
    southwest and then to the Mexican Border. There is a stirring struggle
    for gold, told only as Captain Carson can tell it."

073S.4   The saddle boys at Circle Ranch; or, In at the grand round-up.
(Cupples & Leon, 1913).

    [C&L]: "Here we have lively times at the ranch, and likewise the par-
    ticulars of a grand round-up of cattle and encounters with wild animals
    and also cattle thieves. A story that breathes the very air of the
    plains."

073S.5   The saddle boys on Mexican trails; or, In the hands of the enemy.
(Cupples & Leon, 1915).

    [C&L]: "The scene is shifted in this volume to Mexico. The boys go
    on an important errand, and are caught between the lines of the Mexican

soldiers. They are captured and for a while things look black for
them; but all ends happily."

Nick Carter

Stories about the detective Nick Carter often appeared without a by-line
or with the inscription "by the author of 'Nick Carter.'"* The tales were
turned out by a variety of writers; the best-known were Frederic Van
Rensselaer Dey, John Coryell, and Frederick W. Davis. Coryell created the
character; Dey continued his adventures and produced the bulk of the early
Nick Carter stories; Davis took over after Dey stopped writing the series.
     Other writers also contributed stories to meet the demand. Recent re-
search by J. Randolph Cox in Street & Smith's files shows that Edward
Stratemeyer wrote twenty-two Nick Carter adventures (excluding reprints).
Eighteen of these tales were formerly attributed to Frederic Van Rensselaer
Dey.
     The twenty-two tales first appeared in the NICK CARTER LIBRARY from
May 7, 1892 to August 17, 1895. Most were reprinted in the NICK CARTER
WEEKLY and the MAGNET and NEW MAGNET LIBRARIES between 1898 and 1927.

SERIES PUBLICATIONS

074P   MAGNET LIBRARY

Volumes: 13**
Printed: 1900-1905**
Publisher: Street & Smith
Source of annotations: Street & Smith advertisements [S&S]
Additional information: The MAGNET LIBRARY, a paperback reprint series,
     was published from September 1, 1897 to February 13, 1907, for 483 is-
     sues. It was usually issued weekly, though there were some irregular-
     ities in the publication schedule. On February 20, 1907, the NEW MAG-
     NET LIBRARY began where the MAGNET LIBRARY had stopped--with no. 484--
     and continued until no. 1369, in June 1933. The NEW MAGNET LIBRARY
     was published weekly until 1915, when the schedule changed to biweekly.
        Although stories about other detectives were printed in the MAGNET
     LIBRARY, the majority of the books were reprints of stories about Nick
     Carter that had originally appeared in the NICK CARTER LIBRARY and/or
     the NICK CARTER WEEKLY. Often, two or three stories were spliced to-
     gether (with some editing and with transitions added) to form one long
     adventure per book. Many of these "new" tales were also reprinted in
     the NEW MAGNET LIBRARY.
        There were two methods of reprinting MAGNET LIBRARY titles in the

---

*   "Nick Carter, Detective," no. 1 in the NICK CARTER LIBRARY, was pub-
     lished as by "A Celebrated Author."
**   Number of volumes and years published apply only to titles written by
     Edward Stratemeyer.

NEW MAGNET LIBRARY. The book could simply be reissued with the original
number, but with NEW MAGNET LIBRARY instead of MAGNET LIBRARY on the
cover,* or it could be assigned a new number in the NEW MAGNET LIBRARY
and advertised as a current title. Both methods were sometimes used
on the same title. (Consequently, it is possible to find, for example,
MAGNET LIBRARY no. 286 in an edition marked NEW MAGNET LIBRARY no. 286,
even though it was also reissued as NEW MAGNET LIBRARY no. 1090.)
Series description [S&S]: "The books in this line represent the best works
    of authors of undoubted ability. They are not merely tales of bloodshed
    and crime, but are high-class stories of the adventures of detectives
    who matched their brains rather than their muscles against those of the
    criminals they were obliged to fight. Everyone [sic] of these books is
    so interesting that the reader will be loath to put it down until he has
    finished it. For genuine entertainment, this line cannot be equalled."

074P.1X   Brought to bay.** No. 168. Nov. 14, 1900.

    Contains two Stratemeyer stories, originally published as NICK CARTER
    LIBRARY no. 77, "Baggage check #623; or, Nick Carter among the hotel
    swindlers," Jan. 21, 1893 (076P.7X) and NICK CARTER LIBRARY no. 79,
    "The $35,000 swindle; or, Nick Carter and the insurance frauds," Feb.
    4, 1893 (076P.9X). Reprinted as NEW MAGNET LIBRARY no. 1032, Brought
    to bay,*** July 22, 1920 (075P.3X).

074P.2X   The toss of a coin; or, The man who robbed the mail. No. 248.
August 9, 1902.

    Contains one Stratemeyer story, originally published as NICK CARTER
    LIBRARY no. 172, "The Acquia Creek train robbery; or, The $200,000
    hold-up," Nov. 17, 1894 (076P.16X) and two other Nick Carter stories,
    first published in NICK CARTER LIBRARY no. 33, "The mysterious mail
    bag robbery; or, Nick Carter's great catch," March 19, 1892 and NICK
    CARTER LIBRARY no. 42, "The N. Y. central train; or, The nerviest out-
    law alive," May 21, 1892.

074P.3X   A double handed game; or, The clever "fake" Indian. No. 250.
Aug. 20, 1902

    Contains two Stratemeyer stories, originally published in NICK CARTER
    LIBRARY as no. 40, "The great jewel robbery; or, Nick Carter among the
    hotel thieves," May 7, 1892 (076P.1X), and no. 46, "The gold brick
    swindlers; or, Nick Carter's great exposure," June 18, 1892 (076P.4X),
    and one other Nick Carter story, "Mad Madge, the queen of the crooks;
    or, Fighting an artful foe," first published in NICK CARTER LIBRARY
    no. 30, Feb. 27, 1892. Reprinted as NEW MAGNET LIBRARY no. 1212,
    A double-handed game; or, Hard to win, June 23, 1927 (075P.15X).

074P.4X   The vial of death; or, The poisoner's victim. No. 256. Oct. 1,
1902.

---

*   Many of the Nick Carter titles in the MAGNET LIBRARY were reprinted this
    way. They have not been included in the NEW MAGNET LIBRARY listing,
    which covers only nos. 484-1369. Dates for the NEW MAGNET LIBRARY
    reprints of MAGNET LIBRARY nos. 1-483 are not known.
** Published without a subtitle.
*** Subtitle missing.

Contains one Stratemeyer story originally published as NICK CARTER
LIBRARY no. 112, "Nick Carter among the poisoners; or, The wizard of
death," Sept. 23, 1893 (076P.13X), and two other Nick Carter stories
first published in NICK CARTER LIBRARY as no. 11, "Nick Carter in Boston; or, A clever forger's scheme," Feb. 27, 1892, and as no. 126,
"The heir of Dr. Quartz; or, Nick Carter's game of plots," Dec. 30,
1893. The latter was by Frederic Van Rensselaer Dey. Reprinted as
NEW MAGNET LIBRARY no. 1177, The vial of death; or, Dr. Quartz's last
move, Feb. 18, 1926 (075P.13X).

074P.5X   At the knife's point; or, Chick's clever work. No. 260. Oct.
29, 1902.

Contains one Stratemeyer story originally published as NICK CARTER
LIBRARY no. 166, "The broken arm; or, A brace of cracksmen in a bowery
robbery," Oct. 6, 1894 (076P.15X), and two Frederic Van Rensselaer Dey
stories, first published in NICK CARTER LIBRARY as no. 130, "The meer-
schaum pipe; or, Nick Carter's rescue of a cowboy," Jan. 27, 1894, and
as no. 152, "The face at the window; or, What happened at the lawyer's
office," June 30, 1894. Reprinted as NEW MAGNET LIBRARY no. 1041, At
the knife's point,* Nov. 25, 1920 (075P.4X).

074P.6X   A race track gamble; or, Clever swindlers. No. 282. April 1,
1903.

Contains one Stratemeyer story, first published as NICK CARTER LIBRARY
no. 99, "The book-maker's crime; or, Nick Carter's accidental clew,"
June 24, 1893 (076P.12X). Other contents not known. Reprinted as
NEW MAGNET LIBRARY no. 1099, A race track gamble; or, The hawk and the
jay, Feb. 15, 1923 (075P.11X).

074P.7X   A bonded villain; or, Nick Carter in trouble. No. 286. April 29,
1903.

Contains one Stratemeyer story, originally published as NICK CARTER
LIBRARY no. 160, "The violet ink clew; or, A dangerous woman in the
case," Aug. 25, 1894 (076P.14X), and two Frederic Van Rensselaer Dey
stories, first published in NICK CARTER LIBRARY as no. 196, "The man
with the big head; or, Who opened the combination safe?" May 4, 1895,
and as no. 199, "A swindler in petticoats; or, Nick Carter's pretty
prisoner," May 25, 1895. Reprinted as NEW MAGNET LIBRARY no. 1090,
A bonded villain; or, The long arm of the law, Oct. 12, 1922 (075P.10X).

074P.8X   The cloak of guilt.* No. 320. Dec. 23, 1903.

Contains one Stratemeyer story, originally published as NICK CARTER
LIBRARY no. 207, "Nick Carter's double header; or, The ins and outs of
a Boston sensation," July 20, 1895 (076P.21X), and one Frederic Van
Rensselaer Dey story, NICK CARTER LIBRARY no. 213, "'Mid flying bullets;
or, Lively times on the Chesapeake," Aug. 31, 1895. Reprinted as NEW
MAGNET LIBRARY no. 1075, The cloak of guilt; or, Nick Carter's longest
case, March 16, 1922 (075P.6X).

074P.9X   The "hot air" clew.* No. 324. Jan. 20, 1904.

---

* Subtitle missing.

Contains one Stratemeyer story originally published as NICK CARTER LIBRARY no. 211, "From hotel to prison cell; or, A criminal globe trotter's useless bribe, " Aug. 17, 1895 (076P.22X), and two Frederic Van Rensselaer Dey stories originally published in NICK CARTER LIBRARY as no. 177, "The beautiful shop-lifter; or, Nick Carter's search for an old offender," Dec. 22, 1894, and as no. 182, "Tracked to Union Station; or, The celebrated St. Louis mystery," Jan. 26, 1895. Reprinted as NEW MAGNET LIBRARY no. 1077, The hot air clue; or, Nick Carter's reward, April 13, 1922 (075P.7X).

074P.10X Beyond pursuit.* No. 334. March 30, 1904.

Contains two Stratemeyer stories originally published in NICK CARTER LIBRARY as no. 195, "The mystery of the yellow cab; or, A little setback for Chick," April 27, 1895 (076P.17X), and as no. 197, "Run down in Toronto; or, Nick Carter's work for a friend," May 11, 1895 (076P.18X), and one Frederic Van Rensselaer Dey story first published as NICK CARTER LIBRARY no. 192, "The hole in the bank; or, Nick Carter's campaign against 'Capt. Gold,'" April 6, 1895. Reprinted as NEW MAGNET LIBRARY no. 1081, Beyond pursuit; or, Nick Carter baffled, June 8, 1922 (075P.8X).

074P.11X The wizard of the cue; or, Nick Carter and the pool room case. No. 338. April 27, 1904.

Contains one Stratemeyer story originally published as NICK CARTER LIBRARY no. 198, "The wizard of the cue; or, Nick Carter and the pool room case," May 18, 1895 (076P.19X), and two Frederic Van Rensselaer Dey stories first published in NICK CARTER LIBRARY as no. 158, "Laundry list no. 4575; or, A visit to Nick Carter in the dead of night," Aug. 11, 1894, and as no. 161, "Nick Carter at the wheel; or, The mysterious crew of the Merry Mermaid," Sept. 1, 1894. Reprinted as NEW MAGNET LIBRARY no. 1085, The wizard of the cue; or, A queer criminal, Aug. 3, 1922 (075P.9X).

074P.12X Ahead of the game.* No. 366. Nov. 8, 1904.

Contains one Stratemeyer story originally published as NICK CARTER LIBRARY no. 78, "The concealed booty; or, Nick Carter's first rate find," Jan. 28, 1893 (076P.8X), and one Frederic Van Rensselaer Dey story first published as NICK CARTER LIBRARY no. 109, "Nick Carter after Bob Dalton; or, Tracking the greatest outlaw since Jesse James," Sept. 2, 1893. Reprinted as NEW MAGNET LIBRARY no. 1145, Ahead of the game; or, Nick Carter's bold move, Nov. 20, 1924 (075P.12X).

074P.13X A tangled case.* No. 378. Feb. 1, 1905.

Contains one Stratemeyer story originally published as NICK CARTER LIBRARY no. 205, "A confession by mistake; or, A helping hand to an unwilling prisoner," July 6, 1895 (076P.20X), and two Frederic Van Rensselaer Dey stories first published in NICK CARTER LIBRARY as no. 110, "Among the fire bugs; or, Nick Carter's bravest deed," Sept. 9, 1893, and as no. 180, "Pardoned by the President; or, Nick Carter at the United States Treasury," Jan. 12, 1895. Reprinted as NEW MAGNET

---

* Subtitle missing.

LIBRARY no. 1185, A tangled case; or, Nick Carter's reward, June 10, 1926 (075P.14X).

075P   NEW MAGNET LIBRARY

Volumes: 16*
Printed: 1907-1927*
Publisher: Street & Smith
Source of annotations: Street & Smith advertisements [S&S]
Additional information: The NEW MAGNET LIBRARY printed stories which
    had appeared in the NICK CARTER LIBRARY, the NICK CARTER WEEKLY, the
    MAGNET LIBRARY, and even some of the earlier NEW MAGNET LIBRARY volumes.
    See Nick Carter, MAGNET LIBRARY (074P) for additional information.
Series description [S&S]: "There is no doubt whatever about the ability
    of Street & Smith to publish detective stories that are of absorbing
    interest. We have demonstrated conclusively that no other publisher
    has the facilities for securing this kind of literatre that we have.
    The authors represented are the best that money can secure.
        "Chief among these are the stories of the adventures of Nicholas
    Carter. They are fine examples of how really interesting a detective
    story can be made. Then there are the Harrison Keith stories by the
    same author, as well as those about other detectives by John K. Staf-
    ford, Inspector Stark and Dick Stewart--all writers of prominence.
        "THE NEW MAGNET LIBRARY admirably fills the want of the reader who
    seeks stories that are interesting, true to life and have real literary
    merit. All of these stories are 80,000 words in length, and some of
    them are more. You have your choice of a fine assortment of titles at
    the low price of FIFTEEN CENTS PER COPY."

075P.1X   The worst case on record.** No. 526. Dec. 11, 1907.

    Contains three Stratemeyer stories originally published in NICK CARTER
    LIBRARY as no. 43, "The letters on the floor; or, Nick Carter's clever
    decipher," May 28, 1892 (076P.3X), as no. 76, "A murder in the snow;
    or, Nick Carter's curious case," Jan. 14, 1893 (076P.6X), and as no.
    83, "The freight thieves; or, Nick Carter's expert exposure," March 4,
    1893 (076P.10X). Reprinted as NEW MAGNET LIBRARY no. 1066, The worst
    case on record; or, The crime doctor, Nov. 10, 1921 (075P.5X).

075P.2X   A strike for freedom.** No. 578. Dec. 9, 1908.

    Contains one Stratemeyer story originally published in NICK CARTER
    LIBRARY no. 41, "The fourfold murder; or, Nick Carter's clever work
    in Florida," May 14, 1892 (076P.2X), and one Frederic Van Rensselaer
    Dey story first published in NICK CARTER LIBRARY no. 10, "Nick Carter's
    double game; or, The ghost of Ravenswood House," Oct. 10, 1891. Re-
    printed as NEW MAGNET LIBRARY no. 1213, A strike for freedom; or, The
    crime of a century, July 5, 1927 (075P.16X).***

---

*   Number of volumes and years published apply only to titles written by
      Edward Stratemeyer.
**   Subtitle missing.
***   Date of issue. "Date of delivery" was given as July 1. There was ap-
      parently a disruption in the publication schedule, for the catalogues
      list this as a June title; it should have been published June 30, 1927.

075P.3X   Brought to bay.* No. 1032. July 22, 1920.

> First published as MAGNET LIBRARY no. 168, Brought to bay,** Nov. 14, 1900 (074P.1X).

075P.4X   At the knife's point.* No. 1041. Nov. 25, 1920.

> First published as MAGNET LIBRARY no. 260, At the knife's point; or, Chick's clever work, Oct. 29, 1902 (074P.5X).

075P.5X   The worst case on record; or, The crime doctor. No. 1066. Nov. 10, 1921.

> First published as NEW MAGNET LIBRARY no. 526, The worst case on record,* Dec. 11, 1907 (075P.1X).

075P.6X   The cloak of guilt; or, Nick Carter's longest case. No. 1075. March 16, 1922.

> First published as MAGNET LIBRARY no. 320, The cloak of guilt,* Dec. 23, 1903 (074P.8X).

075P.7X   The hot air clue; or, Nick Carter's reward.*** No. 1077. April 13, 1922.

> First published as MAGNET LIBRARY no. 324, The "hot air" clew,* Jan. 20, 1904 (074P.9X).

075P.8X   Beyond pursuit; or, Nick Carter baffled. No. 1081. June 8, 1922.

> First published as MAGNET LIBRARY no. 334, Beyond pursuit,* March 30, 1904 (074P.10X).

075P.9X   The wizard of the cue; or, A queer criminal. No. 1085. Aug. 3, 1922.

> First published as MAGNET LIBRARY no. 338, The wizard of the cue; or, Nick Carter and the pool room case, April 27, 1904 (074P.11X).

075P.10X   A bonded villain; or, The long arm of the law. No. 1090. Oct. 12, 1922.

> First published as MAGNET LIBRARY no. 286, A bonded villain; or, Nick Carter in trouble, April 29, 1903 (074P.7X).

075P.11X   A race track gamble; or, The hawk and the jay. No. 1099. Feb. 15, 1923.

> First published as MAGNET LIBRARY no. 282, A race track gamble; or, Clever swindlers, April 1, 1903 (074P.6X).

---

*   Subtitle missing.
**   Published without a subtitle.
*** Title listed in Street & Smith advertisements as The hot air clew; the book shows The hot air clue.

075P.12X Ahead of the game; or, Nick Carter's bold move. No. 1145. Nov. 20, 1924.

> First published as MAGNET LIBRARY no. 366, Ahead of the game,* Nov. 8, 1904 (074P.12X).

075P.13X The vial of death; or, Dr Quartz's last move. No. 1177. Feb. 18, 1926.

> First published as MAGNET LIBRARY no. 256, The vial of death; or, The poisoner's victim, Oct. 1, 1902 (074P.4X).

075P.14X A tangled case; or, Nick Carter's reward. No. 1185. June 10, 1926.

> First published as MAGNET LIBRARY no. 378, A tangled case,* Feb. 1, 1905 (074P.13X).

075P.15X A double-handed game; or, Hard to win. No. 1212. June 23, 1927.

> First published as MAGNET LIBRARY no. 250, A double handed game; or, The clever "fake" Indian, Aug. 20, 1902 (074P.3X).

075P.16X A strike for freedom; or, The crime of a century. No. 1213. July 5, 1927.**

> First published as NEW MAGNET LIBRARY no. 578, A strike for freedom,* Dec. 9, 1908 (075P.2X).

076P NICK CARTER LIBRARY

Volumes: 26***
Printed: 1892-1896***
Publisher: Street & Smith
Additional information: The NICK CARTER LIBRARY, a sixteen-page weekly dime
  novel, ran from August 8, 1891 to December 26, 1896. The first three
  issues were titled the Nick Carter Detective Library; the title changed
  with the fourth issue. The last forty issues were reprints of earlier
  issues.
     The majority of the stories in the NICK CARTER LIBRARY were later
  reprinted in the NICK CARTER WEEKLY (077P), the MAGNET LIBRARY (074P),
  and/or the NEW MAGNET LIBRARY (075P).

076P.1X The great jewel robbery; or, Nick Carter among the hotel thieves.#
No. 40. May 7, 1892.

> Reprinted as NICK CARTER LIBRARY no. 270, Oct. 3, 1896 (076P.23X), and

---

*   Subtitle missing.
**   Date of issue. "Date of delivery" was given as July 1. There was ap-
     parently a disruption in the publication schedule, for the catalogues
     list this as a June title, and it should have been issued June 30, 1927.
*** Number of volumes and years published apply only to those titles writ-
     ten by Edward Stratemeyer.
Formerly attributed to Frederic Van Rensselaer Dey.

as NICK CARTER WEEKLY no. 312, "Nick Carter among the jewel thieves; or, The great jewel robbery," Dec. 20, 1902 (077P.17X). Also published as part of MAGNET LIBRARY no. 250, A double handed game; or, The clever "fake" Indian, Aug. 20, 1902 (074P.3X), and as part of NEW MAGNET LIBRARY no. 1212, A double-handed game; or, Hard to win, June 23, 1927 (075P.15X).

076P.2X   The fourfold murder; or, Nick Carter's clever work in Florida.* No. 41. May 14, 1892.

Reprinted as NICK CARTER LIBRARY no. 272, Oct. 17, 1896 (076P.24X), and as NICK CARTER WEEKLY, no. 313, "Nick Carter's fourfold mystery; or, Clever work in Florida," Dec. 27, 1902 (077P.18X). Also reprinted as part of NEW MAGNET LIBRARY no. 578, A strike for freedom,** Dec. 9, 1908 (075P.2X), and as part of NEW MAGNET LIBRARY no. 1213, A strike for freedom; or, The crime of a century, July 5, 1927*** (075P.16X).

076P.3X   The letters on the floor; or, Nick Carter's clever decipher.* No. 43. May 28, 1892.

Reprinted as NICK CARTER LIBRARY no. 274, Oct. 31, 1896 (076P.25X), and as NICK CARTER WEEKLY no. 305, "Nick Carter's clever decipher; or, The letters on the floor," Nov. 1, 1902 (077P.16X). Also reprinted as part of NEW MAGNET LIBRARY no. 526, The worst case on record,** Dec. 11, 1907 (075P.1X), and as part of NEW MAGNET LIBRARY no. 1066, The worst case on record; or, The crime doctor, Nov. 10, 1921 (075P.5X).

076P.4X   The gold brick swindlers; or, Nick Carter's great exposure.* No. 46. June 18, 1892.

Reprinted as NICK CARTER LIBRARY no. 280, "The gold brick swindlers; or, Nick Carter exposing a crime," Dec. 12, 1896 (076P.26X). Also reprinted as part of MAGNET LIBRARY no. 250, A double handed game; or, The clever "fake" Indian, Aug. 20, 1902 (074P.3X), and as part of NEW MAGNET LIBRARY no. 1212, A double-handed game; or, Hard to win, June 23, 1927 (075P.15X).

076P.5X   The Dalton gang wiped out; or, Nick Carter's deadly rifle. No. 67. Nov. 12, 1892.

076P.6X   A murder in the snow; or, Nick Carter's curious case.* No. 76. Jan. 14, 1893.

Reprinted as NICK CARTER WEEKLY no. 100, "Nick assists a body snatcher and saves the life of an innocent man," Nov. 26, 1898 (077P.1X), and as NICK CARTER WEEKLY no. 302, "Nick Carter's queerest case; or, A murder in the snow," Oct. 11, 1902 (077P.15X). Also reprinted as part of NEW MAGNET LIBRARY no. 526, The worst case on record,** Dec. 11, 1907 (075P.1X), and as part of NEW MAGNET LIBRARY no. 1066, The worst case on record; or, The crime doctor, Nov. 10, 1921 (075P.5X).

---

*   Formerly attributed to Frederic Van Rensselaer Dey.
**   Subtitle missing.
***   Date of issue. "Date of delivery" was given as July 1. The catalogues list this as a June title; it should have been issued on June 30, 1927.

076P.7X   Baggage check #623; or, Nick Carter among the hotel swindlers.*
No. 77.   Jan. 21, 1893.

Reprinted as part of MAGNET LIBRARY no. 168, Brought to bay,   Nov.
14, 1900 (074P.1X), and as part of NEW MAGNET LIBRARY no. 1032, Brought
to bay,** July 22, 1920 (075P.3X).

076P.8X   The concealed booty; or, Nick Carter's first rate find.*   No.
78. Jan. 28, 1893.

Reprinted as NICK CARTER WEEKLY no. 102, "Nick Carter shows his nerve
and winds up the case at the freight house," Dec. 10, 1898 (077P.2X).
Also reprinted as part of MAGNET LIBRARY no. 366, Ahead of the game,**
Nov. 8, 1904 (074P.12X), and as part of NEW MAGNET LIBRARY no. 1145,
Ahead of the game; or, Nick Carter's bold move, Nov. 20, 1924 (075P.12X).

076P.9X   The $35,000 swindle; or, Nick Carter and the insurance frauds.*
No. 79.   Feb. 4, 1893.

Reprinted as part of MAGNET LIBRARY no. 168, Brought to bay,   Nov.
14, 1900 (074P.1X), and as part of NEW MAGNET LIBRARY no. 1032, Brought
to bay,** July 22, 1920 (075P.3X).

076P.10X   The freight thieves; or, Nick Carter's expert exposure.*   No.
83. March 4, 1893.

Reprinted as NICK CARTER WEEKLY no. 288, "Nick Carter's expert exposure;
or, Downing the freight thieves," July 5, 1902 (077P.13X).   Also reprinted as part of NEW MAGNET LIBRARY no. 526, The worst case on record,** Dec. 11, 1907 (075P.1X), and as part of NEW MAGNET LIBRARY no.
1066, The worst case on record; or, The crime doctor, Nov. 10, 1921
(075P.5X).

076P.11X   The Turkish bath mystery; or, Nick Carter after a slick pair.*
No. 85.   March 18, 1893.

Reprinted as NICK CARTER WEEKLY no. 106, "Killed at the baths; or,
Nick Carter right on hand," Jan. 7, 1899 (077P.3X), and as NICK CAR-
TER WEEKLY no. 298, "Nick Carter's bath mystery; or, After a slick
pair,"*** Sept. 13, 1902 (077P.14X).

076P.12X   The book-maker's crime; or, Nick Carter's accidental clew.*
No. 99.   June 24, 1893.

Reprinted as NICK CARTER WEEKLY no. 115, "Nick Carter's chance clew;
or, The rogue of the race track," March 11, 1899 (077P.4X).   Also reprinted as part of MAGNET LIBRARY no. 282, A race track gamble; or,
Clever swindlers, April 1, 1903 (074P.6X), and as part of NEW MAGNET
LIBRARY no. 1099, A race track gamble; or, The hawk and the jay, Feb.
15, 1923 (075P.11X).

076P.13X Nick Carter among the poisoners; or, The wizard of death. No.
112. Sept. 23, 1893.

---

*   Formerly attributed to Frederic Van Rensselaer Dey.
**   Subtitle missing.
*** Title page spells subtitle "After a sleek pair."

Reprinted as part of MAGNET LIBRARY no. 256, The vial of death; or, The poisoner's victim, Oct. 1, 1902 (074P.4X), and as part of NEW MAGNET LIBRARY no. 1177, The vial of death; or, Dr. Quartz's last move, Feb. 18, 1926 (075P.13X).

076P.14X The violet ink clew; or, A dangerous woman in the case.* No. 160. Aug. 25, 1894.

Reprinted as NICK CARTER WEEKLY no. 191, "Wanted for embezzlement; or, What became of the treasurer," Aug. 25, 1900 (077P.5X). Also reprinted as part of MAGNET LIBRARY no. 286, A bonded villain; or, Nick Carter in trouble, April 29, 1903 (074P.7X), and as part of NEW MAGNET LIBRARY no. 1090, A bonded villain; or, The long arm of the law, Oct. 12, 1922 (075P.10X).

076P.15X The broken arm; or, A brace of cracksmen in a bowery robbery.* No. 166. Oct. 6, 1894.

Reprinted as NICK CARTER WEEKLY no. 194, "Nick Carter on the bowery; or, A crippled cracksman's detection," Sept. 15, 1900 (077P.6X). Also reprinted as part of MAGNET LIBRARY no. 260, At the knife's point; or, Chick's clever work, Oct. 29, 1902 (074P.5X), and as part of NEW MAGNET LIBRARY no. 1041, At the knife's point,** Nov. 25, 1920 (075P.4X).

076P.16X The Acquia Creek train robbery; or, The $200,000 hold-up. No. 172. Nov. 17, 1894.

Reprinted as part of MAGNET LIBRARY no. 248, The toss of a coin; or, The man who robbed the mail, Aug. 9, 1902 (074P.2X).

076P.17X The mystery of the yellow cab; or, A little set-back for Chick.* No. 195. April 27, 1895.

Reprinted as NICK CARTER WEEKLY no. 209, Dec. 29, 1900 (077P.7X). Also reprinted as part of MAGNET LIBRARY no. 334, Beyond pursuit,** March 30, 1904 (074P.10X), and as part of NEW MAGNET LIBRARY no. 1081, Beyond pursuit; or, Nick Carter baffled, June 8, 1922 (075P.8X).

076P.18X Run down in Toronto; or, Nick Carter's work for a friend.* No. 197. May 11, 1895.

Reprinted as NICK CARTER WEEKLY no. 211, Jan. 12, 1901 (077P.8X). Also reprinted as part of MANGET LIBRARY no. 334, Beyond pursuit,** March 30, 1904 (074P.10X), and as part of NEW MAGNET LIBRARY no. 1081, Beyond pursuit; or, Nick Carter baffled, June 8, 1922 (075P.8X).

076P.19X The wizard of the cue; or, Nick Carter and the pool room case.* No. 198. May 18, 1895.

Reprinted as NICK CARTER WEEKLY no. 212, Jan 19, 1901 (077P.9X). Also reprinted as part of MAGNET LIBRARY no. 338, The wizard of the cue; or, Nick Carter and the pool room case, April 27, 1904 (074P.11X), and as part of NEW MAGNET LIBRARY no. 1085, The wizard of the cue; or, A queer criminal, Aug. 3, 1922 (075P.9X).

---

*   Formerly attributed to Frederic Van Rensselaer Dey.
**   Subtitle missing.

076P.20X A confession by mistake; or, A helping hand to an unwilling prisoner.* No. 205.   July 6, 1895.

> Reprinted as NICK CARTER WEEKLY no. 216, Feb. 16, 1901 (077P.10X).
> Also reprinted as part of MAGNET LIBRARY no. 378, A tangled case,**
> Feb. 1, 1905 (074P.13X), and as part of NEW MAGNET LIBRARY no. 1185,
> A tangled case; or, Nick Carter's reward, June 10, 1926 (075P.14X).

076P.21X Nick Carter's double header; or, The ins and outs of a Boston
sensation.* No. 207.   July 20, 1895.

> Reprinted as NICK CARTER WEEKLY no. 217, Feb. 23, 1901 (077P.11X).
> Also reprinted as part of MAGNET LIBRARY no. 320, The cloak of guilt,**
> Dec. 23, 1903 (074P.8X), and as part of NEW MAGNET LIBRARY no. 1075,
> The cloak of guilt; or, Nick Carter's longest case, March 16, 1922
> (075P.6X)

076P.22X From hotel to prison cell; or, A criminal globe trotter's useless
bribe.* No. 211.   Aug. 17, 1895.

> Reprinted as NICK CARTER WEEKLY no. 219, March 9, 1901 (077P.12X).
> Also reprinted as part of MAGNET LIBRARY no. 324, The "hot air" clew,**
> Jan. 20, 1904 (074P.9X), and as part of NEW MAGNET LIBRARY no. 1077,
> The hot air clue; or, Nick Carter's reward, *** April 13, 1922 (075P.7X).

076P.23X The great jewel robbery; or, Nick Carter among the hotel thieves.
No. 270.   Oct. 3, 1896.

> First printed as NICK CARTER LIBRARY no. 40, May 7, 1892 (076P.1X).

076P.24X The fourfold murder; or, Nick Carter's clever work in Florida.
No. 272.   Oct. 17, 1896.

> First printed as NICK CARTER LIBRARY no. 41, May 14, 1892 (076P.2X).

076P.25X The letters on the floor; or, Nick Carter's clever decipher.
No. 274.   Oct. 31, 1896.

> First printed as NICK CARTER LIBRARY no. 43, May 28, 1892 (076P.3X).

076P.26X The gold brick swindlers; or, Nick Carter exposing a crime.
No. 280.   Dec. 12, 1896.

> First printed as NICK CARTER LIBRARY no. 46, "The gold brick swindlers;
> or, Nick Carter's great exposure," June 18, 1892 (076P.4X).

---

*   Formerly attributed to Frederic Van Rensselaer Dey.
**   Subtitle missing.
*** Street & Smith advertisements list this with the title as The hot air
     clew.

077P   NICK CARTER WEEKLY

Volumes: 18*
Printed: 1898-1902*
Publisher: Street & Smith
Additional information: The NICK CARTER WEEKLY, also called the NEW NICK
    CARTER LIBRARY (nos. 1-7) and the NEW NICK CARTER WEEKLY (nos. 8-42
    and 321-819), was a dime novel series that ran from January 2, 1897
    to September 7, 1912, for 819 issues, and continued the adventures of
    Nick Carter and his companions in both new and reprinted stories. All
    of the stories by Edward Stratemeyer in the NICK CARTER WEEKLY were
    reprints of the NICK CARTER LIBRARY titles (076P). Many of these were
    reissued as part of MAGNET LIBRARY (074P) and NEW MAGNET LIBRARY (075P)
    books.

077P.1X   Nick assists a body snatcher and saves the life of an innocent
man. No. 100. Nov. 26, 1898.

    First published as NICK CARTER LIBRARY no. 76, "A murder in the snow;
    or, Nick Carter's curious case," Jan. 14, 1893 (076P.6X).

077P.2X   Nick Carter shows his nerve and winds up the case at the freight
house. No. 102. Dec. 10, 1898.

    First published as NICK CARTER LIBRARY no. 78, "The concealed booty;
    or, Nick Carter's first rate find," Jan. 28, 1893 (076P.8X).

077P.3X   Killed at the baths; or, Nick Carter right on hand.   No. 106.
Jan. 7, 1899.

    First published as NICK CARTER LIBRARY no. 85, "The Turkish bath mys-
    tery; or, Nick Carter after a slick pair," March 18, 1893 (076P.11X).

077P.4X   Nick Carter's chance clew; or, The rogue of the race track.
No. 115. March 11, 1899.

    First published as NICK CARTER LIBRARY no. 99, "The book-maker's crime;
    or, Nick Carter's accidental clew," June 24, 1893 (076P.12X).

077P.5X   Wanted for embezzlement; or, What became of the treasurer. No.
191. Aug. 25, 1900.

    First published as NICK CARTER LIBRARY no. 160, "The violet ink clew;
    or, A dangerous woman in the case," Aug. 25, 1894 (076P.14X).

077P.6X   Nick Carter on the bowery; or, A crippled cracksman's detection.
No. 194. Sept. 15, 1900.

    First published as NICK CARTER LIBRARY no. 166, "The broken arm; or,
    A brace of cracksmen in a bowery robbery," Oct. 6, 1894 (076P.15X).

077P.7X   The mystery of the yellow cab; or, A little set-back for Chick.
No. 209. Dec. 29, 1900.

---

* Number of volumes and years printed apply only to titles written by
  Edward Stratemeyer.

First published as NICK CARTER LIBRARY no. 195, April 27, 1895 (076P.17X).

077P.8X   Run down in Toronto; or, Nick Carter's work for a friend. No. 211. Jan. 12, 1901.

First published as NICK CARTER LIBRARY no. 197, May 11, 1895 (076P.18X).

077P.9X   The wizard of the cue; or, Nick Carter and the pool room case. No. 212. Jan. 19, 1901.

First published as NICK CARTER LIBRARY no. 198, May 18, 1895 (076P.19X).

077P.10X   A confession by mistake; or, A helping hand to an unwilling prisoner. No. 216. Feb. 16, 1901.

First published as NICK CARTER LIBRARY no. 205, July 6, 1895 (076P.20X).

077P.11X   Nick Carter's double header; or, The ins and outs of a Boston sensation. No. 217. Feb. 23, 1901.

First published as NICK CARTER LIBRARY no. 207, July 20, 1895 (076P.21X).

077P.12X   From hotel to prison cell; or, A criminal globe trotter's useless bribe. No. 219. March 9, 1901,

First published as NICK CARTER LIBRARY no. 211, Aug. 17, 1895 (076P.22X).

077P.13X   Nick Carter's expert exposure; or, Downing the freight thieves. No. 288. July 5, 1902.

First published as NICK CARTER LIBRARY no. 83, "The freight thieves; or, Nick Carter's expert exposure," March 4, 1893 (076P.10X).

077P.14X   Nick Carter's bath mystery; or, After a slick pair.* No. 298 Sept. 13, 1902.

First published as NICK CARTER LIBRARY no. 85, "The Turkish bath mystery; or, Nick Carter after a slick pair," March 18, 1893 (076P.11X).

077P.15X   Nick Carter's queerest case; or, A murder in the snow. No. 302. Oct. 11, 1902.

First published as NICK CARTER LIBRARY no. 76, "A murder in the snow; or, Nick Carter's curious case," Jan. 14, 1893 (076P.6X).

077P.16X   Nick Carter's clever decipher; or, The letters on the floor. No. 305. Nov. 1, 1902.

First published as NICK CARTER LIBRARY no. 43, "The letters on the floor; or, Nick Carter's clever decipher," May 28, 1892 (076P.3X).

077P.17X   Nick Carter among the hotel thieves; or, The great jewel robbery. No. 312. Dec. 20, 1902.

---

* Title page has the subtitle as "After a sleek pair."

First published as NICK CARTER LIBRARY no. 40, "The great jewel robbery; or, Nick Carter among the hotel thieves," May 7, 1892 (076P.1X).

077P.18X Nick Carter's fourfold mystery; or, Clever work in Florida. No. 313. Dec, 27, 1902.

First published as NICK CARTER LIBRARY no. 41, "The fourfold murder; or, Nick Carter's clever work in Florida," May 14, 1892 (076P.2X).

Lester Chadwick

Between 1910 and 1928, Cupples & Leon published twenty series books under the Stratemeyer Syndicate pseudonym Lester Chadwick. All twenty dealt with sports--indeed, some Cupples & Leon advertisements even mentioned that "Mr. Chadwick has played on the diamond and on the gridiron himself." Edward Stratemeyer created the two series published under this pseudonym; Howard Garis contributed to some of the volumes.

SERIES PUBLICATIONS

078S   BASEBALL JOE

Volumes: 14
Printed: 1912-1928
Publisher: Cupples & Leon Company
Illustrator: Walter S. Rogers, vols. 1-5
              R. Emmett Owen, vols. 7-8
              Thelma Gooch, vols. 9-14
Source of annotations: Cupples & Leon Company advertisements [C&L]
Additional information: Howard Garis worked with Edward Stratemeyer on
    some of the titles in this series.
Series description [C&L]: "Ever since the success of Mr. Chadwick's 'Col-
    lege Sports Series' we have been urged to get him to write a series
    dealing exclusively with baseball, a subject in which he is unexcelled
    by any living American author or coach. In this series, Baseball Joe,
    as he is called by all his admirers, advances, step by step, from
    playing on a country town team until he becomes the leading pitcher
    of the Big League."

078S.1   Baseball Joe of the Silver Stars; or, The rivals of Riverside.
(Cupples & Leon, 1912).

[C&L]: "In this volume, the first of the series, Joe is introduced as
an everyday country boy who loves to play baseball and is particularly
anxious to make his mark as a pitcher. He finds it almost impossible
to get on the local nine, but, after a struggle, he succeeds, although
much frowned on by the star pitcher of the club. Some exciting contests
follow, and also a number of other adventures, dear to the hearts of all

young readers. In the end Joe goes in the 'box' as the regular pitcher, however, and helps to win a most exciting contest. A splendid picture of the great national game in the smaller towns of our country, showing how dear it is to all who have good, red blood in their veins."

078S.2   Baseball Joe on the school nine; or, Pitching for the Blue Banner. (Cupples & Leon, 1912).

[C&L]: "Joe's great ambition was to go to boarding school and play on the school team. He got to boarding school but found it harder making the team there than it was getting on the nine at home. He fought his way along, however, and at last saw his chance and took it, and made good. Once he pitched against his old rival from home in an exciting contest. A really remarkable account of how Joe and his companions worked to win the Blue Banner of the Interscholastic League, and a true-to-life story of athletics in a preparatory school.

078S.3   Baseball Joe at Yale; or, Pitching for the college championship. (Cupples & Leon, 1913).

[C&L]: "From a preparatory school Baseball Joe goes to Yale University. He makes the freshman nine and in his second year becomes a varsity pitcher and pitches in several big games."

078S.4   Baseball Joe in the Central League; or, Making good as a professional pitcher. (Cupples & Leon, 1914).

[C&L]: "In this volume the scene of action is shifted from Yale College to a baseball league of our central states. Baseball Joe's work in the box for old Eli had been noted by one of the managers and Joe gets an offer he cannot resist. Joe accepts the offer and makes good."

078S.5   Baseball Joe in the big league; or, A young pitcher's hardest struggles. (Cupples & Leon, 1915).

[C&L]: "From the Central League Joe is drafted into the St. Louis Nationals. At first he has little to do in the pitcher's box, but gradually he wins favor. A corking baseball story that fans, both young and old, will enjoy."

078S.6   Baseball Joe on the Giants; or, Making good as a twirler in the metropolis. (Cupples & Leon, 1916).

[C&L]: "How Joe was traded to the Giants and became their mainstay in the box makes an interesting baseball story."

078S.7   Baseball Joe in the World Series; or, Pitching for the championship. (Cupples & Leon, 1917).

[C&L]: "The rivalry was of course of the keenest, and what Joe did to win the series is told in a manner to thrill the most jaded reader."

078S.8   Baseball Joe around the world; or, Pitching on a grand tour. (Cupples & Leon, 1918).

[C&L]: "The Giants and the All-Americans tour the world, playing in many foreign countries."

078S.9   Baseball Joe, home run king; or, The greatest pitcher and batter on record. (Cupples & Leon, 1922.)

    [C&L]: "Joe becomes the greatest batter in the game."

078S.10   Baseball Joe saving the league; or, Breaking up a great conspiracy. (Cupples & Leon, 1923).

    [C&L]: "Throwing the game meant a fortune but also dishonor and it was a great honor to defeat it."

078S.11   Baseball Joe, captain of the team; or, Bitter struggles on the diamond. (Cupples & Leon, 1924).

    [C&L]: "Joe is elevated to the position of captain."

078S.12   Baseball Joe, champion of the league; or, The record that was worth while. (Cupples & Leon, 1925).

    [C&L]: "A plot is hatched to put Joe's pitching arm out of commission."

078S.13   Baseball Joe, club owner; or, Putting the home town on the map. (Cupples & Leon, 1926).

    [C&L]: "Joe developes [sic] muscle weakness and is ordered off the field for a year."

078S.14   Baseball Joe, pitching wizard; or, Triumphs off and on the diamond (Cupples & Leon, 1928).

079S   COLLEGE SPORTS

Volumes: 6
Printed: 1910-1913
Publisher: Cupples & Leon Company
Illustrator: Charles Nuttall, vols. 1-2
            H. Richard Boehm, vols. 3-6
Source of annotations: Cupples & Leon Company advertisements [C&L]

079S.1   The rival pitchers: A story of college baseball. (Cupples & Leon, 1910).

    [C&L]: "When Tom Parsons went to Randall he was looked upon as a mere country lad, a 'hayseed.' But Tom had played baseball at home and was a good pitcher, and he soon proved his abiiity, and was put on the scrub nine. He had some bitter rivals who tried to keep him down, but he got on the varsity at last. A faithful picture of college life of to-day, with its hazings, its grinds, its pretty girls, and all."

079S.2   A quarterback's pluck: A story of college football. (Cupples & Leon, 1910).

    [C&L]: "Of all college sports, football is undoubtedly king, and in this tale Mr. Chadwick has risen to the occasion by giving us something that is bound to grip the reader from start to finish."

079S.3   Batting to win: A story of college baseball. (Cupples & Leon, 1911).

    [C&L]: "As before, Tom, Phil, and Sid are to the front. Sid, in particular, has developed into a heavy hitter, and the nine depends on him to bring in the needed runs. And then something happens, and poor, misjudged Sid is barred from playing. Then, at the last moment, Sid clears himself and is reinstated, and helps to pound out a victory that will make every reader feel like cheering."

079S.4   The winning touchdown: A story of college football. (Cupples & Leon, 1911).

    [C&L]: "Football was a serious proposition at Randall that year. There had been the loss of several old players, and then, almost at the last moment, another good player had to be dropped. How, in the end, they made that glorious touchdown that won the big game, is told in a way that must be read to be appreciated."

079S.5   For the honor of Randall: A story of college athletics. (Cupples & Leon, 1912).

    [C&L]: "Now the boys of Randall are in a series of athletic contests with rival institutions, and the winning of the hurdle race, hundred-yard dash, and long-distance run, are told in Mr. Chadwick's best style. Mystery, adventure and sports make this one of the best stories Mr. Chadwick has ever written."

079S.6   The eight-oared victors: A story of college water sports. (Cupples & Leon, 1913).

    [C&L]: "Once more we meet the lads of Randall College. This time the scene is shifted to boating and the rivalry on the river is intense."

Allen Chapman

Before the establishment of the Stratemeyer Syndicate, Edward Stratemeyer wrote two stories as Allen Chapman: "For name and fame" in 1896 and The boys of Spring Hill in 1900. He did not use the name again until 1906, when he assigned it to two Syndicate series, the BOYS OF BUSINESS and the RAILROAD series. From 1900 to 1930, forty-four books, excluding reprints, were issued under the pseudomym Allen Chapman. Grosset & Dunlap was the original publisher of twenty-one of these; Cupples & Leon issued another twenty; Mershon was responsible for three titles.

    Even though Grosset & Dunlap published the most books, it handled only two Chapman series: the RADIO BOYS and the RAILROAD series. (It had picked up the latter series with volume three, after Mershon had printed the first two volumes.) Cupples & Leon published five different series by Chapman, none of which went beyond five volumes; Cupples & Leon later combined two series and reissued them as the ten-volume BOYS' POCKET LIBRARY.

    All of the Chapman books except The boys of Spring Hill first appeared in one of seven series: BOYS OF BUSINESS (1906-1908; 4 vols.), BOYS OF

PLUCK (1906-1911; 5 vols.), RAILROAD (1906-1933; 11 vols.*), DAREWELL CHUMS
(1908-1911; 5 vols.), FRED FENTON (1913-1915; 5 vols), TOM FAIRFIELD (1913-
1915; 5 vols.), or RADIO BOYS (1922-1930; 13 vols.). Some of the titles
were later reprinted in Cupples & Leon's BOYS POCKET LIBRARY, Goldsmith's
ALLEN CHAPMAN series, and Donohue's SUCCESS series.

MAGAZINE PUBLICATIONS

080M   "For name and fame; or, Walter Loring's strange quest." Bright
Days, nos. 10-16, Oct. 3-Nov. 14, 1896.

> Reprinted in The boys of Spring Hill; or Bound to Rise, and Walter
> Loring's Career (two books in one) published by Mershon in 1900.
> Reprinted by Chatterton-Peck (091N).

SERIES PUBLICATIONS

081S   ALLEN CHAPMAN

Volumes: 5
Publisher: Goldsmith Publishing Co.
Additional information: This was a reprint of the BOYS OF BUSINESS (082S)
    and the BOYS OF PLUCK (083S) series. The titles were altered slightly;
    in some cases, titles and subtitles were reversed. Goldsmith editions
    were published without illustrations.

081S.1   Bart Stirling's road to success; or, The young express agent.
(Goldsmith).

> First published in 1906 as The young express agent; or, Bart Stirling's
> road to success, vol. 1 of Cupples & Leon's BOYS OF BUSINESS series
> (082S.1).

081S.2   Working hard to win; or, Adventures of two boy publishers.
(Goldsmith).

> First published in 1906 as Two boy publishers; or, From typecase to
> editor's chair, vol. 2 of Cupples & Leon's BOYS OF BUSINESS series
> (082S.2).

081S.3   Bound to succeed; or, Mail-order Frank's chances. (Goldsmith).

> First published in 1907 as Mail order Frank; or, A smart boy and his
> chances, vol. 3 of Cupples & Leon's BOYS OF BUSINESS series (082S.3).

081S.4   The young storekeeper; or, A business boy's pluck. (Goldsmith).

> First published in 1908 as A business boy; or, Winning success, vol.
> 4 of Cupples & Leon's BOYS OF BUSINESS series (082S.4).

* Number of volumes and years published include a four-in-one reprint.

081S.5   Nat Borden's find; or, The young land agent. (Goldsmith).

First published in 1911 as The young land agent; or, The secret of the Borden estate, vol. 5 of Cupples & Leon's BOYS OF PLUCK series (083S.5).

082S   BOYS OF BUSINESS

Volumes: 4
Printed: 1906-1908
Publisher: Cupples & Leon Company
Illustrator: Charles Nuttall, vols. 1-3
            Alex Levy, vol. 4
Source of annotations: Cupples & Leon Company advertisement [C&L]
Additional information: Modelled after several of Stratemeyer's earlier series, the BOYS OF BUSINESS was a group of books that did not share the same central characters but focused on a common theme: success in business.
        The entire series was reprinted by Goldsmith, with altered titles, as the ALLEN CHAPMAN series (081S). Cupples & Leon reprinted the series twice--once as the BOYS OF PLUCK (083S), with the original titles (and with a fifth volume added), and once as part of the BOYS' POCKET LIBRARY (084S), with the Goldsmith titles. Donohue also used three of the books in its SUCCESS series (089S), with two of the original titles.
Series description [C&L]: "ALLEN CHAPMAN is already favorably known to young people, and they are bound to hail this new series by him with immense satisfaction. These stories make the best of reading for boys getting ready to enter business."

082S.1   The young express agent; or, Bart Stirling's road to success. (Cupples & Leon, 1906).

Reprinted as vol. 1 in Cupples & Leon's BOYS OF PLUCK series (083S.1) and as vol. 2 in Donohue's SUCCESS series (089S.2). Also reprinted as Bart Stirling's road to success; or, The young express agent, vol. 1 in Goldsmith's ALLEN CHAPMAN series (081S.1) and, in 1917, vol. 6 in Cupples & Leon's BOYS' POCKET LIBRARY (084S.6).
        [C&L]: "Bart's father was the express agent in a country town. When an explosion of fireworks rendered him unfit for work, the boy took it upon himself to run the express office. The tale gives a good idea of the express business in general."

082S.2   Two boy publishers; or, From typecase to editor's chair. (Cupples & Leon, 1906).

Reprinted as vol. 2 in Cupples & Leon's BOYS OF PLUCK series (083S.2) and as vol. 1 in Donohue's SUCCESS series (089S.1). Also reprinted as Working hard to win; or, Adventures of two boy publishers, vol. 2 in Goldsmith's ALLEN CHAPMAN series (081S.2) and, in 1917, vol. 7 in Cupples & Leon's BOYS' POCKET LIBRARY (084S.7).
        [C&L]: "This tale will appeal strongly to all lads who wish to know how a newspaper is printed and published. The two boy publishers work their way up step by step, from a tiny printing office to the ownership of a town paper."

082S.3   Mail order Frank; or, A smart boy and his chances. (Cupples &
Leon, 1907).

> Reprinted as vol. 3 in Cupples & Leon's BOYS OF PLUCK series (083S.3).
> Also reprinted as Bound to succeed; or, Mail-order Frank's chances,
> vol. 3 in Goldsmith's ALLEN CHAPMAN series (081S.3) and, in 1917, vol.
> 8 of Cupples & Leon's BOYS' POCKET LIBRARY (084S.8).
>   [C&L]: "Here we have a story covering an absolutely new field--
> that of the mail-order business. How Frank started in a small way and
> gradually worked his way up to a business figure of considerable im-
> portance is told in a fascinating manner."

082S.4   A business boy; or, Winning success. (Cupples & Leon, 1908).

> Reprinted as A business boy's pluck; or, Winning success, vol. 4 in Cup-
> ples & Leon's BOYS OF PLUCK series (083S.4) and vol. 3 in Donohue's SUC-
> CESS series (089S.3). Reprinted as The young storekeeper; or, A business
> boy's pluck, vol. 4 in Goldsmith's ALLEN CHAPMAN series (081S.4) and vol.
> 9 in Cupples & Leon's BOYS' POCKET LIBRARY (084S.9).

083S   BOYS OF PLUCK

Volumes: 5
Printed: 1906-1911
Publisher: Cupples & Leon Company
Illustrator: Charles Nuttall, vols. 1-3, 5
              Alex Levy, vol. 4
Source of annotations: Cupples & Leon Company advertisements [C&L]
Additional information: The BOYS OF PLUCK was an expanded (by one volume)
    version of the BOYS OF BUSINESS series (082S). Possibly the first
    title lacked sales appeal, so the series was renamed. The title of
    the fourth volume was also changed.
        Dates for volumes 1 through 3 are from their first issue in the
    BOYS OF BUSINESS series.

083S.1   The young express agent; or, Bart Stirling's road to success.*
(Cupples & Leon, 1906).

> First published as vol. 1 in the BOYS OF BUSINESS series (082S.1).
>   [C&L]: "Bart's father was the express agent in a country town.
> When an explosion of fireworks rendered him unfit for work, the boy
> took it upon himself to run the express office. The tale gives a
> good idea of the express business in general."

083S.2   Two boy publishers; or, From typecase to editor's chair. (Cupples
& Leon, 1906).

> First published as vol. 2 in the BOYS OF BUSINESS series (082S.2).
>   [C&L]: "This tale will appear [sic] strongly to all lads who wish
> to know how a newspaper is printed and published. The two boy pub-
> lishers work their way up, step by step, from a tiny printing office
> to the ownership of a paper."

---

* Cupples & Leon ads also show the subtitle as Bart Stirling's road success.

083S.3   Mail order Frank; or, A smart boy and his chances. (Cupples & Leon, 1907).

First published as vol. 3 in the BOYS OF BUSINESS series (082S.3).
[C&L]: "Here we have a story covering an absolutely new field--that of the mail-order business. How Frank started in a small way and gradually worked his way up to a business figure of considerable importance is told in a fascinating manner."

083S.4   A business boy's pluck; or, Winning success. (Cupples & Leon).

First published as A business boy; or, Winning success, vol. 4 in the BOYS OF BUSINESS series in 1908 (082S.4).
[C&L]: "This relates the ups and downs of a young storekeeper. He has some keen rivals, but 'wins out' in more ways than one. All youths who wish to go into business will want this volume."

083S.5   The young land agent; or, The secret of the Borden estate. (Cupples & Leon, 1911).

Reprinted as Nat Borden's find; or, The young land agent, vol. 5 in Goldsmith's ALLEN CHAPMAN series (081S.5) and vol. 10, in 1917, in Cupples & Leon's BOYS' POCKET LIBRARY (084S.10).
[C&L]: "The young land agent had several rivals, and they did all possible to bring his schemes of selling town lots to naught. But Nat persevered, showed up his rivals in their true light, and not only made a success of the business but likewise cleared up his mother's claim to some valuable real estate."

084S   BOYS' POCKET LIBRARY

Volumes: 10
Printed: 1917
Publisher: Cupples & Leon Company
Illustrator: Clare Angell, vol. 1
              Charles Nuttall, vols. 2-4, 6-10
              H. Richard Boehm, vol. 5
Additional information: This reprint series combined two Allen Chapman series, the DAREWELL CHUMS (085S) and the BOYS OF PLUCK (083S). The titles were altered slightly; often, the original titles and subtitles were reversed.

084S.1   The heroes of the school; or, The Darewell chums through thick and thin. (Cupples & Leon, 1917).

First published in 1908 as The Darewell chums; or, The heroes of the school, vol. 1 of the DAREWELL CHUMS series (085S.1).

084S.2   Ned Wilding's disappearance; or, The Darewell chums in the city. (Cupples & Leon, 1917).

First published in 1908 as The Darewell chums in the city; or, The disappearance of Ned Wilding, vol. 2 of the DAREWELL CHUMS series (085S.2).

084S.3   Frank Roscoe's secret; or, The Darewell chums in the woods. (Cupples & Leon, 1917).

First published in 1908 as The Darewell chums in the woods; or, Frank Roscoe's secret, vol. 3 in the DAREWELL CHUMS series (085S.3).

084S.4   Fenn Masterson's discovery; or, The Darewell chums on a cruise. (Cupples & Leon, 1917).

First published in 1909 as The Darewell chums on a cruise; or, Fenn Masterson's odd discovery, vol. 4 in the DAREWELL CHUMS series (085S.4).

084S.5   Bart Keene's hunting days; or, The Darewell chums in a winter camp. (Cupples & Leon, 1917).

First published in 1911 as The Darewell chums in a winter camp; or, Bart Keene's best shot, vol. 5 in the DAREWELL CHUMS series (085S.5).

084S.6   Bart Stirling's road to success; or, The young express agent. (Cupples & Leon, 1917).

First published in 1906 as The young express agent; or, Bart Stirling's road to success, vol. 1 in the BOYS OF BUSINESS series (082S.1).

084S.7   Working hard to win; or, Adventures of two boy publishers. (Cupples & Leon, 1917).

First published in 1906 as Two boy publishers; or, From typecase to editor's chair, vol. 2 in the BOYS OF BUSINESS series (082S.2).

084S.8   Bound to succeed; or, Mail-order Frank's chances. (Cupples & Leon, 1917).

First published in 1907 as Mail order Frank; or, A smart boy and his chances, vol. 3 in the BOYS OF BUSINESS series (082S.3).

084S.9   The young storekeeper; or, A business boy's pluck. (Cupples & Leon, 1917).

First published in 1908 as A business boy; or, Winning success, vol. 4 in the BOYS OF BUSINESS series (082S.4).

084S.10   Nat Borden's find; or, The young land agent. (Cupples & Leon, 1917).

First published in 1911 as The young land agent; or, The secret of the Borden estate, vol. 5 in the BOYS OF PLUCK series (083S.5).

085S   DAREWELL CHUMS

Volumes: 5
Printed: 1908-1911
Publisher: Cupples & Leon Company
Reprint publisher: Goldsmith Publishing Co., vols. 1-5

Illustrator: Clare Angell, vol. 1
                Charles Nuttall, vols. 2-4
                H. Richard Boehm, vol. 5
Source of annotations: Cupples & Leon Company advertisements [C&L]
Additional information: The DAREWELL CHUMS series was reprinted by Cupples
    & Leon as the first five volumes of the BOYS POCKET LIBRARY (084S) and
    by Goldsmith as the DAREWELL CHUMS series; both reprints had title
    changes, generally with the original subtitles serving as the new
    titles.
        The Goldsmith editions were not illustrated.

085S.1   The Darewell chums; or, The heroes of the school. (Cupples &
Leon, 1908; Goldsmith).

    Reprinted as The heroes of the school; or, The Darewell chums through
    thick and thin, vol. 1 of Goldsmith's series and, in 1917, vol. 1 in
    Cupples & Leon's BOYS' POCKET LIBRARY (084S.1).
        [C&L]: "A bright, lively story for boys, telling the doings of
    four chums, at school and elsewhere. There is a strong holding plot,
    and several characters who are highly amusing. Any youth getting this
    book will consider it a prize and tell all his friends about it."

085S.2   The Darewell chums in the city; or, The disappearance of Ned
Wilding. (Cupples & Leon, 1908; Goldsmith).

    Reprinted as vol. 4 of Donohue's SUCCESS series (089S.4). Also re-
    printed as Ned Wilding's disappearance; or, The Darewell chums in the
    city, vol. 2 in Goldsmith's series and, in 1917, vol. 2 in Cupples &
    Leon's BOYS' POCKET LIBRARY (084S.2).
        [C&L]: "From a country town the scene is changed to a great city.
    One of the chums has disappeared in an extraordinary manner, and the
    others institute a hunt for him. The youths befriend a city waif, who
    in turn makes a revelation which clears up the mystery."

085S.3   The Darewell chums in the woods; or, Frank Roscoe's secret.
(Cupples & Leon, 1908; Goldsmith).

    Reprinted as Frank Roscoe's secret; or, The Darewell chums in the woods,
    vol. 3 in Goldsmith's series and, in 1917, vol. 3 in Cupples & Leon's
    BOYS' POCKET LIBRARY (084S.3).
        [C&L]: "The boys had planned for a grand outing when something
    happened of which none of them had dreamed. They thought one of their
    number had done a great wrong--at least it looked so. But they could
    not really believe the accusations made, so they set to work to help
    Frank all they could. All went camping some miles from home, and when
    not hunting and fishing spent their time in learning the truth of what
    had occurred."

085S.4   The Darewell chums on a cruise; or, Fenn Masterson's odd discovery. (Cupples & Leon, 1909; Goldsmith).

    Reprinted as Fenn Masterson's discovery; or, The Darewell chums on a
    cruise, vol. 4 in Goldsmith's series and, in 1917, vol. 4 in Cupples
    & Leon's BOYS' POCKET LIBRARY (084S.4).
        [C&L]: "A tale of the Great Lakes. The boys run across some Cana-
    dian smugglers and stumble on the secret of a valuable mine."

085S.5   The Darewell chums in a winter camp; or, Bart Keene's best shot. (Cupples & Leon, 1911; Goldsmith).

Reprinted as Bart Keene's hunting days; or, The Darewell chums in a winter camp, vol. 5 in Goldsmith's series and, in 1917, vol. 5 in Cupples & Leon's BOYS' POCKET LIBRARY (085S.5).
[C&L]: "Here is a lively tale of ice and snow, of jolly good times in a winter camp, hunting and trapping, and of taking it easy around a roaring campfire."

086S   FRED FENTON ATHLETIC SERIES

Volumes: 5
Printed: 1913-1915
Publisher: Cupples & Leon Company
Illustrator: Walter S. Rogers, vols. 1-5
Source of annotations: Cupples & Leon Company advertisements [C&L]
Series description [C&L]: "A line of tales embracing school athletics. Fred is a true type of the American schoolboy of to-day."

086S.1   Fred Fenton, the pitcher; or, The rivals of Riverport School. (Cupples & Leon, 1913).

[C&L]: "When Fred came to Riverport none of the school lads knew him, but he speedily proved his worth in the baseball box. A true picture of school baseball."

086S.2   Fred Fenton in the line; or, The football boys of Riverport School. (Cupples & Leon, 1913).

[C&L]: "When Fall came in the thoughts of the boys turned to football. Fred went in the line, and again proved his worth, making a run that helped to win a great game."

086S.3   Fred Fenton on the crew; or, The young oarsmen of Riverport School. (Cupples & Leon, 1913).

[C&L]: "In this volume the scene is shifted to the river, and Fred and his chums show how they can handle the oars. There are many other adventures, all dear to the hearts of boys."

086S.4   Fred Fenton on the track; or, The athletes of Riverport School. (Cupples & Leon, 1913).

[C&L]: "Track athletics form a subject of vast interest to many boys, and here is a tale telling of great running races, high jumping, and the like. Fred again proves himself a hero in the best sense of that term."

086S.5   Fred Fenton, marathon runner; or, The great race at Riverport School. (Cupples & Leon, 1915).

[C&L]: "Fred is taking a post-graduate course at the school when the subject of Marathon running came up. A race is arranged, and Fred shows both his friends and his enemies what he can do. An athletic story of special merit."

087S   RADIO BOYS

Volumes: 13
Printed: 1922-1930
Publisher: Grosset & Dunlap
Illustrator: Walter S. Rogers, vols. 1-13
Source of annotations: Grosset & Dunlap advertisements [G&D]
Additional information: The Stratemeyer Sydndice also produced a four-volume RADIO GIRLS series under the pseudonym Margaret Penrose (212S). It was not published by Grosset & Dunlap, but by Cupples & Leon. Although both radio series started in 1922, the RADIO GIRLS lasted only for two years and four volumes.
Series description [G&D]: "Here is a series that gives full details of radio work both in sending and receiving--how large and small sets can be made and operated, and with this real information there are stories of the radio boys and their adventures. Each story is a record of thrilling adventures--rescues, narrow escapes from death, daring exploits in which the radio plays a main part. Each volume is so thoroughly fascinating, so strictly up-to-date, and accurate that all modern boys will peruse them with delight. Each volume has a foreword by Jack Binns, the well known radio expert."

087S.1   The radio boys' first wireless; or, Winning the Ferberton prize. (Grosset & Dunlap, 1922).

087S.2   The radio boys at Ocean Point; or, The message that saved the ship. (Grosset & Dunlap, 1922).

087S.3   The radio boys at the sending station; or, Making good in the wireless room. (Grosset & Dunlap, 1922).

087S.4   The radio boys at Mountain Pass; or, The midnight call for assistance. (Grosset & Dunlap, 1922).

087S.5   The radio boys trailing a voice; or, Solving a wireless mystery. (Grosset & Dunlap, 1922).

087S.6   The radio boys with the forest rangers; or, The great fire on Spruce Mountain. (Grosset & Dunlap, 1923).

087S.7   The radio boys with the iceberg patrol; or, Making safe the ocean lanes. (Grosset & Dunlap, 1924).

087S.8   The radio boys with the flood fighters; or, Saving the city in the valley. (Grosset & Dunlap, 1925).

087S.9   The radio boys on Signal Island; or, Watching for the ships of mystery. (Grosset & Dunlap, 1926).

087S.10   The radio boys in Gold Valley; or, The mystery of the deserted mining camp. (Grosset & Dunlap, 1927).

087S.11   The radio boys aiding the snowbound; or, Starvation days at Lumber Run. (Grosset & Dunlap, 1928).

087S.12   The radio boys on the Pacific; or, Shipwrecked on an unknown island. (Grosset & Dunlap, 1929).

087S.13   The radio boys to the rescue; or, The search for the Barmore twins. (Grosset & Dunlap, 1930).

088S   RAILROAD (RALPH OF THE RAILROAD)

Volumes: 11*
Printed: 1906-1933*
Publisher: The Mershon Company, vols. 1-2
             Grosset & Dunlap, vols. 3-11X
Reprint publisher: Grosset & Dunlap, vols. 1-2
             Chatterton-Peck Company, vols. 1-2
Illustrator: Clare Angell, vols. 1, 11X
             anonymous, vols. 2, 1iX
             R. M., vols. 3, 11X
             Charles Nuttall, vols. 4, 11X
             H. Richard Boehm, vol. 5
             R. Emmett Owen, vol. 6
             Walter S. Rogers, vols. 7-10
Source of annotations: Grosset & Dunlap advertisements [G&D]
Additional information: The RAILROAD series, also called the RALPH OF THE
    RAILROAD series, was one of several series which were published by
    Mershon, taken over by Chatterton-Peck, involved in the litigation
    between Chatterton-Peck, Stitt, Mershon, and Stratemeyer, and eventually
    reissued by Grosset & Dunlap.
Series description [G&D]:   "Ralph Fairbanks was bound to become a railroad
    man, as his father had been before him. Step by step he worked his way
    upward, serving first in the Roundhouse, cleaning locomotives; then in
    the Switch Tower, clearing the tracks; then on the Engine, as a fireman;
    then as engineer of the Overland Express; and finally as Train Dis-
    patcher.
        "In this line of books there is revealed the whole workings of a
    great American railroad system. There are adventures in abundance--
    railroad wrecks, dashes through forest fires, the pursuit of a 'wild-
    cat' locomotive, the disappearance of a pay car with a large sum of
    money on board--but there is much more than this--the intense rivalry
    among railroads and railroad men, the working out of running schedules,
    the getting through 'on time' in spite of all obstacles, and the ma-
    nipulation of railroad securities by evil men who wish to rule or ruin.
        "Books that every American boy ought to own."

088S.1   Ralph of the round house; or, Bound to become a railroad man.
(Mershon, 1906; Chatterton-Peck, ca1907; Grosset & Dunlap, ca1908).

    Reprinted in 1933 in Ralph on the railroad, a four-in-one reprint
    (088S.11X).

---

*   Number of volumes and years printed include Ralph on the railroad, a
    four-in-one reprint volume.

088S.2   Ralph in the switch tower; or, Clearing the track. (Mershon, 1907; Chatterton-Peck, ca1907; Grosset & Dunlap, ca1908).

Reprinted in 1933 in Ralph on the railroad, a four-in-one reprint (088S.11X).

088S.3   Ralph on the engine; or, The young fireman of the Limited Mail. (Grosset & Dunlap, 1909).

Reprinted in 1933 in Ralph on the railroad, a four-in-one reprint (088S.11X).

088S.4   Ralph on the Overland Express; or, The trials and triumphs of a young engineer. (Grosset & Dunlap, 1910).

Reprinted in 1933 in Ralph on the railroad, a four-in-one reprint (088S.11X).

088S.5   Ralph the train dispatcher; or, The mystery of the pay car. (Grosset & Dunlap, 1911).

088S.6   Ralph on the army train; or, The young railroader's most daring exploit. (Grosset & Dunlap, 1918).

088S.7   Ralph on the Midnight Flyer; or, The wreck at Shadow Valley. (Grosset & Dunlap, 1923).

088S.8   Ralph and the missing mail pouch; or, The stolen government bonds. (Grosset & Dunlap, 1924).

088S.9   Ralph on the mountain division; or, Fighting both flames and flood. (Grosset & Dunlap, 1927).

088S.10   Ralph and the train wreckers; or, The secret of the blue freight cars. (Grosset & Dunlap, 1928).

088S.11X Ralph on the railroad: Four complete adventure books for boys in one big volume. (Grosset & Dunlap, 1933).

Contains Ralph of the roundhouse (088S.1), Ralph in the switch tower (088S.2), Ralph on the engine (088S.3), Ralph on the Overland Express (088S.4). Printed from the original Grosset & Dunlap plates.

089S   SUCCESS

Volumes: 4
Publisher: M. A. Donohue & Company
Additional information: The unusual feature in this reprint series is that it includes one DAREWELL CHUMS title (085S) instead of the third volume of the BOYS OF BUSINESS series (082S). The books were published without subtitles.

089S.1   Two boy publishers. (Donohue).

First published by Cupples & Leon in 1906 as Two boy publishers; or, From typecase to editor's chair, vol. 2 in the BOYS OF BUSINESS series (082S.2).

089S.2   The young express agent. (Donohue).

First published by Cupples & Leon in 1906 as The young express agent; or, Bart Stirling's road to success, vol. 1 of the BOYS OF BUSINESS series (082S.1).

089S.3   A business boy's pluck. (Donohue).

First published by Cupples & Leon in 1908 as A business boy; or, Winning success, vol. 4 of the BOYS OF BUSINESS series (082S.4).

089S.4   The Darewell chums in the city. (Donohue).

First published by Cupples & Leon in 1908 as The Darewell chums in the city; or, The disappearance of Ned Wilding, vol. 2 of the DAREWELL CHUM series (085S.2).

090S   TOM FAIRFIELD

Volumes: 5
Printed: 1913-1915
Publisher: Cupples & Leon Company
Illustrator: Louis Wisa, vols. 1-4
              Walter S. Rogers, vol. 5
Source of annotations: Cupples & Leon Company advertisements [C&L]
Series description [C&L]: "Tom Fairfield is a typical American lad full of life and energy, a boy who believes in doing things. To know Tom is to love him."

090S.1   Tom Fairfield's school days; or, The chums of Elmwood Hall. (Cupples & Leon, 1913).

[C&L]: "Tells of how Tom started for school, of the mystery surroundi one of the Hall seniors, and of how the hero went to the rescue. The first book in a line that is bound to become decidedly popular."

090S.2   Tom Fairfield at sea; or, The wreck of the Silver Star. (Cupple & Leon, 1913).

[C&L]: "Tom's parents had gone to Australia and then been cast away somewhere in the Pacific. Tom set off to find them and was himself cast away. A thrilling picture of the perils of the deep."

090S.3   Tom Fairfield in camp; or, The secret of the old mill. (Cupples & Leon, 1913).

[C&L]: "The boys decided to go camping, and located near an old mill. A wild man resided there and he made it decidedly lively for Tom and his chums. The secret of the old mill adds to the interest of the volume."

090S.4   Tom Fairfield's pluck and luck; or, Working to clear his name. (Cupples & Leon, 1913).

> [C&L]: "While Tom was back at school some of his enemies tried to get him into trouble. Something unusual occurred and Tom was suspected of a crime. How he set to work to clear his name is told in a manner to interest all young readers."

090S.5   Tom Fairfield's hunting trip; or, Lost in the wilderness. (Cupples & Leon, 1915*).

> [C&L]: "Tom was only a schoolboy, but he loved to use a shotgun or a rifle. In this volume we meet him on a hunting trip full of outdoor life and good times around the campfire."

OTHER PUBLICATIONS

091N   Bound to rise; or, The young florists of Spring Hill, and Walter Loring's Career. (Mershon, 1899; Chatterton-Peck, ca1906).

> Two books in one. Bound to rise was first published as "The young florists of Spring Hill; or, The new heliotrope" by Albert Lee Ford in Bright Days, May-July, 1896 (154M). Walter Loring's career was first published as "For name and fame; or, Walter Loring's strange quest" by Allen Chapman in Bright Days, Oct. 3-Nov. 14, 1896 (080M).

092N   The young builders of Swiftdale. (Chatterton-Peck.)**

Louis Charles

Edward Stratemeyer and his brother, Louis Charles Stratemeyer, worked together on at least one book, The land of fire, which Louis Stratmeyer finished. They may also have collaborated for Fortune hunters of the Philippines.

MAGAZINE PUBLICATIONS

093M   "The land of fire; or, A long journey for fortune." Bright Days, nos. 9-16, Sept. 26-Nov. 14, 1896.

> Published in book form by Mershon in 1900 and later by Chatterton-Peck and A. L. Burt, as The land of fire; or, Adventures in underground Africa for all editions (095N).

---

*   This may have been published in 1916.
**   Probably a phantom title.

OTHER PUBLICATIONS

094N   Fortune hunters of the Philippines; or, The treasure of the
burning mountain. (Mershon, 1900; Chatterton-Peck; Burt).

    The Mershon edition is also listed as part of the Boys' Own Series.

095N   The land of fire; or, Adventures in underground Africa. (Mershon,
1900; Chatterton-Peck; Burt).

    First published as "The land of fire; or, A long journey for fortune"
    in Bright Days, Sept. 26–Nov. 14, 1896 (093M).

James A. Cooper

The Stratemeyer Syndicate used the surname "Cooper" with two different
first names: James A. and John R. The former was used on four books set
in Cape Cod and published between 1917 and 1922; the latter appeared on
six baseball stories from 1947 to 1953.

SERIES PUBLICATIONS

096P   HEROINE

Volumes: 2*
Printed: 1933?*
Publisher: World Syndicate Publishing Co.
Additional information: The HEROINE series was a four-volume reprint
    series. The first two volumes were The red lacquer case by H. R.
    Jorgenson and Patty and Jo, detectives by Elsie Wright.

096P.1X   Tobias o' the light: A story of Cape Cod.** (World, 1933).

    Published as vol. 3. First published in 1920 by G. Sully & Co. (100N).

096P.2X   Cap'n Jonah's fortune: A story of Cape Cod. (World, ca1933).

    Published as vol. 4. First published in 1919 by G. Sully & Co. (098N).

---

*   Number of volumes and years printed apply only to titles published
     under the name James A. Cooper.
**   World ads list the title as Tobias.

OTHER PUBLICATIONS

097N   Cap'n Abe, storekeeper: A story of Cape Cod. (Sully & Kleinteich, 1917; G. Sully & Co.; World).

    Sully editions illustrated by A. O. Scott.

098N   Cap'n Jonah's fortune: A story of Cape Cod. (G. Sully & Co., 1919).

    Sully edition illustrated by A. O. Scott. Reprinted as vol. 4 of World's HEROINE series (096P.2X).

099N   Sheila of Big Wreck Cove: A story of Cape Cod. (G. Sully & Co., 1922).

    Illustrated by R. Emmett Owen.

100N   Tobias o' the light: A story of Cape Cod. (G. Sully & Co., 1920).

    Illustrated by Joseph Wykoff. Reprinted as vol. 3 of World's HEROINE series (096P.1X).

John R. Cooper

John R. Cooper, a Stratemeyer Syndicate pseudonym, appeared on one six-volume series, the MEL MARTIN BASEBALL STORIES.

SERIES PUBLICATIONS

101S   MEL MARTIN BASEBALL STORIES

Volumes: 6
Printed: 1947-1953
Publisher: Cupples & Leon Company, vols. 1-2
            Garden City Books, vols. 3-6
Reprint publisher: Garden City Books, vols. 1-2
                    Books, Inc., vols. 1-6
Illustrator: C. R. Schaare, vols. 1-2
Source of annotations: Books, Inc. advertisements [BI]
Additional information: Cupples & Leon began the MEL MARTIN series in
    1947 with the publication of the first two volumes; Garden City Books
    picked up the series in 1952, reissuing the first two volumes and adding
    an additional four. Books, Inc. later reprinted all six volumes in
    paperback and hardcover editions, with unsigned illustrations.
        The books were published without subtitles.
Series description [BI]: "Mel Martin, young right-hander with a quick-

breaking curve, plenty of hop on his fast ball, and good control when the going gets tough, is the main figure in this action-packed series. . . . While baseball is Mel's major interest, somehow mystery and danger seem to follow him and his friends in whatever they do. Mel and the Wright twins constantly find themselves in ticklish situations as Mel's detective work involves them in skirmishes with crooks and mysterious strangers."

101S.1   The mystery at the ball park. (Cupples & Leon, 1947; Garden City, 1952; Books, Inc.).

101S.2   The southpaw's secret. (Cupples & Leon, 1947; Garden City, 1952; Books, Inc.).

101S.3   The phantom homer. (Garden City, 1952; Books, Inc.).

101S.4   First base jinx. (Garden City, 1952; Books, Inc.).

101S.5   The college league mystery. (Garden City, 1953; Books, Inc.).

101S.6   The fighting shortstop. (Garden City, 1953; Books, Inc.).

Jim Daley

This misspelling of Jim Daly appeared on the story "Gentleman Jack's debut; or, The ring champion of the stage" in the New York Five Cent Library, March 18, 1893 (102P.2X). See Jim Daly.

Jim Daly

Jim Daly was a pseudonym used by Edward Stratemeyer for six stories that appeared in the New York Five Cent Library in 1892 and 1893. One of the six stories actually appeared under the name Jim Daley.

SERIES PUBLICATIONS

102P   NEW YORK FIVE CENT LIBRARY

Volumes: 6*
Printed: 1892-1893*
Publisher: Street & Smith
Additional information: See Jim Bowie, NEW YORK FIVE CENT LIBRARY (071P).

---

* Number of volumes and years printed apply only to titles written by Edward Stratemeyer under the name Jim Daly/Jim Daley.

102P.1X   Gentleman Jack; or, From student to pugilist. No. 14. Nov. 12, 1892.

102P.2X   Gentleman Jack's debut; or, The ring champion on the stage. No. 32. March 18, 1893.*

102P.3X   Gentleman Jack's tour; or, The ring champion and his enemies. No. 36. April 15, 1893.

102P.4X   Gentleman Jack's mix-up; or, Settled outside of the prize ring. No. 46. June 24, 1893.

102P.5X   Gentleman Jack's soft mark; or, Knocked out in three rounds. No. 61. Oct. 7, 1893.

102P.6X   Gentleman Jack's big hit; or, Downing the prize ring fakirs. No. 65. Nov. 18, 1893.

Spencer Davenport

The Stratemeyer Syndicate pseudonym Spencer Davenport appeared on the RUSHTON BOYS series, a series that had as many publishers as it did volumes (three).

SERIES PUBLICATIONS

103S   RUSHTON BOYS

Volumes: 3
Printed: 1916
Publisher: Hearst's International Library
Reprint publisher: George Sully & Company, vols. 1-3
                    Whitman Publishing Company, vols. 1-3
Illustrator: Walter S. Rogers, vols. 1-3
Additional information: The same illustrations were used by all three
    publishers.

103S.1   The Rushton boys at Rally Hall; or, Great days in school and out. (Hearst, 1916; Sully, 1918; Whitman, 1940?).

103S.2   The Rushton boys at Treasure Cove; or, The missing oaken chest.** (Hearst, 1916; Sully, 1918; Whitman).

103S.3   The Rushton boys in the saddle; or, The ghost of the plains. (Hearst, 1916; Sully, 1918; Whitman).

---
*   As by Jim Daley.
** Subtitle listed as The missing chest of gold for the Sully editions.

Elmer A. Dawson

Like Lester Chadwick, Elmer A. Dawson was a Stratemeyer Syndicate pseudonym used exclusively for sports stories. The two Dawson series, BUCK AND LARRY BASEBALL STORIES and GARRY GRAYSON FOOTBALL STORIES, were published by Grosset & Dunlap from 1926 to 1932.

SERIES PUBLICATIONS

104S   BUCK AND LARRY BASEBALL STORIES

Volumes: 5
Printed: 1930-1932
Publisher: Grosset & Dunlap
Illustrator: Walter S. Rogers, vols. 1-4
              W. B. Grubb, vol. 5

104S.1   The pick-up nine; or, The Chester boys on the diamond. (Grosset & Dunlap, 1930).

104S.2   Buck's winning hit; or, The Chester boys making a record. (Grosset & Dunlap, 1930).

104S.3   Larry's fadeaway; or, The Chester boys saving the nine. (Grosset & Dunlap, 1930).

104S.4   Buck's home run drive; or, The Chester boys winning against odds. (Grosset & Dunlap, 1931).

104S.5   Larry's speedball; or, The Chester boys and the diamond secret. (Grosset & Dunlap, 1932).

105S   GARRY GRAYSON FOOTBALL STORIES

Volumes: 10
Printed: 1926-1932
Publisher: Grosset & Dunlap
Reprint publisher: Whitman Publishing Company, vols. 8-9*
Illustrator: Walter S. Rogers, vols. 1-9
              G. Condon, vol. 10
Source of annotations: Grosset & Dunlap advertisements [G&D]
Additional information: The Whitman editions were not illustrated.
Series description [G&D]: "Garry Grayson is a football fan, first, last, and all the time. But more than that, he is a wideawake American boy with a 'gang' of chums almost as wideawake as himself.

_____
*   Possibly other volumes as well.

"How Garry organized the first football eleven his grammar school had, how he later played on the High School team, and what he did on the Prep School gridiron and elsewhere, is told in a manner to please all readers and especially those interested in watching a rapid forward pass, a plucky tackle, or a hot run for a touchdown.

"Good, clean football at its best--and in addition, rattling stories of mystery and schoolboy rivalries."

105S.1   Garry Grayson's Hill Street eleven; or, The football boys of Lenox. (Grosset & Dunlap, 1926).

105S.2   Garry Grayson at Lenox High; or, The champions of the football league. (Grosset & Dunlap, 1926).

105S.3   Garry Grayson's football rivals; or, The secret of the stolen signals. (Grosset & Dunlap, 1926).

105S.4   Garry Grayson showing his speed; or, A daring run on the gridiron. (Grosset & Dunlap, 1927).

105S.5   Garry Grayson at Stanley Prep; or, The football rivals of River-view. (Grosset & Dunlap, 1927).

105S.6   Garry Grayson's winning kick; or, Battling for honor. (Grosset & Dunlap, 1928).

105S.7   Garry Grayson hitting the line; or, Stanley Prep on a new gridiron. (Grosset & Dunlap, 1929).

105S.8   Garry Grayson's winning touchdown; or, Putting Passmore Tech on the map. (Grosset & Dunlap, 1930; Whitman).

105S.9   Garry Grayson's double signals; or, Vanquishing the football plotters. (Grosset & Dunlap, 1931; Whitman).

105S.10   Garry Grayson's forward pass; or, Winning in the final quarter. (Grosset & Dunlap, 1932).

Franklin W. Dixon

With eighty-nine books to his credit,* sales of over 50,000,000 copies, and new titles issued annually, Franklin W. Dixon was and is one of the most popular Stratemeyer Syndicate pseudonyms.

The pen name Franklin W. Dixon came into existence in 1927, when Grosset & Dunlap published the first books in two series, TED SCOTT and the HARDY BOYS, both created by Edward Stratemeyer. Writers such as Harriet Adams, Andrew Svenson, and Leslie McFarlane also contributed to the HARDY BOYS series as it progressed. The TED SCOTT series ended after sixteen years and twenty volumes, in 1943; the HARDY BOYS, with fifty-four years and sixty-six titles in 1981, is still growing.

---

* Excluding reprints and revisions.

SERIES PUBLICATIONS

106S   HARDY BOYS

Volumes: 71*
Printed: 1927-
Publisher: Grosset & Dunlap, vols. 1-58, 67X, 70X-71X
            Simon & Schuster, Wanderer Books, vols. 59-66, 68X-69X
Illustrator: Walter S. Rogers, vols. 1-10 (1927-1931)
              J. Clemens Gretter, vols. 11-15 (1932-1936)
              Paul Laune, vols. 16-23 (1937-1944)
              Russell H. Tandy, vols. 24-30 (1945-1951)
              Roy Pell, vols. 31-32 (1952-1953)
              Leslie Morrill, vols. 59-66 (1979-1981)
Source of annotations: Grosset & Dunlap advertisements [G&D], series de-
                        scription and vols. 1-12
                        Library of Congress cataloguing in publication data
                        [LC], vols. 18,20-23,25-26,28,31-36,38,48-64,67X
Additional information: In the fifty-four years since their creation, the
HARDY BOYS have appeared in television shows, comics, cartoons, and
coloring books. The HARDY BOYS series, which has been translated into
French, Italian, Dutch, Norwegian, Swedish, Danish, and other languages,
has sold over 50,000,000 copies; the first volume alone has estimated
sales of approximately 1,500,000 copies. Currently available in paperback and hardcover, and even in special book club editions, the series
has come a long way since its start in 1927.
    The name Frank Hardy originally appeared on the central character
of A young book agent; or, Frank Hardy's road to success, one of the
Stratemeyer Algers, published by Stitt in 1905 as part of the RISE IN
LIFE series (011S.8X). When Edward Stratemeyer created the HARDY BOYS
series, he reused the name, though the two Frank Hardys were not related.
    The first eight** volumes were developed by Edward Stratemeyer be-
fore his death in 1930. Afterward, the Stratemeyer Syndicate continued
the series. An important contributor to the early titles was Leslie
McFarlane, who assisted with volumes 1-11, 15-17, 22, and 24-26.**
Harriet Adams, Edward Stratemeyer's daughter, wrote some of the titles
from this period--volumes 13, 15, 18, 25, 27, and 30, and, later, volumes 35 and 43.** When Andrew Svenson joined the Stratemeyer Syndicate,
he, too, worked on the series and is credited with nine titles--volumes
45, 48 through 50, and the revised editions of volumes 20 through 23.
    In 1959, the Stratemeyer Syndicate began to revise the earlier HARDY
BOYS books. When the revisions ended in 1973, the first thirty-eight
books had been updated, and, in some cases, almost entirely rewritten.***

---

*   As of 1981. Number of volumes also includes related titles, such as
     The Hardy boys detective handbook and two titles based on the television
     series.
**   And possibly several others.
*** A chart, "Dates of originals and rewrites," in the Spring 1981 issue of
     The Mystery and Adventure Series Review describes fifteen of the first
     twenty-four revisions as "wholly different" from the original editions;
     another four are "drastically altered." Only eight of the entire
     thirty-eight revisions are listed as "slightly altered," and six of
     these are for volumes 33-38 (n.p.).

Ethnic slurs, some jokes and characterizations, and extraneous material were removed, highlighting the action and reducing the length of the books by about one-fifth. Harriet Adams was the first to work on this project and is responsible for the new editions of volumes 1, 2, and 38.*

SCHEDULE OF REVISIONS OF THE HARDY BOYS TITLES

BY YEAR OF REVISION:#

Year of revision#	Volume number	Year of revision#	Volume number
1959	1,2	1967	10,13
1960	--	1968	15,29,30
1961	14	1969	18,25,31,32
1962	3,4,11	1970	20,21,23,26,28
1963	5	1971	22,33,34
1964	6,19	1972	35,36
1965	7,9,12,16	1973	38
1966	8,17,24,27,37		

BY VOLUME NUMBER:

Volume number	Year of revision#	Volume number	Year of revision#	Volume number	Year of revision#
1	1959	14	1961	27	1966
2	1959	15	1968	28	1970
3	1962	16	1965	29	1968
4	1962	17	1966	30	1968
5	1963	18	1969	31	1969
6	1964	19	1964	32	1969
7	1965	20	1970	33	1971
8	1966	21	1970	34	1971
9	1965	22	1971	35	1972
10	1967	23	1970	36	1972
11	1962	24	1966	37	1966
12	1965	25	1969	38	1973
13	1967	26	1970		

Year of publication of revised edition

    In 1979 the Stratemeyer Syndicate changed publishers, and the HARDY BOYS, NANCY DREW (193S), and the BOBBSEY TWINS (183S) appeared for the first time in paperback. The names of the illustrators, omitted since 1954, were again included in the books. Wanderer also started an of- ficial NANCY DREW/HARDY BOYS Fan Club in 1979, complete with newsletter and membership card.
    Although their first and probably greatest success has been as series books, the HARDY BOYS have been translated into other formats. Two HARDY BOYS serials, Walt Disney productions, were shown on "The Mickey Mouse Club" in the late 1950s, with Tom Kirk and Tim Considine as Joe and Frank Hardy. One serial was based on The tower treasure. The mystery of the Chinese junk provided the plot for the pilot episode of a HARDY BOYS series aired in September 1967, this time with Tim

---

* Probably other volumes as well.

Matthieson and Rick Gates as Joe and Frank. (The series apparently
never progressed beyond the pilot.) In 1969 a cartoon series based
on the HARDY BOYS occupied half an hour of ABC-TV's Saturday morning
programming. Finally, in January 1977, "The HARDY BOYS Mysteries,"
an hour show with Shaun Cassidy and Parker Stevenson as Joe and Frank,
was televised Sunday nights, again on ABC-TV. The series alternated
with "The NANCY DREW Mysteries" for over a year, then was retitled "The
HARDY BOYS/NANCY DREW Mysteries" in February 1978, and ended within
the next year.
    Four comic books featuring the HARDY BOYS were published by Dell
Comics in the late 1950s, in conjunction with Walt Disney: two were
based on The secret of the old mill and The secret of the caves. Gold
Key also issued HARDY BOYS comics in 1970 and 1971. In 1979 Treasure
Books, a division of Grosset & Dunlap, issued The Hardy boys adventure
pictures to color #1, a coloring book illustrated by Tony Tallarico,
with pictures adapted from illustrations in the series books. A para-
graph on the copyright page noted "If you've read the stories, you can
easily identify the books the Hardy Boys adventure pictures are based
on." A second coloring book, The Hardy boys adventure pictures to color
#2 was also published by Grosset & Dunlap at about the same time.
    Other titles, not properly part of the HARDY BOYS series, have
been issued relating the adventures of the HARDY BOYS:* two handbooks,
one on detection, the other on survival techniques, were published as
by Franklin W. Dixon; a HARDY BOYS "whodunnit" book also lists Dixon
as author. Two HARDY BOYS mystery novels were not published under
the pseudonym Franklin W. Dixon: The haunted house, and Flight to
nowhere (two stories in one book) and The Hardy boys and Nancy Drew
meet Dracula. Both were based on stories from the HARDY BOYS television
series and credit the Stratemeyer Syndicate with the novelizations.
    All of the HARDY BOYS books were published without subtitles. The
revised editions were reillustrated and do not include the artists'
names.
    An R denotes an annotation for a revised edition.
Series description [G&D]: "Frank and Joe Hardy are sons of a celebrated
    detective. Often the boys help him in his investigations. In their
    spare hours and during vacations they follow up clues 'on their own
    hook.' These activities lead them into many strange and dangerous ad-
    ventures in stories that are packed with action, suspense and mystery."

106S.1   The tower treasure. (Grosset & Dunlap, 1927, 1959).

    [G&D]: "A dying criminal confessed that his loot had been secreted
    'in the tower.' It remained for the Hardy Boys to make an astonishing
    discovery that cleared up the mystery."

106S.2   The house on the cliff. (Grosset & Dunlap, 1927, 1959).

    [G&D]: "The house had been vacant and was supposed to be haunted.
    Mr. Hardy started to investigate--and disappeared! An odd tale, with
    plenty of excitement."

106S.3   The secret of the old mill. (Grosset & Dunlap, 1927, 1962**).

---

*   They are included in the listing for the HARDY BOYS because they were
     written by the Stratemeyer Syndicate and feature the HARDY BOYS.
**   Copyrighted 1961.

[G&D]: "Counterfeit money was in circulation, and the limit was reached when Mrs. Hardy took some from a stranger. A tale full of thrills."

106S.4   The missing chums. (Grosset & Dunlap, 1928, 1962).

[G&D]: "Two of the Hardy Boys' chums take a motor trip down the coast. They disappear and are almost rescued by their friends when all are captured. A thrilling story of adventure."

106S.5   Hunting for hidden gold. (Grosset & Dunlap, 1928, 1963).

[G&D]: "Mr. Hardy is injured in tracing some stolen gold. A hunt by the boys leads to an abandoned mine, and there things start to happen. A western story all boys will enjoy."

106S.6   The Shore Road mystery. (Grosset & Dunlap, 1928, 1964).

[G&D]: "Automobiles were disappearing most mysteriously from the Shore Road. It remained for the Hardy Boys to solve the mystery."

106S.7   The secret of the caves. (Grosset & Dunlap, 1929, 1965*).

[G&D]: "The boys follow a trail that ends in a strange and exciting situation."

106S.8   The mystery of Cabin Island. (Grosset & Dunlap, 1929, 1966).

[G&D]: "A story of queer adventures on a rockbound island."

106S.9   The great airport mystery. (Grosset & Dunlap, 1930, 1965).

[G&D]: "The Hardy boys solve the mystery of the disappearance of some valuable mail."

106S.10   What happened at midnight. (Grosset & Dunlap, 1931, 1967).

[G&D]: "The boys follow a trail that ends in a strange and exciting situation."

106S.11   While the clock ticked. (Grosset & Dunlap, 1932, 1962).

[G&D]: "The Hardy boys aid in vindicating a man who has been wrongly accused of a crime."

106S.12   Footprints under the window. (Grosset & Dunlap, 1933, 1965).

[G&D]: "The Smuggling of Chinese into this country is the basis of this story in which the boys find thrills and excitement aplenty."

106S.13   The mark on the door. (Grosset & Dunlap, 1934, 1967).

106S.14   The hidden harbor mystery. (Grosset & Dunlap, 1935, 1961).

106S.15   The sinister signpost. (Grosset & Dunlap, 1936, 1968).

---

* Copyrighted 1964.

106S.16   A figure in hiding. (Grosset & Dunlap, 1937, 1965).

106S.17   The secret warning. (Grosset & Dunlap, 1938, 1966).

106S.18   The twisted claw. (Grosset & Dunlap, 1939, 1969).

[LC]: [R]"The Hardy boys embark on another puzzling mystery when they try to discover who is stealing rare collections of ancient pirate treasure and smuggling them out of the United States."

106S.19   The disappearing floor. (Grosset & Dunlap, 1940, 1964).

106S.20   The mystery of the flying express. (Grosset & Dunlap, 1941, 1970).

[LC]: [R]"After the new hydrofoil they are guarding is stolen, the Hardy boys face frequent danger in solving a mystery involving criminals who operate by sign of the zodiac."

106S.21   The clue of the broken blade. (Grosset & Dunlap, 1942, 1970).

[LC]: [R]"While searching for the guard end of a broken saber that will solve one mystery, the Hardy brothers become involved with a gang of bank robbers."

106S.22   The flickering torch mystery. (Grosset & Dunlap, 1943, 1971).

[LC]: [R]"When two suspicious plane accidents occur near an eastern airport, the two Hardy brothers investigate the case and find themselves in greater danger than they anticipated."

106S.23   The melted coins. (Grosset & Dunlap, 1944, 1970).

[LC]: [R]"Suspecting that their friend has been swindled, the Hardy brothers investigate and find themselves on the trail of a much larger criminal investigation."

106S.24   The short-wave mystery. (Grosset & Dunlap, 1945, 1966).

106S.25   The secret panel. (Grosset & Dunlap, 1946, 1969).

[LC]: [R]"A chance meeting with a stranger on the road provides the Hardy brothers with a clue to a gang of local burglars."

106S.26   The phantom freighter. (Grosset & Dunlap, 1947, 1970).

[LC]: [R]"The Hardy brothers embark on a freighter trip under mysterious circumstances and find themselves involved with a smuggling ring."

106S.27   The secret of Skull Mountain. (Grosset & Dunlap, 1948, 1966).

106S.28   The sign of the crooked arrow. (Grosset & Dunlap, 1949, 1970).

[LC]: [R]"The Hardy brothers interrupt their investigations of jewelry-store holdups to answer a plea from their cousin on a New Mexico cattle ranch."

106S.29   The secret of the lost tunnel. (Grosset & Dunlap, 1950, 1968).

106S.30   The wailing siren mystery. (Grosset & Dunlap, 1951, 1968).

106S.31   The secret of Wildcat Swamp. (Grosset & Dunlap, 1952, 1969).

   [LC]:   [R]"An archaeological expedition in the West turns into a desperate attempt to capture robbers and an escaped convict."

106S.32   The crisscross shadow. (Grosset & Dunlap, 1953, 1969).

   [LC]:   [R]"The Hardy boys find the missing deed to an Indians' [sic] land, prevent a phony salesman from carrying through a reckless scheme, and help their father solve a top-secret case."

106S.33   The yellow feather mystery. (Grosset & Dunlap, 1953, 1971).

   [LC]:   [R]"In trying to trace a missing will, detectives Frank and Joe Hardy trap a dangerous criminal who is willing to risk all--including murder--for money."

106S.34   The hooded hawk mystery. (Grosset & Dunlap, 1954, 1971).

   [LC]:   [R]"When their peregrine falcon brings down a homing pigeon carrying rubies, the Hardy brothers find themselves involved with kidnappers."

106S.35   The clue in the embers. (Grosset & Dunlap, 1955, 1972).

   [LC]:   [R]"In solving the mystery of two medallions missing from an inherited curio collection, the Hardys wind up in a desolate area of Guatemala at the mercy of dangerous thugs."

106S.36   The secret of Pirates' Hill. (Grosset & Dunlap, 1957,* 1972).

   [LC]:   [R]"Hired to locate an old Spanish cannon, the Hardy brothers uncover an even greater treasure after perilous underwater adventures."

106S.37   The ghost at Skeleton Rock. (Grosset & Dunlap, 1958,** 1966).

106S.38   The mystery at Devil's Paw. (Grosset & Dunlap, 1959, 1973).

   [LC]:   [R]"When they journey to Alaska to help a friend who feels his life is in danger, the Hardy brothers find their own lives threatened."

106S.39   The mystery of the Chinese junk. (Grosset & Dunlap, 1960).

106S.40   The mystery of the desert giant. (Grosset & Dunlap, 1961).

106S.41   The clue of the screeching owl. (Grosset & Dunlap, 1962).

106S.42   The Viking symbol mystery. (Grosset & Dunlap, 1963).

---

*   Copyrighted 1956.
**   Copyrighted 1957.

106S.43   The mystery of the Aztec warrior. (Grosset & Dunlap, 1964).

106S.44   The haunted fort. (Grosset & Dunlap, 1965).

106S.45   The mystery of the spiral bridge. (Grosset & Dunlap, 1966).

106S.46   The secret agent on flight 101. (Grosset & Dunlap, 1967).

106S.47   The mystery of the whale tattoo. (Grosset & Dunlap, 1968).

106S.48   The artic patrol mystery. (Grosset & Dunlap, 1969).

> [LC]: "While searching in Iceland for a missing sailor sought by an insurance company, the teen-age detective brothers uncover a plot threatening the life of a United States astronaut and the secrets of NASA's moon project."

106S.49   The Bombay boomerang. (Grosset & Dunlap, 1970).

> [LC]: "The Hardy boys dial a wrong number, get the Pentagon, and suddenly find themselves in a dangerous adventure involving national security."

106S.50   Danger on Vampire Trail. (Grosset & Dunlap, 1971).

> [LC]: "The Hardy boys and two friends take a camping trip to the Rocky Mountains in an attempt to locate a gang of credit-card counterfeiters."

106S.51   The masked monkey. (Grosset & Dunlap, 1972).

> [LC]: "The Hardy brothers' search for the missing son of a wealthy industrialist leads them to Brazil and great danger."

106S.52   The shattered helmet. (Grosset & Dunlap, 1973).

> [LC]: "The Hardy brothers' visiting Greek pen pal enlists their help in searching for a priceless ancient Greek helmet loaned to and lost by a Hollywood movie company years before."

106S.53   The clue of the hissing serpent. (Grosset & Dunlap, 1974).

> [LC]: "Their efforts to recover a stolen ancient chess piece lead the Hardy brothers to Hong Kong where they help smash an international criminal organization."

106S.54   The mysterious caravan. (Grosset & Dunlap, 1975).

> [LC]: "On a winter vacation in Jamaica the Hardy boys begin a dangerous adventure when an ancient bronze death mask is discovered near their beach house."

106S.55   The witchmaster's key. (Grosset & Dunlap, 1976).

> [LC]: "The Hardy boys' investigation of a museum robbery in England arouses the anger of a coven of black witches."

106S.56   The jungle pyramid. (Grosset & Dunlap, 1977).

[LC]: "The search for missing gold takes the Hardy boys to the Yucatan Peninsula where they uncover a second mystery."

106S.57   The firebird rocket. (Grosset & Dunlap, 1978).

[LC]: "Two teenage sleuths help their detective father search for a famous rocket scientist whose disappearance endangers the launching of the Firebird rocket."

106S.58   The sting of the scorpion. (Grosset & Dunlap, 1979).

[LC]: "During their father's investigation of a ruthless gang of terrorists, two young detectives face several adversaries."

106S.59   Night of the werewolf. (Wanderer, 1979).

[LC]: "When a ferocious, wolf-like creature appears in a small town, the Hardy boys are engaged to clear the name of a young man who has a history of werewolves in the family."

106S.60   Mystery of the samurai sword. (Wanderer, 1979).

[LC]: "A Japanese business tycoon mysteriously disappears and, soon after, a rare samurai sword is stolen from an art gallery. Suspecting a connection, the Hardy boys try to solve the mystery."

106S.61   The Pentagon spy. (Wanderer, 1979).

[LC]: "Valuable antique weathervanes are being stolen in the Pennsylvania Dutch country. A Navy employee removes a top secret document from the Pentagon. The Hardy brothers try to solve these two seemingly unrelated mysteries."

106S.62   The apeman's secret. (Wanderer, 1980).

[LC]: "A 'monster' who terrorizes Bayport and a girl who runs away to join a cult are the subjects of the Hardy boys' sleuthing."

106S.63   The mummy case. (Wanderer, 1980).

[LC]: "Called in to investigate the theft of some statuettes stolen from the Egyptian museum in New York, the Hardy brothers become involved in a deepening mystery which includes the possible overthrow of another country's government."

106S.64   The mystery of Smuggler's Cove. (Wanderer, 1980).

[LC]: "The art collector who suspects the Hardy boys of stealing one of his valuable paintings offers them a chance to prove their innocence by hiring them to find the painting and the real culprits."

106S.65   The mystery of the stone idol. (Wanderer, 1981).

106S.66   The vanishing thieves. (Wanderer, 1981).

106S.67X   The Hardy boys' detective handbook. (Grosset & Dunlap, 1959, 1972).

   "In consultation with Special Agent William F. Flynn, Federal Bureau
of Investigation, Retired." 1972 edition revised.
      [LC]:   [R]"Relates seven cases in which the Hardy brothers use
police technology to track down criminals. Details of these techniques
and procedures are given in the last five chapters."

106S.68X   The Hardy boys' handbook: Seven stories of survival. (Wanderer,
1980).

   "By Franklin W. Dixon with Sheila Link."

106S.69X   The Hardy boys' who-dunnit mystery book. (Wanderer, 1980).

106S.70X   The Hardy boys and Nancy Drew meet Dracula. (Grosset & Dunlap,
1978).

   Novelization by the Stratemeyer Syndicate. "Based on the Universal
Television Series HARDY BOYS/NANCY DREW MYSTERIES Developed for Television by Glen A. Larson[.]   Based on the HARDY BOYS Books by Franklin
W. Dixon and the NANCY DREW Books by Carolyn Keene[.] Adapted from
the episodes THE HARDY BOYS AND NANCY DREW MEET DRACULA (Parts I and
II) Written by Glen A. Larson and Michael Sloan." Illustrated with
photographs copyrighted by Universal City Studios, Inc.

106S.71X   The haunted house and Flight to nowhere. (Grosset & Dunlap, 1978).

   Two stories in one book. "The Haunted House By Stratemeyer Syndicate[.]
Based on the Universal Television Series HARDY BOYS/NANCY DREW MYSTERIES
Developed for Television by Glen A. Larson[.] Based on the HARDY BOYS
books by Franklin W. Dixon[.] Adapted from the episode THE HOUSE ON
POSSESSED HILL Written by Michael Sloan[.] Flight to Nowhere by Strate-
meyer Syndicate[.] Based on the Universal Television Series HARDY BOYS/
NANCY DREW MYSTERIES Developed for Television by Glen A. Larson[.]
Adapted from the episode THE FLICKERING TORCH MYSTERY Written by James
Henerson." Illustrated with photographs copyrighted by Universal City
Studios, Inc.

107S   TED SCOTT FLYING SERIES

Volumes: 20
Printed: 1927-1943
Publisher: Grosset & Dunlap
Illustrator: Walter S. Rogers, vols. 1-14
              J. Clemens Gretter, vols. 15-18
              I. B. Hazelton, vols. 19-20
Source of annotations: Grosset & Dunlap advertisements [G&D]
Series description [G&D]: "No subject has so thoroughly caught the imagi-
   nation of young America as aviation. This series has been inspired
   by recent daring feats of the air, and is dedicated to Lindbergh, Byrd,
   Chamberlin and other heroes of the skies."
      [Another advertisement] [G&D]: "The thrilling adventures of a
   daring young aviator as an air mail pilot, racer and pioneer flyer."

107S.1   Over the ocean to Paris; or, Ted Scott's daring long distance flight. (Grosset & Dunlap, 1927).

107S.2   Rescued in the clouds; or, Ted Scott, hero of the air. (Grosset & Dunlap, 1927).

107S.3   Over the Rockies with the air mail; or, Ted Scott lost in the wilderness. (Grosset & Dunlap, 1927).

107S.4   First stop Honolulu; or, Ted Scott over the Pacific. (Grosset & Dunlap, 1927).

107S.5   The search for the lost flyers; or, Ted Scott over the West Indies. (Grosset & Dunlap, 1928).

107S.6   South of the Rio Grande; or, Ted Scott on a secret mission. (Grosset & Dunlap, 1928).

107S.7   Across the Pacific; or, Ted Scott's hop to Australia. (Grosset & Dunlap, 1928).

107S.8   The lone eagle of the border; or, Ted Scott and the diamond smugglers. (Grosset & Dunlap, 1929).

107S.9   Flying against time; or, Ted Scott breaking the ocean to ocean record. (Grosset & Dunlap, 1929).

107S.10   Over the jungle trails; or, Ted Scott and the missing explorers. (Grosset & Dunlap, 1929).

107S.11   Lost at the South Pole; or, Ted Scott in blizzard land. (Grosset & Dunlap, 1930).

107S.12   Through the air to Alaska; or, Ted Scott's search in Nugget Valley. (Grosset & Dunlap, 1930).

107S.13   Flying to the rescue; or, Ted Scott and the big dirigible. (Grosset & Dunlap, 1930).

107S.14   Danger trails of the sky; or, Ted Scott's great mountain climb. (Grosset & Dunlap, 1931).

107S.15   Following the sun shadow; or, Ted Scott and the great eclipse. (Grosset & Dunlap, 1932).

107S.16   Battling the wind; or, Ted Scott flying around Cape Horn. (Grosset & Dunlap, 1933).

107S.17   Brushing the mountain top; or, Aiding the lost traveler. (Grosset & Dunlap, 1934).

107S.18   Castaways of the stratosphere; or, Hunting the vanquished balloonist. (Grosset & Dunlap, 1935).

107S.19   Hunting the sky spies; or, Testing the invisible plane. (Grosset & Dunlap, 1941).

107S.20   The pursuit patrol; or, Chasing the platinum pirates.   (Grosset
& Dunlap, 1943).

OTHER PUBLICATIONS

108N   A superboy, supergirl anthology: Selected chapters from the
earlier works of Victor Appleton, Franklin W. Dixon, and Carolyn Keene.
Edited by Stephen Dunning and Henry B. Maloney. Scholastic Book Services,
1971.

Julia K. Duncan

The Stratemeyer Syndicate pseudonym Julia K. Duncan appeared on one four-
volume girls' series, DORIS FORCE, published by Altemus in 1931 and 1932.
Walter Karig contributed to the series.

SERIES PUBLICATIONS

109S   DORIS FORCE

Volumes: 4
Printed: 1931-1932
Publisher: Henry Altemus Company
Reprint publisher: M. A. Donohue & Company, vols. 1, 4*
                    Goldsmith Publishing Co., vols. 2-4*
Illustrator: Thelma Gooch, vols. 1-4
Source of annotations: Henry Altemus Company advertisements [HA]
Additional information: Walter Karig assisted the Stratemeyer Syndicate
    with the books in this series.
        Donohue editions also had Thelma Gooch illustrations; Goldsmith
    editions were not illustrated.
Series description [HA]: "Doris Force is a charming and plucky girl of
    sixteen who, in trying to help others, finds herself having many in-
    teresting adventures. In each book she is confronted with a mystery,
    but this up-to-date miss is able to solve each one."

109S.1   Doris Force at Locked Gates; or, Saving a mysterious fortune.
(Altemus, 1931; Donohue).

    [HA]: "The Misses Azalea and Iris Gates, the white-haired twins who
    lived shut away from the world, summon Doris to help them out of an
    unusual circumstance."

_____
* Possibly others as well.

109S.2   Doris Force at Cloudy Cove; or, The old miser's signature.
(Altemus, 1931; Goldsmith).

[HA]: "Further adventures await Doris and her interesting friends when
they attempt to uncover the secret concerning an old uncle who has not
been heard of in thirty years."

109S.3   Doris Force at Raven Rock; or, Uncovering the secret oil well.
(Altemus, 1932; Goldsmith).

109S.4   Doris Force at Barry Manor; or, Mysterious adventures between
classes. (Altemus, 1932; Goldsmith; Donohue).

Theodore Edison

Edward Stratemeyer's one story as Theodore Edison first appeared in a boys'
story paper in 1895 and was reprinted as a book by Roy Rockwood in 1900.

MAGAZINE PUBLICATIONS

110M   "The wizard of the deep; or, Over and under the ocean in search
of the $1,000,000 pearl." Young Sports of America, nos. 11-16, Aug. 10-
Sept. 14, 1895.

    Reprinted in book form as The wizard of the sea; or, A trip under the
    ocean by Roy Rockwood, first by Mershon in 1900 and later by Chatter-
    ton-Peck and A. L. Burt (240N).

Julia Edwards

Julia Edwards was a Street & Smith house name used for serials in the New
York Weekly, many of which were reprinted in paperback libraries such as
the CLOVER SERIES (141PQ), the EAGLE and NEW EAGLE LIBRARIES (142PQ), the
Far and Near Series, the FAVORITE LIBRARY (143PQ), and the Select Series.
The first Julia Edwards story serialized in the New York Weekly ran in 1877;
the last, in 1907. The pseudonym was especially popular in the New York
Weekly during the last decade of the nineteenth century: from September
26, 1891 to December 1, 1894, every issue carried an installment of at least
one Julia Edwards serial (and sometimes two); from December 1, 1894 to April
2, 1898, all but eight or ten issues included Julia Edwards romances. The
paperback libraries reprinted the stories as early as 1890 and as late as
1932.
    Edward Stratemeyer's exact connection with Julia Edwards has not yet
been established. In The fiction factory, Quentin Reynolds mentions that
Stratemeyer, "who had begun [at Street & Smith] by editing Good News, was

now . . . writing dime novels under the names of Jim Bowie, Nat Woods and
Jim Daly, and writing serials aimed at women for the Weekly under the name
of Julie [sic] Edwards."* If this is true, some of the stories printed as
by Julia Edwards are Stratemeyer's work: the question, of course, is which
ones. Obviously, none of the tales prior to late 1889 are Stratemeyer's,
since his first published story did not appear until November 1889.** No
new Julia Edwards serials were printed between April 1900 and September
1906; since Stratemeyer had stopped working for Street & Smith in 1896 and
formed his Literary Syndicate about 1906, it seems rqasonable to assume that
he did not pen any Julia Edwards tales after 1900. This leaves the thirty
stories published from 1890 to 1900. Some of these may have been Stratemeyer's work, though it is impossible to assign him specific titles without
more evidence.***

  For reference' sake, the list below includes all of the Julia Edwards
stories first published between 1890 to 1900 although they are certainly
not all by Stratemeyer.

MAGAZINE PUBLICATIONS

111MQ   "Beautiful Aldine; or, Shackles of gold." New York Weekly, vol.
46, nos. 5-10, Nov. 29, 1890-Jan. 3, 1891.

112MQ   "Beautiful Viola, the cloak maker's model; or, Did she marry for
love?" New York Weekly, vol. 47, nos. 25-48, April 16-Sept. 24, 1892.

113MQ   "The belle of the wheel; or, The secret of the camera." New York
Weekly, vol. 49, no. 47-vol. 50, no. 10, Sept. 15-Dec. 29, 1894.

114MQ   "Bonnie little Bluebell; or, The schoolmaster's sweetheart." New
York Weekly, vol. 50, nos. 39-50, July 20-Oct. 5, 1895.

  Reprinted in Street & Smith's NEW EAGLE SERIES as Bonnie Bluebell,#
  no. 1014, Sept. 1918 (142PQ.9X) and no. 1343, May 1931 (142PQ.13X).
  Both editions had the same title.

115MQ   "Carolyn, the factory girl; or, The waters of death." New York
Weekly, vol. 52, no. 44-vol. 53, no. 7, Aug. 21-Dec. 4, 1897.

116MQ   "The East River mystery; or Murder will out." New York Weekly,
vol. 53, nos. 8-24, Dec. 11, 1897-April 2, 1898.

---

*   The fiction factory; or, From Pulp Row to Quality Street (New York:
     Random House, 1955), p. 116.
**   The Julia Edwards serials published in the New York Weekly before 1889
     are often attributed to John Coryell.
*** If Reynolds's quote is construed to indicate that Stratemeyer was writ-
     ing as Julia Edwards, Jim Daly, Nat Woods, and Jim Bowie concurrently,
     then Stratemeyer's Julia Edwards stories may have been serialized
     during 1892 and 1893; however, it should also be noted that an Edna
     Winfield romance attributed to Stratemeyer was not published in the
     Weekly until 1896, which might suggest a later date for the Julia
     Edwards romances.
Subtitle missing.

117MQ   "Estelle's millionaire lover; or, The prettiest typewriter in New York." New York Weekly, vol. 48, nos. 12-31, Jan. 14-May 27, 1893.

Reprinted as no. 90 in Street & Smith's CLOVER SERIES,* May 14, 1896 (141PQ.3X), as no. 27 in Street & Smith's EAGLE LIBRARY, Aug. 30, 1897 (142PQ.2X), and as part of American News Company's FAVORITE LIBRARY* (143PQ.3X).

118MQ   "Evelyn, the pretty factory girl; or, Married at the loom." New York Weekly, vol. 47, no. 48-vol. 48, no. 16, Sept. 24, 1892-Feb. 11, 1893.

119MQ   "Fairest of the fair; or, How true-hearted Tess won the love of a handsome millionaire." New York Weekly, vol. 51, nos. 38-49, July 11-Sept. 26, 1896.

Reprinted in Street & Smith's NEW EAGLE SERIES as no. 974,* Jan. 1917 (142PQ.6X), and as no. 1292,* May 1929 (142PQ.10X).

120MQ   "The forsaken bridegroom; or, Bonnie Claribel's handsome lover." New York Weekly, vol. 52, nos. 25-40, April 10-July 24, 1897.

121MQ   "Forsaken on her wedding night."** New York Weekly, vol. 50, nos. 10-25, Dec. 29, 1894-April 13, 1895.

122MQ   "He loves me, he loves me not; or, The life and love of Violet Lee. One of the most romantic stories ever written." New York Weekly, vol. 46, no. 48-vol. 47, no. 10, Sept. 26, 1891-Jan. 2, 1892.

Reprinted as no. 47 in Street & Smith's CLOVER SERIES,* May 11, 1895 (141PQ.2X), as no. 3 in Street & Smith's EAGLE LIBRARY,* March 15, 1897, as He loves me, he loves me not,* and later with the title The love of Violet Lee* (142PQ.1X). Also reprinted as no. 102 in American News Company's FAVORITE LIBRARY* (143PQ.2X), and as no. 1369, The love of Violet Lee,* in NEW EAGLE SERIES, May 1932 (142PQ.14X).

123MQ   "His little darling." New York Weekly, vol. 53, no. 32. May 28, 1898.

124MQ   "Lauretta is my darling; or, Loved in New York and won at the World's Fair." New York Weekly, vol. 48, nos. 31-47. May 27-Sept. 16, 1893.

125MQ   "The love that won; or, The misadventures of a willful little schoolma'am." New York Weekly, vol. 52, nos. 9-23, Dec. 19, 1896-March 27, 1897.

126MQ   "Madcap Merribel, the sauciest little model that ever posed for an artist. A strangely thrilling tale of rapturous love and mad jealousy." New York Weekly, vol. 48, no. 48-vol. 49, no. 11, Sept. 23, 1893-Jan. 6, 1894.

Reprinted in Street & Smith's NEW EAGLE SERIES as no. 1007,* May 1918 (142PQ.8X), and as no. 1336,* Feb. 1931 (142PQ.12X).

---

*   Subtitle missing.
**   No subtitle. Title may be "Forsaken on her wedding morn."

127MQ   "One girl's heart."* New York Weekly, vol. 52, nos. 41-42, July 31-Aug. 7, 1897.

128MQ   "Only a country girl; or, Little Nellie's city lovers, false and true." New York Weekly, vol. 51, nos. 23- ?,** March 28- ?, 1896.**

Reprinted as no. 997*** in Street & Smith's NEW EAGLE SERIES, Dec. 1917 (142PQ.7X).

129MQ   "Plighted hearts and broken vows; or, Pretty Pansy's temptations." New York Weekly, vol. 53, no. 51-vol. 54, no. 15, Oct. 8, 1898-Jan. 28, 1899.

Reprinted in Street & Smith's NEW EAGLE SERIES as no. 948,*** Dec. 1915 (142PQ.5X), and as no. 1310,*** Feb. 1930 (142PQ.11X).

130MQ   "The prettiest girl awheel; or, The romance of Muriel Dene." New York Weekly, vol. 51, no. 46-vol. 52, no. 9, Sept. 5-Dec. 19, 1896.

131MQ   "A princess in calico." New York Weekly, vol. 55, nos. 11-22, Dec. 30, 1899-March 17, 1900.

132MQ   "Rescued by love; or, Out of a tangled web." New York Weekly, vol. 54, nos. 16-30, Feb. 4-May 13, 1899.

133MQ   "She loved, but left him; or, The beautiful working-girl's battle for honor's sake." New York Weekly, vol. 49, nos. 10-32, Dec. 30, 1893-June 2, 1894.

Reprinted in Street & Smith's EAGLE SERIES as no. 209,*** Feb. 25, 1901 (142PQ.4X), and in American News Company's FAVORITE LIBRARY as no. 56*** (143PQ.1X).

134MQ   "Stella Sterling; or, A beautiful girl's struggles with fate. The most thrilling and pathetic love story ever written." New York Weekly, vol. 46, nos. 21-32, March 21-June 6, 1891.

Reprinted in Street & Smith's CLOVER SERIES as no. 46,*** May 4, 1895 (141PQ.1X), in Street & Smith's EAGLE LIBRARY as no. 62,*** May 2, 1898 (142PQ.3X), and in American New's Company's FAVORITE LIBRARY*** (143PQ.4X).

135MQ   "Tempted to leave her lover; or, The life romance of Lillie Goldie. A love story of entrancing interest." New York Weekly, vol. 47, nos. 11-36, Jan. 9-July 2, 1892.

136MQ   "They fell in love at the sea-shore: An absorbing romance of love and mystery." New York Weekly, vol. 49, nos. 33-44, June 9-Aug. 25, 1894.

137MQ   "Trixie's lovers; or, A strange wooing." New York Weekly, vol. 51, nos. 10-21, Dec. 28, 1895-March 14, 1896.

---

*   No subtitle.
**   Serial ended between nos. 30-34 (vol. 51), May 18-June 13, 1896.
*** Subtitle missing.

138MQ   "The web of fate; or, The sunshine of the mill." New York Weekly,
vol. 53, nos. 26-42, April 16-Aug. 6, 1898.

139MQ   "A wild marriage; or, They loved in spite of all." New York
Weekly, vol. 50, no. 49-vol. 51, no. 12, Sept. 28, 1895-Jan. 11, 1896.

140MQ   "The wizard of the wheel; or, Two true hearts against the world."
New York Weekly, vol. 50, nos. 26-38, April 20-July 13, 1895.

SERIES PUBLICATIONS

141PQ CLOVER SERIES

Volumes: 3*
Printed: 1895-1896*
Publisher: Street & Smith
Additional information: The paperback CLOVER SERIES reprinted love stories,
    many of which had appeared earlier in the New York Weekly. Issued
    weekly, the series began on June 23, 1894, and continued until at least
    January 16, 1897 (134 issues). A complete list of titles has not been
    seen, but Edward T. LeBlanc's bibliographic listing shows seven Julia
    Edwards titles from March 30, 1895 through May 11, 1895 (nos. 41-47).
    An eighth title was no. 90 in the series. Five of the books first
    appeared in the New York Weekly before 1890 and are not Stratemeyer's
    work. Some or all of the other three may be by Edward Stratemeyer.

141PQ.1X Stella Sterling.** No. 46. May 4, 1895.

    First published as "Stella Sterling; or, A beautiful girl's struggles
    with fate. The most thrilling and pathetic love story ever written"
    in the New York Weekly, March 21-June 6, 1891 (134MQ).

141PQ.2X He loves me, he loves me not.** No. 47. May 11, 1895.

    First published as "He loves me, he loves me not; or, The life and
    love of Violet Lee. One of the most romantic stories ever written"
    in the New York Weekly, Sept. 26, 1891-Jan. 2, 1892 (122MQ).

141PQ.3X Estelle's millionaire lover.** No. 90. May 14, 1896.

    First published as "Estelle's millionaire lover; or, The prettiest
    typewriter in New York" in the New York Weekly, Jan. 14-May 27, 1893
    (117MQ).

142PQ EAGLE LIBRARY/EAGLE SERIES/NEW EAGLE SERIES

Volumes: 14*
Printed: 1897-1932*

---
* Number of volumes and years published apply only to Julia Edwards titles
    originally published in the New York Weekly between 1890 and 1900.
** Subtitle missing.

Publisher: Street & Smith
Source of annotations: Street & Smith advertisements [S&S]
Additional information: The EAGLE LIBRARY, a line of paperback reprints, was issued every week (with some breaks in the schedule) from March 1, 1897 through March 31, 1915 (no. 931), and then every other week until the final issue, no. 1385, in December 1932. The series went through three titles in thirty-five years: the EAGLE LIBRARY (nos. 1-153), the EAGLE SERIES (nos. 154-552), and the NEW EAGLE SERIES (nos. 553-1385).

   Much of the material for the series was taken from the New York Weekly; some of the stories had already been reprinted in the CLOVER (141PQ), Far and Near, and/or Select Series. Among the stories reprinted from the New York Weekly were thirteen romances under the name Julia Edwards; six of the thirteen were published twice* in the EAGLE LIBRARY/EAGLE SERIES/NEW EAGLE SERIES, for a total of nineteen volumes by Julia Edwards.** Five had first appeared in the Weekly prior to 1890 and are thought to be by John Coryell; some of the remaining fourteen titles may be Stratemeyer's work.

   One volume in the EAGLE LIBRARY was written by Edward Stratemeyer under the name Edna Winfield (346P.1X).

   Some of the earlier titles in the EAGLE LIBRARY and EAGLE SERIES may have been reissued with the original numbers, but with NEW EAGLE SERIES on the covers.

Series description [S&S]: "Carefully selected love stories.
   "There is such a profusion of good books in this list, that it is an impossibility to urge you to select any particular title or author's work. All that we can say is that any line that contains the complete works of Mrs. Georgie Sheldon, Charles Garvice, Mrs. Harriet Lewis, May Agnes Fleming, Wenona Gilman, Mrs. Alex McVeigh Miller, and other writers of the same type, is worthy of your attention."

142PQ.1X He loves me, he loves me not.*** No. 3. March 15, 1897.

   Reissued with the same number but with the title The love of Violet Lee.# First published as "He loves me, he loves me not; or, The life and love of Violet Lee. One of the most romantic stories ever written in the New York Weekly, Sept. 26, 1891-Jan. 2, 1892 (122MQ).

142PQ.2X Estelle's millionaire lover; or, The prettiest typewriter in New York. No. 27. August 30, 1897.

   First published in the New York Weekly, Jan. 14-May 27, 1893 (117MQ).

142PQ.3X Stella Sterling.*** No. 62. May 2, 1898.

---

*   With two different volume numbers, that is.
** An additional four titles by Julia Edwards that have not yet been trac to an earlier publication date were issued between 1915 and 1918. Thr of these were again reprinted in the NEW EAGLE SERIES (with new volume numbers) in 1929 and 1930.
*** Subtitle missing.
#   The title may have been changed after the publication of no. 328, He loves me, he loves me not by Charles Garvice (June 8, 1903), to prevent confusion. (The Garvice title is apparently not the same story as the Edwards title.)

First published as "Stella Sterling; or, A beautiful girl's struggles
with fate. The most thrilling and pathetic love story ever written"
in the New York Weekly, March 21-June 6, 1891 (134MQ).

142PQ.4X She loved, but left him.* No. 209. Feb. 25, 1901.

First published as "She loved, but left him; or, The beautiful working-
girl's battle for honor's sake" in the New York Weekly, Dec. 30, 1893-
June 2, 1894 (133M).

142PQ.5X Plighted hearts and broken vows.* No. 948. Dec. 1915.

First published as "Plighted hearts and broken vows; or, Pretty Pansy's
temptations" in the New York Weekly Oct. 8, 1898-Jan. 28, 1899 (129MQ).

142PQ.6X Fairest of the fair.* No. 974. Jan. 1917.

First published as "Fairest of the fair; or, How true-hearted Tess won
the love of a handsome millionaire" in the New York Weekly, July 11-
Sept. 26, 1896 (119MQ).

142PQ.7X Only a country girl.* No. 997. Dec. 1917.

First published as "Only a country girl; or, Little Nellie's city
lovers, true and false" in the New York Weekly, March 28- ?, 1896**
(128MQ).

142PQ.8X Madcap Merribel.* No. 1007. May 1918.

First published as "Madcap Merribel, the sauciest little model that
ever posed for an artist. A strangely thrilling tale of rapturous
love and mad jealousy" in the New York Weekly, Sept. 23, 1893-Jan. 6,
1894 (126MQ).

142PQ.9X Bonnie Bluebell.* No. 1014. Sept. 1918.

First published as "Bonnie little Bluebell; or, The schoolmaster's
sweetheart" in the New York Weekly, July 20-Oct. 5, 1895 (114MQ).

142PQ.10X Fairest of the fair.* No. 1292. May 1929.

First published as "Fairest of the fair; or, How true-hearted Tess won
the love of a handsome millionaire" in the New York Weekly, July 11-
Sept. 26, 1896 (119MQ).

142PQ.11X Plighted hearts and broken vows.* No. 1310. Feb. 1930.

First published as "Plighted hearts and broken vows; or, Pretty Pansy's
temptations" in the New York Weekly Oct. 8, 1898-Jan. 28, 1899 (129MQ).

142PQ.12X Madcap Merribel.* No. 1336. Feb. 1931.

First published as "Madcap Merribel, the sauciest little model that

---

* Subtitle missing.
** Serial ended between nos. 30-34 (vol. 51), May 18-June 13, 1896.

ever posed for an artist. A strangely thrilling tale of rapturous love and mad jealousy" in the New York Weekly, Sept. 23, 1893-Jan. 6, 1894 (126MQ).

142PQ.13X Bonnie Bluebell.* No. 1343. May 1931.

First published as "Bonnie little Bluebell; or, The schoolmaster's sweetheart" in the New York Weekly, July 20-Oct. 5, 1895 (114MQ).

142PQ.14X The love of Violet Lee.* No. 1369. May 1932.

First published as "He loves me, he loves me not; or, The life and love of Violet Lee. One of the most romantic stories ever written" in the New York Weekly, Sept. 26, 1891-Jan. 2, 1892 (122MQ).

143PQ   FAVORITE LIBRARY

Volumes: 4**
Printed: ca1902-1905?**
Publisher: American News Company
Additional information: The American News Company issued the FAVORITE LIBRARY, a paperback reprint series of at least 251 volumes. The United States Catalogue supplement: Books published 1902-1905 shows eight titles by Julia Edwards in the FAVORITE LIBRARY; four of these have been credited to John Coryell. Other Julia Edwards books may have appeared in this series: a complete list of titles has not been seen.

143PQ.1X She loved but left him.* No. 56. ca1902-1905?

First published as "She loved, but left him; or, The beautiful working-girl's battle for honor's sake" in the New York Weekly, Dec. 30, 1893-June 2, 1894 (133MQ).

143PQ.2X He loves me, he loves me not.* No. 102. ca1902-1905?

First published as "He loves me, he loves me not; or, The life and love of Violet Lee. One of the most romantic stories ever written" in the New York Weekly, Sept. 26, 1891-Jan. 2, 1892 (122MQ).

143PQ.3X Estelle's millionaire lover.*** ca1902-1905?

First published as "Estelle's millionaire lover; or, The prettiest type-writer in New York" in the New York Weekly, Jan. 14-May 27, 1893 (117MQ).

143PQ.4X Stella Sterling.*** ca1902-1905?

First published as "Stella Sterling; or, A beautiful girl's struggles with fate. The most thrilling and pathetic love story ever written" in the New York Weekly, March 21-June 6, 1891 (134MQ).

---

*   Subtitle missing.
**   Number of volumes and years published apply only to Julia Edwards titles originally published in the New York Weekly between 1890 and 1900.
*** Subtitle and volume number missing.

Alice B. Emerson

The forty-five books in the two girls' series BETTY GORDON and RUTH FIELDING, published by Cupples & Leon from 1913 to 1934, were the only titles written under the Stratemeyer Syndicate pseudonym Alice B. Emerson. W. Bert Foster helped the Stratemeyer Syndicate with some volumes in the two series.

SERIES PUBLICATIONS

144S   BETTY GORDON

Volumes: 15
Printed: 1920-1932
Publisher: Cupples & Leon Company
Illustrator: Thelma Gooch, vols. 1-6
              Walter S. Rogers, vol. 7
              Ernest Townsend, vols. 8, 11
              anonymous, vol. 9
              Bess Goe Willis, vol. 10
              Russell H. Tandy, vols. 12-13
              A. Suk, vol. 14
Source of annotations: Cupples & Leon Company advertisements [C&L]
Series description [C&L]: "A new series of stories bound to make this
    writer more popular than ever with her host of girl readers. Every
    one will want to know Betty Gordon, and every one will be sure to love
    her."

144S.1   Betty Gordon at Bramble Farm; or, The mystery of a nobody. (Cupples & Leon, 1920).

    Reprinted in Mystery and adventure stories for girls, ca1934 (146N).
        [C&L]: "At the age of twelve Betty is left an orphan in the care
    of her bachelor uncle. He is interested in oil properties and so sends
    the girl off to live with a married woman who years before had been
    his school companion. Betty finds life at Bramble Farm exceedingly
    hard."

144S.2   Betty Gordon in Washington; or, Strange adventures in a great
city. (Cupples & Leon, 1920).

    [C&L]: "In this volume Betty goes to the national capitol to find her
    uncle. She falls in with a number of strangers and has several unusual
    adventures, one of which comes close to ending disastrously. A splendid
    picture of life at our national capitol."

144S.3   Betty Gordon in the land of oil; or, The farm that was worth a
fortune. (Cupples & Leon, 1920).

    [C&L]: "From Washington the scene is shifted to the great oil fields
    of our country. Betty has followed her uncle to a new oil locality.

Betty having overheard some conversation which proves that a particular farm is rich in oil, informs her uncle. A splendid picture of the oil field operations of today."

144S.4   Betty Gordon at boarding school; or, The treasure of Indian Chasm. (Cupples & Leon, 1921).

[C&L]: "An up-to-date tale of school life. Betty made many friends but a jealous girl tried to harm her. Seeking the treasure of Indian Chasm makes an exceedingly interesting incident."

144S.5   Betty Gordon at mountain camp; or, The mystery of Ida Bellethorne. (Cupples & Leon, 1922).

[C&L]: "At Mountain Camp Betty found herself in the midst of a mystery involving a girl whom she had previously met in Washington."

144S.6   Betty Gordon at Ocean Park; or, School chums on the boardwalk.* (Cupples & Leon, 1923).

[C&L]: "A glorious outing that Betty and her chums never forgot."

144S.7   Betty Gordon and her school chums; or, Bringing the rebels to terms. (Cupples & Leon, 1924).

[C&L]: "Rebellious students, disliked teachers and mysterious robberies make a fascinating story."

144S.8   Betty Gordon at Rainbow Ranch; or, Cowboy Joe's secret. (Cupples & Leon, 1925).

[C&L]: "Betty and her chums have a grand time in the saddle."

144S.9   Betty Gordon in Mexican wilds; or, The secret of the mountains. (Cupples & Leon, 1926).

[C&L]: "Betty receives a fake telegram and finds both Bob and herself held for ransom in a mountain cave."

144S.10   Betty Gordon and the lost pearls; or, A mystery of the seaside. (Cupples & Leon, 1927).

[C&L]: "Betty and her chums go to the ocean shore for a vacation and there Betty becomes involved in the disappearance of a string of pearls worth a fortune."

144S.11   Betty Gordon on the campus; or, The secret of the trunk room. (Cupples & Leon, 1928).

[C&L]: "An up-to-date college story with a strange mystery that is bound to fascinate any girl reader."

144S.12   Betty Gordon and the Hale twins; or, An exciting vacation. (Cupples & Leon, 1929).

---

* Subtitle also listed as Gay days on the boardwalk.

144S.13   Betty Gordon at mystery farm; or, Strange doings at Rocky Ridge. (Cupples & Leon, 1930).

144S.14   Betty Gordon on No-trail Island; or, Uncovering a queer secret. (Cupples & Leon, 1931).

144S.15   Betty Gordon and the mystery girl; or, The secret at Sundown Hall. (Cupples & Leon, 1932).

145S   RUTH FIELDING

Volumes: 30
Printed: 1913-1934
Publisher: Cupples & Leon Company
Illustrator: anonymous, vols. 1-3, 5, 13, 15, 20-22, 25-26
            WB [WR?], vol. 4
            Walter S. Rogers, vols. 6, 8-10
            W. Ru...[illegible], vol. 7
            R. Emmett Owen, vols. 11-12, 14, 16
            Thelma Gooch, vols. 17-19
            Bess Goe Willis, vol. 23
            Ernest Townsend, vol. 24
            M. J. LeBeuthillier, vol. 27
            Russell H. Tandy, vols. 28-30
Source of annotations: Cupples & Leon Company advertisements [C&L]
Series description [C&L]: "Ruth Fielding was an orphan and came to live
    with her miserly uncle. By her sunny disposition she melted the old
    miller's heart. Her adventures and travels make stories that will hold
    the interest of every reader. The Ruth Fielding series is the biggest
    and best selling series of books for girls ever published. Ruth Field-
    ing is a character that will live in juvenile fiction."

145S.1   Ruth Fielding of the red mill; or, Jasper Parloe's secret. (Cupples & Leon, 1913).

    Reprinted in Popular stories for girls (147N).
       [C&L]: "Telling how Ruth, an orphan girl, came to live with her
    miserly uncle, and how the girl's sunny disposition melted the old
    miller's heart. A great flood, and the disappearance of the miser's
    treasure box, add to the interest of the volume."

145S.2   Ruth Fielding at Briarwood Hall; or, Solving the campus mystery. (Cupples & Leon, 1913).

       [C&L]: "Ruth was sent by her uncle to boarding school to get an edu-
    cation. She made many friends and also one enemy, and the latter made
    much trouble for her. The mystery of the school campus is a most un-
    usual one."

145S.3   Ruth Fielding at Snow Camp; or, Lost in the backwoods. (Cupples & Leon, 1913).

       [C&L]: "A thrilling tale of adventures in the backwoods in winter.
    How Ruth went to the camp, and how she fell in with some very strange
    people, is told in a manner to interest every girl."

145S.4   Ruth Fielding at Lighthouse Point; or, Nita, the girl castaway.*
(Cupples & Leon, 1913).

 [C&L]: "From boarding school the scene is shifted to the Atlantic
 Coast, where Ruth goes for a summer vacation with some chums. There
 is a storm and a wreck, and Ruth aids in rescuing a girl from the sea."

145S.5   Ruth Fielding at Silver Ranch; or, Schoolgirls among the cowboys.
(Cupples & Leon, 1913).

 [C&L]: "A story with a western flavor--but one which is up-to-date and
 free from sensationalism. How the girls came to the rescue of Bashful
 Ike, the cowboy, and aided him and Sally, his 'gal,' is told in a way
 that is most absorbing."

145S.6   Ruth Fielding on Cliff Island; or, The old hunter's treasure box.
(Cupples & Leon, 1915).

 [C&L]: "Ruth and her friends go to Cliff Island, and there have many
 good times during the winter season."

145S.7   Ruth Fielding at Sunrise Farm; or, What became of the Ruby or-
phans. (Cupples & Leon, 1915).

 [C&L]: "Jolly good times at a farmhouse in the country, where Ruth
 rescues two orphan children who ran away."

145S.8   Ruth Fielding and the gypsies; or, The missing pearl necklace.
(Cupples & Leon, 1915).

 [C&L]: "This volume tells of stirring adventures at a gypsy encampment,
 of a missing heirloom, and how Ruth has it restored to its owner."

145S.9   Ruth Fielding in moving pictures; or, Helping the dormitory fund.
(Cupples & Leon, 1916).

145S.10   Ruth Fielding down in Dixie; or, Great days in the land of cotton.
(Cupples & Leon, 1916).

145S.11   Ruth Fielding at college; or, The missing examination papers.
(Cupples & Leon, 1917).

145S.12   Ruth Fielding in the saddle; or, College girls in the land of
gold. (Cupples & Leon, 1917).

145S.13   Ruth Fielding in the Red Cross; or, Doing her best for Uncle Sam.
(Cupples & Leon, 1918).

145S.14   Ruth Fielding at the war front; or, The hunt for the lost soldier.
(Cupples & Leon, 1918).

145S.15   Ruth Fielding homeward bound; or, a Red Cross worker's ocean
perils. (Cupples & Leon, 1919).

---

* Subtitle also listed in ads as Nita, the girl runaway.

145S.16   Ruth Fielding down east; or, The hermit of Beach Plum Point. (Cupples & Leon, 1920).

145S.17   Ruth Fielding in the great Northwest; or, The Indian girl star of the movies. (Cupples & Leon, 1921).

145S.18   Ruth Fielding on the St. Lawrence; or, The queer old man of the Thousand Islands. (Cupples & Leon, 1922).

145S.19   Ruth Fielding treasure hunting; or, A moving picture that became real. (Cupples & Leon, 1923).

145S.20   Ruth Fielding in the far North; or, The lost motion picture company. (Cupples & Leon, 1924).

145S.21   Ruth Fielding at Golden Pass; or, The perils of an artificial avalanche. (Cupples & Leon, 1925).

145S.22   Ruth Fielding in Alaska; or, The miners of Snow Mountain. (Cupples & Leon, 1926).

145S.23   Ruth Fielding and her great scenario; or, Striving for the motion picture prize. (Cupples & Leon, 1927).

145S.24   Ruth Fielding at Cameron Hall; or, A mysterious disappearance. (Cupples & Leon, 1928).

145S.25   Ruth Fielding clearing her name; or, The rivals of Hollywood. (Cupples & Leon, 1929).

145S.26   Ruth Fielding in talking pictures; or, The prisoners of the tower. (Cupples & Leon, 1930).

145S.27   Ruth Fielding and Baby June.* (Cupples & Leon, 1931).

145S.28   Ruth Fielding and her double.* (Cupples & Leon, 1932).

145S.29   Ruth Fielding and her greatest triumph; or, Saving her company from disaster. (Cupples & Leon, 1933).

145S.30   Ruth Fielding and her crowning victory; or, Winning honors abroad. (Cupples & Leon, 1934).

OTHER PUBLICATIONS

146N   Mystery and adventure stories for girls. (Cupples & Leon, ca1934).

   Contains Two girls and a mystery by May Hollis Barton, published in 1928 (032S.8); Maxie, an adorable girl by Elsie Bell Gardner, published in 1932; Betty Gordon at Bramble Farm by Alice B. Emerson, published in 1920 (144S.1); Jane Allen of the sub-team by Edith Bancroft, published in 1917. Printed from the original plates.

---

* Published without a subtitle.

147N   Popular stories for girls. (Cupples & Leon, ca1934).

Contains Ruth Fielding of the red mill by Alice B. Emerson, published
in 1913 (145S.1); Peggy and Michael of the coffee plantation by Anna
Andrews, published in 1931; The Linger-nots and the mystery house by
Agnes Miller, published in 1923; Billie Bradley and her inheritance*
by Janet D. Wheeler, published in 1920 by G. Sully & Co., and ca1928
by Cupples & Leon (320S.1). Printed from the original plates.

Ruth Belmore Endicott

Dodd, Mead & Co., and later Grosset & Dunlap, published the two-volume
CAROLYN series, the only books written under the Stratemeyer Syndicate
house name Ruth Belmore Endicott.

SERIES PUBLICATIONS

148S   CAROLYN

Volumes: 2
Printed: 1918-1919
Publisher: Dodd, Mead & Co.
Reprint publisher: Grosset & Dunlap, vols. 1-2
Illustrator: Edward C. Caswell, vols. 1-2
Additional information: The books were published without subtitles.

148S.1   Carolyn of the corners. (Dodd, Mead, 1918; Grosset & Dunlap,
1919).

148S.2   Carolyn of the sunny heart. (Dodd, Mead, 1919; Grosset & Dunlap,
1920).

James Cody Ferris

From 1926 to 1942, the Stratemeyer Syndicate used the pseudonym James Cody
Ferris for the twenty-one X BAR X BOYS books, a western adventure series
published by Grosset & Dunlap. Leslie McFarlane, Roger Garis (the son of
Howard Garis), and Walter Karig assisted with titles in this series.

---

*   Title page spells this Billy Bradley and her inheritance.

SERIES PUBLICATIONS

149S   X BAR X BOYS (X-X BOYS)

Volumes: 21
Printed: 1926-1942
Publisher: Grosset & Dunlap
Illustrator: Walter S. Rogers, vols. 1-10
              J. Clemens Gretter, vols. 11-15
              Paul Laune, vols. 16-21
Source of annotations: Grosset & Dunlap advertisements [G&D]
Additional information: The Stratemeyer Syndicate received assistance from
    several writers for this series: Leslie McFarlane contributed to one
    volume, Roger Garis helped with some titles, and Walter Karig worked
    on volumes 14 and 15.
        Volume 21, the last book in the series, advertises The X Bar X boys
    with the border patrol as volume 22. This volume was probably never
    published and is considered a phantom title.
        The books were published without subtitles.
Series description [G&D]: "Thrilling tales of the great west, told pri-
    marily for boys but which will be read by all who love mystery, rapid
    action, and adventures in the great open spaces.
        "The Manley Boys, Roy and Teddy, are the sons of an old ranchman,
    the owner of many thousands of heads of cattle. The lads know how to
    ride, how to shoot, and how to take care of themselves under any and
    all circumstances.
        "The cowboys of the X Bar X ranch are real cowboys, on the job when
    required but full of fun and daring--a bunch any reader will be de-
    lighted to know."

149S.1   The X Bar X boys on the ranch. (Grosset & Dunlap, 1926).

149S.2   The X Bar X boys in Thunder Canyon. (Grosset & Dunlap, 1926).

149S.3   The X Bar X boys on Whirlpool River. (Grosset & Dunlap, 1926).

149S.4   The X Bar X boys on Big Bison Trail. (Grosset & Dunlap, 1927).

149S.5   The X Bar X boys at the round-up. (Grosset & Dunlap, 1927).

149S.6   The X Bar X boys at Nugget Camp. (Grosset & Dunlap, 1928).

149S.7   The X Bar X boys at Rustlers' Gap. (Grosset & Dunlap, 1929).

149S.8   The X Bar X boys at Grizzly Pass. (Grosset & Dunlap, 1929).

149S.9   The X Bar X boys lost in the Rockies. (Grosset & Dunlap, 1930).

149S.10   The X Bar X boys riding for life. (Grosset & Dunlap, 1931).

149S.11   The X Bar X boys in Smoky Valley. (Grosset & Dunlap, 1932).

149S.12   The X Bar X boys at Copperhead Gulch. (Grosset & Dunlap, 1933).

149S.13   The X Bar X boys branding the wild herd. (Grosset & Dunlap, 1934)

149S.14   The X bar X boys at the strange rodeo. (Grosset & Dunlap, 1935).

149S.15   The X bar X boys with the secret rangers. (Grosset & Dunlap, 1936).

149S.16   The X Bar X boys hunting the prize mustangs. (Grosset & Dunlap, 1937).

149S.17   The X Bar X boys at Triangle Mine. (Grosset & Dunlap, 1938).

149S.18   The X Bar X boys and the sagebrush mystery. (Grosset & Dunlap, 1939).

149S.19   The X Bar X boys in the haunted gully. (Grosset & Dunlap, 1940).

149S.20   The X Bar X boys seeking the lost troopers. (Grosset & Dunlap, 1941).

149S.21   The X Bar X boys following the stampede. (Grosset & Dunlap, 1942).

Graham B. Forbes

Two series were published as by the Stratemeyer Syndicate pseudonym Graham
B. Forbes: the eight-volume BOYS OF COLUMBIA HIGH series, published by
Grosset & Dunlap from 1912 to 1920, and the seventeen-volume FRANK ALLEN
series, printed by Garden City in 1926 and 1927. The latter series in-
cluded retitled editions of the BOYS OF COLUMBIA HIGH books. St. George
Rathborne assisted with some BOYS OF COLUMBIA HIGH titles.

SERIES PUBLICATIONS

150S   BOYS OF COLUMBIA HIGH

Volumes: 8
Printed: 1912-1920
Publisher: Grosset & Dunlap
Illustrator: Walter S. Rogers, vols. 1-8*
Source of annotations: Grosset & Dunlap advertisements [G&D]
Additional information: The books in this series were retitled and reissue
    in 1926 by Garden City as volumes 1 through 7 and 11 of the FRANK ALLEI
    series. St. George Rathborne contributed to some volumes in this seri(

*   Harry K. Hudson's Bibliography of hard-cover boys' books (Tampa: Data
     Print, 1977) notes "It is believed that W. S. Rogers did all of the
     illustrations" (p. 60).

Series description [G&D]: "Never was there a cleaner, brighter, more manly
    boy than Frank Allen, the hero of this series of boys' tales, and never
    was there a better crowd of lads to associate with than the students of
    the School. All boys will read these stories with deep interest. The
    rivalry between the towns along the river was of the keenest, and plots
    and counterplots to win the championships, at baseball, at football, at
    boat racing, at track athletics, and at ice hockey, were without number.
    Any lad reading one volume of this series will surely want the others."

150S.1   The boys of Columbia High; or, The all around rivals of the
school. (Grosset & Dunlap, 1912*).

    Reprinted by Garden City in 1926 as Frank Allen's schooldays; or, The
    all-around rivals of Columbia High, vol. 1 in the FRANK ALLEN series
    (151S.1).

150S.2   The boys of Columbia High on the diamond; or, Winning out by
pluck. (Grosset & Dunlap, 1912*).

    Reprinted by Garden City in 1926 as Frank Allen--pitcher; or, The boys
    of Columbia High on the diamond, vol. 5 in the FRANK ALLEN series
    (151S.5).

150S.3   The boys of Columbia High on the river; or, The boat race plot
that failed. (Grosset & Dunlap, 1912*).

    Reprinted by Garden City in 1926 as Frank Allen--head of the crew; or,
    The boys of Columbia High on the river, vol. 6 of the FRANK ALLEN
    series (151S.6).

150S.4   The boys of Columbia High on the gridiron; or, The struggle for
the silver cup. (Grosset & Dunlap, 1912*).

    Reprinted by Garden City in 1926 as Frank Allen--captain of the team;
    or, The boys of Columbia High on the gridiron, vol. 11 of the FRANK
    ALLEN series (151S.11).

150S.5   The boys of Columbia High on the ice; or, Out for the hockey
championship. (Grosset & Dunlap, 1912*).

    Reprinted by Garden City in 1926 as Frank Allen playing to win; or, The
    boys of Columbia High on the ice, vol. 2 of the FRANK ALLEN series
    (151S.2).

150S.6   The boys of Columbia High in track athletics; or, A long run that
won. (Grosset & Dunlap, 1913).

    Reprinted by Garden City in 1925 as Frank Allen and his rivals; or,
    The boys of Columbia High in track athletics, vol. 4 of the FRANK AL-
    LEN series (151S.3).

150S.7   The boys of Columbia High in winter sports; or, Stirring doings
on skates and iceboats. (Grosset & Dunlap, 1915).

---

* Copyrighted 1911.

Reprinted by Garden City in 1926 as Frank Allen in winter sports; or, Columbia High on skates and iceboats, vol. 3 of the FRANK ALLEN series (151S.3).

150S.8   The boys of Columbia High in camp; or, The rivalry of the old school league. (Grosset & Dunlap, 1920).

Reprinted by Garden City in 1926 as Frank Allen in camp; or, Columbia High and the school league rivals, vol. 7 of the FRANK ALLEN series (151S.7).

151S   FRANK ALLEN

Volumes: 17*
Printed: 1926-1927
Publisher: Garden City Publishing Company
Source of annotations: Garden City Publishing Company advertisements [GC]
Additional information: Volumes 1 through 7 and 11 were reprinted from the BOYS OF COLUMBIA HIGH plates. The books were retitled, the series order was rearranged, and some new titles were added to form the FRANK ALLEN series, which was published in hardcover and paperback editions. The paperback volumes were issued monthly, with the exception of the first two volumes, which were both issued in January, and possibly the last two volumes, which may have been phantom titles. For further information on Garden City's publishing schedule, see Victor Appleton, MOVIE BOYS (019S).
     St. George Rathborne assisted with some of the volumes published in the BOYS OF COLUMBIA HIGH series.
Series description [GC]: "Frank is a Columbia High boy who knows how to play hockey to win, how to pitch, how to row, and how to make a winning run on the gridiron. And he also knows how to camp out, how to shoot-- and above all how to take care of himself in any and every emergency."

151S.1   Frank Allen's schoolday's; or, The all-around rivals of Columbia High. (Garden City, 1926).

First published by Grosset & Dunlap in 1912** as The boys of Columbia High; or, The all around rivals of the school, vol. 1 of the BOYS OF COLUMBIA HIGH series (150S.1).
     [GC]: "A clean-cut school story, full of pep and ginger from beginning to end. Frank is such a manly, outspoken lad that to know him is to cotton to him at once. How Frank befriended an unknown lad, and what came of it, is delightfully told. The first of a series bound to become tremendously popular with all boys."

151S.2   Frank Allen playing to win; or, The boys of Columbia High on the ice. (Garden City, 1926).

First published by Grosset & Dunlap in 1912** as The boys of Columbia High on the ice; or, Out for the hockey championship, vol. 5 of the BOYS OF COLUMBIA HIGH series (150S.5).

---

* The last two volumes may never have been published.
** Copyrighted 1911.

[GC]: "Snow and snowballing, sledding and skating, and then some thrilling games of ice hockey, and a daring ice-boat race that will hold the readers breathless. And through it all a curious mystery that no boy will want to leave until it is unravelled."

151S.3   Frank Allen in winter sports; or, Columbia High on skates and iceboats. (Garden City, 1926).

First published by Grosset & Dunlap in 1915 as The boys of Columbia High in winter sports; or, Stirring doings on skates and iceboats, vol. 7 of the BOYS OF COLUMBIA HIGH series (150S.7).
[GC]: "More doings in mid-winter and again Frank Allen is to the front in a new series of thrilling adventures. In this volume Frank proves himself a hero in more ways than one and shows up his enemies as they were never shown up before."

151S.4   Frank Allen and his rivals; or, The boys of Columbia High in track athletics. (Garden City, 1926).

First published by Grosset & Dunlap in 1913 as The boys of Columbia High in track athletics; or, A long run that won, vol. 6 of the BOYS OF COLUMBIA HIGH series (150S.6).

151S.5   Frank Allen--pitcher; or, The boys of Columbia High on the diamond. (Garden City, 1926).

First published by Grosset & Dunlap in 1912* as The boys of Columbia High on the diamond; or, Winning out by pluck, vol. 2 of the BOYS OF COLUMBIA HIGH series (150S.2).

151S.6   Frank Allen--head of the crew; or, The boys of Columbia High on the river. (Garden City, 1926).

First published by Grosset & Dunlap in 1912* as The boys of Columbia High on the river; or, The boat race plot that failed, vol. 3 of the BOYS OF COLUMBIA HIGH series (150S.3).

151S.7   Frank Allen in camp; or, Columbia High and the school league rivals. (Garden City, 1926).

First published by Grosset & Dunlap in 1920 as The boys of Columbia High in camp; or, The rivalry of the old school league, vol. 8 of the BOYS OF COLUMBIA HIGH series (150S.8).

151S.8   Frank Allen at Rockspur Ranch; or, The old cowboy's secret. (Garden City, 1926).

151S.9   Frank Allen at Gold Fork; or, Locating the lost claim.   (Garden City, 1926).

151S.10   Frank Allen and his motor boat; or, Racing to save a life. (Garden City, 1926).

151S.11   Frank Allen--captain of the team; or, The boys of Columbia High on the gridiron. (Garden City, 1926).

---

* Copyrighted 1911.

First published by Grosset & Dunlap in 1912* as <u>The boys of Columbia</u> <u>High</u> <u>on</u> <u>the</u> <u>gridiron</u>; <u>or</u>, <u>The struggle for the silver cup</u>, vol. 4 of the the BOYS OF COLUMBIA HIGH series (150S.4).

151S.12   Frank Allen at Old Moose Lake; or, The trail in the snow.   (Garden City, 1926).

151S.13   Frank Allen at Zero Camp; or, The queer old man of the hills. (Garden City, 1926).

151S.14   Frank Allen snowbound; or, Fighting for life in the big blizzard. (Garden City, 1927).

151S.15   Frank Allen after big game; or, With guns and snowshoes in the Rockies.   (Garden City, 1927).

151S.16   Frank Allen with the circus; or, The old ringmaster's secret. (Garden City, 1927).**

151S.17   Frank Allen pitching his best; or, The baseball rivals of Columbia High.   (Garden City, 1927).**

Albert Lee Ford

In 1895 and 1896, Edward Stratemeyer wrote three stories under the name Albert Lee Ford. Two were later reprinted in book form under other pseudonyms.

MAGAZINE PUBLICATIONS

152M   "A New Year's hold-up; or, A brave boy's reward." <u>Young People</u> <u>of America</u>, no. 32, Jan. 4, 1896.

153M   "Poor but plucky; or, The mystery of a flood." <u>Young People of</u> <u>America</u>, nos. 23-30, Nov. 3-Dec. 21, 1895.

Reprinted in 1897 in book form with Arthur M. Winfield as author, as vol. 8 in W. L. Allison's BOUND TO WIN series (330S.3X) and in 1905, still with Winfield as author, as vol. 1 in Allison's, and later Donohue's, BRIGHT AND BOLD series (334S.1).

154M   "The young florists of Spring Hill; or, The new heliotrope." <u>Bright Days</u>, nos. 2-4, May-July, 1896.

Reprinted in book form by Mershon in 1900 in <u>Bound to rise</u>; <u>or</u>, <u>The</u> <u>young florists of Spring Hill</u>, <u>and Walter Loring's career</u> (two books in one) by Allen Chapman; also reprinted by Chatterton-Peck (091N).

---
* Copyrighted 1911.
** Possibly never published.

Frederick Gordon

Frederick Gordon was one of two Stratemeyer Syndicate pseudonyms used on series published by Graham & Matlack, and later by C. E. Graham Co. (The other was Raymond Stone.) The pseudonym lasted for five years and six books, excluding reprints.

SERIES PUBLICATIONS

155S   FAIRVIEW BOYS

Volumes: 6
Printed: ca1914-1917
Publisher: Graham & Matlack, vols. 1-5
            C. E. Graham Co., vol. 6
Reprint publisher: C. E. Graham Co., vols. 1-5
Illustrator: anonymous, vols. 1-3
              R. Menel [Mencl?], vols. 4-5
              R. Emmett Owen, vol. 6
Additional information: Volumes 1, 2, and 3 were first published by Graham
    & Matlack in 1912 as the UP AND DOING series (156S), then retitled and
    reissued as part of the FAIRVIEW BOYS series between 1912 and 1917,
    possibly in 1914, when volumes 4 and 5 of the FAIRVIEW BOYS series were
    published. In 1917 C. E. Graham Co. issued the sixth volume; volumes
    1 through 5 may have been reprinted about that time.

155S.1   The Fairview boys afloat and ashore; or, The young Crusoes of
Pine Island. (Graham & Matlack, ca1914; Graham, ca1917).

    First published by Graham & Matlack in 1912 as The young Crusoes of
    Pine Island; or, The wreck of the Puff, vol. 1 of the UP AND DOING
    series (156S.1).

155S.2   The Fairview boys on Eagle Mountain; or, Sammy Brown's treasure
hunt. (Graham & Matlack, ca1914; Graham, ca1917).

    First published by Graham & Matlack in 1912 as Sammy Brown's treasure
    hunt; or, Lost in the mountains, vol. 2 of the UP AND DOING series
    (156S.2).

155S.3   The Fairview boys and their rivals; or, Bob Bouncer's schooldays.
(Graham & Matlack, ca1914; Graham, ca1917).

    First published by Graham & Matlack in 1912 as Bob Bouncer's schooldays;
    or, The doings of a real, live everyday boy, vol. 3 of the UP AND DOING
    series (156S.3).

155S.4   The Fairview boys at Camp Mystery; or, The old hermit and his
secret. (Graham & Matlack, 1914; Graham, ca1917).

155S.5   The Fairview boys at Lighthouse Cove; or, Carried out to sea.
(Graham & Matlack, 1914; Graham, ca1917).

155S.6   The Fairview boys on a ranch; or, Riding with the cowboys.
(Graham, 1917).

156S   UP AND DOING

Volumes: 3
Printed: 1912
Publisher: Graham & Matlack
Illustrator: anonymous, vols. 1-3
Additional information: The series was reprinted as volumes 1, 2, and 3
    of the FAIRVIEW BOYS series (155S), with the original titles serving
    as the new subtitles.

156S.1   The young Crusoes of Pine Island; or, The wreck of the Puff.
(Graham & Matlack, 1912).

    Reprinted by Graham & Matlack, ca1914, and by C. E. Graham Co, ca1917,
    as The Fairview boys afloat and ashore; or, The young Crusoes of Pine
    Island, vol. 1 of the FAIRVIEW BOYS series (155S.1).

156S.2   Sammy Brown's treasure hunt; or, Lost in the mountains. (Graham
& Matlack, 1912).

    Reprinted by Graham & Matlack, ca1914, and by C. E. Graham, ca1917,
    as The Fairview boys on Eagle Mountain; or, Sammy Brown's treasure
    hunt, vol. 2 of the FAIRVIEW BOYS series (155S.2).

156S.3   Bob Bouncer's schooldays; or, The doings of a real, live everyday
boy. (Graham & Matlack, 1912).

    Reprinted by Graham & Matlack, ca1914, and by C. E. Graham, ca1917,
    as The Fairview boys and their rivals; or, Bob Bouncer's schooldays,
    vol. 3 of the FAIRVIEW BOYS series (155S.3).

Ralph Hamilton

Between 1890 and 1895, Golden Days serialized four different stories by Edward Stratemeyer under the house name Ralph Hamilton.* Three were reprinted in Golden Days between 1903 and 1907: one with Stratemeyer listed
as author, two without a specific author named.** A fifth story, printed
in 1891 and reprinted as by Dr. Willard MacKenzie in 1903, is considered

---

*   Actually, one of the four began as by Ralph Hamilton, but the author
      was changed to Edward Stratemeyer for the second and succeeding in-
      stallments.
**   As by "the author of 'Clearing His Name'" and as by "the author of
      'Captain Bob's Secret.'"

a possible Stratemeyer, but not a proven one.

Since Ralph Hamilton was a Golden Days house name, it was used by several writers, not just Stratemeyer, and appeared on serials as early as 1882, seven years before Stratemeyer's first published story. One Ralph Hamilton title too early to be Stratemeyer's work, but sometimes incorrectly attributed to him, is "Off to the Southwest; or, The adventures of the twin Manlys," published in Golden Days in August 1884 (and reprinted in November 1899 as by Franklin Calkins).*

MAGAZINE PUBLICATIONS

157M   "Alvin Chase's search; or, The mystery of Cedar Cove." Golden Days, vol. 11, no. 46–vol. 12, no. 4, Oct. 11–Dec. 20, 1890.

   Reprinted as by "the author of 'Clearing His Name'" in Golden Days, Sept. 11–Nov. 12, 1904 (158M). ("Clearing his name" was serialized in Golden Days twice: in 1891, with Ralph Hamilton as author [159M], and in 1903 with Edward Stratemeyer as author [265M].)

158M   "Alvin Chase's search; or, The mystery of Cedar Cove." Golden Days, vol. 25, no. 45–vol. 26, no. 1, Sept. 11–Nov. 12, 1904.

   Published with the author listed as "the author of 'Clearing His Name.'" ("Clearing his name" appeared in Golden Days twice: with Ralph Hamilton as author in 1891 [159M], and with Edward Stratemeyer as author in 1903 [265M].) First published with Ralph Hamilton listed as author in Golden Days, Oct. 11–Dec. 20, 1890 (157M).

159M   "Clearing his name: A midwinter story." Golden Days, vol. 12, nos. 39–45, Aug. 22–Oct. 3, 1891.

   Reprinted with Edward Stratemeyer listed as author in Golden Days, Feb. 21–April 4, 1903 (265M).

160MQ   "The hermit's protege; or, The mystery of Wind Ridge." Golden Days, vol. 13, nos. 4–14, Dec. 19, 1891–Feb. 27, 1892.

   Reprinted with Dr. Willard MacKenzie listed as author in Golden Days, Nov. 14, 1903–Jan. 23, 1904 (200MQ).

161M   "Judge Dockett's grandson." Golden Days, vol. 13, nos. 33–43, July 9–Sept. 17, 1892.

   Reprinted with the author listed as "the author of 'Captain Bob's Secret'" in Golden Days, Oct. 27, 1906–Jan. 5, 1907 (271M). ("Captain Bob's secret" was serialized twice in Golden Days: in 1890 with Edward Stratemeyer listed as author [263M], and in 1905 with the author given as "the author of 'Clearing His Name'" (264M). "Clearing his name" also appeared in Golden Days twice—in 1891 with Ralph Hamilton as author [159M], and in 1903 with Edward Stratemeyer as author [265M].)

---

* Because of this, Franklin Calkins is sometimes listed as a Stratemeyer pseudonym. This is highly unlikely. There was, however, a real Franklin Calkins (1857–1928) who wrote Western adventure stories.

162M   "Paul Raymond's rovings; or, In quest of name and fortune."
Golden Days, vol. 16, nos. 36-46, July 27-Oct. 5, 1895.

> No. 36 lists Ralph Hamilton as author; nos. 37-46 show the author as
> Edward Stratemeyer (276M).

Robert W. Hamilton

The Stratemeyer Syndicate pseudonym Robert W. Hamilton was used for only
one book, Belinda of the Red Cross.

OTHER PUBLICATIONS

163N   Belinda of the Red Cross.*   (Sully & Kleinteich, 1917; A. L. Burt,
1918; World).

> The first two editions were illustrated by A. O. Scott.

Alice Dale Hardy

Alice Dale Hardy was the Stratemeyer Syndicate pseudonym that appeared on
two children's series, the three-volume FLYAWAYS and the six-volume RIDDLE
CLUB series, published by Grosset & Dunlap from 1924-1929.

SERIES PUBLICATIONS

164S   FLYAWAYS

Volumes: 3
Printed: 1925
Publisher: Grosset & Dunlap
Illustrator: Walter S. Rogers, vols. 1-3
Source of annotations: Grosset & Dunlap advertisements [G&D]
Additional information: This was the only fantasy series (excluding science
    fiction) written by the Stratemeyer Syndicate that featured humans as
    the main characters. (Two other series, Richard Barnum's KNEETIME ANI-
    MAL STORIES [026S] and Laura Lee Hope's MAKE-BELIEVE STORIES [185S] re-
    lated the adventures of animals and toys, respectively.) The books
    were published without subtitles.

---

*   No subtitle.

Series description [G&D]: "A splendid new line of interesting tales for
the little ones, introducing many of the well known characters of fairyland in a series of novel adventures. The Flyaways are a happy family
and every little girl and boy will want to know them."

164S.1   The Flyaways and Cinderella. (Grosset & Dunlap, 1925).

[G&D]: "How the Flyaways went to visit Cinderella only to find that
Cinderella's Prince had been carried off by the Three Robbers, Rumbo,
Hibo, and Jobo. 'I'll rescue him!' cried Pa Flyaway and then set out
for the stronghold of the robbers. A splendid continuation of the
original story of Cinderella."

164S.2   The Flyaways and Little Red Riding Hood. (Grosset & Dunlap, 1925).

[G&D]: "On their way to visit Little Red Riding Hood the Flyaways fell
in with Tommy Tucker and The Old Woman Who Lived in a Shoe. They told
Tommy about the Magic Button on Red Riding Hood's cloak. How the wicked
Wolf stole the Magic Button and how the wolves plotted to eat up Little
Red Riding Hood and all her family, and how the Flyaways and King Cole
sent the wolves flying, makes a story no children will want to miss."

164S.3   The Flyaways and Goldilocks. (Grosset & Dunlap, 1925).

[G&D]: "The Flyaways wanted to see not only Goldilocks but also the
Three Bears and they took a remarkable journey through the air to do
so. Tommy even rode on a Rocket and met the monstrous Blue Frog. When
they arrived at Goldilock's house they found that the Three Bears had
been there before them and mussed everything up, much to Goldilock's
despair. 'We must drive those bears out of the country!' said Pa
Flyaway. Then they journeyed underground to the Yellow Palace, and oh!
so many things happened after that!"

165S   RIDDLE CLUB

Volumes: 6
Printed: 1924-1929
Publisher: Grosset & Dunlap
Illustrator: Walter S. Rogers, vols. 1-6
Source of annotations: Grosset & Dunlap advertisements [G&D]
Series description [G&D]: "Here is as ingenious a series of books for little folks as has ever appeared since 'Alice in Wonderland.' The idea
of the Riddle books is a little group of children--three girls and three
boys decide to form a riddle club. Each book is full of the adventures'
and doings of these six youngsters, but as an added attraction each book
is filled with a lot of the best riddles you ever heard."

165S.1   The Riddle Club at home: How the club was formed, what riddles
were asked and how the members solved a mystery. (Grosset & Dunlap, 1924).

[G&D]: "An absorbing tale that all boys and girls will enjoy reading.
How the members of the club fixed up a clubroom in the Larue barn, and
how they, later on, helped solve a most mysterious happening, and how
one of the members won a valuable prize, is told in a manner to please
every young reader."

165S.2   The Riddle Club in camp: How they journeyed to the lake, what happened around the campfire and how a forgotten name was recalled. (Grosset & Dunlap, 1924).

> [G&D]: "The club members went into camp on the edge of a beautiful lake. Here they had rousing good times swimming, boating and around the campfire. They fell in with a mysterious old man known as The Hermit of Triangle Island. Nobody knew his real name or where he came from until the propounding of a riddle solved these perplexing questions."

165S.3   The Riddle Club through the holidays: The club and its doings, how the riddles were solved and what the snowman revealed. (Grosset & Dunlap, 1924).

> [G&D]: "This volume takes in a great number of winter sports, including skating and sledding and the building of a huge snowman. It also gives the particulars of how the club treasurer lost the dues entrusted to his care and what the melting of the great snowman revealed."

165S.4   The Riddle Club at Sunrise Beach: How they toured to the shore, what happened on the sand and how they solved the mystery of Rattlesnake Island. (Grosset & Dunlap, 1925).

> [G&D]: "This volume tells how the club journeyed to the seashore and how they not only kept up their riddles but likewise had good times on the sand and in the water. Once they got lost in a fog and are marooned on an island. Here they made a discovery that greatly pleased the folks at home."

165S.5   The Riddle Club at Shadybrook: Why they went there, what happened on the way and what occurred during their absence from home. (Grosset & Dunlap, 1926).

165S.6   The Riddle Club at Rocky Falls: How they went up the river, what adventures they had in the woods and how they solved the mystery of the deserted hotel. (Grosset & Dunlap, 1929).

Hal Harkaway

Edward Stratemeyer was one of the writers whose stories were printed in Golden Hours under the pen name Hal Harkaway. One Harkaway story was definitely written by Stratemeyer; another is considered possible, but not proven.

MAGAZINE PUBLICATIONS

166MQ   "Bob Ready, reporter; or, The mystery of the poisoned dagger." Golden Hours, nos. 686-693, March 23-May 11, 1901.

167M   "Holland, the destroyer; or, America against the world." <u>Golden</u>
<u>Hours</u>, nos. 669-676, Nov. 24, 1900–Jan. 12, 1901.

> Reprinted in book form in 1902 by Thompson & Thomas as <u>The young naval</u>
> <u>captain; or, The war of all nations</u> by Captain Ralph Bonehill (070N).
> Also reprinted as <u>Oscar the naval cadet; or, Under the sea</u>, still with
> Bonehill as author, as vol. 1 of Donohue's LAND AND SEA series (058P.1).

Ralph Harrington

Ralph Harrington is not a proven Stratemeyer pseudonym. Three stories that
appeared in <u>Bright Days</u> in 1896 as by Ralph Harrington are thought to be
possible Stratemeyer titles; none are proven. One of the three was later
included in <u>The rival bicyclists</u>, which was written by Edward Stratemeyer
and published under the name Captain Ralph Bonehill (047S.3X; 049P.1X;
065S.1).

MAGAZINE PUBLICATIONS

168MQ   "Lost in a coal mine." <u>Bright Days</u>, no. 2, May 1896.

> Later reprinted as part of <u>The rival bicyclists; or, Fun and adven-</u>
> <u>ture on the wheel</u> by Captain Ralph Bonehill. The book was published
> in 1897 as vol. 9 of W. L. Allison's BOUND TO WIN series (047S.3X),
> and later as vol. 1 of Allison's YOUNG SPORTSMAN'S series and vol. 1
> of Donohue's YOUNG SPORTSMAN'S series (065S.1), and as vol. 14 of Dono-
> hue's BOYS' LIBERTY series* (049P.1X). All editions had the same author
> and title. The title story was first published as "Joe Johnson, the
> bicycle wonder; or, Riding for the championship of the world" by Roy
> Rockwood in <u>Young Sports of America</u>, June 1–July 13, 1895 (218M).

169MQ   "On to Cuba; or, Nellie and Nat Denham in search of their father."
<u>Bright Days</u>, nos. 14-18, Oct. 31–Nov. 28, 1896.

> Reprinted as a short story in G. A. Henty's <u>The golden canyon</u>, published
> by Mershon in 1899 (171NQ).

170MQ   "The stone chest; or, The secret of Cedar Island." <u>Bright Days</u>,
nos. 7-12, Sept. 12–Oct. 17, 1896.

> Reprinted as a short story in G. A. Henty's <u>The golden canyon</u>, published
> by Mershon in 1899 (171NQ), and later by Donohue (172NQ).

---

* Subtitle missing.

OTHER PUBLICATIONS

171NQ   The golden canyon. (Mershon, 1899).

> By G. A. Henty. Contains "The golden canyon" by G. A. Henty, and "The stone chest" and "On to Cuba" by Ralph Harrington. "The stone chest" was originally published as "The stone chest; or, The secret of Cedar Island" in Bright Days, Sept. 12-Oct. 17, 1896 (170MQ); "On to Cuba" was originally published as "On to Cuba; or, Nellie and Nat Denham in search of their father" in Bright Days, Oct. 31-Nov. 28, 1896 (171MQ).

172NQ   The golden canyon. (Donohue).

> By G. A. Henty. Contains "The golden canyon" by G. A. Henty, "The stone chest" by Ralph Harrington, and "The solid muldoon." "The stone chest" was originally published as "The stone chest; or, The secret of Cedar Island" in Bright Days, Sept. 12-Oct. 17, 1896 (170MQ).

Mabel C. Hawley

Mabel C. Hawley was a Stratemeyer Syndicate pseudonym assigned to one series for children, the FOUR LITTLE BLOSSOMS. The series was published by three different publishers but never went beyond seven volumes.

SERIES PUBLICATIONS

173S   FOUR LITTLE BLOSSOMS

Volumes: 7
Printed: 1920-1930
Publisher: George Sully & Company, vols. 1-5
            Cupples & Leon Company, vols. 6-7
Reprint publisher: Cupples & Leon Company, vols. 1-5
                    Saalfield Publishing Co., vols. 1-6
Illustrator: Robert Gaston Herbert, vols. 1-3
              Walter F. Rodgers, vol. 4
              H, vol. 7
Source of annotations: Cupples & Leon Company advertisments [C&L]
Additional information: Books were published without subtitles.

173S.1   Four little Blossoms at Brookside Farm. (Sully, 1920; Cupples & Leon; Saalfield, 1938).

> [C&L]: "Mother called them her Four Little Blossoms, but Daddy Blossom called them Bobby, Meg, and the twins. The twins, Twaddles and Dot, were a comical pair and always getting into mischief. The children had heaps of fun around the big farm."

173S.2   Four little Blossoms at Oak Hill School. (Sully, 1920; Cupples & Leon; Saalfield, 1938).

[C&L]: "In the Fall, Bobby and Meg had to go to school. It was good fun, for Miss Mason was a kind teacher. Then the twins insisted on going to school, too, and their appearance quite upset the class. In school something very odd happened."

173S.3   Four little Blossoms and their winter fun. (Sully, 1920; Cupples & Leon; Saalfield, 1938).

[C&L]: "Winter came and with it lots of ice and snow, and oh! what fun the Blossoms had skating and sledding. And once Bobby and Meg went on an errand and got lost in a sudden snowstorm."

173S.4   Four little Blossoms on Appletree Island. (Sully, 1921; Cupples & Leon; Saalfield, 1938).

[C&L]: "The Four Little Blossoms went to a beautiful island in the middle of a big lake and there had a grand time on the water and in the woods. And in a deserted cabin they found some letters which helped an old man to find his missing wife."

173S.5   Four little Blossoms through the holidays. (Sully, 1922; Cupples & Leon; Saalfield).

[C&L]: "The story starts at Thanksgiving. They went skating and coasting, and they built a wonderful snowman, and one day Bobby and his chums visited a carpenter shop on the sly, and that night the shop burnt down, and there was trouble for the boys."

173S.6   Four little Blossoms at Sunrise Beach. (Cupples & Leon, 1929; Saalfield).

[C&L]: "The Four Little Blossoms start on the happy road to fun and vacation at Sunrise Beach. Their delightful adventures will amuse and interest you."

173S.7   Four little Blossoms indoors and out. (Cupples & Leon, 1930).

Brooks Henderley

A short-lived Stratemeyer Syndicate pseudonym, Brooks Henderley lasted for two years and three books.

SERIES PUBLICATIONS

174S   Y.M.C.A. BOYS

Volumes: 3
Printed: 1916-1917
Publisher: Cupples & Leon Company
Illustrator: Walter S. Rogers, vol. 1
              R. Emmett Owen, vols. 2-3
Source of annotations: Cupples & Leon Company advertisements [C&L]
Series description [C&L]: "This new series relates the doings of a wide-
    awake boys' club of the Y.M.C.A., full of good times and every-day
    practical Christianity. Clean, elevating and full of fun and vigor,
    books that should be read by every boy."

174S.1   The Y.M.C.A. boys of Cliffwood; or, The struggle for the Holwell
prize. (Cupples & Leon, 1916).

    [C&L]: "Telling how the boys of Cliffwood were a wild set and how, on
    Hallowe'en, they turned the home town topsy-turvy. This led to an or-
    ganization of a boys' department in the local Y.M.C.A. When the lads
    realized what was being done for them, they joined in the movement with
    vigor and did all they could to help the good cause. To raise funds
    they gave a minstrel show and other entertainments, and a number of
    them did their best to win a gold medal offered by a local minister
    who was greatly interested in the work of up-building youthful char-
    acter."

174S.2   The Y.M.C.A. boys on Bass Island; or, The mystery of Russabaga
Camp. (Cupples & Leon, 1916).

    [C&L]: "Summer was at hand, and at a meeting of the boys of the
    Y.M.C.A. of Cliffwood, it was decided that a regular summer camp should
    be instituted. This was located at a beautiful spot on Bass Island,
    and there the lads went boating, swimming, fishing and tramping to
    their heart's [sic] content. There were a great many surprises, but
    in the end the boys managed to clear up a mystery of long standing.
    Incidentally, the volume gives a clear insight into the workings of
    the now justly popular summer camps of the Y.M.C.A., throughout the
    United States."

174S.3   The Y.M.C.A. boys at football; or, Lively doings on and off the
gridiron. (Cupples & Leon, 1917).

    [C&L]: "This volume will add greatly to the deserved success of this
    well-written series. The Y.M.C.A. boys are plucky lads--clean-minded
    and true as steel. They have many ups and downs, but in the end they
    'win out' in the best meaning of the term."

D. T. Henty

D. T. Henty is not a proven Stratemeyer pseudonym. One magazine story
and the resulting book may have been the work of Edward Stratemeyer.

MAGAZINE PUBLICATIONS

175MQ   "Malcolm, the waterboy; or, A mystery of old London." Bright
Days, nos. 15-22, Nov. 7-Dec. 26, 1896.

   Reprinted by Mershon in 1901 (176NQ).

OTHER PUBLICATIONS

176NQ   Malcolm the waterboy; or, A mystery of old London. (Mershon,
1901).

   First published in Bright Days, Nov. 7-Dec. 26, 1896 (175MQ).

Harvey Hicks

Edward Stratemeyer was one of the writers whose boys' stories were serialized in Good News under the pseudonym Harvey Hicks. Early bibliographies
often labeled some of the Mat Merrian and Tom Truxton stories, as well
as a story titled "Ned Purcell, the boy engineer," as possible Stratemeyers,
but research in Street & Smith's records has shown that only two Hicks
stories were actually penned by Edward Stratemeyer: "The tour of the
Zero Club," in 1894 and 1895, and "By pluck alone," in 1895.*
   Both tales were reissued in book form under different pseudonyms.
"The tour of the Zero Club; or, Perils by ice and snow" became The tour of
the Zero Club; or, Adventures amid ice and snow by Captain Ralph Bonehill,
while "By pluck alone; or, Ralph Nelson's upward struggle" was changed to
The young bridge tender; or, Ralph Nelson's upward struggle by Arthur M.
Winfield. The two titles were included in Street & Smith's MEDAL LIBRARY
(059P.1X; 337P.1X), Street & Smith's BOYS' OWN LIBRARY (051P.2X; 333P.3X),
McKay's BOYS' OWN LIBRARY (050P.2X; 332P.3X), and Caldwell's FAMOUS BOOKS
FOR BOYS (054P.1X; 336P.2X). In addition, each received its own series--
though neither series progressed beyond a single title. (Hence, The tour
of the Zero Club was the entire ZERO CLUB series [066S.1], and The young
bridge tender, the entire SILVER LAKE series [340S.1].) The tour of the
Zero Club was also reprinted as part of Street & Smith's ROUND THE WORLD

* Dr. John T. Dizer, Jr., reported some of the findings from J. Randolph
  Cox's research in "Street & Smith Box M58" (Dime Novel Round-Up 46,
  no. 4 [Aug. 1977]: 78-84).

LIBRARY (063P.1X; 063P.2X). The two stories, then, were reprinted twelve times, in seven different series.

MAGAZINE PUBLICATIONS

177M   "By pluck alone; or, Ralph Nelson's upward struggle." Good News, vol. 11, nos. 277-289, Aug. 24-Nov. 16, 1895.

Reprinted in book form as The young bridge-tender; or, Ralph Nelson's upward struggle by Arthur M. Winfield for all editions: as part of Street & Smith's BOYS' OWN LIBRARY (333P.3X), part of McKay's BOYS' OWN LIBRARY (332P.3X), and vol. 1 of Street & Smith's SILVER LAKE series (340S.1), all in 1902; as no. 249 in Street & Smith's paperback MEDAL LIBRARY in 1904 (337P.1X); as part of Caldwell's FAMOUS BOOKS FOR BOYS in 1905 (336P.2X).

178M   "The tour of the Zero Club; or, Perils by ice and snow." Good News, vol. 10, nos. 243-255, Dec. 29, 1894-March 23, 1895.

Reprinted in book form as The tour of the Zero Club; or, Adventures amid ice and snow by Captain Ralph Bonehill for all editions: as part of Street & Smith's BOYS' OWN LIBRARY (051P.2X), part of McKay's BOYS' OWN LIBRARY (050P.2X), and vol. 1 of Street & Smith's ZERO CLUB series (066S.1), all in 1902; as no. 241 in Street & Smith's paperback MEDAL LIBRARY in 1904 (059P.1X); as part of Caldwell's FAMOUS BOOKS FOR BOYS in 1905 (054P.1X); as no. 67* and no. 180* in Street & Smith's paperback ROUND THE WORLD LIBRARY in 1927 and 1931 (063P.1X; 063P.2X).

Grace Brooks Hill

The CORNER HOUSE GIRLS, a thirteen-volume series which ran from 1915 to 1926, was the only series issued under the Stratemeyer Syndicate pseudonym Grace Brooks Hill.

SERIES PUBLICATIONS

179S   CORNER HOUSE GIRLS

Volumes: 13
Printed: 1915-1926
Publisher: Barse & Hopkins
Reprint publisher: Grosset & Dunlap, some vols.**

---

*   Subtitle missing.
**   Grosset & Dunlap reprinted some Barse & Co. series. Volumes 4 and 11 of the CORNER HOUSE GIRLS have been seen in Grosset & Dunlap editions.

Illustrator: R. Emmett Owen, vols. 1-9*
              Thelma Gooch, vols. 10-12*
              Howard L. Hastings, vol. 13
Source of annotations: Barse & Hopkins advertisements [B&H]
Series description [B&H]: "Four girls from eight to fourteen years of age
    receive word that a rich bachelor uncle has died, leaving them the old
    Corner House he occupied. They move into it and then the fun begins.
    What they find and do will provoke many a hearty laugh. Later, they
    enter school and make many friends. One of these invites the girls to
    spend a few weeks at a bungalow owned by her parents, and the adventures
    they meet with make very interesting reading. Clean, wholesome stories
    of humor and adventures, sure to appeal to all young girls."

179S.1   The Corner House girls: How they moved to Milton, what they
found, and what they did. (Barse & Hopkins, 1915).

179S.2   The Corner House girls at school: How they entered, whom they
met, and what they did. (Barse & Hopkins, 1915).

179S.3   The Corner House girls under canvas: How they reached Pleasant
Cove and what happened afterward. (Barse & Hopkins, 1915).

179S.4   The Corner House girls in a play: How they rehearsed, how they
acted, and what the play brought in. (Barse & Hopkins, 1916; Grosset &
Dunlap).

179S.5   The Corner House girls' odd find: Where they made it, and what
the strange discovery led to. (Barse & Hopkins, 1916).

179S.6   The Corner House girls on a tour: Where they went, what they
saw, and what they found. (Barse & Hopkins, 1917).

179S.7   The Corner House girls growing up: What happened first, what
came next, and how it ended. (Barse & Hopkins, 1918).

179S.8   The Corner House girls snowbound: How they went away, what they
discovered, and how it ended. (Barse & Hopkins, 1919).

179S.9   The Corner House girls on a houseboat: How they sailed away,
what happened on the voyage, and what they discovered. (Barse & Hopkins,
1920).

179S.10   The Corner House girls among the gypsies: How they met, what
happened, and how it ended. (Barse & Hopkins, 1921).

179S.11   The Corner House girls on Palm Island: Looking for adventure,
how they found it, and what happened. (Barse & Hopkins, 1922; Grosset &
Dunlap).

179S.12   The Corner House girls solve a mystery: What it was, where it
was, and who found it. (Barse & Hopkins, 1923).

179S.13   The Corner House girls facing the world: Why they had to, how
they did it, and what came of it. (Barse & Hopkins, 1926).

_____
* Grosset & Dunlap volumes, too.

Thomas K. Holmes

The Stratemeyer Syndicate used the name Thomas K. Holmes on two books originally published by G. Sully & Co. in 1919 and 1921, and reprinted by A. L. Burt in 1922 and 1923.

OTHER PUBLICATIONS

180N   The heart of Canyon Pass.* (Sully, 1921; Burt, 1923).

181N   The man from tall timber.* (Sully, 1919; Burt, 1922).

Laura Lee Hope

Far and away the most long-lived and prolific Stratemeyer Syndicate pseudo- nym, Laura Lee Hope "wrote" 164 volumes (excluding reprints and revisions) over a period of seventy-seven years.** All the Laura Lee Hope titles were published as series books and featured either girls, young children of both sexes, or toys as central characters. Her series about young children were the most popular: the BOBBSEY TWINS (1904-), BUNNY BROWN AND HIS SISTER SUE (1916-1931), and the SIX LITTLE BUNKERS (1918-1930) reached a combined total of 110 volumes. The girls' series, the OUTDOOR GIRLS (1913-1933), the MOVING PICTURE GIRLS (1914-1916), and the BLYTHE GIRLS (1925-1932), accounted for forty-two volumes, while the MAKE-BELIEVE series (1920-1923) featuring toys lasted for twelve titles.

Edward Stratemeyer created the pseudonym and all seven series; Lillian and Howard Garis assisted with some volumes in the BOBBSEY TWINS, OUTDOOR GIRLS, SIX LITTLE BUNKERS, and BUNNY BROWN AND HIS SISTER SUE series. Harriet Adams, and later Andrew Svenson and Nancy Axelrad, continued the BOBBSEY TWINS series after Stratemeyer's death.

Grosset & Dunlap was the original publisher for all but seven Laura Lee Hope titles.***

SERIES PUBLICATIONS

182S   BLYTHE GIRLS

Volumes: 12
Printed: 1925-1932

---

*   No subtitle.
**   Some BOBBSEY TWINS books were even copyrighted under Laura Lee Hope.
*** Volumes 1 and 2 of the BOBBSEY TWINS were published by Mershon; volume
     3, by Chatterton-Peck; volumes 73X-76X by Wanderer Books.

Reprint publisher: Whitman Publishing Company, vols. 1-4
Illustrator: Thelma Gooch, vols. 1-12
Source of annotations: Grosset & Dunlap advertisements [G&D]
Additional information: The series followed a pattern: first, a title
    about all three girls, followed by books centering on Margy, Rose, and
    Helen (in that order), then the cycle was repeated.
Series description [G&D]: "These stories relate the experiences of the
    three Blythe girls who were left alone to make their way in the big
    city of New York. Every young girl will want to know how they suc-
    ceeded."

182S.1   The Blythe girls: Helen, Margy and Rose; or, Facing the great
world. (Grosset & Dunlap, 1925; Whitman).

    [G&D]: "The Blythe girls, three in number, were left alone in New York
    City. Helen, who went in for art and music, kept the little flat up-
    town, while Margy, just out of a business school, obtained a position
    as a private secretary and Rose, plain spoken and businesslike, took
    what she called a 'job' in a department store."

182S.2   The Blythe girls: Margy's queer inheritance; or, The worth of
a name. (Grosset & Dunlap, 1925; Whitman).

    [G&D]: "The girls had a peculiar old aunt and when she died she left
    an unusual inheritance. This tale continues the struggles of all the
    girls for existence."

182S.3   The Blythe girls: Rose's great problem; or, Face to face with a
crisis. (Grosset & Dunlap, 1925; Whitman).

    [G&D]: "Rose, still at work in the big department store, is one day
    faced with the greatest problem of her life. A tale of mystery as well
    as exciting girlish happenings."

182S.4   The Blythe girls: Helen's strange boarder; or, The girl from
Bronx Park. (Grosset & Dunlap, 1925; Whitman).

    [G&D]: "Helen, out sketching, goes to the assistance of a strange girl,
    whose real identity is a puzzle to all the Blythe girls. Who the girl
    really was comes as a tremendous surprise."

182S.5   The Blythe girls: Three on a vacation; or, The mystery at Peach
Farm. (Grosset & Dunlap, 1925).

    [G&D]: "The girls close their flat and go to the country for two weeks
    --and fall in with all sorts of curious and exciting happenings. How
    they came to the assistance of Joe Morris, and solved a queer mystery,
    is well related."

182S.6   The Blythe girls: Margy's secret mission; or, Exciting days at
Shadymore. (Grosset & Dunlap, 1926).

    [G&D]: "Of course we cannot divulge the big secret, but nevertheless
    the girls as usual have many adventures."

182S.7   The Blythe girls: Rose's odd discovery; or, The search for Irene
Conroy. (Grosset & Dunlap, 1927).

[G&D]: "A very interesting story, telling how Rose aided an old man in the almost hopeless search for his daughter."

182S.8   The Blythe girls: The disappearance of Helen; or, The art shop mystery. (Grosset & Dunlap, 1928).

[G&D]: "Helen calls on the art dealer on business and finds the old fellow has made a wonderful discovery."

182S.9   The Blythe girls; Snowbound in camp; or, The mystery at Elk Lodge. (Grosset & Dunlap, 1929).

[G&D]: "An absorbing tale of winter happenings, full of excitement."

182S.10   The Blythe girls: Margy's mysterious visitor; or, Guarding the Pepper fortune. (Grosset & Dunlap, 1930).

182S.11   The Blythe girls: Rose's hidden talent.* (Grosset & Dunlap, 1931).

182S.12   The Blythe girls: Helen's wonderful mistake; or, The mysterious necklace. (Grosset & Dunlap, 1932).

183S   BOBBSEY TWINS

Volumes: 76**
Printed: 1904-
Publisher: The Mershon Company, vols. 1-2
            Chatterton-Peck Company, vol. 3
            Grosset & Dunlap, vols. 4-72
            Simon & Schuster, Wanderer Books, vols. 73X-76X
Reprint publisher: Chatterton-Peck Company, vols. 1-2
            Grosset & Dunlap, vols. 1-3
            Simon & Schuster, Wanderer Books, vols. 1-3
            M. A. Donohue & Company, vols. 1-3
            Goldsmith Publishing Co., vols. 1-3
            Saalfield Publishing Co., vols. 1-3,
            Whitman Publishing Company, vols. 1-3
            Wonder Books, vol. 1
Illustrator: A [enclosed in a triangle}, vol. 1
            Charles Nuttall, vols. 2-3
            anonymous, vol. 5
            Walter S. Rogers, vols. 1, 8-15, 17, 22-24*** (Grosset &
                Dunlap)
            Marie Schubert, vols. 1-2, 4, 25, 27-30, 32-37*** (Grosset
                & Dunlap)
            Margaret Temple Braley, vol. 26
            C. G., vol. 44
            Gloria Singer, vol. 73X
            Ruth Sanderson, vols. 74X-76X

---

*   No subtitle.
**   As of 1981. The series is still in progress.
*** Possibly other volumes as well.

Illustrator: Martha E. Miller, vols. 1-3 (Saalfield)
                 Henry E. Vallely, vol. 1 (Whitman, 1940)
                 Janet Laura Scott, vols. 1-3 (Whitman)
                 Corinne Dillon, vol. 1 (Wonder Books)
Source of annotations: Grosset & Dunlap advertisements [G&D], series de-
                 scription, vols. 4-8
                 Library of Congress cataloguing in publication data
                 [LC], vols. 18-20, 24, 62-64, 66-70, 73X-76X
Additional information: The publishing history of the BOBBSEY TWINS is an
impressive one. Three-quarters of a century old in 1979, the BOBBSEY
Twins has the most volumes, the most reprint publishers, the most title
changes, the most revisions of a single volume, and the longest run of
any Stratemeyer or Stratemeyer Syndicate series. The series has sold
roughly 50,000,000 copies and has been translated into Dutch, German,
and other languages.

     The BOBBSEY TWINS began in 1904, when Edward Stratemeyer wrote The
Bobbsey twins; or, Merry days indoors and out (the only BOBBSEY TWINS
book with a subtitle). Mershon published the first volume and its
sequel, The Bobbsey twins in the country, in 1904; a third title was
added in 1907 after Chatterton-Peck became the publisher for the series.
In 1908, following legal action between Mershon, Stitt, Chatterton-Peck,
and Edward Stratemeyer, Grosset & Dunlap acquired the rights to the
series, adding a fourth volume in 1913. Fifteen years and sixteen volumes later, in 1928, Grosset & Dunlap published a "new and enlarged"
edition of the first title. During these early years, Lillian Garis
(with some help from her husband, Howard Garis) was assisting with some
titles in the series.

     The BOBBSEY TWINS flourished, and in 1940 Donohue and Saalfield
(and possibly Goldsmith) published editions of the first three volumes.*
In 1950, Whitman reprinted the first three books, and Grosset & Dunlap
issued revised editions of the same three volumes. By 1954, when Whitman again reprinted volumes 1, 2, and 3, the series had reached forty-
eight volumes. At least fifteen of these were written by Harriet Adams
(volumes 33, and 35 through 48).

     Like the HARDY BOYS (106S) and NANCY DREW (193S), the BOBBSEY TWINS
underwent extensive revision in the 1950s, 1960s, and 1970s. Most of
the first twenty-five titles were updated, and, in some cases, almost
entirely rewritten;** even the 1950 editions of the first three books
were revised again in 1961 and 1962. The two pairs of BOBBSEY TWINS
jumped from ages four and eight to ages six and twelve; the roles of
some characters were altered; ethnic slurs, dated references, and extraneous material were removed; the length of the books was reduced by
about one-fifth. Starting in 1960, the titles were often changed, too,
occasionally merely by adding the word "mystery" or "adventure" to the
existing title. Harriet Adams was responsible for some of the revised
editions, including volumes 6 and 14.

     Not all of the earlier titles were updated; instead, many were
allowed to go out of print. A Grosset & Dunlap catalogue for 1979-1980
lists the "complete collection" as only forty-nine books: volumes 1-20,

*   Whitman also issued an edition of volume 1 in 1940.
**   The Bobbsey twins' adventures with Baby May (originally titled The Bobbsey twins and Baby May) is an example of one of the more drastic revisions. The original had the Bobbsey twins discovering and caring for
an abandoned infant; the revised edition concerns a theft and a stolen
elephant.

24-25, 27, and 49-72. Some of these titles were written by Stratemeyer
Syndicate partners Andrew Svenson and Nancy Axelrad.

SCHEDULE OF REVISIONS OF THE BOBBSEY TWINS TITLES

BY YEAR OF REVISION:

Year of revision	Volume number	Year of revision	Volume number
1950	1,2,3	1965	11
1955	6,16	1966	13
1959	10	1967	14
1960	5,8,9,15,25	1968	17,18,19
1961	1,2	1969	--
1962	3,4,24	1970	--
1963	7,12	1971	20
1964	--		

BY VOLUME NUMBER:

Volume number	Year of revision	Volume number	Year of revision
1	1928,1950,1961	12	1963
2	1950,1961	13	1966
3	1950,1962	14	1967
4	1962	15	1960
5	1960	16	1955
6	1955	17	1968
7	1963	18	1968
8	1960	19	1968
9	1960	20	1971
10	1959	24	1962
11	1965	25	1960

In 1979 Wanderer Books, Simon & Schuster's juvenile imprint, issued
commemorative editions of the first three titles, using the original
texts and illustrations. The following year marked the first paperback
editions of the BOBBSEY TWINS--technically, volumes 73, 74, and 75 in
the series, but renumbered by Wanderer Books as volumes 1, 2, and 3.
    Illustrators: The Mershon, Chatterton-Peck, and early Grosset &
Dunlap editions of The Bobbsey twins all had the same illustrations,
signed with an A enclosed in a triangle. The Bobbsey twins in the
country appeared in Mershon, Chatterton-Peck, and early Grosset & Dunlap editions with artwork by Charles Nuttall; the Chatterton-Peck and
early Grosset & Dunlap editions of The Bobbsey twins at the seashore
also had Nuttall illustrations.
    Walter S. Rogers illustrated many (but not all) of the BOBBSEY
TWINS titles published by Grosset & Dunlap from 1916 to 1931. During
this time he also reillustrated the first volume--possibly in 1928,
for his artwork appeared in the "new and enlarged edition" published
that year. From 1932 until at least 1944, Marie Schubert provided
drawings for many (but not all) of the volumes Grosset & Dunlap added
to the series; she also reillustrated some of the earlier titles for
Grosset & Dunlap, including the first two volumes.
    In the late 1940s or early 1950s, the Grosset & Dunlap BOBBSEY
TWINS BOOKS began to appear regularly with unsigned illustrations;

when the books were revised, they received new artwork, but the artists
still remained anonymous. In 1980, when Wanderer Books began to publish the series, the illustrators were again named: Gloria Singer for
the first Wanderer title and Ruth Sanderson for the others.

The first three BOBBSEY TWINS titles were also reprinted by other
publishing houses, generally with new illustrations. The 1940 Whitman
edition of The Bobbsey Twins had illustrations by Henry E. Vallely;
editions from 1950 and after were reillustrated by Janet Laura Scott
(for not only the first volume, but also the second and third titles).
Martha E. Miller illustrated the Saalfield editions; the Goldsmith
titles were published without illustrations. Only the Wanderer commemorative editions used the original Mershon and Chatterton-Peck
artwork.

Except for the first volume, books were published without subtitles.
An R denotes an annotation for a revised edition.

Series description [G&D]: "Copyright publications which cannot be obtained
elsewhere. Books that charm the hearts of the little ones, and of
which they never tire. Many of the adventures are comical in the extreme, and all the accidents that ordinarily happen to youthful personages happened to these many-sided little mortals. Their haps and
mishaps make decidedly entertaining reading."

[G&D] [R]: "Meet Freddie, Flossie, Nan and Bert, the two sets of
twins, as they go from one exciting adventure to another."

183S.1   The Bobbsey twins; or, Merry days indoors and out. (Mershon,
1904, 1905; Chatterton-Peck, ca1907; Grosset & Dunlap, ca1908, 1928, 1950,
1961, 196-?; Donohue, ca1940; Goldsmith; Saalfield, 1940; Whitman, 1940,
1950, 1954?; Wonder Books, 1954; Wanderer, 1979).

1928 Grosset & Dunlap edition "new and enlarged;" 1950 edition revised
and published without the subtitle; 1961 edition revised and retitled
The Bobbsey twins of Lakeport. Also published by Grosset & Dunlap
in The Bobbsey twins mystery stories, containing The Bobbsey twins of
Lakeport, The Bobbsey twins' adventure in the country (183S.2), and
The Bobbsey twins' secret at the seashore (183S.3). Donohue edition
published as a "jumbo juvenile," with three books in one: The Bobbsey
twins; The Bobbsey twins in the country (183S.2); The Bobbsey twins at
the seashore (183S.3). 1940 Whitman edition published as "Laura Lee
Hope's The Bobbsey twins," retold by Bennett Kline in 96 pages. Wonder
Books edition published as Meet the Bobbsey twins, as Wonder Books no.
623. Wanderer edition published as part of a three-book boxed set,
including The Bobbsey twins in the country (183S.2) and The Bobbsey
twins at the seashore (183S.3); all three books used the original texts
and illustrations.

183S.2   The Bobbsey twins in the country. (Mershon, 1904; Chatterton-
Peck, 1907; Grosset & Dunlap, ca1908, 1950, 1961, 196-?; Donohue, ca1940;
Goldsmith; Saalfield, 1940; Whitman, 1950, 1954; Wanderer, 1979).

1950 Grosset & Dunlap edition revised; 1961 Grosset & Dunlap edition
revised and retitled as The Bobbsey twins' adventure in the country.
Also published by Grosset & Dunlap in The Bobbsey twins mystery stories,
containing The Bobbsey twins of Lakeport (183S.1), The Bobbsey twins'
adventure in the country, and The Bobbsey twins' secret at the seashore
(183S.3). Donohue edition published as a "jumbo juvenile," with three
books in one: The Bobbsey twins (183S.1), The Bobbsey twins in the

country, and The Bobbsey twins at the seashore (183S.3). Wanderer edition published as part of a three-book boxed set, including The Bobbsey twins (183S.1) and The Bobbsey twins at the seashore (183S.3); all three books used the original texts and illustrations.

183S.3   The Bobbsey twins at the seashore. (Chatterton-Peck, 1907; Grosset & Dunlap, ca1908; 1950, 1962, 196-?; Donohue, ca1940; Goldsmith; Saalfield, 1940; Whitman, 1950, 1954; Wanderer, 1979).

1950 Grosset & Dunlap edition revised; 1962 edition revised and retitled The Bobbsey twins' secret at the seashore. Also published by Grosset & Dunlap in The Bobbsey twins mystery stories, containing The Bobbsey twins (183S.1), The Bobbsey twins' adventure in the country (183S.2), and The Bobbsey twins' secret at the seashore. Donohue edition published as a "jumbo juvenile," with three books in one: The Bobbsey twins (183S.1), The Bobbsey twins in the country (183S.2), and The Bobbsey twins at the seashore. Wanderer edition published as part of a three-book boxed set, including The Bobbsey twins (183S.1) and The Bobbsey twins in the country (183S.2); all three books used the original texts and illustrations.

183S.4   The Bobbsey twins at school. (Grosset & Dunlap, 1913, 1941,* 1962).

1962 edition titled The Bobbsey twins' mystery at school.
    [G&D]: "Telling how they got home from the seashore; went to school and were promoted, and of their many trials and tribulations."

183S.5   The Bobbsey twins at Snow Lodge. (Grosset & Dunlap, 1913, 1960).

1960 edition titled The Bobbsey twins and the mystery at Snow Lodge.
    [G&D]: "Telling of the winter holidays and of the many fine times and adventures the twins had at a winter lodge in the woods."

183S.6   The Bobbsey twins on a houseboat. (Grosset & Dunlap, 1915, 1955)

    [G&D]: "Mr. Bobbsey obtains a houseboat, and the whole family go off on a tour."

183S.7   The Bobbsey twins at Meadow Brook. (Grosset & Dunlap, 1915, 1963)

1963 edition titled The Bobbsey twins' mystery at Meadowbrook.
    [G&D]: "The young folks visit the farm again and have plenty of good times and several adventures."

183S.8   The Bobbsey twins at home. (Grosset & Dunlap, 1916, 1920?, 1944, 1960).

1960 edition titled The Bobbsey twins' big adventure at home.
    [G&D]: "The twins get into all sorts of trouble--and out again-- also bring aid to a poor family."

183S.9   The Bobbsey twins in a great city. (Grosset & Dunlap, 1917, 1945 1960).

---

* Recopyrighted.

1960 edition titled <u>The Bobbsey twins' search in the great city</u>.

183S.10   The Bobbsey twins on Blueberry Island. (Grosset & Dunlap, 1917, 1945,* 1959).

183S.11   The Bobbsey twins on the deep blue sea. (Grosset & Dunlap, 1918, 1946,* 1965).

1965 edition titled <u>The Bobbsey twins' mystery on the deep blue sea</u>.

183S.12   The Bobbsey twins in Washington. (Grosset & Dunlap, 1919, 1938?, 1945,* 1963).

1963 edition titled <u>The Bobbsey twins' adventure in Washington</u>.

183S.13   The Bobbsey twins in the great West. (Grosset & Dunlap, 1920, 1966).

1966 edition titled <u>The Bobbsey twins' visit to the great West</u>.

183S.14   The Bobbsey twins at Cedar Camp. (Grosset & Dunlap, 1921, 1967).

1967 edition titled <u>The Bobbsey twins and the Cedar Camp mystery</u>.

183S.15   The Bobbsey twins at the county fair. (Grosset & Dunlap, 1922, 1960).

1960 edition titled <u>The Bobbsey twins and the county fair mystery</u>.

183S.16   The Bobbsey twins camping out. (Grosset & Dunlap, 1923, 1955).

183S.17   The Bobbsey twins and Baby May. (Grosset & Dunlap, 1924, 1968).

1968 edition titled <u>The Bobbsey twins' adventures with Baby May</u>.

183S.18   The Bobbsey twins keeping house. (Grosset & Dunlap, 1925, 1968).

1968 edition titled <u>The Bobbsey twins and the play house secret</u>.
    [LC]: [R]"The toy the Bobbsey twins buy as a Valentine gift soon puts them on the trail of two men conducting a fradulent antique business."

183S.19   The Bobbsey twins at Cloverbank. (Grosset & Dunlap, 1926, 1968).

1968 edition titled <u>The Bobbsey twins and the four-leaf clover mystery</u>.
    [LC]: [R]"The Bobbsey twins stay on a Pennsylvania farm and become involved with a mysteriously vanishing prowler and a search for a golden birthday present. "

183S.20   The Bobbsey twins at Cherry Corners. (Grosset & Dunlap, 1927, 1971).

1971 edition titled <u>The Bobbsey twins' mystery at Cherry Corners</u>.
    [LC]: [R]"A vacation turns into an investigation of a haunted school house and a chase after a kidnapped monkey."

---

*   Recopyrighted.

183S.21   The Bobbsey twins and their schoolmates. (Grosset & Dunlap, 1928).

183S.22   The Bobbsey twins treasure hunting. (Grosset & Dunlap, 1929).

183S.23   The Bobbsey twins at Spruce Lake. (Grosset & Dunlap, 1930).

183S.24   The Bobbsey twins' wonderful secret. (Grosset & Dunlap, 1931, 1962).

     1962 edition titled The Bobbsey twins' wonderful winter secret.
        [LC]: [R]"When the Bobbsey twins ponder the perfect gift for
     Mother and Father, they decide on Project Santa Claus."

183S.25   The Bobbsey twins at the circus. (Grosset & Dunlap, 1932, 1960).

     1960 edition titled The Bobbsey twins and the circus surprise.

183S.26   The Bobbsey twins on an airplane trip. (Grosset & Dunlap, 1933).

183S.27   The Bobbsey twins solve a mystery. (Grosset & Dunlap, 1934).

183S.28   The Bobbsey twins on a ranch. (Grosset & Dunlap, 1935).

183S.29   The Bobbsey twins in Eskimo land. (Grosset & Dunlap, 1936).

183S.30   The Bobbsey twins in a radio play. (Grosset & Dunlap, 1937).

183S.31   The Bobbsey twins at Windmill Cottage. (Grosset & Dunlap, 1938).

183S.32   The Bobbsey twins at Lighthouse Point. (Grosset & Dunlap, 1939).

183S.33   The Bobbsey twins at Indian Hollow. (Grosset & Dunlap, 1940).

183S.34   The Bobbsey twins at the ice carnival. (Grosset & Dunlap, 1941).

183S.35   The Bobbsey twins in the land of cotton. (Grosset & Dunlap, 1942, 1957?).

183S.36   The Bobbsey twins in Echo Valley. (Grosset & Dunlap, 1943).

183S.37   The Bobbsey twins on the pony trail. (Grosset & Dunlap, 1944).

183S.38   The Bobbsey twins at mystery mansion. (Grosset & Dunlap, 1945).

183S.39   The Bobbsey twins at Sugar Maple Hill. (Grosset & Dunlap, 1946).

183S.40   The Bobbsey twins in Mexico. (Grosset & Dunlap, 1947).

183S.41   The Bobbsey twins' toy shop. (Grosset & Dunlap, 1948).

183S.42   The Bobbsey twins in Tulip Land. (Grosset & Dunlap, 1949).

183S.43   The Bobbsey twins in Rainbow Valley. (Grosset & Dunlap, 1950).

183S.44   The Bobbsey twins' own little railroad. (Grosset & Dunlap, 1951).

183S.45   The Bobbsey twins at Whitesail Harbor. (Grosset & Dunlap, 1952).

183S.46   The Bobbsey twins and the horseshoe riddle. (Grosset & Dunlap, 1953).

183S.47   The Bobbsey twins at Big Bear Pond. (Grosset & Dunlap, 1953).

183S.48   The Bobbsey twins on a bicycle trip. (Grosset & Dunlap, 1954).

183S.49   The Bobbsey twins' own little ferryboat. (Grosset & Dunlap, 1956).

183S.50   The Bobbsey twins at Pilgrim Rock. (Grosset & Dunlap, 1957*).

183S.51   The Bobbsey twins' forest adventure. (Grosset & Dunlap, 1958**).

183S.52   The Bobbsey twins at London Tower. (Grosset & Dunlap, 1959).

183S.53   The Bobbsey twins in the mystery cave. (Grosset & Dunlap, 1960).

183S.54   The Bobbsey twins in volcano land. (Grosset & Dunlap, 1961).

183S.55   The Bobbsey twins and the goldfish mystery. (Grosset & Dunlap, 1962).

183S.56   The Bobbsey twins and the big river mystery. (Grosset & Dunlap, 1963).

183S.57   The Bobbsey twins and the Greek hat mystery. (Grosset & Dunlap, 1964).

183S.58   The Bobbsey twins' search for the green rooster. (Grosset & Dunlap, 1965).

183S.59   The Bobbsey twins and their camel adventure. (Grosset & Dunlap, 1966).

183S.60   The Bobbsey twins' mystery of the king's puppet. (Grosset & Dunlap, 1967).

183S.61   The Bobbsey twins and the secret of Candy Castle. (Grosset & Dunlap, 1968).

183S.62   The Bobbsey twins and the doodlebug mystery. (Grosset & Dunlap, 1969).

[LC]: "When their new friend, an Indian girl, is falsely accused of theft, the Bobbsey twins proceed to find out why."

183S.63   The Bobbsey twins and the talking fox mystery. (Grosset & Dunlap, 1970).

[LC]: "The twins solve a baffling mystery, make several people happy,

---

* Copyrighted 1956.
** Copyrighted 1957.

and return a homeless St. Bernard and a stuffed fox to their rightful owners."

183S.64   The red, white, and blue mystery. (Grosset & Dunlap, 1971).

[LC]: "The Bobbsey twins' vacation in Colonial Williamsburg takes an exciting turn when they catch a thief, discover a howling monster, and find an old American flag hidden during the Revolution."

183S.65   The Bobbsey twins: Dr. Funnybone's secret. (Grosset & Dunlap, 1972).

183S.66   The Bobbsey twins and the tagalong giraffe. (Grosset & Dunlap, 1973).

[LC]: "While on safari to Africa, the Bobbsey twins help capture a gang of poachers."

183S.67   The Bobbsey twins and the Flying Clown. (Grosset & Dunlap, 1974).

[LC]: "The Bobbsey twins travel to World of Fun in Florida where they investigate danger threatening a boy named Howie and his sister, an airplane pilot called the Flying Clown.

183S.68   The Bobbsey twins on the Sun-Moon cruise. (Grosset & Dunlap, 1975).

[LC]: "When the Bobbsey twins take an ocean voyage to view a solar eclipse, they become involved in a mystery concerning damaged equipment and missing papers."

183S.69   The Bobbsey twins: The freedom bell mystery. (Grosset & Dunlap, 1976).

[LC]: "The Bobbsey Twins hope to expose some rather suspicious activities in the Silver Town Mint Center."

183S.70   The Bobbsey twins and the Smoky Mountain mystery. (Grosset & Dunlap, 1977).

[LC]: "The four twin detectives investigate the mysterious thefts and vandalism that threaten to close a Smoky Mountain crafts market."

183S.71   The Bobbsey twins in a TV mystery show. (Grosset & Dunlap, 1978).

183S.72   The Bobbsey twins: The coral turtle mystery. (Grosset & Dunlap, 1979).

183S.73X   The Bobbsey twins: The blue poodle mystery. (Wanderer, 1980).

Issued as volume 1.
    [LC]: "The Bobbsey twins search for a poodle that interrupted a ballet performance and then was stolen."

183S.74X   The Bobbsey twins: The secret in the pirate's cave. (Wanderer, 1980).

Issued as volume 2.
[LC]: "While vacationing in Bermuda, the four Bobbsey twins become involved with a pair of thieves trying to steal valuable artifacts from the local museum."

183S.75X The Bobbsey twins: The dune buggy mystery. (Wanderer, 1980).

Issued as volume 3.
[LC]: "The mystery surrounding a dune buggy bought at the town dump deepens when the vehicle is stolen."

183S.76X The Bobbsey twins: The missing pony mystery. (Wanderer, 1981).

Issued as volume 4.
[LC]: "The Bobbsey twins try to track down a missing pony and saddlebag."

184S   BUNNY BROWN AND HIS SISTER SUE

Volumes: 20
Printed: 1916-1931
Publisher: Grosset & Dunlap
Illustrator: Florence England Nosworthy, vols. 1-7
              Thelma Gooch, vol. 8
              Walter S. Rogers, vols. 9-20
Source of annotations: Grosset & Dunlap advertisements [G&D]
Additional information: Howard Garis assisted with some of the volumes
    in this series, which was created by Edward Stratemeyer.
        Books were published without subtitles.
Series description [G&D]: "These stories by the author of the 'Bobbsey
    Twins' Books are eagerly welcomed by little folks from about five to
    ten years of age. Their eyes fairly dance with delight at the lively
    doings of inquisitive little Bunny Brown and his cunning, trustful
    sister Sue."

184S.1   Bunny Brown and his sister Sue. (Grosset & Dunlap, 1916).

[G&D]: "Bunny was a lively little boy, very inquisitive. When he did
anything, Sue followed his leadership. They had many adventures, some
comical in the extreme."

184S.2   Bunny Brown and his sister Sue on Grandpa's farm. (Grosset &
Dunlap, 1916).

[G&D]: "How the youngsters journeyed to the farm in an auto, and what
good times followed, is realistically told."

184S.3   Bunny Brown and his sister Sue playing circus. (Grosset & Dunlap,
1916).

[G&D]: "First the children gave a little affair, but when they obtained
an old army tent the show was truly grand."

184S.4   Bunny Brown and his sister Sue at Camp Rest-A-While. (Grosset
& Dunlap, 1916).

[G&D]: "The family go into camp on the edge of a beautiful lake, and
Bunny and his sister have more good times and some adventures."

184S.5   Bunny Brown and his sister Sue at Aunt Lu's city home. (Grosset
& Dunlap, 1916).

[G&D]: "The city proved a wonderful place to the little folks. They
took in all the sights and helped a colored girl who had run away from
home."

184S.6   Bunny Brown and his sister Sue in the big woods. (Grosset &
Dunlap, 1917).

[G&D]: "As usual, Bunny gets into plenty of queer situations and Sue
dutifully follows."

184S.7   Bunny Brown and his sister Sue on an auto tour. (Grosset & Dunlap, 1917).

[G&D]: "The youngsters go on a fine trip with their parents and have
a good time."

184S.8   Bunny Brown and his sister Sue and their Shetland pony. (Grosset
& Dunlap, 1918).

184S.9   Bunny Brown and his sister Sue giving a show. (Grosset & Dunlap
1919).

184S.10   Bunny Brown and his sister Sue at Christmas Tree Cove. (Grosset
& Dunlap, 1920).

184S.11   Bunny Brown and his sister Sue in the sunny South. (Grosset &
Dunlap, 1921).

184S.12   Bunny Brown and his sister Sue keeping store. (Grosset & Dunlap
1922).

184S.13   Bunny Brown and his sister Sue and their trick dog. (Grosset &
Dunlap, 1923).

184S.14   Bunny Brown and his sister Sue at a sugar camp. (Grosset & Du
lap, 1924).

184S.15   Bunny Brown and his sister Sue on the rolling ocean. (Grosset
& Dunlap, 1925).

184S.16   Bunny Brown and his sister Sue on Jack Frost Island. (Grosset
& Dunlap, 1927).

184S.17   Bunny Brown and his sister Sue at Shore Acres. (Grosset & Dunlap, 1928).

184S.18   Bunny Brown and his sister Sue at Berry Hill. (Grosset & Dunla
1929).

184S.19   Bunny Brown and his sister Sue at Sky Top. (Grosset & Dunlap, 1930).

184S.20   Bunny Brown and his sister Sue at the summer carnival. (Grosset & Dunlap, 1931).

185S   MAKE-BELIEVE STORIES

Volumes: 12
Printed: 1920-1923
Publisher: Grosset & Dunlap
Illustrator: Harry L. Smith, vols. 1-12
Source of annotations: Grosset & Dunlap advertisements [G&D]
Additional information: Books were published without subtitles.
Series description [G&D]: "In this fascinating line of books Miss Hope
    has the various toys come to life 'when nobody is looking' and she
    puts them through a series of adventures as interesting as can possibly
    be imagined."

185S.1   The story of a sawdust doll. (Grosset & Dunlap, 1920).

    [G&D]: "How the toys held a party at the Toy Counter; how the Sawdust
    Doll was taken to the home of a nice little girl, and what happened to
    her there."

185S.2   The story of a white rocking horse. (Grosset & Dunlap, 1920).

    [G&D]: "He was a bold character and a man purchased him for his son's
    birthday. Once the Horse had to go to the Toy Hospital, and my! what
    sights he saw there."

185S.3   The story of a lamb on wheels. (Grosset & Dunlap, 1920).

    [G&D]: "She was a dainty creature and a sailor bought her and took her
    to a little girl relative and she had a great time."

185S.4   The story of a bold tin soldier. (Grosset & Dunlap, 1920).

    [G&D]: "He was Captain of the Company and marched up and down in the
    store at night. Then he went to live with a little boy and had the
    time of his life."

185S.5   The story of a candy rabbit. (Grosset & Dunlap, 1920).

    [G&D]: "He was continually in danger of losing his life by being eaten
    up. But he had plenty of fun, and often saw his many friends from the
    Toy Counter."

185S.6   The story of a monkey on a stick. (Grosset & Dunlap, 1920).

    [G&D]: "He was mighty lively and could do many tricks. The boy who
    owned him gave a show, and many of the Monkey's friends were among the
    actors."

185S.7   The story of a calico clown. (Grosset & Dunlap, 1920).

    [G&D]: "He was a truly comical chap and all the other toys loved him greatly."

185S.8   The story of a nodding donkey. (Grosset & Dunlap, 1921).

    [G&D]: "He made happy the life of a little lame boy and did lots of other good deeds."

185S.9   The story of a china cat. (Grosset & Dunlap, 1921).

    [G&D]: "The China Cat had many adventures, but enjoyed herself most of the time."

185S.10   The story of a plush bear. (Grosset & Dunlap, 1921).

    [G&D]: "This fellow came from the North Pole, stopped for a while at the toy store, and was then taken to the seashore by his little master."

185S.11   The story of a stuffed elephant. (Grosset & Dunlap, 1922).

    [G&D]: "He was a wise looking animal and had a great variety of adventures."

185S.12   The story of a woolly dog. (Grosset & Dunlap, 1923).

186S   MOVING PICTURE GIRLS

Volumes: 7
Printed: 1914-1916
Publisher: Grosset & Dunlap
Reprint publisher: Goldsmith Publishing Co., vols. 2-4*
                        World Syndicate Publishing Co., vols. 1-7
Illustrator: Walter S. Rogers, vols. 1-7
Source of annotations: Grosset & Dunlap advertisements [G&D]
Additional information: The Stratemeyer Syndicate created four series about motion pictures: the MOTION PICTURE CHUMS (018S), the MOVING PICTURE BOYS (020S), the MOTION PICTURE COMRADES (024S), and the MOVING PICTURE GIRLS. Only the girls acted in films; the boys were either filmmakers or theater owners.
      World editions also had illustrations by Walter S. Rogers.
Series description [G&D]: "The adventures of Ruth and Alice DeVere. Their father, a widower, is an actor who has taken up work for the 'movies.' Both girls wish to aid him in his work and visit various localities to act in all sorts of pictures."

186S.1   The moving picture girls; or, First appearances in photo dramas.
(Grosset & Dunlap, 1914; World).

    [G&D]: "Having lost his voice, the father of the girls goes into the movies and the girls follow. Tells how many 'parlor dramas' are filmed

---
* Possibly other volumes as well.

186S.2   The moving picture girls at Oak Farm; or, Queer happenings while taking rural plays. (Grosset & Dunlap, 1914; Goldsmith; World).

[G&D]: "Full of fun in the country, the haps and mishaps of taking film plays, and giving an account of two unusual discoveries."

186S.3   The moving picture girls snowbound; or, The proof on the film. (Grosset & Dunlap, 1914; Goldsmith; World).

[G&D]: "A tale of winter adventures in the wilderness, showing how the photo-play actors sometimes suffer."

186S.4   The moving picture girls under the palms; or, Lost in the wilds of Florida. (Grosset & Dunlap, 1914; Goldsmith; World).

[G&D]: "How they went to the land of palms, played many parts in dramas before the camera; were lost, and aided others who were also lost."

186S.5   The moving picture girls at Rocky Ranch; or, Great days among the cowboys. (Grosset & Dunlap, 1914; World).

[G&D]: "All who have ever seen moving pictures of the great West will want to know just how they are made. This volume gives every detail and is full of clean fun and excitement."

186S.6   The moving picture girls at sea; or, A pictured shipwreck that became real. (Grosset & Dunlap, 1915; World).

[G&D]: "A thrilling account of the girls' experiences on the water."

186S.7   The moving picture girls in war plays; or, The sham battles at Oak Farm. (Grosset & Dunlap, 1916; World).

[G&D]: "The girls play important parts in big battles scenes and have plenty of hard work along with considerable fun."

187S   OUTDOOR GIRLS

Volumes: 23
Printed: 1913-1933
Publisher: Grosset & Dunlap
Reprint publisher: Whitman Publishing Company, vols. 19-22*
Illustrator: anonymous, vols. 1-5
              Walter S. Rogers, vols. 6-8, 10-21
              R. Emmett Owen, vol. 9
              Margaret Temple Braley, vols. 22-23
Source of annotations: Grosset & Dunlap advertisements [G&D]
Additional information: Lillian Garis assisted the Stratemeyer Syndicate with some of the titles in this series. Howard Garis often helped her.
Series description [G&D]: "These are the tales of the various adventures participated in by a group of bright, fun-loving girls who have a common bond in their fondness for outdoor life, camping, travel, and adventure. They are clean and wholesome and free from sensationalism."

* Possibly other volumes as well.

187S.1   The outdoor girls of Deepdale; or, Camping and tramping for fun and health. (Grosset & Dunlap, 1913).

[G&D]: "Telling how the girls organized their Camping and Tramping Club, how they went on a tour, and of various adventures which befell them."

187S.2   The outdoor girls at Rainbow Lake; or, The stirring cruise of the motor boat Gem. (Grosset & Dunlap, 1913).

[G&D]: "One of the girls becomes the proud possessor of a motor boat and invites her club members to take a trip down the river to Rainbow Lake, a beautiful sheet of water lying between the mountains."

187S.3   The outdoor girls in a motor car; or, The haunted mansion of Shadow Valley. (Grosset & Dunlap, 1913).

[G&D]: "One of the girls has learned to run a big motor car, and she invites the club to go on a tour to visit some distant relatives. On the way they stop at a deserted mansion and make a surprising discovery."

187S.4   The outdoor girls in a winter camp; or, Glorious days on skates and iceboats. (Grosset & Dunlap, 1913).

[G&D]: "In this story, the scene is shifted to a winter season. The girls have some jolly times skating and ice boating, and visit a hunters' camp."

187S.5   The outdoor girls in Florida; or, Wintering in the sunny South. (Grosset & Dunlap, 1913).

[G&D]: "The parents of one of the girls have bought an orange grove in Florida, and her companions are invited to visit the place. They take a trip into the interior, where several unusual things happen."

187S.6   The outdoor girls at Ocean View; or, The box that was found in the sand. (Grosset & Dunlap, 1915).

[G&D]: "The girls have great fun and solve a mystery while on an outing along the New England coast."

187S.7   The outdoor girls on Pine Island; or, A cave and what it contained (Grosset & Dunlap, 1916).

[G&D]: "A bright, healthful story, full of good times at a bungalow camp on Pine Island."

187S.8   The outdoor girls in army service; or, Doing their bit for the soldier boys. (Grosset & Dunlap, 1918).

187S.9   The outdoor girls at the hostess house; or, Doing their best for the soldiers. (Grosset & Dunlap, 1919).

187S.10   The outdoor girls at Bluff Point; or, A wreck and a rescue. (Grosset & Dunlap, 1920).

187S.11   The outdoor girls at Wild Rose Lodge; or, The hermit of Moonlight Falls. (Grosset & Dunlap, 1921).

187S.12   The outdoor girls in the saddle; or, The girl miner of Gold Run. (Grosset & Dunlap, 1922).

187S.13   The outdoor girls around the campfire; or, The old maid of the mountains. (Grosset & Dunlap, 1923).

187S.14   The outdoor girls on Cape Cod; or, Sally Ann of Lighthouse Rock. (Grosset & Dunlap, 1924).

187S.15   The outdoor girls at Foaming Falls; or, Robina of Red Kennels. (Grosset & Dunlap, 1925).

187S.16   The outdoor girls along the coast; or, The cruise of the motor boat Liberty. (Grosset & Dunlap, 1926).

187S.17   The outdoor girls at Spring Hill Farm; or, The ghost of the old milk house. (Grosset & Dunlap, 1927).

187S.18   The outdoor girls at New Moon Ranch; or, Riding with the cowboys. (Grosset & Dunlap, 1928).

187S.19   The outdoor girls on a hike; or, The mystery of the deserted airplane. (Grosset & Dunlap, 1929; Whitman).

187S.20   The outdoor girls on a canoe trip; or, The secret of the brown mill. (Grosset & Dunlap, 1930; Whitman).

187S.21   The outdoor girls at Cedar Ridge; or, The mystery of the old windmill. (Grosset & Dunlap, 1931; Whitman).

187S.22   The outdoor girls in the air; or, Saving the stolen invention. (Grosset & Dunlap, 1932; Whitman).

187S.23   The outdoor girls in Desert Valley; or, Strange happenings in a cowboy camp. (Grosset & Dunlap, 1933).

188S   SIX LITTLE BUNKERS

Volumes: 15*
Printed: 1918-1933*
Publisher: Grosset & Dunlap
Illustrator: R. Emmett Owen, vols. 1-6
              Walter S. Rogers, vols. 7-14
Source of annotations: Grosset & Dunlap advertisements [G&D]
Additional information: Howard Garis contributed to some volumes in the
     series. The books were published without subtitles.
Series description [G&D]: "Delightful stories for little boys and girls
     which sprung into immediate popularity. To know the six little Bunkers

---

* Number of volumes and years published includes Six little Bunkers, the
   four-in-one reprint (188S.15X).

is to take them at once to your heart, they are so intensely human, so full of fun and cute sayings. Each story has a little plot of its own --one that can be easily followed--and all are written in Miss Hope's most entertaining manner. Clean, wholesome volumes which ought to be on the bookshelf of every child in the land."

188S.1   Six little Bunkers at Grandma Bell's. (Grosset & Dunlap, 1918).

188S.2   Six little Bunkers at Aunt Jo's. (Grosset & Dunlap, 1918).

188S.3   Six little Bunkers at Cousin Tom's. (Grosset & Dunlap, 1918).

188S.4   Six little Bunkers at Grandpa Ford's. (Grosset & Dunlap, 1918).

188S.5   Six little Bunkers at Uncle Fred's. (Grosset & Dunlap, 1918).

188S.6   Six little Bunkers at Captain Ben's. (Grosset & Dunlap, 1920).

188S.7   Six little Bunkers at Cowboy Jack's. (Grosset & Dunlap, 1921).

188S.8   Six little Bunkers at Mammy June's. (Grosset & Dunlap, 1922).

188S.9   Six little Bunkers at Farmer Joel's. (Grosset & Dunlap, 1923).

188S.10   Six little Bunkers at Miller Ned's. (Grosset & Dunlap, 1924).

188S.11   Six little Bunkers at Indian John's. (Grosset & Dunlap, 1925).

188S.12   Six little Bunkers at Happy Jim's. (Grosset & Dunlap, 1928).

188S.13   Six little Bunkers at Skipper Bob's. (Grosset & Dunlap, 1929).

188S.14   Six little Bunkers at Lighthouse Nell's. (Grosset & Dunlap, 1930).

188S.15X   Six little Bunkers. (Grosset & Dunlap, 1933).

     Four-in-one reprint.

Francis Hunt

Francis Hunt, a Stratemeyer Syndicate pen name, appeared on the five-volume MARY AND JERRY MYSTERY STORIES, published by Grosset & Dunlap from 1935 to 1937.

SERIES PUBLICATIONS

189S   MARY AND JERRY MYSTERY STORIES

Volumes: 5
Printed: 1935-1937
Publisher: Grosset & Dunlap
Illustrator: Margaret Ayer, vols. 1-5
Source of annotations: Grosset & Dunlap advertisements [G&D]
Additional information: Books were published without subtitles.
Series description [G&D]: "Introducing The DENTON Children who LOVE TO
   SOLVE MYSTERIES.
      "Mary and Jerry have an interesting hobby--they love to solve mys-
   teries. Between school hours and on weekends they follow clue upon
   clue, each more puzzling than the last, through a whole series of
   strange adventures."

189S.1   The messenger dog's secret. (Grosset & Dunlap, 1935).

   [G&D]: "The big police dog Flanders carried a strange message in his
   collar. By following its directions, Mary and Jerry Denton were able
   to bring a lost fortune to someone in need."

189S.2   The mystery of the toy bank. (Grosset & Dunlap, 1935).

   [G&D]: "Jerry Denton was saving for a bicycle, but when his little
   bank strangely disappeared he had a big mystery to solve. With the
   aid of Mary, several chums and a queer old sailor, this eager lad
   brought about a happy solution."

189S.3   The story the parrot told. (Grosset & Dunlap, 1935).

   [G&D]: "A fire in a pet shop started a long chain of adventures for
   Mary and Jerry Denton. The tale the talking parrot told caused plenty
   of excitement and mystery before the bird was restored to its rightful
   owner."

189S.4   The secret of the missing clown. (Grosset & Dunlap, 1936).

   [G&D]: "Mary and Jerry have many happy adventures at the circus while
   searching for the missing clown and his beautiful pony, Silverfeet."

189S.5   The mystery of the crooked tree. (Grosset & Dunlap, 1937).

Captain Lew James

As Captain Lew James, Edward Stratemeyer wrote eight stories published
in the LOG CABIN LIBRARY in 1892 and 1893. He was not the only writer
to use this pseudonym.

SERIES PUBLICATIONS

190P   LOG CABIN LIBRARY

Volumes: 8*
Printed: 1892-1893*
Publisher: Street & Smith
Additional information: The LOG CABIN LIBRARY, a weekly dime novel series,
    was published from March 21, 1889, to December 8, 1897, for a total of
    456 issues. Eight of the early issues were written by Edward Strate-
    meyer under the name Captain Lew James.

190P.1X   Cool Dan, the sport; or, The crack shot of Creede. No. 180.
Aug. 25, 1892.

190P.2X   Crazy Bob, the terror of Creede; or, Cool Dan the sport again to
the front. No. 186. Oct. 6, 1892.**

190P.3X   Cool Dan the sport's wonderful nerve; or, The madman's matchless
mine. No. 190. Nov. 3, 1892.**

190P.4X   The Collis Express robbers; or, Hunting down two desperate criminals. No. 193. Nov. 26, 1892.

190P.5X   Cool Dan the sport's contest; or, Fighting the Creede combination.
No. 210.   March 23, 1893.

190P.6X   Ouray Jack, the go-it-lively sport; or, A winner from the start.
No. 211.   March 30, 1893.

190P.7X   Two old sports; or, Pards in every deal. No. 213. April 13,
1893.

190P.8X   Straight-flush Lou, the man from Denver; or, Playing for a triple
stake. No. 217. May 11, 1893.

Frances K. Judd

Frances K. Judd was the Stratemeyer Syndicate pen name used for the eighteen-
volume KAY TRACEY MYSTERY STORIES, published by Cupples & Leon from 1934 to
1942. The series was reprinted by five other publishers from 1951 to 1980.

---

*   Number of volumes and years published apply only to titles written by
      Edward Stratemeyer under the name Captain Lew James.
**   Also on microfilm--Library of Congress Photoduplication Service, 1976.

SERIES PUBLICATIONS

191S   KAY TRACEY MYSTERY STORIES

Volumes: 18
Printed: 1934-1942
Publisher: Cupples & Leon Company
Reprint publisher: Garden City Books, vols. 1-2, 5-12, 14-18
            Books, Inc., vols. 1-2, 5-12, 14-18
            Berkley Publishing Corporation, vols. 2, 5-6, 9, 14,
              16-18
            Lamplight Publishing, Inc., vols. 5-6, 9, 12, 16-17
            Bantam Books, vols. 5-6, 9, 12, 16-17
Illustrator: Furman [Turman?], vols. 1-10
            anonymous, vols. 11-18
Source of annotations: Cupples & Leon Company advertisements [C&L]
Additional information: Five different publishers reprinted the KAY TRACEY
    MYSTERY STORIES, each time altering the original format, series order,
    and series length.   Garden City Books reprinted fifteen volumes from
    1951 to 1953, with new illustrations and a new series order; Books,
    Inc., later published the same fifteen titles, with a different series
    order, in both paperback and hardcover editions.   The dust jackets for
    the Books, Inc., editions were identical to Garden City's dust jackets;
    the same illustrations were also used for the covers of the Books, Inc.
    paperback editions, and later for the hardcover editions as well.   Six
    of these titles reappeared circa 1961 as Berkley Medallion paperbacks;
    Berkley also published two other titles in paperback in 1964; however,
    these may not have been Medallion books.   Again, the series order was
    rearranged.
        About this time,   Berkley reissued five of the eight titles in
    Berkley Highland paperback editions.   Then in 1978, Lamplight Publish-
    ing, Inc., reprinted six KAY TRACEY books in hardcover editions with
    the same cover illustrations as the Garden City editions, but with a
    different series order.   In 1980, Bantam Books published Bantam Skylark
    paperback editions of the same six titles with a new series order,
    but with cover illustrations similar to Berkley's cover illustrations.

CHANGES IN KAY TRACEY SERIES ORDER

Cupples & Leon volume:	1	2	3	4	5	6	7	8	9
BECOMES									
Garden City volume:	15	14	--	--	3	13	8	12	11
Books, Inc., volume:	13	12	--	--	4	11	10	7	8
Berkley volume:	--	7	--	--	3	5	--	--	8
Lamplight volume:	--	--	--	--	2	6	--	--	5
Bantam volume:	--	--	--	--	3	5	--	--	6

Cupples & Leon volume:	10	11	12	13	14	15	16	17	18
BECOMES									
Garden City volume:	9	6	4	--	2	10	7	1	5
Books, Inc., volume:	9	5	2	--	1	15	14	3	6
Berkley volume:	--	--	--	--	4	--	6	1	2
Lamplight volume:	--	--	3	--	--	--	4	1	--
Bantam volume:	--	--	2	--	--	--	1	4	--

Five titles--volumes 5, 6, 9, 16, and 17--were included in the series each time it was reprinted; three others--volumes 3, 4, and 13--were not reprinted at all. Only one title was changed: <u>Beneath the crimson briar bush</u> became <u>The crimson briar bush</u> and then <u>The crimson briar bush</u>.

The first two Cupples & Leon volumes had illustrations signed by Furman (or, possibly, Turman). The first letter of the name was in script, in an inverted triangle. Volumes 3 through 10 in Cupples & Leon editions were signed only with the initial in an inverted triangle; volumes 11 through 18 were unsigned. None of the other editions had signed illustrations; the Berkley editions had no illustrations, except on the cover.

The books were published without subtitles.

Series description [C&L]: "Meet clever Kay Tracey, who, though only sixteen, solves mysteries in a surprising manner. Working on clues which she assembles, this surprising heroine supplies the solution to cases that have baffled professional sleuths. The KAY TRACEY MYSTERY STORIES will grip a reader from start to finish."

191S.1   The secret of the red scarf. (Cupples & Leon, 1934; Garden City, 1953; Books, Inc.).

Garden City edition published as vol. 15; Books, Inc. edition, as vol. 13.

[C&L]: "A case of mistaken identity at a masquerade leads Kay into a delightful but mysterious secret."

191S.2   The strange echo. (Cupples & Leon, 1934; Garden City, 1953; Books, Inc.; Berkley, 1964).

Garden City edition published as vol. 14; Books, Inc. edition, as vol. 12; Berkley edition, as vol. 7, no. Y797, and later as Highland no. F1475.

[C&L]: "Lost Lake had two mysteries--an old one and a new one. Kay, visiting there, solves both of them by deciphering a strange echo."

191S.3   The mystery of the swaying curtains. (Cupples & Leon, 1935).

[C&L]: "Heavy draperies swaying in a lonely mansion give the clue which is needed to solve a mystery that has defied professional investigators but proves to be fun for the attractive and clever Kay Tracey."

191S.4   The shadow on the door. (Cupples & Leon, 1935).

[C&L]: "Was the shadow on the door made by a human being or an animal? Apparently without explanation Kay Tracey, after some exciting work, solved the mystery and was able to help a small child out of an unfortunate situation."

191S.5   The six-fingered glove mystery. (Cupples & Leon, 1936; Garden City, 1951; Books, Inc.; Berkley, ca1961; Lamplight, 1978; Bantam, 1980).

Garden City edition published as vol. 3; Books, Inc. edition, as vol. 4; Berkley edition, as vol. 3, Medallion no. G592, Highland no. F1113; Lamplight edition, as vol. 2; Bantam Skylark, as vol. 3.

191S.6   The green cameo mystery. (Cupples & Leon, 1936; Garden City, 1951; Books, Inc.; Berkley, ca1961; Lamplight, 1978; Bantam, 1980).

Garden City edition published as vol. 13; Books, Inc. edition, as vol. 11; Berkley edition, as vol. 5, Medallion no. G592, Highland no. F113; Lamplight edition, as vol. 6; Bantam Skylark edition, as vol. 5.

191S.7   The secret at the windmill. (Cupples & Leon, 1937; Garden City, 1952; Books, Inc.).

Garden City edition published as vol. 8; Books, Inc. edition, as vol. 10.

191S.8   Beneath the crimson briar bush. (Cupples & Leon, 1937; Garden City, 1952; Books, Inc.).

Garden City edition published as vol. 12, as The crimson briar bush; Books, Inc. edition published as vol. 7, as The crimson brier bush.

191S.9   The message in the sand dunes. (Cupples & Leon, 1938; Garden City, 1952; Books, Inc.; Berkley, 1964; Lamplight, 1978; Bantam, 1980).

Garden City edition published as vol. 11; Books, Inc. edition, as vol. 8; Berkley edition, as vol. 8, no. Y980, Highland no. F1476; Lamplight edition, as vol. 5; Bantam Skylark edition, as vol. 6.

191S.10   The murmuring portrait. (Cupples & Leon, 1938; Garden City, 1951; Books, Inc.).

Garden City edition published as vol. 9; Books, Inc. edition also vol. 9.

191S.11   When the key turned. (Cupples & Leon, 1939; Garden City, 1951; Books, Inc.).

Garden City edition published as vol. 6; Books, Inc. edition, as vol. 5.

191S.12   In the sunken garden. (Cupples & Leon, 1939; Garden City, 1951; Books, Inc.; Lamplight, 1978; Bantam, 1980).

Garden City edition published as vol. 4; Books, Inc. edition, as vol. 2; Lamplight edition, as vol. 3; Bantam Skylark edition, as vol. 2.

191S.13   The forbidden tower. (Cupples & Leon, 1940).

191S.14   The sacred feather. (Cupples & Leon, 1940; Garden City, 1951; Books, Inc.; Berkley, ca1961).

Garden City edition published as vol. 2; Books, Inc. edition, as vol. 1; Berkley edition, as vol. 4, Medallion no. G458.

191S.15   The lone footprint. (Cupples & Leon, 1941; Garden City, 1952; Books, Inc.).

Garden City edition published as vol. 10; Books, Inc. edition, as vol. 15.

191S.16   The double disguise. (Cupples & Leon, 1941; Garden City, 1952; Books, Inc.; Berkley, 1961; Lamplight, 1978; Bantam, 1980).

Garden City edition published as vol. 7; Books, Inc. edition, as vol. 14; Berkley edition, as vol. 6, Medallion no. G593, Lamplight edition, as vol. 4; Bantam Skylark edition, as vol. 1.

191S.17   The mansion of secrets. (Cupples & Leon, 1942; Garden City, 1951; Books, Inc.; Berkley, ca1961; Lamplight, 1978; Bantam, 1980).

Garden City edition published as vol. 1; Books, Inc. edition, as vol. 3; Berkley edition, as vol. 1, Medallion no. G455, Highland no. F1459, Lamplight edition, as vol. 1; Bantam Skylark edition, as vol. 4.

191S.18   The mysterious neighbors. (Cupples & Leon, 1942; Garden City, 1951; Books, Inc.; Berkley, ca1961).

Garden City edition published as vol. 5; Books, Inc. edition, as vol. 6; Berkley edition, as vol. 2, Medallion no. G456.

Carolyn Keene

For over half a century, the Stratemeyer Syndicate pseudonym Carolyn Keene has appeared on girls' mystery series. Her two series, NANCY DREW and the DANA GIRLS, began in 1930 and 1934, respectively, and have reached a combined total of ninety-nine volumes;* all but five were published by Grosset & Dunlap. The first three NANCY DREW books were created by Edward Stratemeyer; Harriet Adams has worked on all the other titles, including the revised editions.

SERIES PUBLICATIONS

192S   DANA GIRLS

Volumes: 34**
Printed: 1934- **
Publisher: Grosset & Dunlap
Illustrator: Ferdinand E. Warren, vols. 1-12
              Russell H. Tandy, vol. 13
Source of annotations: Grosset & Dunlap advertisements [G&D], series de-
                        scription

---

*   Count inlcudes related volumes, such as The Nancy Drew cookbook and the NANCY DREW PICTURE BOOKS (194S), but not reprints, revised editions, or The Hardy Boys and Nancy Drew meet Dracula. (The latter was not published under the pseudonym Carolyn Keene.)
**   As of 1981. The series may still be in progress, although the most recent title was published in 1979.

Source of annotations: Library of Congress cataloguing in publication data
[LC], vols. 17, 20-34X
Additional information: Harriet Adams wrote the titles in this series;
Leslie McFarlane may have contributed to the first four volumes.
From 1972 to 1975, the DANA GIRLS series was renumbered: the first
sixteen volumes and volume 18 were allowed to go out of print, while
volumes 17, and 19 through 30 were reissued as volumes 1 through 13,
with a slightly different series order.

SCHEDULE OF VOLUME NUMBER CHANGES IN THE DANA GIRLS SERIES

Year of change	New number	Former number	Year of change	New number	Former number
1972	1	25	1973	8	21
1972	2	26	1973	9	22
1972	3	27	1973	10	23
1972	4	28	1974	11	24
1972	5	29	1974	12	19
1972	6	30	1975	13	17
1973	7	20			

Series description [G&D]: "Readers of NANCY DREW need no assurance that
the adventures of resourceful Louise Dana and her irresponsible sister
Jean are packed with thrills, excitement and mystery. Every girl will
love these fascinating stories which tell how the Dana girls, like
Nancy Drew herself, meet and match the challenge of each strange new
mystery."
[Later advertisement] [G&D]: "Another exciting Carolyn Keene series! Mysteries have a way of rising up to challenge Louise and Jean
Dana, attractive teen-age sisters, wherever they go. At home and on
vacation the modern young detectives encounter dangerous adventures and
solve baffling mysteries. All girls who enjoy action and suspense will
thrill to these fascinating stories."

192S.1   By the light of the study lamp. (Grosset & Dunlap, 1934).

192S.2   The secret at Lone Tree Cottage. (Grosset & Dunlap, 1934).

192S.3   In the shadow of the tower. (Grosset & Dunlap, 1934).

192S.4   A three-cornered mystery. (Grosset & Dunlap, 1935).

192S.5   The secret at the Hermitage. (Grosset & Dunlap, 1936, 1949).

192S.6   The circle of footprints. (Grosset & Dunlap, 1937, 1949).

192S.7   The mystery of the locked room. (Grosset & Dunlap, 1938, 1950).

192S.8   The clue in the cobweb. (Grosset & Dunlap, 1939, 1950).

192S.9   The secret at the gatehouse. (Grosset & Dunlap, 1940).

192S.10   The mysterious fireplace. (Grosset & Dunlap, 1941).

192S.11   The clue of the rusty key. (Grosset & Dunlap, 1942, 1951).

192S.12   The portrait in the sand. (Grosset & Dunlap, 1943, 1951).

192S.13   The secret in the old well. (Grosset & Dunlap, 1944).

192S.14   The clue in the ivy. (Grosset & Dunlap, 1952).

192S.15   The secret of the jade ring. (Grosset & Dunlap, 1953).

192S.16   The mystery at the crossroads. (Grosset & Dunlap, 1954).

192S.17   The ghost in the gallery. (Grosset & Dunlap, 1955, 1975).

   1975 edition sometimes listed as The ghosts in the gallery. Reissued
   as volume 13.
      [LC]: "Rehearsing for a musical and writing songs prove to be
   frightening experiences for the two Dana sisters, as there are ghosts
   in the theater, or are there?"

192S.18   The clue of the black flower. (Grosset & Dunlap, 1956).

192S.19   The winking ruby mystery. (Grosset & Dunlap, 1957, 1974).

   1974 edition reissued as volume 12.

192S.20   The secret of the Swiss chalet. (Grosset & Dunlap, 1958, 1973).

   1973 edition reissued as volume 7.
      [LC]: "While vacationing in Europe, the Dana sisters agree to help
   a former Austrian prince locate his family's long lost heirlooms, a
   search that takes them into the dangerous snow-covered Swiss Alps."

192S.21   The haunted lagoon. (Grosset & Dunlap, 1959, 1973).

   1973 edition reissued as volume 8.
      [LC]: "The Dana girls and their friends try to locate a missing
   sea captain last seen on Chincoteague Island off the Virginia Coast."

192S.22   Mystery of the bamboo bird. (Grosset & Dunlap, 1960, 1973).

   1973 edition reissued as volume 9.
      [LC]: "Attempting to recover a sacred gold statue stolen from a
   friend, the Dana sisters track the thief to Thailand where they encounter a series of harrowing experiences."

192S.23   The Sierra gold mystery. (Grosset & Dunlap, 1961, 1973).

   1973 edition reissued as volume 10.
      [LC]: "The search for a stolen sapphire ring, a missing grand-
   father, and a lost chest of gold nuggets leads the Dana sisters to
   California's gold country in the Sierra Nevada mountains."

192S.24   The secret of Lost Lake. (Grosset & Dunlap, 1963, 1974).

   1974 edition reissued as volume 11.
      [LC]: "While attempting to locate a lost dog, the Dana sisters
   become involved in the mystery surrounding a reclusive mountain woman."

192S.25   Mystery of the stone tiger. (Grosset & Dunlap, 1963, 1972).

    1972 edition reissued as volume 1.
        [LC]: "The Dana girls unravel a mystery involving a marble tiger from India."

192S.26   The riddle of the frozen fountain. (Grosset & Dunlap, 1964, 1972).

    1972 edition reissued as volume 2.
        [LC]: "When asked to trace the writer of a threatening note, the Dana sisters become enmeshed in a mystery concerning a bronze fountain."

192S.27   The secret of the silver dolphin. (Grosset & Dunlap, 1965, 1972).

    1972 edition reissued as volume 3.
        [LC]: "Two girls' search for a silver dolphin mentioned in a will is hindered by a hostile fortune-teller and an elusive thief."

192S.28   Mystery of the wax queen. (Grosset & Dunlap, 1966, 1972).

    1972 edition reissued as volume 4.
        [LC]: "The Dana sisters spend their spring vacation solving a mystery involving a phony automobile raffle, a wax bust of Queen Victoria, a stolen diamond, and a sculptress."

192S.29   The secret of the minstrel's guitar. (Grosset & Dunlap, 1967, 1972).

    1972 edition reissued as volume 5.
        [LC]: "The Dana girls, who are sailing for Portugal to solve the thefts of cork from a warehouse, find an even more baffling mystery aboard ship."

192S.30   The phantom surfer. (Grosset & Dunlap, 1968, 1972).

    1972 edition reissued as volume 6.
        [LC]: "While spending spring vacation at an ocean resort, the Dana girls encounter the mystery of the nocturnal surfer who disappears into the sea."

192S.31X   The curious coronation. (Grosset & Dunlap, 1976).

    Issued as volume 14.
        [LC]: "The Dana girls turn their attention to the thefts, kidnapping, and other mysterious events which surround a teenage pageant."

192S.32X   The hundred-year mystery. (Grosset & Dunlap, 1977).

    Issued as volume 15.
        [LC]: "The Dana sisters study ancient Viking symbols and customs in order to interpret several clues connected to a buried treasure."

192S.33X   Mountain-peak mystery. (Grosset & Dunlap, 1978).

Issued as volume 16.
[LC]: "Two teenagers searching for a duplicate manuscript containing the secret disclosure of an orphan's grandfather realize dangers from unknown enemies who are also hunting for the document."

192S.34X The witch's omen. (Grosset & Dunlap, 1979).

Issued as volume 17.
[LC]: "After an uninvited witch interrupts their Halloween party, two teenage detectives unravel a mystery involving an international gang and contraband cargo at a waterfront."

193S NANCY DREW MYSTERY STORIES

Volumes: 64*
Printed: 1930-
Publisher: Grosset & Dunlap, vols. 1-56, 61X-62X, 64X
            Simon & Schuster, Wanderer Books, vols. 57-60, 63X
Illustrator: Russell H. Tandy, vols. 1-23 (1930-1946)
            Polly Bolian, vols. 1-2, 27-36 (1959-1960)
            Ruth Sanderson, vols. 57-60
Source of annotations: Grosset & Dunlap advertisements [G&D], series description, vols. 1-8
            Library of Congress cataloguing in publication data [LC], vols. 12-24, 30-34, 46-55, 57-59, 61X-62X
Additional information: With sales of approximately 60,000,000 copies and translations available in Danish, Dutch, French,** German, Italian, Norwegian, Swedish, and other languages, NANCY DREW is well-established as the Stratemeyer Syndicate's most popular girls' series.
    The first three NANCY DREW books, created by Edward Stratemeyer, were published in 1930. Since then, Edward Stratemeyer's daughter Harriet Adams has written the series, including the revised editions. Grosset & Dunlap published the NANCY DREW books until 1979, when Wanderer Books issued the first paperback NANCY DREW titles.
    The first thirty-four NANCY DREW titles were revised from 1959 to 1977. Some of these books have three copyright dates--the original, the revision, and a 1959 or 1960 date as well. The latter appears to reflect new illustrations by Polly Bolian copyrighted by Grosset & Dunlap, rather than a revised text.*** The revised editions of the NANCY DREW books were

_____

* As of 1981. Volume count also includes related titles, such as The Nancy Drew cook book and The Hardy boys and Nancy Drew meet Dracula, but not the two NANCY DREW PICTURE BOOKS (194S), which have their own listing.
** In France, Nancy Drew is Alice Roy, and Carolyn Keene, Caroline Quine.
*** Some--possibly all--of the Polly Bolian illustrations appeared in color in book club editions. There were apparently three different book club editions of Nancy Drew, all showing Grosset & Dunlap as publisher. The earliest, cal959-1960, have grey covers with a picture of a locket on the front, and color illustrations by Polly Bolian; the next set, probably issued in the 1960s, have the standard pictorial covers, but include the words "book club" on the title page; the last, offered by several book clubs from about 1977 to the present, consist of a set of the first three titles, with plain blue covers and with dust jackets showing the illustrations from the regular pictorial covers.

approximately twenty to forty pages shorter than the original editions. The plots, characters, and settings were updated and sometimes almost wholly altered. Generally, the changes were similar to those occurring in the HARDY BOYS (106S) and the BOBBSEY TWINS (183S) series--indeed, like the BOBBSEY TWINS, NANCY DREW became a little older in the revisions: age eighteen instead of age sixteen.

SCHEDULE OF REVISIONS OF THE NANCY DREW TITLES

BY YEAR OF REVISION:

Year of revision	Volume number	Year of revision	Volume number
1959	1,2	1969	16,19,30
1960	3	1970	14,21
1961	4,6	1971	18
1962	7	1972	12,15,20
1963	--	1973	22,23
1964	--	1974	13,31,32
1965	5,11	1975	33,34
1966	10	1976	17
1967	25,26,27	1977	24
1968	8,9,28,29		

BY VOLUME NUMBER:

Volume number	Year of revision	Volume number	Year of revision	Volume number	Year of revision
1	1959	13	1974	24	1977
2	1959	14	1970	25	1967
3	1960	15	1972	26	1967
4	1961	16	1969	27	1967
5	1965	17	1976	28	1968
6	1961	18	1971	29	1968
7	1962	19	1969	30	1969
8	1968	20	1972	31	1974
9	1968	21	1970	32	1974
10	1966	22	1973	33	1975
11	1965	23	1973	34	1975
12	1972				

NANCY DREW has also appeared on film. Four NANCY DREW movies were produced by Warner Bros. in 1938 and 1939, all with Bonita Granville as NANCY DREW: Nancy Drew, Detective (1938),* Nancy Drew--Reporter (1939), Nancy Drew--Troubleshooter (1939), and Nancy Drew and the Hidden Staircase (1939). In February 1977, "The NANCY DREW Mysteries" appeared on ABC-TV on Sunday nights, alternating with "The HARDY BOYS Mysteries." The two series merged in February 1978, to become "The HARDY BOYS/NANCY DREW Mysteries." Pamela Sue Martin starred as NANCY DREW in 1977 and 1978, but left shortly after the shows were combined; Janet Louise Johnson then took the role of NANCY DREW.

Four NANCY DREW filmstrips, with accompanying cassettes, were issued in 1979 by the Society for Visual Education. Each was an adaption of a NANCY DREW book: The secret of the old clock, Nancy's mysterious

---

* Based on The password to Larkspur Lane. Screenplay by Kenneth Gamet.

letter, The mysterious mannequin, and The sky phantom. In addition,
a tape recording of The clue in the old stagecoach was made in 1972.
     NANCY DREW's name has appeared on several other products, including
The NANCY DREW Mystery Game, a boxed game issued by Parker Brothers in
1958 and 1959,* and My Nancy Drew private eye diary and My Nancy Drew
date book and homework planner, both published by Wanderer Books in
1979. Wanderer also sponsored a NANCY DREW/HARDY BOYS fan club, formed
in 1979, which included a newsletter, The Nancy Drew/Hardy boys mystery
reporter, and a membership card. Two coloring books, Nancy Drew mystery pictures to color #1 and Nancy Drew mystery pictures to color #2,
were published by Grosset & Dunlap in 1979, with illustrations by Tony
Tallarico based on the NANCY DREW series books.
     Grosset & Dunlap also published The Nancy Drew cookbook and The
Nancy Drew sleuth book, two non-fiction works inspired by the NANCY
DREW series, while Wanderer Books issued an activity book, The Nancy
Drew book of hidden clues; all were published under the pseudonym Carolyn Keene. Two NANCY DREW PICTURE BOOKS appeared in 1977, also with
Carolyn Keene listed as author; both were original NANCY DREW stories,
not adaptions of previously published titles, but were written for a
younger audience.
     Books were published without subtitles. An R denotes an annotation
for a revised edition.
Series description [G&D]: "Here is a thrilling series of mystery stories
     for girls. Nancy Drew, ingenious, alert, is the daughter of a famous
     criminal lawyer and she herself is deeply interested in his mystery
     cases. Her interest involves her often in some very dangerous and
     exciting cases."

193S.1   The secret of the old clock. (Grosset & Dunlap, 1930, 1959,
1960**).

     Also published in a two-in-one edition with The hidden staircase in
     the early 1970s; 1959 plates were used.
     [G&D]: "Nancy, unaided, seeks to locate a missing will and finds
     herself in the midst of adventure."

193S.2   The hidden staircase. (Grosset & Dunlap, 1930, 1959, 1960**).

     Also published in a two-in-one edition, The secret of the old clock
     [and] The hidden staircase, in the early 1970s; 1959 plates were used.
     [G&D]: "Mysterious happenings in an old stone house mansion lead
     to an investigation by Nancy."

193S.3   The bungalow mystery. (Grosset & Dunlap, 1930, 1960).

     [G&D]: "Nancy has some perilous adventures around a deserted bungalow."

193S.4   The mystery at Lilac Inn. (Grosset & Dunlap, 1930, 1961).

     [G&D]: "Quick thinking and quick action were needed for Nancy to ex-
     tricate herself from a dangerous situation."

---

*   The design on the box changed in 1959: the 1958 edition had Nancy Drew
     wearing a rainhat, with her flashligh beam pointed toward a house on a
     hill. When the box was redesigned, the hat, house, and hill disappeared
**   Published with illustrations by Polly Bolian.

193S.5   The secret at Shadow Ranch. (Grosset & Dunlap, 1930, 1965).

   1965 edition titled The secret of Shadow Ranch.
      [G&D]: "On a vacation in Arizona Nancy uncovers an old mystery and
   solves it."

193S.6   The secret of Red Gate Farm. (Grosset & Dunlap, 1931, 1961).

   [G&D]: "Nancy exposes the doings of a secret society on an isolated
   farm."

193S.7   The clue in the diary. (Grosset & Dunlap, 1932, 1962).

   [G&D]: "A fascinating and exciting story of a search for a clue to a
   surprising mystery."

193S.8   Nancy's mysterious letter. (Grosset & Dunlap, 1932, 1968).

   [G&D]: "Nancy receives a letter informing her that she is heir to a
   fortune. This story tells of her search for another Nancy Drew."

193S.9   The sign of the twisted candles. (Grosset & Dunlap, 1933, 1959?,
1968).

193S.10   The password to Larkspur Lane. (Grosset & Dunlap, 1933, 1960?,
1966).

193S.11   The clue of the broken locket. (Grosset & Dunlap, 1934, 1965).

193S.12   The message in the hollow oak. (Grosset & Dunlap, 1935, 1972).

   [LC]: [R]"Nancy Drew tackles a mystery professional detectives failed
   to solve--finding a valuable centuries-old message in a hollow oak tree
   in Illinois."

193S.13   The mystery of the ivory charm. (Grosset & Dunlap, 1936, 1974).

   [LC]: [R]"Nancy Drew determines if an ivory elephant charm really
   protects its wearer from harm when she investigates the involvement
   of a member of the Bengleton Wild-Animal Show in a mysterious scheme."

193S.14   The whispering statue. (Grosset & Dunlap, 1937, 1970).

   [LC]: [R]"Nancy and her friends establish headquarters in a seaside
   yacht club to investigate strange happenings in a book store and the
   disappearance of a marble statue."

193S.15   The haunted bridge. (Grosset & Dunlap, 1937, 1972).

   [LC]: [R]"Nancy Drew becomes involved in a double mystery concerning
   a haunted bridge and jewel thieves."

193S.16   The clue of the tapping heels. (Grosset & Dunlap, 1939, 1969).

   [LC]: [R]"Nancy Drew tries to find a clue to the strange tapping
   sounds in the home of a retired actress."

193S.17   The mystery of the brass bound trunk. (Grosset & Dunlap, 1940, 1976).

    [LC]:   [R]"A brass-bound trunk mistakenly delivered to Nancy's cabin on a New York-bound ocean liner becomes the first clue leading her to suspect that international jewel thieves are aboard."

193S.18   The mystery at the moss-covered mansion. (Grosset & Dunlap, 1941, 1971).

    [LC]:   [R]"Nancy Drew sets out to prove that her father's client was unjustly accused of trying to sabotage the United States space program."

193S.19   The quest of the missing map. (Grosset & Dunlap, 1942, 1969).

    [LC]:   [R]"The eighteen-year-old girl detective must find a man who has been missing for years in order to locate the other half of a treasure map."

193S.20   The clue in the jewel box. (Grosset & Dunlap, 1943, 1972).

    [LC]:   [R]"Nancy and her friends help a woman search for her missing grandson."

193S.21   The secret in the old attic. (Grosset & Dunlap, 1944, 1970).

    [LC]:   [R]"Nancy Drew must use clues in a dead man's letters to find some unpublished musical manuscripts that will save an old man and his granddaughter from financial ruin."

193S.22   The clue in the crumbling wall. (Grosset & Dunlap, 1945, 1973).

    [LC]:   [R]"While trying to locate a missing dancer who is about to gain a large inheritance, Nancy Drew finds a clue leading to the solution of yet another mystery."

193S.23   The mystery of the tolling bell. (Grosset & Dunlap, 1946, 1973).

    [LC]:   [R]"Nancy Drew and her two friends help uncover a gang of swindlers while vacationing in a seaside town."

193S.24   The clue in the old album. (Grosset & Dunlap, 1947, 1977).

    [LC]:   [R]"At a doll collector's request for help, a young sleuth searches for an old album, a lost doll, and a missing gypsy violinist."

193S.25   The ghost of Blackwood Hall. (Grosset & Dunlap, 1948, 1967).

193S.26   The clue of the leaning chimney. (Grosset & Dunlap, 1949, 1967).

193S.27   The secret of the wooden lady. (Grosset & Dunlap, 1950, 1960,* 1967).

193S.28   The clue of the black keys. (Grosset & Dunlap, 1951, 1960,* 1968

---

* Published with illustrations by Polly Bolian.

193S.29   The mystery at the ski jump. (Grosset & Dunlap, 1952, 1960,*
1968).

193S.30   The clue of the velvet mask. (Grosset & Dunlap, 1953, 1959,*
1969).

[LC]: [R]"When a gang that uses parties as a cover for robberies vic-
timizes a masquerade party Nancy is attending, the teen-age detective
switches identity with her girlfriend to solve the case."

193S.31   The ringmaster's secret. (Grosset & Dunlap, 1953, 1959,* 1974).

[LC]: [R]"Nancy Drew joins the circus in order to investigate the
mystery surrounding a gold charm bracelet and a young orphaned aeri-
alist."

193S.32   The scarlet slipper mystery. (Grosset & Dunlap, 1954, 1959,*
1974).

[LC]: [R]"Nancy Drew comes to the aid of the owners of a local dancing
school when they receive an anonymous note threatening their lives."

193S.33   The witch tree symbol. (Grosset & Dunlap, 1955, 1959,* 1975).

[LC]: [R]"An unusual hex sign leads Nancy Drew to Pennsylvania Dutch
country in pursuit of a thief who stops at nothing to get rid of her."

193S.34   The hidden window mystery. (Grosset & Dunlap, 1957,** 1959,* 1975).

[LC]: [R]"Nancy Drew visits her cousin in Virginia hoping to locate
a missing stained-glass window."

193S.35   The haunted showboat. (Grosset & Dunlap, 1958,*** 1959*).

193S.36   The secret of the golden pavilion. (Grosset & Dunlap, 1959,
1960*).

193S.37   The clue in the old stagecoach. (Grosset & Dunlap, 1960).

193S.38   The mystery of the fire dragon. (Grosset & Dunlap, 1961).

193S.39   The clue of the dancing puppet. (Grosset & Dunlap, 1962).

193S.40   The Moonstone Castle mystery. (Grosset & Dunlap, 1963).

193S.41   The clue of the whistling bagpipes. (Grosset & Dunlap, 1964).

193S.42   The phantom of Pine Hill. (Grosset & Dunlap, 1965).

193S.43   The mystery of the 99 steps. (Grosset & Dunlap, 1966).

193S.44   The clue in the crossword cipher. (Grosset & Dunlap, 1967).

---

*   Published with illustrations by Polly Bolian.
**   Copyrighted 1956.
*** Copyrighted 1957.

193S.45   The spider sapphire mystery. (Grosset & Dunlap, 1968).

193S.46   The invisible intruder. (Grosset & Dunlap, 1969).

[LC]: "Nancy Drew and her friends go on a ghost hunting expedition and become involved with a gang of thieves who concentrate their activities on collectors of valuable shells."

193S.47   The mysterious mannequin. (Grosset & Dunlap, 1970).

[LC]: "The gift of an Oriental rug with a coded message woven into its border and the disappearance of a Turkish client start Nancy Drew on a new search for a missing mannequin."

193S.48   The crooked banister. (Grosset & Dunlap, 1971).

[LC]: "While helping the police find the owner of a mysterious house with a crooked staircase and an unpredictable robot, Nancy Drew, girl detective, also helps capture a swindler."

193S.49   The secret of Mirror Bay. (Grosset & Dunlap, 1972).

[LC]: "When Nancy Drew and her friends go to a lake in New York to investigate reports of a woman gliding over water, they discover a treasure underwater."

193S.50   The double jinx mystery. (Grosset & Dunlap, 1973).

[LC]: "Nancy and her friends find they have to overcome people's superstitions and fears in solving the case of a 'jinxed' and threatened bird farm."

193S.51   The mystery of the glowing eye. (Grosset & Dunlap, 1974).

[LC]: "A fiery glowing eye in a museum, the abduction of Ned, the code name Cyclops, and a pilotless helicopter draw Nancy and her friends into a dangerous investigation."

193S.52   The secret of the forgotten city. (Grosset & Dunlap, 1975).

[LC]: "Nancy and her friends become involved in a search for lost treasure."

193S.53   The sky phantom. (Grosset & Dunlap, 1976).

[LC]: "While vacationing in the Midwest with her friends, Nancy Drew investigates a mysterious magnetic cloud, searches for a hijacked plane, and hunts a horse thief."

193S.54   The strange message in the parchment. (Grosset & Dunlap, 1977).

[LC]: "While trying to recover a set of stolen parchment paintings, Nancy Drew becomes involved in tracking a kidnapper and extortionist."

193S.55   The mystery of Crocodile Island. (Grosset & Dunlap, 1978).

[LC]: "A young detective's attempts to uncover a group of poachers on Crocodile Island in Florida involve her with kidnapping, reptiles, enemy boats, and a sinister racket."

193S.56   The thirteenth pearl. (Grosset & Dunlap, 1979).

193S.57   The triple hoax. (Wanderer, 1979).

[LC]: "Nancy Drew and friends Bess and George track a group of swindlers and kidnappers from New York to Mexico City to Los Angeles where they finally solve the mystery of the Triple Hoax."

193S.58   The flying saucer mystery. (Wanderer, 1980).

[LC]: "Nancy and friends, in search of information about a UFO, become involved in another mystery involving the inheritance of an old man who lives in the forest."

193S.59   The secret in the old lace. (Wanderer, 1980).

[LC]: "While in Belgium investigating the mystery surrounding an antique cross, Nancy and her friends learn that her entry in a short story contest may somehow be involved."

193S.60   The Greek symbol mystery. (Wanderer, 1981).

193S.61X The Nancy Drew cookbook: Clues to good cooking. (Grosset & Dunlap, 1973).

[LC]: "More than one hundred easy recipes, some with Nancy's special cooking secret. Includes 'Detective Burgers,' 'Double Jinx Salad,' 'Twisted Candles Peach Crisp,' and many more."

193S.62X The Nancy Drew sleuth book: Clues to good sleuthing. (Grosset & Dunlap, 1979).

[LC]: "In solving a series of mysteries, Nancy Drew and her Detective Club study techniques of criminal investigation involving handwriting, fingerprints, codes, and moulages."

193S.63X Nancy Drew book of hidden clues. (Wanderer, 1980).

193S.64X The Hardy boys and Nancy Drew meet Dracula. (Grosset & Dunlap, 1978).

Novelization by Stratemeyer Syndicate. "Based on the Universal Television Series HARDY BOYS/NANCY DREW MYSTERIES Developed for Television by Glen A. Larson[.] Based on the HARDY BOYS Books by Franklin W. Dixon and the NANCY DREW Books by Carolyn Keene[.] Adapted from the episodes THE HARDY BOYS AND NANCY DREW MEET DRACULA (Parts I and II) Written by Glen A. Larson and Michael Sloan." Illustrated with photographs copyrighted by Universal City Studios, Inc.

194S   NANCY DREW PICTURE BOOKS

Volumes: 2
Printed: 1977
Publisher: Grosset & Dunlap
Illustrator: Tom O'Sullivan, vols. 1-2
Source of annotations: Grosset & Dunlap advertisements, vol. 1
                        Library of Congress cataloguing in publication data
                        [LC], vol. 2
Additional information: The two books are short stories (approximately
    sixty pages) featuring NANCY DREW. They are new stories, not adaptions
    of previously published books.
        The books were published without subtitles.

194S.1   Mystery of the lost dogs. (Grosset & Dunlap, 1977).

    [G&D]: "In the very first exciting Nancy Drew mystery for younger
    children, Nancy's young friends ask her to find their missing dogs.
    Then Nancy discovers that Togo, her own bull-terrier, has disappeared.
    Is a very clever dognapping ring operating in River Heights?"

194S.2   The secret of the twin puppets. (Grosset & Dunlap, 1977).

    [LC]: "Two little girls ask Nancy to solve the mystery of two oddly
    behaving puppets."

OTHER PUBLICATIONS

195N   A superboy, supergirl anthology: Selected chapters from the
earlier works of Victor Appleton, Franklin W. Dixon, and Carolyn Keene.
Edited by Stephen Dunning and Henry B. Maloney. (Scholastic Book Services
1971).

Jack Lancer

Jack Lancer was a Stratemeyer Syndicate pseudonym used for only one six-
volume boys' spy series.

SERIES PUBLICATIONS

196S   CHRISTOPHER COOL/TEEN AGENT

Volumes: 6
Printed: 1967-1969
Publisher: Grosset & Dunlap

Illustrator: anonymous, vols. 1-6
Source of annotations: Grosset & Dunlap advertisements [G&D], series de-
                        scription, vols. 1-3
                        Library of Congress cataloguing in publication data
                        [LC], vols. 4, 6
Additional information: This series appeared when "The Man from U.N.C.L.E."
    and other television shows about espionage were popular. TEEN was an
    acronym for Top-secret Educational Espionage Network.
         Books were published without subtitles.
Series description [G&D]: "MEET . . . CHRISTOPHER COOL/TEEN AGENT as he
    plays the deadliest game of all--international intrigue--in America's
    newest exciting spy stories.
         "Christopher Cool and his Apache Indian roommate, Geronimo Johnson
    --sophomores at an Ivy League university--combine their campus lives
    with undercover assignments for a vital arm of U. S. Intelligence:
    Top-Secret Educational Espionage Network.
         "Expertly schooled in all the arts of espionage, the two daring
    TEEN agents work closely with red-haired Spice Carter, a clever coed
    agent, to thwart enemy spies in trouble spots throughout the world."

196S.1   X marks the spy. (Grosset & Dunlap, 1967).

    [G&D]: "Chris flies to France to ferret out a secret device which could
    change the balance of power in the cold war."

196S.2   Mission: Moonfire. (Grosset & Dunlap, 1967).

    [G&D]: "A flaming crescent moon and the trail of fanatical thugs take
    Chris to Turkey, to hunt down a renegade scientist known as Dr. Death."

196S.3   Department of danger. (Grosset & Dunlap, 1967).

    [G&D]: "In London, Chris poses an enemy agent in order to intercept
    a deadly formula which threatens the free world with a horrifying
    plague."

196S.4   Ace of shadows. (Grosset & Dunlap, 1968).

    [LC]: "Two TEEN agents try to discover the connection between the
    accidental death of a German count and the activities of an enemy
    agent known as the Ace of Shadows."

196S.5   Heads you lose, (Grosset & Dunlap, 1968).

196S.6   Trial by fury. (Grosset & Dunlap, 1969).

    [LC]: "Djakarta is only one stop in this worldwide trek of TEEN agent
    Christopher Cool and his partner Geronimo as they seek a fanatic Orien-
    tal assassin."

Clinton W. Locke

The Stratemeyer Syndicate pseudonym Clinton W. Locke appeared on the four books in the PERRY PIERCE MYSTERY STORIES from 1931 to 1934.

SERIES PUBLICATIONS

197S   PERRY PIERCE MYSTERY STORIES

Volumes: 4
Printed: 1931-1934
Publisher: Henry Altemus Company
Reprint publisher: M. A. Donohue & Company, vols. 1-4
                     Goldsmith Publishing Company, vols. 1-4
Illustrator: Russell H. Tandy, vols. 1-3
               C. C. Stevens, vol. 4
Source of annotations: Henry Altemus Company advertisements [HA]
Series description [HA]:   "As leader [of the Skull Mystery Club] Perry
    reminds his fellow-members that he must solve at least one mystery a
    year to remain in good standing. Perry and his chums start a summer
    vacation looking for a mystery and are rewarded beyond their hopes."

197S.1   Who closed the door; or, Perry Pierce and the old storehouse
mystery. (Altemus, 1931; Donohue; Goldsmith).

    [HA]: "The ancient Sunflower Storehouse is to be torn down in a month,
    but before the time is up, many queer happenings take place there."

197S.2   Who opened the safe; or, Perry Pierce and the secret cipher mystery. (Altemus, 1931; Donohue; Goldsmith).

    [HA]: "A valuable safe disappears in a strange way. Perry and his
    chums in the Skull Mystery Club offer to hunt for it, but when they
    locate it they find that the real mystery has just begun."

197S.3   Who hid the key; or, Perry Pierce tracing the counterfeit money.
(Altemus, 1932; Donohue; Goldsmith).

197S.4   Who took the papers; or, Perry Pierce gathering the printed clues
(Altemus, 1934; Donohue; Goldsmith).

Helen Beecher Long

Six books for girls (the DO SOMETHING series and one non-series title)
were written under the Stratemeyer Syndicate pseudonym Helen Beecher Long
between 1914 and 1919.

SERIES PUBLICATIONS

198S   DO SOMETHING (JANICE DAY)

Volumes: 5
Printed: 1914-1919
Publisher: Sully & Kleinteich, vols. 1-4
            George Sully & Company, vol. 5
Reprint publisher: George Sully & Company, vols. 1-4
                    The Christian Herald, vol. 1
                    Goldsmith Publishing Co., vols. 1-5
                    Grosset & Dunlap, vol. 1*
                    Saalfield Publishing Co., vols. 1-5
Illustrator: Walter S. Rogers, vol. 1
              Corinne Turner, vols. 2-5
Source of annotations: Goldsmith Publishing Co. advertisements [G]
Additional information: George Sully & Co. published popular editions of
    all five DO SOMETHING books in 1919.
        The Saalfield and Goldsmith editions had a slightly different se-
    ries order; The Christian Herald's edition had the Walter S. Rogers
    illustrations.
Series description [G]: "Janice Day is a character that will live long in
    juvenile fiction. . . .There is an abundance of humor, quaint situations,
    and worth-while effort, and likewise plenty of plot and mystery."

198S.1   Janice Day at Poketown.   (Sully & Kleinteich, 1914; Grosset &
Dunlap, 1916;* Sully, 1919; Christian Herald; Goldsmith; Saalfield).

    Title also listed as Janice Day. Goldsmith and Saalfield editions
    listed as vol. 2.

198S.2   The testing of Janice Day. (Sully & Kleinteich, 1915; Sully,
1918?, 1919; Goldsmith; Saalfield).

    Saalfield and Goldsmith editions listed as vol. 3.

198S.3   How Janice Day won. (Sully & Kleinteich, 1916; Sully, 1919;
Goldsmith; Saalfield).

    Saalfield and Goldsmith editions listed as vol. 4.

198S.4   The mission of Janice Day. (Sully & Kleinteich, 1917; Sully,
1919; Goldsmith; Saalfield).

    Saalfield and Goldsmith editions listed as vol. 5.

198S.5   Janice Day, the young homemaker. (Sully, 1919; Goldsmith; Saalfield).

    Saalfield and Goldsmith editions listed as vol. 1.

----

* Possibly a phantom edition.

OTHER PUBLICATIONS

199N   The girl he left behind.* (Sully, 1918).

Dr. Willard Mackenzie

Dr. Willard Mackenzie was a house name for Golden Days and is not a proven
Stratemeyer pseudonym. One serial, a reprint of a boys' story that origi-
nally appeared under the name Ralph Hamilton, is sometimes credited to
Edward Stratemeyer.

MAGAZINE PUBLICATIONS

200MQ   "The hermit's protege; or, The mystery of Wind Ridge." Golden
Days, vol. 25, nos. 1-11, Nov. 14, 1903-Jan. 23, 1904.

   First published with the same title, but with Ralph Hamilton listed as
   author, in Golden Days, Dec. 19, 1891-Feb. 27, 1892 (160MQ).

Amy Bell Marlowe

The Stratemeyer Syndicate pseudonym Amy Bell Marlowe appeared on ten girls'
series books in two series, AMY BELL MARLOWE'S BOOKS FOR GIRLS and the
ORIOLE series, printed between 1914 and 1927, and reprinted in two omnibus
volumes in 1933.

SERIES PUBLICATIONS

201S   AMY BELL MARLOWE'S BOOKS FOR GIRLS

Volumes: 8**
Printed: 1914-1933**
Publisher: Grosset & Dunlap
Illustrator: Walter S. Rogers, vols. 1-3, 7
             WR, vol. 6
Source of annotations: Grosset & Dunlap advertisements [G&D]

---

*   Illustrated by R. Emmett Owen.
**   Number of volumes and years published include the four-in-one reprint,
     Sunset Ranch, published in 1933.

Additional information: AMY BELL MARLOWE'S BOOKS FOR GIRLS was a series
only in that all the books were published and advertised under the
heading AMY BELL MARLOWE'S BOOKS FOR GIRLS. The books did not share
the same characters or focus on a single theme.

    The three ORIOLE books (202S) were often included under the heading
AMY BELL MARLOWE'S BOOKS FOR GIRLS, but since they were also advertised
as the ORIOLE books, and since they all had ORIOLE as the central character, they have been given a separate listing.

Series description [G&D]: "Charming, fresh and original stories. Miss
Marlowe's books for girls are somewhat of the type of Miss Alcott, but
all are thoroughly up-to-date and wholly American in scene and action."

201S.1   The oldest of four; or, Natalie's way out. (Grosset & Dunlap,
1914).

    [G&D]: "A sweet story of the struggles of a live girl to keep a family
from want, the father having disappeared during a wreck at sea."

201S.2   The girls of Hillcrest Farm; or, The secret of the rocks. (Grosset & Dunlap, 1914).

    [G&D]: "Relating the trials of two girls who take boarders on an old
farm. The secret of the rocks is a most unusual one."

201S.3   A little Miss Nobody; or, With the girls of Pinewood Hall.
(Grosset & Dunlap, 1914).

    [G&D]: "A pathetic tale of a school girl who was literally a nobody.
How she solved the mystery of her identity, is most absorbing."

201S.4   The girl from Sunset Ranch; or, Alone in a great city. (Grosset
& Dunlap, 1914).

    [G&D]: "A ranch girl comes to New York to meet relatives she has never
seen and to vindicate her family honor. Her adventures in a great city
make unusually good reading."

201S.5   Wyn's camping days; or, The outing of the Go-Ahead Club. (Grosset & Dunlap, 1914).

    [G&D]: "A tale of happy days on the water and under canvas, with a
touch of mystery and considerable excitement."

201S.6   Frances of the ranges; or, The old ranchman's treasure. (Grosset
& Dunlap, 1915).

    [G&D]: "A vivid picture of life on the great cattle ranges of the West.
Frances undertakes a mission for her sick father that has many perils,
but there are also many amusing incidents."

201S.7   The girls of Rivercliff School; or, Beth Baldwin's resolve.
(Grosset & Dunlap, 1916).

    Reprinted in Oriole's adventures, a four-in-one reprint, in 1933
(202S.4).

[G&D]: "This is one of the most entertaining stories centering about a girl's school that has ever been written."

201S.8X   Sunset Ranch. (Grosset & Dunlap, 1933).

A four-in-one reprint. Contents not certain.

202S   ORIOLE

Volumes: 4*
Printed: 1920-1933*
Publisher: Grosset & Dunlap
Illustrator: Walter S. Rogers, vols. 1-4X
Source of annotations: Grosset & Dunlap advertisements [G&D]
Additional information: Books were published without subtitles.

202S.1   When Oriole came to Harbor Light. (Grosset & Dunlap, 1920).

Reprinted in Oriole's adventures, a four-in-one reprint, in 1933 (202S.4X).
[G&D]: "The story of a young girl, cast up by the sea, and rescued by the old lighthouse keeper."

202S.2   When Oriole traveled westward. (Grosset & Dunlap, 1921).

Reprinted in Oriole's adventures, a four-in-one reprint, in 1933 (202S.4X).
[G&D]: "Oriole visits the family of a rich ranchman and enjoys herself immensely."

202S.3   When Oriole went to boarding school. (Grosset & Dunlap, 1927).

Reprinted in Oriole's adventures, a four-in-one reprint, in 1933 (202S.4X).
[G&D]: "How this brave girl bears up under the most trying experiences, makes very interesting reading."

202S.4X   Oriole's adventures: Four complete adventure books for girls in one big volume. (Grosset & Dunlap, 1933).

Contains When Oriole came to Harbor Light, published in 1920 (202S.1); When Oriole traveled westward, published in 1921 (202S.2); When Oriole went to boarding school, published in 1927 (202S.3), and The girls of Rivercliff School, published in 1916 (201S.7).

---

*   Number of volumes and years published include Oriole's adventures, a four-in-one reprint published in 1933.

Eugene Martin

Eugene Martin's four-volume SKY FLYERS series was published by Altemus in the 1930s. It was the only series attributed to this Stratemeyer Syndicate pseudonym.

SERIES PUBLICATIONS

203S   SKY FLYERS (RANDY STARR)

Volumes: 4
Printed: 1931-ca1933
Publisher: Henry Altemus Company
Reprint publisher: Saalfield Publishing Co., vols. 1-3
Illustrator: Howard L. Hastings, vols. 1-3
Source of annotations: Henry Altemus Company advertisements [HA]
Series description [HA]:   "Readers of the Randy Starr books will become
    acquainted with a hero who yearns for what nearly every American boy
    does--a pilot's license.   How he works for this, how he tries to win
    an airplane, and how he becomes involved in many adventures, form the
    subject-matter of these stories."

203S.1   Randy Starr after an air prize; or, The sky flyers in a dash down
the States. (Altemus, 1931; Saalfield).

    [HA]:   "The story of a prize race from Maine to Miami."

203S.2   Randy Starr above stormy seas; or, The sky flyers on a perilous
journey. (Altemus, 1931; Saalfield).

    [HA]:   "Randy and his chums render a Spanish mine-owner a great service."

203S.3   Randy Starr leading the air circus; or, The sky flyers in a daring
stunt. (Altemus, 1932; Saalfield).

203S.4   Randy Starr tracing the air spy; or, The sky flyers seeking the
stolen plane. (Altemus, ca1933).

Fenworth Moore

Fenworth Moore was a short-lived Stratemeyer Syndicate pseudonym that was credited with one four-volume series, the JERRY FORD WONDER STORIES, published in 1931 and 1932 (and reprinted in 1937).

SERIES PUBLICATIONS

204S   JERRY FORD WONDER STORIES

Volumes: 5*
Printed: 1931-1937*
Publisher: Cupples & Leon Company
Illustrator: Russell H. Tandy, vols. 1-4
Source of annotations: Cupples & Leon Company advertisements [C&L]
Series description [C&L]: "A new series with plenty of action and adventure
    It is lively and full of real situations that relate in an entertaining
    way how Jerry Ford overcame his obstacles."

204S.1   Wrecked on Cannibal Island; or, Jerry Ford's adventure among
savages. (Cupples & Leon, 1931).

    Reprinted in Thrilling stories for boys, published in 1937 (204S.5X),
    and in Popular stories for boys, published ca1934 (205N), both four-
    in-one reprints.
        [C&L]: "Jerry Ford's inheritance was stolen by an unscrupulous
    lawyer, and he had many thrilling adventures before the thief was
    finally captured."

204S.2   Lost in the caves of gold; or, Jerry Ford among the mountains of
mystery. (Cupples & Leon, 1931).

    Reprinted in Thrilling stories for boys, a four-in-one reprint published
    in 1937 (204S.5X).
        [C&L]: "The finding of the trunks in which the stolen fortune was
    hidden, and the discovery of a Pirate's treasure in some underground
    caves."

204S.3   Cast away in the land of snow; or, Jerry Ford among the polar
bears. (Cupples & Leon, 1931).

    Reprinted in Thrilling stories for boys, a four-in-one reprint published
    in 1937 (204S.5X).
        [C&L]: "While returning home with the treasure, the ship is cap-
    tured by pirates in the middle of the Pacific Ocean. Plenty of action
    and excitement follows."

204S.4   Prisoners on the pirate ship; or, Jerry Ford and the yellow men.
(Cupples & Leon, 1932).

    Reprinted in Thrilling stories for boys, a four-in-one reprint published
    in 1937 (204S.5X).
        [C&L]: "This story offers a thrill in a life time. Jerry Ford,
    and his pals, recapture the pirate ship and again secure their missing
    treasure."

204S.5X   Thrilling stories for boys. (Cupples & Leon, 1937).

----

*   Number of volumes and years published include Thrilling stories for boy
    the four-in-one reprint published in 1937.

Contains <u>Wrecked</u> <u>on</u> <u>Cannibal</u> <u>Island</u> (204S.1), <u>Lost</u> <u>in</u> <u>the</u> <u>caves</u> <u>of</u> <u>gold</u> (204S.2), <u>Cast</u> <u>away</u> <u>in</u> <u>the</u> <u>land</u> <u>of</u> <u>snow</u> (204S.3), all published in 1931, and <u>Prisoners</u> <u>on</u> <u>the</u> <u>pirate</u> <u>ship</u>, published in 1932 (204S.4).

OTHER PUBLICATIONS

205N   Popular stories for boys. (Cupples & Leon, ca1934).

Contains <u>Bomba</u> <u>the</u> <u>jungle</u> <u>boy</u> by Roy Rockwood, published in 1926 (226S.1); <u>Sky</u> <u>riders</u> <u>of</u> <u>the</u> <u>Atlantic</u> by Richard H. Stone, published in 1930 (259S.1); <u>Wrecked</u> <u>on</u> <u>Cannibal</u> <u>Island</u> by Fenworth Moore, published in 1931 (204S.1), and <u>Bob</u> <u>Dexter</u> <u>and</u> <u>the</u> <u>clubhouse</u> <u>mystery</u> by Willard Baker, published in 1925.

Gertrude W. Morrison

The Stratemeyer Syndicate pseudonym Gertrude W. Morrison was used for a seven-volume girls' adventure and sports series, the GIRLS OF CENTRAL HIGH, published from 1914 to 1919.

SERIES PUBLICATIONS

206S   GIRLS OF CENTRAL HIGH

Volumes: 7
Printed: 1914-1919
Publisher: Grosset & Dunlap
Reprint publisher: Goldsmith Publishing Co., vols. 1-5*
                    Saalfield Publishing Co., vols. 1-7
                    World Syndicate Publishing Co., vols. 1-7
Illustrator: Dick Richards, vols. 1, 4
              Jim H.[?] Richards, vol. 2
              anonymous, vols. 3, 5
              Walter S. Rogers, vol. 6
              R. Emmett Owen, vol. 7
Source of annotations: Grosset & Dunlap advertisements [G&D]
Additional information: Some (possibly all) Goldsmith editions have covers
    which show the title as "Central High Girls" instead of "Girls of Cen-
    tral High."
Series description [G&D]: "Here is a series full of the spirit of high
    school life of today. The girls are real flesh-and-blood characters,
    and we follow them with interest in school and out.
        "There are many contested matches on track and field, and on the
    water, as well as doings in the classroom and on the school stage.

---

*   Possibly volumes 6 and 7 as well.

There is plenty of fun and excitement, all clean, pure and wholesome."

206S.1   The girls of Central High; or, Rivals for all honors. (Grosset & Dunlap, 1914; Goldsmith; Saalfield; World).

[G&D]: "A stirring tale of high school life, full of fun, with a touch of mystery and a strange initiation."

206S.2   The girls of Central High on Lake Luna; or, The crew that won. (Grosset & Dunlap, 1914; Goldsmith; Saalfield; World).

[G&D]: "Telling of water sports and fun galore, and of fine times in camp."

206S.3   The girls of Central High at basketball; or, The great gymnasium mystery. (Grosset & Dunlap, 1914; Goldsmith; Saalfield; World).

[G&D]: "Here we have a number of thrilling contests at basketball and in addition, the solving of a mystery which had bothered the high school authorities for a long while."

206S.4   The girls of Central High on the stage; or, The play that took the prize. (Grosset & Dunlap, 1914; Goldsmith; Saalfield; World).

[G&D]: "How the girls went in for theatricals and how one of them wrote a play which afterward was made over for the professional stage and brought in some much-needed money."

206S.5   The girls of Central High on track and field; or, The girl champions of the school league. (Grosset & Dunlap, 1914; Goldsmith; Saalfield; World).

[G&D]: "This story takes in high school athletics in their most approved and up-to-date fashion. Full of fun and excitement."

206S.6   The girls of Central High in camp; or, The old professor's secret (Grosset & Dunlap, 1915; Saalfield; World).

[G&D]: "The girls went camping on Acorn Island and had a delightful time at boating, swimming and picnic parties."

206S.7   The girls of Central High aiding the Red Cross; or, Amateur theatricals for a worthy cause. (Grosset & Dunlap, 1919, 1921?; Saalfield, World).

Oliver Optic

Oliver Optic was a pseudonym for William Taylor Adams. His last book, An undivided union, was completed by Edward Stratemeyer.

SERIES PUBLICATIONS

207S   THE BLUE AND THE GRAY SERIES--ON LAND

Volumes: 1*
Printed: 1899*
Publisher: Lee and Shepard
Additional information: This was a six-volume series: all the other titles
    were written by William Taylor Adams as Oliver Optic. Only the first
    book had a sub-title. The other five titles were:
    1. Brother against brother; or, The war on the border (1894)
    2. In the saddle (1895)
    3. A lieutenant at eighteen (1895)
    4. On the staff (1896)
    5. At the front (1897)

207S.1   An undivided union. (Lee & Shepard, 1899).

    Completed by Edward Stratemeyer.

Peter Pad

Several writers, including Edward Stratemeyer, used the pseudonym Peter
Pad. Stratemeyer's only publication under this name was a dime novel published in the NEW YORK FIVE CENT LIBRARY in 1893.

SERIES PUBLICATIONS

208P   NEW YORK FIVE CENT LIBRARY

Volumes: 1**
Printed: 1893**
Publisher: Street & Smith
Additional information: See Jim Bowie, NEW YORK FIVE CENT LIBRARY (071P).

208P.1X   Mayor Liederkranz of Hoboken; or, The jolly captain of the pretzel
schuten corps. No. 40. May 13, 1893.

---

* Number of volumes and years published apply only to those titles written
   by Edward Stratemeyer.
** Number of volumes and years published apply only to those titles written
   by Edward Stratemeyer under the name Peter Pad.

Margaret Penrose

Twenty-seven books, excluding reprints and revisions, were published under
the Stratemeyer Syndicate pseudonym Margaret Penrose, all as part of three
girls' series published by Cuppies & Leon: DOROTHY DALE (1908-1924; 13
vols.), the MOTOR GIRLS (1910-1917; 10 vols.), and the RADIO GIRLS (1922-
1924; 4 vols.). One series, the RADIO GIRLS, was retitled and reprinted
by Goldsmith in 1930 as the CAMPFIRE GIRLS series.
    Lillian Garis assisted Edward Stratemeyer with some titles published
under this pseudonym.

SERIES PUBLICATIONS

209S   CAMPFIRE GIRLS

Volumes: 4
Printed: 1930
Publisher: Goldsmith Publishing Co.
Additional information: This series was printed from the plates for the
    RADIO GIRLS series (212S), which was first published from 1922 to 1924.
    Although the covers and title pages had the new CAMPFIRE GIRLS titles,
    the page tops still showed the original RADIO GIRLS titles.
        The books were published without illustrations.

209S.1   The Campfire girls of Roselawn; or, A strange message from the
air. (Goldsmith, 1930).

    First published by Cuppies & Leon in 1922 as The radio girls of Rose-
    lawn; or, A strange message from the air, vol. 1 of the RADIO GIRLS
    series (212S.1).

209S.2   The Campfire girls on the program; or, Singing and reciting at
the sending station. (Goldsmith, 1930).

    First published by Cuppies & Leon in 1922 as The radio girls on the
    program; or, Singing and reciting at the sending station, vol. 2 of
    the RADIO GIRLS series (212S.2).

209S.3   The Campfire girls on Station Island; or, The wireless from the
steam yacht. (Goldsmith, 1930).

    First published by Cuppies & Leon in 1922 as The radio girls on Station
    Island; or, The wireless from the steam yacht, vol. 3 of the RADIO
    GIRLS series (212S.3).

209S.4   The Campfire girls at Forest Lodge; or, The strange hut in the
swamp. (Goldsmith, 1930).

    First published by Cuppies & Leon in 1924 as The radio girls at Forest
    Lodge; or, The strange hut in the swamp, vol. 4 of the RADIO GIRLS
    series (212S.4)

210S   DOROTHY DALE

Volumes: 13
Printed: 1908–1924
Publisher: Cupples & Leon Company
Illustrator: Charles Nuttall, vols. 1-5
            H. Richard Boehm, vol. 6
            anonymous, vols. 7-8
            Walter S. Rogers, vols. 9-10
            R. Emmett Owen, vols. 11-12
Source of annotations: Cupples & Leon advertisements [C&L]
Additional information: Lillian Garis contributed to some of the volumes
   in this series; Howard Garis sometimes helped her.
        The books were published without subtitles.
Series description [C&L]: "Dorothy Dale is the daughter of an old Civil
   War veteran who is running a weekly newspaper in a small Eastern town.
   Her sunny disposition, her fun-loving ways and her trials and triumphs
   make clean, interesting and fascinating reading. The Dorothy Dale series is one of the most popular series of books for girls ever published."

210S.1   Dorothy Dale, a girl of today. (Cupples & Leon, 1908).

   [C&L]: "Dorothy is the daughter of an old Civil War veteran who is
   running a weekly newspaper in a small Eastern town. When her father
   falls sick, the girl shows what she can do to support the family."

210S.2   Dorothy Dale at Glenwood School. (Cupples & Leon, 1908).

   [C&L]: "More prosperous times have come to the Dale family, and Major
   Dale resolves to send Dorothy to a boarding school to complete her
   education. At Glenwood School the girl makes a host of friends and
   has many good times. But some girls are jealous of Dorothy's popularity, and they seek to get her into trouble in more ways than one."

210S.3   Dorothy Dale's great secret. (Cupples & Leon, 1909).

   [C&L]: "A splendid story of one girl's devotion to another. Dorothy's
   chum ran away to join a theatrical company. What Dorothy did, and how
   she kept the secret, make a tale no girl will care to miss."

210S.4   Dorothy Dale and her chums. (Cupples & Leon, 1909).

   [C&L]: "A story of a school life, and of strange adventures among the
   gypsies. Dorothy befriends a little French girl and also a gypsy waif,
   in a manner sure to touch the hearts of all readers."

210S.5   Dorothy Dale's queer holidays. (Cupples & Leon, 1910).

   [C&L]: "Relates the details of a mystery that surrounded Tanglewood
   Park. There is a great snowstorm, and the young folks become snowbound, much to their dismay."

210S.6   Dorothy Dale's camping days. (Cupples & Leon, 1911).

[C&L]: "A great variety of things happen in this volume, from the moment Dorothy and her chums are met coming down the hillside on a treacherous load of hay, until all the various complications are cleared up in the final chapter."

210S.7   Dorothy Dale's school rivals. (Cupples & Leon, 1912).

[C&L]: "Dorothy and her chum, Tavia, return to Glenwood School. One of the new students becomes Dorothy's bitter rival and troubles at home add to her difficulties. A splendid story, showing Dorothy's sterling character."

210S.8   Dorothy Dale in the city. (Cupples & Leon, 1913).

[C&L]: "Dorothy is invited to New York City by her Aunt. This tale presents a clever picture of life in New York as it appears to one who has never before visited the Metropolis."

210S.9   Dorothy Dale's promise. (Cupples & Leon, 1914).

210S.10   Dorothy Dale in the West. (Cupples & Leon, 1915).

210S.11   Dorothy Dale's strange discovery. (Cupples & Leon, 1916).

210S.12   Dorothy Dale's engagement. (Cupples & Leon, 1917).

210S.13   Dorothy Dale to the rescue. (Cupples & Leon, 1924).

211S   MOTOR GIRLS

Volumes: 10
Printed: 1910-1917
Publisher: Cupples & Leon Company
Reprint publisher: Goldsmith Publishing Co., vols. 1-10
Illustrator: G. M. Kaiser, vol. 1
              Charles Nuttall, vol. 2
              anonymous, vols. 3-6
              Walter S. Rogers, vols. 7-9
              R. Emmett Owen, vol. 10
Source of annotations: Cupples & Leon Company advertisements [C&L]
Additional information: Lillian Garis assisted Edward Stratemeyer with
    some of the books in this series, possibly with help from Howard Garis.
    Howard Garis also worked with Edward Stratemeyer on titles in the MOTOR
    BOYS series (354S), published by Cupples & Leon from 1906 to 1924.
        The Goldsmith editions were published without illustrations.
Series description [C&L]: "Since the enormous success of our 'Motor Boys
    Series' by Clarence Young, we have been asked to get out a similar se-
    ries for girls. No one is better equipped to furnish these tales than
    Mrs. Penrose, who, besides being an able writer, is an expert auto-
    mobilist."

211S.1   The motor girls; or, A mystery of the road. (Cupples & Leon,
1910; Goldsmith).

[C&L]: "When Cora Kimball got her touring car she did not imagine so many adventures were in store for her. During a trip from one city to another, a rich young man lost a pocketbook containing valuable stocks and much cash. Later, to the surprise of everybody, the empty pocketbook was found in the tool box of Cora's automobile. A fine tale that all wide-awake girls will appreciate."

211S.2   The motor girls on a tour; or, Keeping a strange promise. (Cupples & Leon, 1910; Goldsmith).

[C&L]: "A great many things happen in this volume, starting with the running over of a hamper of good things lying in the road. A precious heirloom is missing, and how it was traced up is told with absorbing interest."

211S.3   The motor girls at Lookout Beach; or, In quest of the runaways. (Cupples & Leon, 1911; Goldsmith).

[C&L]: "There was great excitement when the Motor Girls decided to go to Lookout Beach for the summer. Just previous to departing, they visited a strawberry farm, and there fell in with two little girls who were accused by a rich boarder of stealing a pair of diamond earrings. They befriended the little runaways, and at last proved their innocence."

211S.4   The motor girls through New England; or, Held by the gypsies. (Cupples & Leon, 1911; Goldsmith).

[C&L]: "A strong story and one which will make this series more popular than ever. There is a robbery at the cottage where the Motor Girls are staying and one of them sees the burglar, who escapes. Later, the man, who is a gypsy, is captured. The girls go on a motoring trip through New England, and there the girl who saw the burglar is abducted and held by the Gypsies so that she cannot go into court to testify against the captured member of the band."

211S.5   The motor girls on Cedar Lake; or, The hermit of Fern Island. (Cupples & Leon, 1912; Goldsmith).

[C&L]: "How Cora and her chums went camping on the lake shore, how they took trips in their motor boat, how they met the strange hermit and his daughter and how they aided the hermit in establishing his innocence, are told with a vim and vigor all girls enjoy."

211S.6   The motor girls on the coast; or, The waif from the sea. (Cupples & Leon, 1913; Goldmsith).

[C&L]: "From a lake the scene is shifted to the sea coast where the girls pay a visit. They have their motor boat with them and go out for many good times.

211S.7   The motor girls on Crystal Bay; or, The secret of the red oar. (Cupples & Leon, 1914; Goldsmith).

[C&L]: "More jolly times on the water and at a cute little bungalow on the shore of the bay. A tale that will interest all girls."

211S.8   The motor girls on waters blue; or, The strange cruise of the
Tartar. (Cupples & Leon, 1915; Goldsmith).

    [C&L]: "Before the girls started on a long cruise down to the West
Indies, they fell in with a foreign girl and she informed them that
her father was being held a political prisoner on one of the islands.
A story that is full of fun as well as mystery."

211S.9   The motor girls at Camp Surprise; or, The cave in the mountains.
(Cupples & Leon, 1916; Goldsmith).

211S.10   The motor girls in the mountains; or, The gypsy girl's secret.
(Cupples & Leon, 1917; Goldsmith).

212S   RADIO GIRLS

Volumes: 4
Printed: 1922-1924
Publisher: Cupples & Leon Company
Illustrator: Thelma Gooch, vols. 1-3
Source of annotations: Cupples & Leon Company advertisements [C&L]
Additional information: Like the MOTOR GIRLS (211S), the RADIO GIRLS also
    had male counterparts in a boys' series: the RADIO BOYS (087S),
    a Stratemeyer Syndicate series published under the pseudonym Allen
    Chapman. Although the two series both started in 1922, the RADIO BOYS,
    a Grosset & Dunlap series, was the more successful series and lasted
    for thirteen volumes (1922-1930).
        Goldsmith reprinted the RADIO GIRLS series as the CAMPFIRE GIRLS
    series (209S) in 1930, substituting the word "Campfire" for the word
    "radio" in all the titles.
Series description [C&L]: "A new and up-to-date series, taking in the
    activities of several bright girls who become interested in radio.
    The stories tell of thrilling exploits, out-door life and the great
    part the Radio plays in the adventures of the girls and in solving
    their mysteries. Fascinating books that girls of all ages will want
    to read."

212S.1   The radio girls of Roselawn; or, A strange message from the air.
(Cupples & Leon, 1922).

    Reprinted by Goldsmith in 1930 as The Campfire girls of Roselawn; or,
A strange message from the air, vol. 1 of the CAMPFIRE GIRLS series
(209S.1).
    [C&L]: "Showing how Jessie Norwood and her chums became interested
in radiophoning, how they gave a concert for a worthy local charity,
and how they received a sudden and unexpected call for help out of the
air. A girl who was wanted as a witness in a celebrated law case had
disappeared, and how the radio girls went to the rescue is told in an
absorbing manner."

212S.2   The radio girls on the program; or, Singing and reciting at the
sending station. (Cupples & Leon, 1922).

    Reprinted by Goldsmith in 1930 as The Campfire girls on the program;

or, Singing and reciting at the sending station, vol. 2 of the CAMPFIRE GIRLS series (209S.2).

[C&L]: "When listening in on a thrilling recitation or a superb concert number who of us has not longed to 'look behind the scenes' to see how it was done? The girls had made the acquaintance of a sending station manager and in this volume are permitted to get on the program, much to their delight. A tale full of action and not a little fun."

212S.3   The radio girls on Station Island; or, The wireless from the steam yacht. (Cupples & Leon, 1922).

Reprinted by Goldsmith in 1930 as The Campfire girls on Station Island; or, The wireless from the steam yacht, vol. 3 of the CAMPFIRE GIRLS series (209S.3).

[C&L]: "In this volume the girls travel to the seashore and put in a vacation on an island where is located a big radio sending station. The big brother of one of the girls owns a steam yacht and while out with a pleasure party those on the island receive word by radio that the yacht is on fire. A tale thrilling to the last page."

212S.4   The radio girls at Forest Lodge; or, The strange hut in the swamp. (Cupples & Leon, 1924).

Reprinted by Goldsmith in 1930 as The Campfire girls at Forest Lodge; or, The strange hut in the swamp, vol. 4 of the CAMPFIRE GIRLS series (209S.4).

[C&L]: "The Radio Girls spend several weeks on the shores of a beautiful lake and with their radio get news of a great forest fire. It also aids them in rounding up some undesirable folks who occupy the strange hut in the swamp."

Peter

Edward Statemeyer used the pen name Peter for two magazine stories serialized in Good News in 1895 and 1896.

MAGAZINE PUBLICATIONS

213M   "Dot poy Hans." Good News, vol. 12, nos. 289-299, Nov. 23, 1895-Jan. 25, 1896.

214M   "That coon Rastus." Good News, vol. 11, nos. 277-288, Aug. 24-Nov. 9, 1895.

Nat Ridley, Jr.

Nat Ridley, Jr., sometimes listed as Nat Ridley, was the pen name for the
NAT RIDLEY RAPID FIRE DETECTIVE STORIES, a Stratemeyer Syndicate series
published in 1926 and 1927 by the Garden City Publishing Company.

SERIES PUBLICATIONS

215S   NAT RIDLEY RAPID FIRE DETECTIVE STORIES

Volumes: 17
Printed: 1926-1927
Publisher: Garden City Publishing Company
Source of annotations: Garden City Publishing Company advertisements [GC]
Additional information: This series appeared only in paperback. The first
    volume was issued on January 2, 1926; subsequent volumes were published
    on the 21st of each month. See Victor Appleton, MOVIE BOYS (019S) for
    further information about Garden City's publishing schedule.
        Except for the cover artwork, the books were published without il-
    lustrations.
Series description [GC]: "Do you like detective stories that are swift in
    action, full of mystery and absorbing from start to finish? If so read
    THE NAT RIDLEY Rapid Fire DETECTIVE STORIES By Nat Ridley, Jr."

215S.1   Guilty or not guilty? or, Nat Ridley's great race track case.
(Garden City, 1926).

    [GC]: "A thrilling horse race--the winning of thousands of dollars--
    then darkness and a mysterious murder on the lonely road. Who was
    guilty, tramps, a rival horseman, or the young college boy who was in
    debt and who was also in love with the murdered man's beautiful daugh-
    ter?"

215S.2   Tracked to the West; or, Nat Ridley at the Magnet Mine. (Garden
City, 1926).

    [GC]: "A rich mine owner comes from the West to New York to dispose
    of his holdings--and mysteriously disappears. The wife calls upon Nat
    Ridley to solve this mystery. From New York Bay the scene shifts to
    the gold mines of Montana, and the great detective finds himself en-
    gulfed in one perilous situation after another."

215S.3   In the nick of time; or, Nat Ridley saving a life. (Garden City,
1926).

    [GC]: "Once again Nat Ridley finds himself confronted by a most per-
    plexing puzzle. Who was guilty and why was this awful crime committed?
    The detective's enemies set a trap for him--and Nat was caught. But he
    turned the trick in a manner to make every reader sit up and take no-
    tice."

215S.4   The crime on the Limited; or, Nat Ridley in the Follies. (Garden City, 1926).

215S.5   A daring abduction; or, Nat Ridley's biggest fight. (Garden City, 1926).

215S.6   The stolen nuggets of gold; or, Nat Ridley on the Yukon. (Garden City, 1926).

215S.7   A secret of the stage; or, Nat Ridley and the bouquet of death. (Garden City, 1926).

215S.8   The great circus mystery; or, Nat Ridley on a crooked trail. (Garden City, 1926).

215S.9   A scream in the dark; or, Nat Ridley's crimson clue. (Garden City, 1926).

215S.10   The race track crooks; or, Nat Ridley's queerest puzzle. (Garden City, 1926).

215S.11   The stolen liberty bonds; or, Nat Ridley's circle of clues. (Garden City, 1926).

215S.12   In the grip of the kidnappers; or, Nat Ridley in high society. (Garden City, 1926).

215S.13   The double dagger; or, Nat Ridley's Mexican trail. (Garden City, 1926).

215S.14   The mountain inn mystery; or, Nat Ridley with the forest rangers. (Garden City, 1927).

215S.15   The Western Express robbery; or, Nat Ridley and the mail thieves. (Garden City, 1927).

215S.16   Struck down at midnight; or, Nat Ridley and his rivals. (Garden City, 1927).

215S.17   Detective against detective; or, Nat Ridley showing his nerve. (Garden City, 1927).

Roy Rockwood

Edward Stratemeyer first used the pseudonym Roy Rockwood in 1895, on a story that appeared in Young Sports of America. Eighty-three years later, in 1978, the pseudonym was revived when Grosset & Dunlap reissued the first volumes of the BOMBA THE JUNGLE BOY series.

Between 1895 and 1978, ten magazine stories, six series, and four individual titles were published under this pseudonym. Nine of the magazine stories (including one reprint) were written by Edward Stratemeyer and appeared in boys' story papers from 1895 to 1901; the tenth, serialized in

Banner Weekly in 1895, is considered a probable, but not a proven, Stratemeyer. Roy Rockwood's six series were first published between 1905 and
1936. Stitt and Grosset & Dunlap issued the first series, the DEEP SEA
books (later retitled the SEA TREASURE series), from 1905 to 1908; Cupples
& Leon printed the most series: GREAT MARVEL (1906-1935), DAVE DASHAWAY
(1913-1915), SPEEDWELL BOYS (1913-1915), and BOMBA THE JUNGLE BOY (1926-
1938); Sully and Garden City published the remaining series, DAVE FEARLESS,
from 1918 to 1927. Grosset & Dunlap later reprinted some BOMBA THE JUNGLE
BOY titles--once in 1953 and again in 1978.
    After 1904 or 1905, Roy Rockwood became a Stratemeyer Syndicate house
name, and Howard Garis and Leslie McFarlane, among others, assisted Edward
Stratemeyer with some Roy Rockwood titles.

MAGAZINE PUBLICATIONS

216M   "Brave Larry Barlow; or, The fire fighters of New York." Golden
Hours, nos. 693-702, May 11-July 13, 1901.

    Published in book form in 1902 by Saalfield as Larry Barlow's ambition;
    or, The adventures of a young fireman by Arthur M. Winfield; reprinted
    by Caldwell with the new author and title (343N). Also issued as vol.
    1 in Saalfield's WINFIELD series, still with the new author and title
    (341S.1).

217MQ   "Flyer Fred, the cyclist ferret; or, Running down the rough and
ready rascals," Banner Weekly, vol. 14, nos. 722-727, Sept. 12-Oct. 17,
1896.

    Reprinted on Aug. 17, 1897 by Beadle & Adams as no. 1047 of the HALF-
    DIME LIBRARY (232PQ.1X).

218M   "Joe Johnson, the bicycle wonder; or, Riding for the championship
of the world." Young Sports of America, nos. 2-7, June 1-July 13, 1895.

    Reprinted as "The rival bicyclists; or, Fun and adventure on the wheel"
    in Bright Days, nos. 1-3, April-June 1896 (221M). Published in book
    form in 1897 by W. L. Allison with the new title and Captain Ralph
    Bonehill as author, as vol. 9 in the BOUND TO WIN series (047S.3X).
    Also published as vol. 1 of Allison's (and later Donohue's) YOUNG
    SPORTSMAN'S series (065S.1), and as vol. 14 of Donohue's BOYS' LIBERTY
    series* (049P.1X), all with the new author and title.

219M   "Lost in the land of ice; or, Bob Baxter at the South Pole."
Golden Hours, nos. 670-678, Dec. 1, 1900-Jan. 26, 1901.

    Published in book form in 1902 by A. Wessels as Lost in the land of
    ice; or, Daring adventures around the South Pole by Captain Ralph Bone-
    hill; reprinted by Chatterton-Peck with the new author and title ca1907
    (068N). Also published by Grosset & Dunlap as volume 7 or 8 in the
    ENTERPRISE series, still with the new author and title (053P.1X).
    Printed in paperback by Street & Smith in 1920 as Lost in the land of

---

* Subtitle missing. Title listed as Rival cyclists.

ice; or, Under the northern lights by Edward Stratemeyer, no. 122 in the ALGER SERIES (289P.25X).

220M   "Nat Donald, king of the air; or, The marvelous adventures of a young balloonist." Young Sports of America, nos. 9-13, July 20-Aug. 24, 1895.

221M   "The rival bicyclists; or, Fun and adventure on the wheel." Bright Days, nos. 1-3, April-June, 1896.

First published as "Joe Johnson, the bicycle wonder; or, Riding for the championship of the world" in Young Sports of America, June 1-July 13, 1895 (218M).

222M   "The rival ocean divers; or, A boy's daring search for sunken treasure." Golden Hours, nos. 675-682, Jan. 5-Feb. 23, 1901.

Published in book form by Stitt in 1905 as The rival ocean divers; or, The search for a sunken treasure, vol. 1 in the DEEP SEA series; reprinted by Chatterton-Peck and Grosset & Dunlap with the new title, still as vol. 1 in the DEEP SEA series (229S.1). Also reprinted by Grosset & Dunlap, still with the new title, as vol. 3 of the SEA TREAS-URE series (234S.3). Published by G. Sully & Co. in 1918 and reprinted by Garden City in 1926, both times as Dave Fearless after a sunken treasure; or, The rival ocean divers, vol. 1 of the DAVE FEARLESS series (228S.1).

223M   "The schoolboy cadets; or, Fun and mystery at Washington Hall." Bright Days, nos. 6-10, Sept. 5-Oct. 3, 1896.

224M   "The schoolboy's mutiny; or, Lively times at Riverdale." Bright Days, nos. 16-20, Nov. 14-Dec. 12, 1896.

225M   "Tom Fairwood's schooldays; or, The boys of Riverdale." Bright Days, nos. 11-15, Oct. 10-Nov. 7, 1896.

SERIES PUBLICATIONS

226S   BOMBA THE JUNGLE BOY

Volumes: 20
Printed: 1926-1938
Publisher: Cupples & Leon Company
Reprint publisher: McLoughlin Bros., Clover Books, vols. 1-9
                    Grosset & Dunlap, vols. 1-10
Illustrator: Walter S. Rogers, vols. 1-6
              Howard L. Hastings, vols. 7-11, 13-20
              A. Suk, vol. 12
Source of annotations: Cupples & Leon Company advertisements [C&L]
Additional information: Twelve BOMBA THE JUNGLE BOY movies were made be-
    tween 1949 and 1952, directed by Ford Beebe and starring Johnny Shef-
    field as BOMBA. The movies were loosely based on the series and in-
    cluded Bomba the jungle boy (1949), Bomba on Panther Island (1949),

Bomba in the hidden city (1950), Bomba and the African treasure (1951), Bomba and the elephant stampede (also titled Elephant stampede) (1951), Bomba and the lion hunters (1951), Bomba and the lost volcano (1951), and Bomba and the jungle girl (1952).

Clover books were published without subtitles or illustrations, as were the 1953 Grosset & Dunlap editions.

Series description [C&L]: "Bomba lived far back in the jungles of the Amazon with a half-demented naturalist who told the lad nothing of his past. The jungle boy was a lover of birds, and hunted animals with a bow and arrow and his trusty machete. He had a primitive education in some things, and his daring adventures will be followed with breathless interest by thousands."

226S.1   Bomba the jungle boy; or, The old naturalist's secret. (Cupples & Leon, 1926; McLoughlin, Grosset & Dunlap, 1953, 1978).

1978 edition published without the subtitle. Reprinted in Popular books for boys, a four-in-one reprint, ca1934 (238N).
    [C&L]: "In this volume the reader is taken into the depth of the jungle when he meets Bomba in a life replete with thrilling situations. Once the jungle boy saves the lives of two American rubber hunters who ask him who he is. That sets Bomba to thinking. Who is he and how had he come to the jungle? He knew that he was not of the natives, for he loved the birds and wild animals better. The old naturalist gives him a hint of his father and his mother, and Bomba sets off to solve the mystery of his identity."

226S.2   Bomba the jungle boy at the moving mountain; or, The mystery of the caves of fire. (Cupples & Leon, 1926; McLoughlin; Grosset & Dunlap, 1953, 1978).

1978 edition titled Bomba the jungle boy: The moving mountain.
    [C&L]: "Bomba travels many miles through the jungle, with many encounters with wild beasts and hostile natives. At last he reaches the Andes and presently trails the old man of the burning mountain to his caves of fire and learns more concerning himself. Weird adventures underground."

226S.3   Bomba the jungle boy at the giant cataract; or, Chief Nascanora and his captives. (Cupples & Leon, 1926; McLoughlin; Grosset & Dunlap, 1953).

[C&L]: "From the Moving Mountain Bomba travels to the Giant Cataract, still searching out his parentage. Among the Pilati Indians he finds some white captives. He finds, too, an aged woman who had at one time been a great operatic singer, and she is the first to give Bomba real news of his forebears."

226S.4   Bomba the jungle boy on Jaguar Island; or, Adrift on the river of mystery. (Cupples & Leon, 1927; McLoughlin; Grosset & Dunlap, 1953).

[C&L]: "Jaguar Island was a spot as dangerous as it was mysterious and Bomba was warned to keep away. But the plucky boy sallied forth and met adventures galore."

226S.5   Bomba the jungle boy in the abandoned city; or, A treasure 10,000 years old. (Cupples & Leon, 1927; McLoughlin; Grosset & Dunlap, 1953).

[C&L]: "Years ago this great city had sunk out of sight beneath the trees of the jungle. A wily half-breed and his tribe thought to carry away its treasure of gold and precious stones. Bomba follows."

226S.6   Bomba the jungle boy on Terror Trail; or, The mysterious men from the sky. (Cupples & Leon, 1928; McLoughlin; Grosset & Dunlap, 1953).

226S.7   Bomba the jungle boy in the swamp of death; or, The sacred alligators of Abarago. (Cupples & Leon, 1929; McLoughlin; Grosset & Dunlap, 1953).

226S.8   Bomba the jungle boy among the slaves; or, Daring adventures in the valley of skulls. (Cupples & Leon, 1929; McLoughlin; Grosset & Dunlap, 1953).

226S.9   Bomba the jungle boy on the underground river; or, The cave of bottomless pits. (Cupples & Leon, 1930; McLoughlin; Grosset & Dunlap, 1953).

226S.10   Bomba the jungle boy and the lost explorers; or, A wonderful revelation. (Cupples & Leon, 1930; Grosset & Dunlap, 1953).

226S.11   Bomba the jungle boy in a strange land; or, Facing the unknown. (Cupples & Leon, 1931).

226S.12   Bomba the jungle boy among the pygmies; or, Battling with stealthy foes. (Cupples & Leon, 1931).

226S.13   Bomba the jungle boy and the cannibals; or, Winning against native dangers. (Cupples & Leon, 1932).

226S.14   Bomba the jungle boy and the painted hunters; or, A long search rewarded. (Cupples & Leon, 1932).

226S.15   Bomba the jungle boy and the river demons; or, Outwitting the savage medicine man. (Cupples & Leon, 1933).

226S.16   Bomba the jungle boy and the hostile chieftain; or, A hazardous trek to the sea. (Cupples & Leon, 1934).

226S.17   Bomba the jungle boy trapped by the cyclone; or, Shipwrecked on the swirling seas. (Cupples & Leon, 1935).

226S.18   Bomba the jungle boy in the land of burning lava; or, Outwitting superstitious natives. (Cupples & Leon, 1936).

226S.19   Bomba the jungle boy in the perilous kingdom; or, Braving strange hazards. (Cupples & Leon, 1937).

226S.20   Bomba the jungle boy in the steaming grotto; or, Victorious through flame and fury. (Cupples & Leon, 1938).

227S   DAVE DASHAWAY

Volumes: 5
Printed: 1913-1915
Publisher: Cupples & Leon Company
Illustrator: R. Blass, vols. 1-5
Source of annotations: Cupples & Leon Company advertisements [C&L]
Series description [C&L]: "Never was there a more clever young aviator
    than Dave Dashaway. All up-to-date lads will surely wish to read about
    him."

227S.1   Dave Dashaway, the young aviator; or, In the clouds for fame and
fortune. (Cupples & Leon, 1913).

    [C&L]: "This initial volume tells how the hero ran away from his mi-
    serly guardian, fell in with a successful airman, and became a young
    aviator of note."

227S.2   Dave Dashaway and his hydroplane; or, Daring adventures over the
Great Lakes. (Cupples & Leon, 1913).

    [C&L]: "Showing how Dave continued his career as a birdman and had
    many adventures over the Great Lakes, and how he foiled the plans of
    some Canadian smugglers."

227S.3   Dave Dashaway and his giant airship; or, A marvelous trip across
the Atlantic. (Cupples & Leon, 1913).

    [C&L]: "How the giant airship was constructed and how the daring young
    aviator and his friends made the hazardous journey through the clouds
    from the new world to the old, is told in a way to hold the reader
    spellbound."

227S.4   Dave Dashaway around the world; or, A young Yankee aviator among
many nations. (Cupples & Leon, 1913).

    [C&L]: "An absorbing tale of a great air flight around the world, of
    adventures in Alaska, Siberia and elsewhere. A true to life picture
    of what may be accomplished in the near future."

227S.5   Dave Dashaway, air champion; or, Wizard work in the clouds.
(Cupples & Leon, 1915).

    [C&L]: "Dave makes several daring trips, and then enters a contest for
    a big prize. An aviation tale thrilling in the extreme."

228S   DAVE FEARLESS

Volumes: 17*
Printed: 1918-1927
Publisher: George Sully & Company, vols. 1-3
          Garden City Publishing Company, vols. 4-17*

---

*   The last two volumes may be phantom titles.

Reprint publisher: Garden City Publishing Company, vols. 1-3
Illustrator: A. B. Shute, vol. 1
               Clare Angell, vol. 2
               Charles Nuttall, vol. 3
Source of annotations: Garden City Publishing Company advertisements [GC]
Additional information: The first three DAVE FEARLESS titles, published
   by Sully in 1918, were reprints of volumes 1, 2, and 3 of the DEEP SEA
   series (229S). Sully's DAVE FEARLESS series stopped after three titles,
   but eight years later Garden City published a paperback edition of the
   first DAVE FEARLESS book on January 2, 1926. The second and third volumes appeared in paperback on January 14, 1926, and February 14, 1926;
   after that, the Stratemeyer Syndicate produced new titles, which were
   issued monthly until either February or March 1927.* Leslie McFarlane,
   who had just begun to work for the Stratemeyer Syndicate, contributed
   to volumes 10, 11, and 12. For further information on the publishing
   history of the first three titles, see DEEP SEA series (229S); for more
   information on Garden City's publishing schedules, see Victor Appleton,
   MOVIE BOYS (019S).
      Except for the cover artwork, the Garden City editions were pub-
   lished without illustrations.

228S.1   Dave Fearless after a sunken treasure; or, The rival ocean divers.
(Sully, 1918; Garden City, 1926).

   First published as "The rival ocean divers; or, A boy's daring search
   for sunken treasure" in Golden Hours, Jan. 5-Feb. 23, 1901 (222M).
      [GC]: "A million dollars at the bottom of the ocean! Could the
   old diver and his son get to it and bring it to the surface! Rivals
   heard of this treasure on the bottom of the Pacific--and at once there
   began a race to see who could reach the treasure first. A rattling
   ocean yarn."

228S.2   Dave Fearless on a floating island; or, The cruise of the treasure
ship. (Sully, 1918; Garden City, 1926).

   First published by Mershon in 1906 as The cruise of the treasure ship;
   or, The castaways of floating island (236N).
      [GC]: "On the lonely ocean and with a treasure aboard, Dave Fear-
   less and his father have another fight with their enemies. Then a stop
   is made at an unknown island and to the amazement of all this island
   begins to float away! A yarn as thrilling as it is amazing."

228S.3   Dave Fearless and the cave of mystery; or, Adrift on the Pacific.**
(Sully, 1918; Garden City, 1926).

   First published by Grosset & Dunlap in 1908 as Adrift on the Pacific,
   or; The secret of the island cave, vol. 3 of the DEEP SEA series (229S.3).

      [GC]: "The treasure seekers find themselves cast away on an island
   infested by savages ruled over for years by a quaint Irishman. This
   King, as he calls himself, tries to befriend the whites and thereby

---

*   Although the Garden City advertisements list seventeen titles, the last
    two volumes may not have been published.
** Garden City cover reads Dave Fearless and a mystery cave; title page
    has Dave Fearless and the mystery cave.

calls down the wrath of the tribe, and the Americans have to flee for their lives."

228S.4   Dave Fearless among the icebergs; or, The secret of the eskimo igloo. (Garden City, 1926).

228S.5   Dave Fearless wrecked among savages; or, The captives of the head hunters. (Garden City, 1926).

228S.6   Dave Fearless and his big raft; or, Alone on the broad Pacific. (Garden City, 1926).

228S.7   Dave Fearless on volcano island; or, The magic cave of blue fire. (Garden City, 1926).

228S.8   Dave Fearless captured by apes; or, In gorilla land. (Garden City, 1926).

228S.9   Dave Fearless and the mutineers; or, Prisoners on the ship of death. (Garden City, 1926).

228S.10   Dave Fearless under the ocean; or, The treasure of the lost submarine. (Garden City, 1926).

228S.11   Dave Fearless in the black jungle; or, Lost among the cannibals. (Garden City, 1926).

228S.12   Dave Fearless near the South Pole; or, The giant whales of Snow Island. (Garden City, 1926).

228S.13   Dave Fearless caught by Malay pirates; or, The secret of Bamboo Island. (Garden City, 1926).

228S.14   Dave Fearless on the ship of mystery; or, The strange hermit of Shark Cove. (Garden City, 1927).

228S.15   Dave Fearless on the lost brig; or, Abandoned in the big hurricane. (Garden City, 1927).

228S.16   Dave Fearless at Whirlpool Point; or, The mystery of the water cave. (Garden City, 1927).*

228S.17   Dave Fearless among the cannibals; or, The defense of the hut in the swamp. (Garden City, 1927).*

229S   DEEP SEA

Volumes: 4
Printed: 1905-1908
Publisher: Stitt Publishing Company, vols. 1-2
            Grosset & Dunlap, vols. 3-4
Reprint publisher: Grosset & Dunlap, vols. 1-2

---

* Possibly a phantom title.

Reprint publisher: Chatterton-Peck, vols. 1-2
Illustrator: A. B. Shute, vol. 1
              Clare Angell, vol. 2
              Charles Nuttall, vols. 3-4
Additional information: Although the DEEP SEA series was issued from 1905
    to 1908, the publishing history of its four books spans twenty-five
    years. The first volume originally appeared as a story in Golden Hours
    in 1901, four years before Stitt reprinted it in book form as part of
    the series. In 1906, Mershon published The cruise of the treasure ship
    as an individual title; within a year, Stitt reissued it as volume 2
    in the series. Chatterton-Peck acquired the DEEP SEA series in 1907
    or 1908, but did not add any new titles.
        In March 1908, a Grosset & Dunlap advertisement announced that Gros-
    set & Dunlap had "taken over the publication" of some of Stratemeyer's
    books (following litigation between Stratemeyer and Mershon, Stitt, and
    Chatterton-Peck); the DEEP SEA series and Jack North's treasure hunt
    were among the books involved in the transfer. Grosset & Dunlap then
    added two more volumes to the series: Adrift on the Pacific, published
    for the first time, and Jack North's treasure hunt, originally published
    by Chatterton-Peck in 1907 as a non-series title. Soon after, Grosset
    & Dunlap changed the series title to the SEA TREASURE series (234S) and
    advertised the four books with a slightly different series order. Gros-
    set & Dunlap also reprinted Jack North's treasure hunt in the ENTERPRISE
    series (230S).
        In 1918 the first three books in the DEEP SEA series appeared with
    new titles--as George Sully & Company's three-volume DAVE FEARLESS se-
    ries (228S). Eight years later, Garden City reprinted the volumes,
    using the new titles, when it began to publish the paperback DAVE FEAR-
    LESS series. The three Sully and Garden City volumes were printed from
    plates for the earlier editions: the new covers and title pages showed
    the DAVE FEARLESS titles, but the page tops still had the original DEEP
    SEA titles.
        The Stitt, Chatterton-Peck, and Grosset & Dunlap editions all had
    the same illustrations.

229S.1   The rival ocean divers; or, The search for a sunken treasure.
(Stitt, 1905; Chatterton-Peck, ca1907; Grosset & Dunlap, ca1908).

    First published as "The rival ocean divers; or, A boy's daring search
    for sunken treasure" in Golden Hours, Jan. 5-Feb. 23, 1901 (222M).

229S.2   The cruise of the treasure ship; or, The castaways of floating
island. (Stitt, ca1907; Chatterton-Peck, 1907; Grosset & Dunlap, ca1908).

    First published by Mershon in 1906 (236N).

229S.3   Adrift on the Pacific; or, The secret of the island cave. (Grosset & Dunlap, 1908).

    Reprinted by Grosset & Dunlap as vol. 1 in the SEA TREASURE series
    (234S.1); later reprinted by Sully in 1918 and Garden City in 1926,
    both times as Dave Fearless and the cave of mystery; or, Adrift on
    the Pacific, vol. 3 of the DAVE FEARLESS series (228S.3).

229S.4   Jack North's treasure hunt; or, Daring adventures in South America. (Grosset & Dunlap, ca1908).

First published by Chatterton-Peck in 1907 (237N).

230P   ENTERPRISE

Volumes: 1*
Publisher: Grosset & Dunlap
Source of annotations: Grosset & Dunlap advertisements [G&D]
Additional information: See Captain Ralph Bonehill, ENTERPRISE series
    (053P).

230P.1X   Jack North's treasure hunt; or, Daring adventures in South America. (Grosset & Dunlap).

    Published as vol. 7 or 8. Ads list subtitle as A story of South Amer-
    ican adventure. First published by Chatterton-Peck in 1907 (237N).
        [G&D]: "Jack is sent to South America on a business trip, and while
    there he hears of the wonderful treasure of the Incas located in the
    Andes. He learns also of a lake that appears and disappears. He re-
    solves to investigate, and organizes an expedition for that purpose.
    The book is a thriller."

231S   GREAT MARVEL

Volumes: 9
Printed: 1906-1935
Publisher: Cupples & Leon Company
Reprint publisher: Whitman Publishing Company, vols. 3-6, 8-9
Illustrator: Charles Nuttall, vols. 1-3
              G. M. Kizer, vol. 4
              anonymous, vols. 5-6
              Ernest Townsend, vol. 7
              Ed Whittemore, vol. 8
              C. R. Shaare, vol. 9
Source of annotations: Cupples & Leon Company advertisements [C&L]
Additional information: Howard Garis contributed to the first eight vol-
    umes in this series, and possibly the ninth as well.
Series description [C&L]: "Since the days of Jules Verne, tales of flying
    machines and submarine boats have enjoyed increasing popularity. Sto-
    ries of adventures, in strange places, with peculiar people and queer
    animals, make this series noteworthy and popular."

231S.1   Through the air to the North Pole; or, The wonderful cruise of
the electric monarch. (Cupples & Leon, 1906).

    [C&L]: "The tale of a trip to the frozen North with a degree of reality
    that is most convincing."

231S.2   Under the ocean to the South Pole; or, The strange cruise of the
submarine wonder. (Cupples & Leon, 1907).

* Number of volumes applies only to titles published under the pseudonym
  Roy Rockwood.

[C&L]: "The vessel moves from the coast of Maine to the boiling sea of the South Pole, and during the trip the voyagers visit the bottom of the ocean--the graveyard of many ships--and have numerous stirring encounters with deep-sea monsters."

231S.3   Five thousand miles underground; or, The mystery of the center of the earth. (Cupples & Leon, 1908; Whitman).

[C&L]: "A craft is built which will sail both in the air and under the water, and in this the adventurers descend to the interior of our globe by means of a hole found at an island in the ocean."

231S.4   Through space to Mars; or, The most wonderful trip on record. (Cupples & Leon, 1910; Whitman).

[C&L]: "A thrilling tale of a visit to the planet Mars. The adventurers meet with many happenings out of the ordinary. The volume reads like the record of a real trip."

231S.5   Lost on the moon; or, In quest of the field of diamonds. (Cupples & Leon, 1911; Whitman).

[C&L]: "In a like manner to their visit to Mars, the heroes visit the Moon. They search for a field of diamonds and find the moon to be a land of desolation and silence. They almost perish from cold and hunger. A startling romance that will hold and charm every reader."

231S.6   On a torn-away world; or, Captives of the great earthquake. (Cupples & Leon, 1913; Whitman).

[C&L]: "After a tremendous convulsion of nature the adventurers find themselves captives on a vast 'island in the air.'"

231S.7   The city beyond the clouds; or, Captured by the red dwarfs. (Cupples & Leon, 1925).

[C&L]: "The City Beyond the Clouds is a weird place, full of surprises, and the impish Red Dwarfs caused no end of trouble. There is a fierce battle in the woods and in the midst of this a volcanic eruption sends the Americans sailing away in a feverish endeavor to save their lives."

231S.8   By air express to Venus; or, Captives of a strange people. (Cupples & Leon, 1929; Whitman).

[C&L]: "Our heroes are captured by strange inhabitants of the inside world and have a series of adventures as wonderful as they are absorbing."

231S.9   By space ship to Saturn; or, Exploring the ringed planet. (Cupples & Leon, 1935; Whitman).

[C&L]: "After a rocket ship race to Saturn, two boys have harrowing adventures with snakes at the Boiling Lake in this Land of Vapors."

232PQ   HALF-DIME LIBRARY

Volumes: 1*
Printed: 1897*
Publisher: Beadle & Adams
Additional information: The HALF-DIME LIBRARY, a dime novel series, began
    on October 15, 1877, and continued through December 1905, for 1168 is-
    sues. Edward Stratemeyer may have written one title in this series.

232PQ.1X Flyer Fred, the cyclist ferret; or, Running down the rough and
ready rascals. No. 1047. Aug. 17, 1897.

    First published in the Banner Weekly, Sept. 12-Oct. 17, 1896 (217MQ).

233P   OUTDOOR

Volumes: 1*
Publisher: World Syndicate Publishing Co.
Additional information: Volumes 1 and 2 in this series were the Stratemeyer
    Syndicate's work; volumes 2 through 6 were printed in the ENTERPRISE
    series. The seven volumes in this publisher's series were:
    1. Andy at Yale by Roy Eliot Stokes
    2. Jack North's treasure hunt by Roy Rockwood
    3. The crimson banner by William D. Moffat
    4. Andy the acrobat by Peter T. Harkness
    5. Two boys and a fortune by Matthiew White, Jr.
    6. Canoe boys and campfires by William Murry Graydon
    7. Adventures of a boy reporter by H. St. Morrison

233P.1X   Jack North's treasure hunt; or, Daring adventures in South America. (World).

    Issued as volume 2. First published by Chatterton-Peck in 1907 (237N).

234S   SEA TREASURE

Volumes: 4
Publisher: Grosset & Dunlap
Illustrator: Charles Nuttall, vols. 1, 4
              Clare Angell, vol. 2
              A. Burnham Shute, vol. 3
Source of annotations: Grosset & Dunlap advertisements [G&D]
Additional information: First published as the DEEP SEA series (229S).
Series description [G&D]: "No manly boy ever grew tired of sea stories--
    there is a fascination about them, and they are a recreation to the
    mind. These books are especially interesting and are full of adventure
    clever dialogue and plenty of fun."

_____

* Number of volumes and years published apply only to titles published
   under the pseudonym Roy Rockwood.

234S.1   Adrift on the Pacific; or, The secret of the island cave. (Grosset & Dunlap).

> First published by Grosset & Dunlap in 1908, as vol. 3 in the DEEP SEA series (229S.3).

234S.2   The cruise of the treasure ship; or, The castaways of floating island. (Grosset & Dunlap).

> First published by Mershon in 1906 (236N).

234S.3   The rival ocean divers; or, The search for a sunken treasure. (Grosset & Dunlap).

> First published as "The rival ocean divers; or, A boy's daring search for sunken treasure" in Golden Hours, Jan. 5-Feb. 23, 1901 (222M).

234S.4   Jack North's treasure hunt; or, Daring adventures in South America. (Grosset & Dunlap).

> First published by Chatterton-Peck in 1907 (237N).

235S   SPEEDWELL BOYS

Volumes: 5
Printed: 1913-1915
Publisher: Cupples & Leon Company
Illustrator: Walter S. Rogers, vols. 1-5
Source of annotations: Cupples & Leon Company advertisements [C&L]
Series description [C&L]: "All boys who love to be on the go will welcome the Speedwell boys. They are clean cut and loyal to the core--youths worth knowing."

235S.1   The Speedwell boys on motorcycles; or, The mystery of a great conflagration. (Cupples & Leon, 1913).

> [C&L]: "The lads were poor, but they did a rich man a great service and he presented them with their motor cycles. What a great fire led to is exceedingly well told."

235S.2   The Speedwell boys and their racing auto; or, A run for the golden cup. (Cupples & Leon, 1913).

> [C&L]: "A tale of automobiling and of intense rivalry on the road. There was an endurance run and the boys entered the contest. On the run they rounded up some men who were wanted by the law."

235S.3   The Speedwell boys and their power launch; or, To the rescue of the castaways. (Cupples & Leon, 1913).

> [C&L]: "Here is a water story of unusual interest. There was a wreck and the lads, in their power launch, set out to the rescue. A vivid picture of a great storm adds to the interest of the tale."

235S.4   The Speedwell boys in a submarine; or, The treasure of Rocky Cove.
(Cupples & Leon, 1913).

> [C&L]: "An old sailor knows of a treasure lost under water because of
> a cliff falling into the sea. The boys get a chance to go out in a sub-
> marine and they make a hunt for the treasure. Life under the water is
> well described."

235S.5   The Speedwell boys and their ice racer; or, Lost in the great
blizzard. (Cupples & Leon, 1915).

> [C&L]: "The boys had an idea for a new sort of iceboat, to be run by
> combined wind and motor power. How they built the craft, and what fine
> times that had on board of it, is well related."

OTHER PUBLICATIONS

236N   The cruise of the treasure ship; or, The castaways of floating
island. (Mershon, 1906).

> Reprinted by Stitt ca1907, Chatterton-Peck in 1907, and Grosset & Dun-
> lap ca1908, all as vol. 2 of the DEEP SEA series (229S.2). Later re-
> printed by Grosset & Dunlap as vol. 2 of the SEA TREASURE series
> (234S.2). Also published by G. Sully & Co. in 1918 and Garden City
> in 1926, both times as Dave Fearless on a floating island; or, The
> cruise of the treasure ship, vol. 2 of the DAVE FEARLESS series
> (228S.2).

237N   Jack North's treasure hunt; or, Daring adventures in South America. (Chatterton-Peck, 1907; Goldsmith).

> Reprinted by Grosset & Dunlap ca1908 as vol. 4 of the DEEP SEA series
> (229S.4) and later as vol. 4 of the SEA TREASURE series (234S.4) and
> as vol. 7 or 8 of the ENTERPRISE series (230P.1X). World edition
> published as vol. 2 of the OUTDOOR series (233P.1X); Goldsmith edition
> published as a non-series title.

238N   Popular stories for boys. (Cupples & Leon, ca1934).

> Contains Bomba the jungle boy by Roy Rockwood, published in 1926
> (226S.1); Sky riders of the Atlantic by Richard H. Stone, published
> in 1930 (259S.1); Bob Dexter and the club house mystery by Willard F.
> Baker, published in 1925; and Wrecked on Cannibal Island by Fenworth
> Moore, published in 1931 (204S.1). Printed from the original plates.

239N   A schoolboy's pluck; or, The career of a nobody. (Mershon, 1900;
Chatterton-Peck).

> First published as "A nobody schoolboy; or, Backbone against the world,
> by Philip A. Alyer, in Young People of America, Dec. 7, 1895-Feb. 22,
> 1896 (016M).

240N   The wizard of the sea; or, A trip under the ocean. (Mershon,
1900; Chatterton-Peck; A. L. Burt).

First published as "The wizard of the deep; or, Over and under the ocean in search of the $1,000,000 pearl," by Theodore Edison, in Young Sports of America, Aug. 10-Sept. 14, 1895 (110M).

Harry Mason Roe

Harry Mason Roe was a Stratemeyer Syndicate pseudonym used for only one series, the three-volume LANKY LAWSON stories, printed in 1929 and 1930.

SERIES PUBLICATIONS

241S   LANKY LAWSON

Volumes: 4*
Printed: 1929-1930
Publisher: Barse & Company
Illustrator: David Randolph, vols. 1-3
Source of annotations: Barse & Company advertisements [B&C]
Series description [B&C]: "In this series of books Lanky Lawson tells his
    own story and does it in his own way. Of unknown parentage, he is keen,
    quick and full and [sic] dry humor--and honest to the core. He is al-
    ways willing to aid a friend and equally willing to give an enemy what
    he deserves, but often in a laughable way. He is knocked around from
    pillar to post, trying all sorts of jobs and making all sorts of odd
    acquaintances. He helps to bring a swindler to justice, falls in with
    an aviator who takes him skyward and he becomes an attache of a small
    circus that is on the verge of going to pieces.
        "Every boy who reads about Lanky Lawson and his doings will take
    Lanky right to his heart--'And that's O.K. with me,' as Lanky would
    say."

241S.1   Lanky Lawson, the boy from nowhere: How he arrived at Beanville,
what Beanville did to him, and what he did to Beanville. (Barse, 1929).

241S.2   Lanky Lawson with the one-ring circus: How he joined the show,
what he did to the wild animals, what happened when the circus collapsed.
(Barse, 1929).

241S.3   Lanky Lawson and his trained zebra: How he happened to get the
beast, how the cantankerous animal performed, and what happened at the
county fair. (Barse, 1930).

241S.4   Lanky Lawson somewhere on the ocean.** (Barse, ca1930).*

----

*   The fourth volume may never have been published.
** Subtitle missing.

Ned St. Meyer

Ned St. Meyer, Edward Stratemeyer's first pseudonym, appeared on two stories published in the NUGGET LIBRARY in 1890; one was serialized in 1903.

MAGAZINE PUBLICATIONS

242M   "Match as a fakir; or, The Pumpkinville country fair." Boys of America, nos. 71-74, Feb. 7-Feb. 28, 1903.

   First published as no. 56 in Street & Smith's NUGGET LIBRARY, Aug. 28, 1890 (243P.2X).

SERIES PUBLICATIONS

243P   NUGGET LIBRARY

Volumes: 2*
Printed: 1890*
Publisher: Street & Smith
Additional information: The NUGGET LIBRARY was a weekly dime novel series that began on August 29, 1889 and continued until August 11, 1892, for a total of 167 issues.

243P.1X   Match; or, The golden wedding at Turkey Hollow. No. 50. July 17, 1890.

243P.2X   Match as a fakir; or, The Pumpkinville county fair. No. 56. Aug 28, 1890.

   Reprinted in Boys of America, Feb. 7-Feb. 28, 1903 (242M).

Dan Scott

A western series, the BRET KING MYSTERY STORIES, was the only series published under the Stratemeyer Syndicate pseudonym Dan Scott. Andrew Svenson was responsible for some of the volumes in this series.

---

*   Number of volumes and years published apply only to titles written by Edward Stratemeyer under the pseudonym Ned St. Meyer.

SERIES PUBLICATIONS

244S   BRET KING MYSTERY STORIES

Volumes: 9
Printed: 1960-1964
Publisher: Grosset & Dunlap
Illustrator: Joe Beeler, vols. 1-3, 5-9
            Santo Sorrentino, vol. 4
Source of annotations: Grosset & Dunlap advertisements [G&D]
Additional information: Andrew Svenson wrote some of the books in this
    series, including volume 9. The books were published without subtitles.
Series description [G&D]: "Today's West is just as fascinating as the Old
    West ever was. The new Bret King mystery series takes you along on the
    action-packed adventures of a modern young cowboy and his friends on
    Rimrock Ranch in New Mexico. Stories of the great outdoors, written by
    one of America's most famous Western authors."

244S.1   The mystery of Ghost Canyon. (Grosset & Dunlap, 1960).

    [G&D]: "Truck rustlers butcher cattle on Rimrock Ranch, confronting
    Bret with Western outlaws who combine thievery with science to outwit
    the law."

244S.2   The secret of Hermit's Peak. (Grosset & Dunlap, 1960).

    [G&D]: "When a wild mountain lion and a gang of thieves invade Deso-
    lation Peak at the same time, Bret unlocks the fascinating secret of
    the mountain."

244S.3   The range rodeo mystery. (Grosset & Dunlap, 1960).

    [G&D]: "From the moment the cow town of Tovar plans a revival of its
    colorful local rodeo, trouble stampedes Rimrock Ranch, until Bret out-
    smarts a band of big-time gangsters."

244S.4   The mystery of Rawhide Gap. (Grosset & Dunlap, 1960).

    [G&D]: "Bret and his plane become involved in an international mix-up,
    uncovering a bizarre underground plot aimed at the federal government
    of the United States."

244S.5   The mystery at Blizzard Mesa. (Grosset & Dunlap, 1961).

244S.6   The secret of Fort Pioneer. (Grosset & Dunlap, 1961).

244S.7   The mystery of the Comanche caves. (Grosset & Dunlap, 1962).

244S.8   The phantom of Wolf Creek. (Grosset & Dunlap, 1963).

244S.9   The mystery of Bandit Gulch. (Grosset & Dunlap, 1964).

Walden F. Sharpe

One story that appeared in Good News under the pseudonym Walden F. Sharpe was actually written by Edward Stratemeyer. Other stories listed as by Walden F. Sharpe may have been the work of William Wallace Cook.

MAGAZINE PUBLICATIONS

245M   "For his honor's sake; or, The richest boy detective in New York." Good News, vol. 11, nos. 271-283, July 13-Oct. 5, 1895.

Ann Sheldon

The LINDA CRAIG series, published under the Stratemeyer Syndicate pseudonym Ann Sheldon, seems to be the female equivalent of the BRET KING series (244S). First published in the early 1960s, the LINDA CRAIG series, western mystery and adventure tales, lasted for two years and six volumes. Harriet Adams wrote several of the books in the series.

SERIES PUBLICATIONS

246S   LINDA CRAIG

Volumes: 6
Printed: 1962-1964
Publisher: Doubleday & Company, Inc.
Reprint publisher: Simon & Schuster, Wanderer Books, vols. 1-4
Source of annotations: Doubleday & Company, Inc. advertisements [Dd]
Additional information: Harriet Adams wrote at least four, and possibly all six, titles in this series, which was published in hardcover by Doubleday and reprinted in paperback by Wanderer Books.
    The books were published without subtitles; Doubleday editions were not illustrated.
Series description [Dd]: "GIRLS! Saddle up and ride into a thrilling new mystery series with Linda Craig and her prize-winning palomino, Chica d'Oro. . . . Watch for more of these exciting mystery stories filled with danger, adventure and great horsemanship!"

246S.1   Linda Craig and the palomino mystery. (Doubleday, 1962; Wanderer, 1981).

Wanderer edition titled Linda Craig: The palomino mystery.

246S.2   Linda Craig and the clue on the desert trail. (Doubleday, 1962; Wanderer, 1981).

Wanderer edition titled Linda Craig: The clue on the desert trail and published as vol. 3.

246S.3   Linda Craig and the secret of Rancho del Sol. (Doubleday, 1963; Wanderer, 1981).

Wanderer edition titled Linda Craig: The secret of Rancho del Sol and published as vol. 2.

246S.4   Linda Craig and the mystery of Horseshoe Canyon. (Doubleday, 1963; Wanderer, 1981).

Wanderer edition titled Linda Craig: The mystery of Horseshoe Canyon.

246S.5   Linda Craig and the ghost town treasure. (Doubleday, 1964).

246S.6   Linda Craig and the mystery in Mexico. (Doubldeay, 1964).

Eric Speed

A recent Stratemeyer Syndicate pseudonym, Eric Speed combined Andrew Svenson's plots and editing with Sylvia Wilkerson's racing knowledge, for one series--the WYNN AND LONNY books. As the pseudonym's surname suggests, the series was about speed--motor-car racing.

SERIES PUBLICATIONS

247S   WYNN AND LONNY

Volumes: 6
Printed: 1975-1978
Publisher: Grosset & Dunlap
Source of annotations: Library of Congress cataloguing in publication
                        data [LC]
Additional information: Andrew Svenson and Sylvia Wilkerson worked together
    on some titles in this series. Books were published without subtitles.

247S.1   ·The Mexicali 1000. (Grosset & Dunlap, 1975).

[LC]: "Wynn and Lonny become involved with Mexican smugglers when they enter their buggy in the thousand-mile-off-road race down the Baja Peninsula of southern California."

247S.2   Road race of champions. (Grosset & Dunlap, 1975).

[LC]: "Wynn and Lonny build their own Formula Vee racer, compete on the southern circuit, and gain the finals in the Race of Champions at Road Atlanta."

247S.3   GT challenge. (Grosset & Dunlap, 1976).

[LC]: "Two young drivers set their sights on the GT racing series but encounter difficulty linked to stolen cars and sabotage."

247S.4   Gold cup rookies. (Grosset & Dunlap, 1976).

[LC]: "Despite incidents of sabotage and spying, two young men compete in the Gold Cup racing series hoping to overcome the unbeatable champion."

247S.5   Dead heat at Le Mans. (Grosset & Dunlap, 1977).

[LC]: "Despite incidents of sabotage and terrorism, Wynn and Lonny realize their lifelong dream and compete in the auto race at Le Mans, France."

247S.6   The midnight rally. (Grosset & Dunlap, 1978).

Raymond Sperry

Several bibliographies list Raymond Sperry as a Stratemeyer Syndicate house name, while simultaneously noting that the books published under this pseudonym were the work of Howard Garis. While the two conditions are not mutually exclusive, the circumstances surrounding the use of Raymond Sperry suggest that the Stratemeyer Syndicate had little or no connection with the actual creation of the Sperry books.

Six of the eight books eventually published under the pseudonym Raymond Sperry have a tangled publishing history. The first two volumes were published by Chatterton-Peck in 1907 as the Newspaper series or the Great Newspaper series, with Howard Garis as author. In 1908, after legal problems between Edward Stratemeyer and several publisher had been resolved, a Grosset & Dunlap advertisement in Publishers' Weekly announced that Grosset & Dunlap had "just completed an arrangement with Mr. Edward Stratemeyer, owner of the plates and copyrights, and the publishing house of Chatterton-Peck, whereby we [Grosset & Dunlap] have taken over the publication of the following well known books. . ." Included in the list that followed were the first two Great Newspaper series titles. Grosset & Dunlap then published the first two volumes, still as the Great Newspaper series, and added four more titles: one from 1907, two in 1912, and one in 1915, all with Howard Garis as author.

G. Sully & Company reprinted all six volumes, changing the titles slightly and calling the series the Young Reporter series, but still listing the author as Howard Garis. Then, in 1926, Garden City Publishing Company reprinted the six books in paperback, changing the titles again and calling the series the Larry Dexter series. (For most volumes, this was the third title.) The biggest change was in the author's name: it was given as Raymond Sperry. In 1927, two new volumes were added to the series, still with

Raymond Sperry as author. The series stopped after eight volumes:

1. Larry Dexter at the big flood; or, The perils of a reporter (originally From office boy to reporter; or, The first step in journalism; also published as The young reporter at the big flood; or, The perils of news gathering)

2. Larry Dexter and the land swindlers; or, Queer adventures in a great city (originally Larry Dexter, the young reporter; or, Strange adventures in a great city; also published as The young reporter and the land swindlers; or, Queer adventures in a great city)

3. Larry Dexter and the missing millionaire; or, The great search (originally Larry Dexter's great search; or, The hunt for a missing millionaire; also published as The young reporter and the missing millionaire; or, A strange disappearance)

4. Larry Dexter and the bank mystery; or, Exciting days in Wall Street (originally Larry Dexter and the bank mystery; or, A young reporter in Wall Street; also published as The young reporter and the bank mystery; or, Stirring doings in Wall Street)

5. Larry Dexter and the stolen boy; or, A chase on the Great Lakes (originally Larry Dexter and the stolen boy; or, A young reporter on the lakes; also published as The young reporter and the stolen boy; or, A chase on the Great Lakes)

6. Larry Dexter at the battle front; or, A war correspondent's double mission (originally Larry Dexter in Belgium; or, A young war correspondent's double mission; also published as The young reporter at the battle front; or, A war correspondent's double mission)

7. Larry Dexter and the Ward diamonds; or, The young reporter at Sea Cliff

8. Larry Dexter's great chase; or, The young reporter across the continent

It is possible that the Stratemeyer Syndicate helped Howard Garis plot the first six Larry Dexter books, but improbable. They were published under Garis's name originally, and it seems reasonable to assume that they were entirely his creation. The last two Larry Dexter books, the only two that never appeared under Garis's name, may have been the work of the Stratemeyer Syndicate (and/or Howard Garis, who was still assisting with several Stratemeyer Syndicate series at the time).

Although the Grosset & Dunlap advertisement referred to Edward Stratemeyer as the "owner of the plates and copyrights," this does not necessarily mean that he was the author of the books, as he had purchased the plates and copyrights to several series from Chatterton-Peck. The first two volumes of the Dorothy Chester series and the entire ENTERPRISE series were also listed in the Grosset & Dunlap advertisement, yet five of the eight ENTERPRISE books and both Dorothy Chester titles are not Stratemeyer Syndicate creations. While the similarity between the names Raymond Sperry and Raymond Sperry, Jr., (the latter a Stratemeyer Syndicate house name) cannot be overlooked, it is possible that Edward Stratemeyer (who owned the rights to at least two titles), Howard Garis, and/or Garden City decided to change the author's name in order to give the series a new look and simply chose a pseudonym related to an existing Stratemeyer Syndicate house name.

Raymond Sperry, Jr.

The Stratemeyer Syndicate pseudonym Raymond Sperry, Jr., had the somewhat dubious honor of authoring the WHITE RIBBON BOYS series, which Fortune called the series books' "worst failure." This was the only series credited to this pseudonym.

SERIES PUBLICATIONS

248S   WHITE RIBBON BOYS

Volumes: 2*
Printed: 1915-1916*
Publisher: Cupples & Leon Company
Illustrator: Walter S. Rogers, vol. 1
Source of annotations: Cupples & Leon Company advertisements [C&L]
Additional information: Despite the advertising annotation, the second
    volume in this series may never have been published.
Series description [C&L]: "This new series deals with the great modern
    movement for temperance. Clean-cut, up-to-date stories that will please
    all growing boys and do them a world of good."

248S.1   The white ribbon boys of Chester; or, The old tavern keeper's
secret. (Cupples & Leon, 1915).

    [C&L]: "Chester was a typical factory town with its quota of drinking
    places. The father of one of the boys was a foreman in one of the fac-
    tories, and he advocated temperance so strongly that some of the men,
    urged on by an old tavern keeper, plotted so that he lost his position.
    One day, when partly intoxicated, the tavern keeper's son climbs in a
    factory window, smashes things, and is badly burned by acid. He is
    rescued by the boys who are advocating temperance, who take him to his
    mother. When the tavern keeper sees the condition of his son, he breaks
    down, and confesses to the plot against the discharged foreman. Tem-
    perance wins out, and the town of Chester becomes far more prosperous
    than before."

248S.2   The white ribbon boys at Long Shore; or, To the rescue of Dan
Bates. (Cupples & Leon, 1916).*

    [C&L]: "In this tale the scene is shifted to the seashore, where the
    boys are having a vacation for the summer. Encouraged by the temperance
    work done in their home town, they join a local crusade to close the
    various drinking and gambling houses. They fall in with another lad,
    the son of a well-known drunkard of the summer resort, and do all they
    can to aid him. A good, clean-cut boys' story, full of life and action,
    not at all preachy, but teaching the best of morals."

---

* The second volume is generally considered a phantom title.

Chester K. Steele

Six adult mysteries were published under the Stratemeyer Syndicate pseudonym Chester K. Steele between 1911 and 1928.

SERIES PUBLICATIONS

249P   DETECTIVE LIBRARY

Volumes: 1*
Publisher: World Syndicate Publishing Company
Additional information: This series was composed of mystery stories for adults.

249P.1X   The golf course mystery: Being a somewhat different detective story. (World).

First published by George Sully & Company in 1919 (252N).

OTHER PUBLICATIONS

250N   The crime at Red Towers.** (E. J. Clode, Inc., 1927; A. L. Burt, 1930).

251N   The diamond cross mystery: Being a somewhat different detective story. (G. Sully & Co., 1918).

    Illustrated by Frances Edwina Dunn.

252N   The golf course mystery: Being a somewhat different detective story. (G. Sully & Co., 1919).

    Illustrated by A. O. Scott. Reprinted by World Syndicate as part of the DETECTIVE LIBRARY (249P.1X).

253N   The great radio mystery: A detective story. (Chelsea House, 1928).

254N   The house of disappearances: A detective story. (Chelsea House, 1927).

255N   The mansion of mystery: Being a certain case of importance, taken from the notebook of Adam Adams, investigator and detective. (Cupples & Leon, 1911; International Fiction Library).

---

*   Number of volumes applies only to titles published under the pseudonym Chester K. Steele.
**   Subtitle missing.

Roy Eliot Stokes

The two-volume UNIVERSITY series was the only series published under the Stratemeyer Syndicate pseudonym Roy Eliot Stokes.

SERIES PUBLICATIONS

256S   UNIVERSITY

Volumes: 2
Printed: 1914
Publisher: Sully & Kleinteich
Reprint publisher: George Sully & Company, vols. 1-2
Illustrator: H. Richard Boehm, vols. 1-2

256S.1   Andy at Yale; or, The great quadrangle mystery. (Sully & Kleinteich, 1914; G. Sully & Co., 1918).

Also reprinted by World and Goldsmith as a non-series title.

256S.2   Chet at Harvard; or, A young freshman's triumph. (Sully & Kleinteich, 1914; G. Sully & Co., ca1918).

Alan Stone

Alan Stone was the Stratemeyer Syndicate pseudonym used by Andrew Svenson when he wrote the three volumes in the TOLLIVER ADVENTURE SERIES in 1967.

SERIES PUBLICATIONS

257S   TOLLIVER ADVENTURE SERIES

Volumes: 3
Printed: 1967
Publisher: World Publishing Company
Illustrator: Mel Bolden, vols. 1-3
Additional information: Andrew Svenson, a partner in the Stratemeyer Syndicate, wrote all three books in this series about a black family. The books were published without subtitles; each book was listed as "A Holly Book."

257S.1   The Tollivers and the mystery of the lost pony. (World, 1967).

257S.2   The Tollivers and the mystery of Pirate Island. (World, 1967).

257S.3   The Tollivers and the mystery of the old jalopy. (World, 1967).

Raymond Stone

The Stratemeyer Syndicate combined the surname Stone with three different first names: Alan, Raymond, and Richard. Each pseudonym was used for one series. Raymond was the earliest of the three, appearing from 1912 to 1917, and was one of the two Stratemeyer Syndicate pen names published by Graham & Matlack. (The other was Frederick Gordon.)

SERIES PUBLICATIONS

258S   TOMMY TIPTOP

Volumes: 6
Printed: 1912-1917
Publisher: Graham & Matlack, vols. 1-5
            C. E. Graham Co., vol. 6
Reprint publisher: C. E. Graham Co., vols. 1-5
Illustrator: anonymous, vols. 1-4
              R. Menel [Mencl?], vol. 5
              R. Emmett Owen, vol. 6
Source of annotations: C. E. Graham Co. advertisements [CG]
Series description [CG]: "A new series for outdoor boys, that fairly bris-les
    tles with boyish humanness. The writer . . . takes one through Tommy
    Tiptop's career as a little organizer of games and clubs and always a
    leader of boys."

258S.1   Tommy Tiptop and his baseball nine; or, The boys of Riverdale and their good times. (Graham & Matlack, 1912; Graham, ca1917).

258S.2   Tommy Tiptop and his football eleven; or, A great victory and how it was won. (Graham & Matlack, 1912; Graham, ca1917).

258S.3   Tommy Tiptop and his winter sports; or, Jolly times on the ice and in camp. (Graham & Matlack, 1912; Graham, ca1917).

258S.4   Tommy Tiptop and his boat club; or, The young hunters of Hemlock Island. (Graham & Matlack, 1914; Graham, ca1917).

258S.5   Tommy Tiptop and his boy scouts; or, The doings of the Silver Fox Patrol. (Graham & Matlack, 1915; Graham, ca1917).

258S.6   Tommy Tiptop and his great show; or, Raising some money that was needed. (Graham, 1917).

Richard H. Stone

Richard H. Stone appeared on one aviation series, the SLIM TYLER AIR STORIES, in the 1930s. The Stratemeyer Syndicate produced six volumes, excluding reprints, under this pseudonym.

SERIES PUBLICATIONS

259S   SLIM TYLER AIR STORIES

Volumes: 7*
Printed: 1930-1936*
Publisher: Cupples & Leon Company
Illustrator: anonymous, vols. 1-6
Source of annotations: Cupples & Leon Company advertisements [C&L]
Series description [C&L]: "A new group of stories for boys by a new author
    whose excellent air adventures are so realistically written and so up
    to the minute in all their implications as to win ready admiration from
    all readers."

259S.1   Sky riders of the Atlantic; or, Slim Tyler's first trip in the
clouds. (Cupples & Leon, 1930).

    Reprinted in Aviation stories for boys in 1936 (259S.7X) and in Popular
    stories for boys ca1934 (260N), both four-in-one reprints.
        [C&L]: "Slim Tyler though but a boy, finds himself confronted by
    troubles and by enemies that might well have dismayed a man. By pluck
    and straight thinking he fights clear of entanglements and gains a
    place he has long coveted among flyers."

259S.2   Lost over Greenland; or, Slim Tyler's search for Dave Boyd. (Cupples & Leon, 1930).

    Reprinted in Aviation stories for boys, a four-in-one reprint, in 1936
    (259S.7X).
        [C&L]: "Slim Tyler sets out in search of his friend and patron who
    is lost over Greenland, and in so doing has many hair-raising adventures
    that make an absorbing story."

259S.3   An air cargo of gold; or, Slim Tyler, special bank messenger.
(Cupples & Leon, 1930).

    Reprinted in Aviation stories for boys, a four-in-one reprint, in 1936
    (259S.7X).
        [C&L]: "Quick-witted and resourceful, Slim, after strenuous efforts
    to gain the world's endurance record, faces more odds when he makes a
    perilous trip carrying a cargo of gold."

---

* Number of volumes and years published include Aviation stories for boys,
  a four-in-one reprint published in 1936.

259S.4   Adrift over Hudson Bay; or, Slim Tyler in the land of ice. (Cupples & Leon, 1931).

Reprinted in Aviation stories for boys, a four-in-one reprint, in 1936 (259S.7X).
[C&L]: "Blazing the great Northeastern trail against great odds, this story will captivate the hearts of the boys."

259S.5   An airplane mystery; or, Slim Tyler on the trail. (Cupples & Leon, 1931).

[C&L]: "The story of the rescue, after the flyers had been given up for lost, was a 'whale' of a story."

259S.6   Secret sky express; or, Slim Tyler saving a fortune. (Cupples & Leon, 1932).

[C&L]: "A story of many episodes and thrills against great odds."

259S.7X   Aviation stories for boys. (Cupples & Leon, 1936).

Contains: Sky riders of the Atlantic (259S.1), Lost over Greenland (259S.2), An air cargo of gold (259S.3), all published in 1930, and Adrift over Hudson Bay (259S.4), published in 1931.

OTHER PUBLICATIONS

260N   Popular stories for boys. (Cupples & Leon, ca1934).

Contains Bomba the jungle boy by Roy Rockwood, published in 1926 (226S.1); Sky riders of the Atlantic by Richard H. Stone, published in 1930 (259S.1); Bob Dexter and the club house mystery by Willard F. Baker, published in 1925; and Wrecked on Cannibal Island by Fenworth Moore, published in 1931 (204S.1). Printed from the original plates.

Edward Stratemeyer

Despite his wide assortment of pseudonyms, Edward Stratemeyer managed to write twenty-five magazine stories (including reprints) under his own name, as well as seventy-seven different books (some of which had been previously published under other pseudonyms and/or as magazine stories). The majority of the books appeared in one or more of sixteen series between 1894 and 1920: BOUND TO SUCCEED (1894-1899; 3 vols.), SHIP AND SHORE (1894-1900; 3 vols.), BOUND TO WIN (1897; 4 vols),* MINUTE BOYS (1898-1899; 2 vols.),* OLD GLORY (1898-1901; 6 vols.), WORKING UPWARD (ca1898-1903; 6 vols.), SOLDIERS OF FORTUNE (1900-1904; 4 vols.), AMERICAN BOYS' BIOGRAPHICAL SERIES (1901-1904; 2 vols.), COLONIAL (1901-1906; 6 vols.), PAN-AMERICAN (1902-

---

* Number of volumes and years published apply only to titles published as by Edward Stratemeyer.

1911; 6 vols.), GREAT AMERICAN INDUSTRIES (1903; 1 vol.), DAVE PORTER (1905-1919; 15 vols.), LAKEPORT (1908-1912; 6 vols.), MEXICAN WAR (1909; 3 vols.), ALGER SERIES (1919-1920; 26 vols.),* STRATEMEYER POPULAR SERIES (15 vols.). Merriam published the first two volumes in Stratemeyer's first two series; Lee & Shepard (later Lothrop, Lee & Shepard) completed the series and was the publisher for all the other series except the BOUND TO WIN series (Allison), the first four volumes of the WORKING UPWARD series (Allison), the MINUTE BOYS (Estes & Lauriat), and the ALGER SERIES (Street & Smith—a paperback reprint series).

Edward Stratemeyer's first published story was "Victor Horton's idea" in Golden Days, November 2 through November 30, 1889.

MAGAZINE PUBLICATIONS

261M   "Building the line." The Popular Magazine, vol. 2, nos. 3-4, July-Aug. 1904.

262M   "Camera Bob; or, The thrilling adventures of a travelling photographer." Good News, vol. 7, nos. 179-194, Oct. 7, 1893-Jan 20, 1894.

Published in book form by A. Wessels in 1902, by Stitt in 1905, by Chatterton-Peck ca1906, and by Grosset & Dunlap, all as Bob, the photographer; or, A hero in spite of himself by Arthur M. Winfield (342N). Grosset & Dunlap edition published as vol. 6 of the ENTERPRISE series (335P.1X). Also published by Street & Smith as Bob the photographer; or, Strictly on the job by Edward Stratemeyer, no. 123 in the ALGER SERIES (289P.26X).

263M   "Captain Bob's secret; or, The treasures of Bass Island." Golden Days, vol. 11, nos. 16-26, March 15-May 24, 1890.

Reprinted with the same title, but with the author as "the author of 'Clearing His Name,'" in Golden Days, Sept. 23-Nov. 25, 1905 (264M).

264M   "Captain Bob's secret; or, The treasures of Bass Island." Golden Days, vol. 26, no. 46-vol. 27, no. 3, Sept. 23-Nov. 25, 1905.

Author listed as "by the author of 'Clearing His Name.'" ("Clearing his name" was first published with Ralph Hamilton as author [159M] and reprinted with Edward Stratemeyer as author [265M].)
First published with the same title, but with Edward Stratemeyer as author, in Golden Days, March 15-May 24, 1890 (263M).

265M   "Clearing his name: A midwinter story." Golden Days, vol. 24, nos. 15-21, Feb. 21-April 4, 1903.

First published with Ralph Hamilton listed as author, in Golden Days, Aug. 22-Oct. 3, 1891 (159M).

266M   "In defense of his flag." The American Boy, May 1906-June 1907.

---

* Number of volumes and years published apply only to titles published as by Edward Stratemeyer.

Reprinted in book form by Lothrop, Lee & Shepard in 1907 as <u>Defending</u> <u>his</u> <u>flag</u>; <u>or</u>, <u>A</u> <u>boy</u> <u>in</u> <u>blue</u> <u>and</u> <u>a</u> <u>boy</u> <u>in</u> <u>gray</u> (306N).

267M   "The island of caves; or, The remarkable adventures of the Bixby twins." <u>Bright</u> <u>Days</u>, nos. 1-3, April-June, 1896.

268M   "Jack, the inventor; or, The trials and triumphs of a young machinist." <u>The</u> <u>Holiday</u>, vol. 3, nos. 18-25, April 25-June 3, 1891.

Reprinted in <u>Good</u> <u>News</u>, Jan. 23-April 2, 1892 (269M). Also partly reprinted as "A young inventor's pluck; or, The Wellington legacy" (unfinished) in <u>Bright</u> <u>Days</u>, Feb. 20-Feb. 27, 1897 (288M). Published in book form by Saalfield in 1901 with the new title and with Arthur M. Winfield as author, and by Caldwell (344N); reprinted by Saalfield, still with the new author and title, in the WINFIELD series (341S.2).

269M   "Jack, the inventor; or, The trials and triumphs of a young machinist." <u>Good</u> <u>News</u>, vol. 4, nos. 90-100, Jan. 23-April 2, 1892.

First published in <u>The</u> <u>Holiday</u>, April 25-June 3, 1891 (268M).

270M   "Joe, the surveyor; or, The value of a lost claim." <u>Good</u> <u>News</u>, vol. 9, nos. 209-221, May 5-July 28, 1894.

Published in book form by Lee & Shepard in 1903, and later by Grosset & Dunlap (308N). Reprinted by Lothrop, Lee & Shepard in the STRATEMEYER POPULAR SERIES (303S.11X), and by Street & Smith as no. 108 in the ALGER SERIES (289P.11X).

271M   "Judge Dockett's grandson." <u>Golden</u> <u>Days</u>, vol. 27, no. 51-vol. 28, no. 9, Oct. 27, 1906-Jan. 5, 1907.

Author listed as "by the author of 'Captain Bob's secret.'" ("Captain Bob's secret" first published with Edward Stratemeyer as author [263M].)
     First published with Ralph Hamilton as author in <u>Golden</u> <u>Days</u>, July 9-Sept. 17, 1892 (161M).

272M   "Just from the farm; or, Don Borden's metropolitan adventures." <u>Bright</u> <u>Days</u>, nos. 6-13, Sept. 5-Oct. 3, 1896.

273M   "Larry the wanderer; or, The ups and downs of a knockabout." <u>Good</u> <u>News</u>, vol. 9, nos. 223-235, Aug. 11-Nov. 3, 1894.

Published in book form as <u>Larry</u> <u>the</u> <u>wanderer</u>; <u>or</u>, <u>The</u> <u>rise</u> <u>of</u> <u>a</u> <u>nobody</u> by Lee & Shepard in 1904; reprinted by Grosset & Dunlap (309N). Also published by Lothrop, Lee & Shepard in the STRATEMEYER POPULAR SERIES (303S.12X), and, in 1920, by Street & Smith as no. 109 in the ALGER SERIES (289P.12), both times with the new title.

274M   "Luke Foster's grit; or, The last cruise of the Spitfire." <u>Argosy</u>, vol. 13, nos. 477-487, Jan. 23-April 2, 1892.

Published in book form by Merriam in 1894 and by Lee & Shepard in 1900 (the latter as a revised edition), both times as vol. 1 of the SHIP AND SHORE series, with the title <u>The</u> <u>last</u> <u>cruise</u> <u>of</u> <u>the</u> <u>Spitfire</u>; <u>or</u>, <u>Luke</u> <u>Foster's</u> <u>strange</u> <u>voyage</u> (303S.1). Also published with the new title for the next three editions: as vol. 1 of Lothrop, Lee & Shepard's STRATEMEYER POPULAR SERIES (303S.1); as a non-series title by Grosset & Dunlap; as no. 98 in Street & Smith's ALGER SERIES, in 1919 (289P.1X).

275M   "On Sam's point." Good News, vol. 10, no. 238, Nov. 24, 1894.

Reprinted with Ed Ward as author in Young Sports of America, June 22, 1895 (314M).

276M   "Paul Raymond's rovings; or, In quest of name and fortune." Golden Days, vol. 16, nos. 36-46, July 27-Oct. 5, 1895.

No. 36 has Ralph Hamilton as author (162M); nos. 37-46 list Edward Stratemeyer.

277M   "Reuben Stone's discovery; or, The young miller of Torrent Bend." Argosy, vol. 14, nos. 503-515, July 23-Oct 15, 1892.

Published in book form by Merriam in 1895, as vol. 2 of the SHIP AND SHORE series; revised edition published in 1900 by Lee & Shepard, still as vol. 2 of the SHIP AND SHORE series (301S.2). Also published by Lothrop, Lee & Shepard as vol. 2 of the STRATEMEYER POPULAR SERIES (303S.2), by Grosset & Dunlap as a non-series title, and by Street & Smith as no. 99 in the ALGER SERIES (289P.2X). The Street & Smith edition was published in 1919.

278M   "Richard Dare's venture; or, Striking out for himself." Argosy, vol. 11, nos. 423-433, Jan. 10-March 21, 1891.

Published in book form by Merriam in 1894 as vol. 1 of the BOUND TO SUCCEED series; revised edition published by Lee & Shepard in 1899, also as vol. 1 of the BOUND TO SUCCEED series (291S.1). Reprinted as part of Lee & Shepard's WORKING UPWARD series in 1903 (304S.6X), and later as vol. 4 of Lothrop, Lee & Shepard's STRATEMEYER POPULAR SERIES (303S.4), and a non-series title by Grosset & Dunlap. Published in 1919 by Street & Smith as no. 101 in the ALGER SERIES (289P.4X).

279M   "Shorthand Tom; or, The exploits of a young reporter." Good News, vol. 8, nos. 196-207, Feb. 3-April 21, 1894.

Published in book form by W. L. Allison in 1897 as vol. 4 in the BOUND TO WIN series (292S.2X). Also published by W. L. Allison, by M. A. Donohue, and by Lee & Shepard (the latter in 1903) all as Shorthand Tom the reporter; or, The exploits of a bright boy, vol. 3 in the WORKING UPWARD series (304S.3). The new title was also used for the next three editions: by Lothrop, Lee & Shepard as part of the STRATE-MEYER POPULAR SERIES (303S.9X); by Grosset & Dunlap as a non-series title; and by Street & Smith as no. 106 in the ALGER SERIES, in 1920 (289P.9X).

280M   "Snow Lodge." The Popular Magazine. vol. 1, nos. 2-3, Dec. 1903-Jan. 1904.

First published in book form by A. S. Barnes & Co. in 1904 as The island camp; or, The young hunters of Lakeport by Captain Ralph Bonehill, vol

1 of the OUTDOOR series (061S.1). Reprinted by Lothrop, Lee & Shepard as The gun club boys of Lakeport; or, The island camp by Edward Stratemeyer, vol. 1 of the LAKEPORT series (296S.1).

281M   "Three ranch boys; or, The great Winthrop claim." Young People of America, nos. 27-37, Nov. 30, 1895-Feb. 8, 1896.

Published in book form by Saalfield in 1901 as Three young ranchmen; or, Daring adventures in the great West by Captain Ralph Bonehill, and later by Caldwell (069N). Reprinted as vol. 1 of Saalfield's ADVENTURE series (045S.1X) and vol. 2 of Saalfield's BONEHILL series (046S.2), both times with the new author and title.

282M   "The tin box mystery; or, The stolen railroad bonds." Good News, vol. 6, nos. 154-164, April 15-June 24, 1893.

Published in book form as The missing tin box; or, The stolen railroad bonds by Arthur M. Winfield in 1897 as vol. 5 of W. L. Allison's BOUND TO WIN series (330S.2X). Also published by Allison and by Donohue as vol. 4 in the BRIGHT AND BOLD series (334S.4), and by Donohue in the BOYS' LIBERTY series* (331P.1X). All editions had the new author and title.

283M   "True to himself; or, Roger Strong's struggle for place." Argosy, vol. 13, nos. 463-475, Oct. 17, 1891-Jan. 9, 1892.

Published in book form by Lee & Shepard in 1900 as vol. 3 of the SHIP AND SHORE series (301S.3). Also published by Grosset & Dunlap as a non-series title; and by Lothrop, Lee & Shepard as vol. 3 of the STRATEMEYER POPULAR series (303S.3); and by Street & Smith as no. 100 in the ALGER SERIES, in 1919 (289P.3X).

284M   "Victor Horton's idea." Golden Days, vol. 10, no. 49-vol. 11, no. 1, Nov. 2-Nov. 30, 1889.

Reprinted with the same title, but with no author listed, in Golden Days, Dec. 9, 1905-Jan. 6, 1906 (285M).

285M   "Victor Horton's idea." Golden Days, vol. 27, nos. 5-9, Dec. 9, 1905-Jan. 6, 1906.

Published anonymously.
    First published in Golden Days, Nov. 2-Nov. 30, 1889 with Edward Stratemeyer listed as author (284M).

286M   "The young auctioneer; or, The polishing of a rolling stone." Good News, vol. 10, nos. 241-253, Dec. 15, 1894-March 9, 1895.

Published in book form in 1897 as vol. 7 of W. L. Allison's BOUND TO WIN series, The young auctioneers; or, The polishing of a rolling stone (292S.3X). Published with the original title by Allison, Donohue, and Lee & Shepard, all as vol. 1 of the WORKING UPWARD series (304S.1). Also published by Grosset & Dunlap as a non-series title; by Lothrop, Lee & Shepard as part of the STRATEMEYER POPULAR series (303S.7X); and by Street & Smith as no. 104 of the ALGER SERIES, in 1920 (289P.7X),

---

* Subtitle missing.

all with the original title.

287M   "The young civil engineer; or, The perils of the backwoods."
Bright Days, nos. 13-21, Oct. 24-Dec. 19, 1896.

288M   "A young inventor's pluck; or, The Wellington legacy." Bright
Days, nos. 30-31, Feb. 20-Feb. 27, 1897.

Unfinished story.
First published as "Jack, the inventor; or, The trials and triumphs
of a young machinist" in The Holiday, April 25-June 3, 1891 (268M).

SERIES PUBLICATIONS

289P   ALGER SERIES

Volumes: 26*
Printed: 1919-1920*
Publisher: Street & Smith
Additional information: Numbers 113 through 122 previously appeared in
     book form with Captain Ralph Bonehill as author; number 123, with Arthur
     M. Winfield as author. The Street & Smith editions changed the titles
     of many of the last fourteen volumes.
          When the ALGER SERIES was reprinted from 1928 to 1933, the first
     four Stratemeyer titles were replaced with four of Alger's works. For
     further information, see Horatio Alger, Jr., ALGER SERIES (010P).

289P.1X   The last cruise of the Spitfire; or, Luke Foster's strange voyage.
No. 98. Nov. 17, 1919.

First published as "Luke Foster's grit; or, The last cruise of the
Spitfire" in Argosy, Jan. 23-April 2, 1892 (274M).

289P.2X   Reuben Stone's discovery; or, The young miller of Torrent Bend.
No. 99. Dec. 1, 1919.

First published in Argosy, July 23-Oct. 15, 1892 (277M).

289P.3X   True to himself; or, Roger Strong's struggle for place. No. 100.
Dec. 15, 1919.

First published in Argosy, Oct. 17, 1891-Jan. 9, 1892 (283M).

289P.4X   Richard Dare's venture; or, Striking out for himself. No. 101.
Dec. 29, 1919.

First published in Argosy, Jan. 10-March 21, 1891 (278M).

289P.5X   Oliver Bright's search; or, The mystery of a mine. No. 102.
Jan. 12, 1920; Jan. 1932.

---

* Number of volumes and years published apply only to titles published
   as by Edward Stratemeyer.

First published as "One boy in a thousand; or, The mystery of the Aurora Mine" by Arthur M. Winfield in Argosy, Nov. 12, 1892-Feb. 4, 1893 (327M).

289P.6X   To Alaska for gold; or, The fortune hunters of the Yukon.   No. 103.   Jan. 26, 1920; Jan. 1932.

First published by Lee & Shepard in 1899 as vol. 3 of the BOUND TO SUCCEED series (291S.3).

289P.7X   The young auctioneer; or, The polishing of a rolling stone.   No. 104.   Feb. 9, 1920; Feb. 1932.

First published in Good News, Dec. 15, 1894-March 9, 1895 (286M).

289P.8X   Bound to be an electrician; or, Franklin Bell's success.   No. 105.   Feb. 23, 1920; Feb. 1932.

First published as "Bound to be an electrician; or, A clear head and a stout heart" by Arthur M. Winfield in Bright Days, April-Aug. 1896 (323M).

289P.9X   Shorthand Tom the reporter; or, The exploits of a bright boy.*   No. 106.   March 8, 1920; March 1932.

First published as "Shorthand Tom; or, The exploits of a young reporter" in Good News, Feb. 3-April 21, 1894 (279M).

289P.10X   Fighting for his own; or, The fortunes of a young artist.   No. 107.   March 22, 1920; March 1932.

First published in Argosy, May 21-July 23, 1892, with Arthur M. Winfield as author (324M).

289P.11X   Joe the surveyor; or, The value of a lost claim.   No. 108.   April 5, 1920; April 1932.

First published in Good News, May 5-July 28, 1894 (270M).

289P.12X   Larry the wanderer; or, The rise of a nobody.   No. 109.   April 19, 1920; April 1932.

First published as "Larry the wanderer; or, The ups and downs of a knockabout" in Good News, Aug. 11-Nov. 3, 1894 (273M).

289P.13X   The young ranchman; or, Between Boer and Briton.   No. 110.   May 3, 1920; May 1932.

First published as Between Boer and Briton; or, Two boys' adventures in South Africa, a non-series title, by Lee & Shepard in 1900 (305N).

289P.14X   The young lumberman; or, Out for fortune.   No. 111.   May 17, 1920; May 1932.

First published by Lee & Shepard in 1903 as Two young lumbermen; or, From Maine to Oregon, the GREAT AMERICAN INDUSTRIES series (295S.1).

---

* Cover and spine read Shorthand Tom; title page has the full title.

289P.15X The young explorers; or, Adventures above the Arctic Circle. No. 112. May 31, 1920; May 1932.

First published by Lothrop, Lee & Shepard in 1909 as First at the North Pole; or, Two boys in the Arctic Circle (307N).

289P.16X Boys of the wilderness; or, Down in old Kentucky. No. 113. June 14, 1920; June 1932.

First published by Mershon in 1903 as With Boone on the frontier; or, The pioneer boys of old Kentucky by Captain Ralph Bonehill, vol. 1 of the FRONTIER series (057S.1).

289P.17X Boys of the great Northwest; or, Across the Rockies. No. 114. June 28, 1920; June 1932.

First published by Mershon in 1904 as Pioneer boys of the great North-west; or, With Lewis and Clark across the Rockies by Captain Ralph Bonehill, vol. 2 of the FRONTIER series (057S.2).

289P.18X Boys of the gold fields; or, The nugget hunters. No. 115. July 12, 1920; July 1932.

First published by Stitt in 1906 as Pioneer boys of the gold fields; or, The nugget hunters of '49 by Captain Ralph Bonehill, vol. 3 of the FRONTIER series (057S.3).

289P.19X For his country; or, The adventures of two chums. No. 116. July 26, 1920; July 1932.

First published by Mershon in 1899 as When Santiago fell; or, The war adventures of two chums by Captain Ralph Bonehill, vol. 1 of the FLAG OF FREEDOM series (056S.1).

289P.20X Comrades in peril; or, Afloat on a battleship. No. 117. Aug. 9, 1920; Aug. 1932.

First published by Mershon in 1899 as A sailor boy with Dewey; or, Afloat in the Philippines by Captain Ralph Bonehill, vol. 2 of the FLAG OF FREEDOM series (056S.2).

289P.21X The young pearl hunters; or, In Hawaiian waters. No. 118. Aug. 23, 1920; Aug. 1932.

First published by Mershon in 1899 as Off for Hawaii; or, The mystery of a great volcano by Captain Ralph Bonehill, vol. 3 of the FLAG OF FREEDOM series (056S.3).

289P.22X The young bandmaster; or, Against big odds. No. 119. Sept. 6, 1920; Sept. 1932.

First published as "The young bandmaster; or, Solving a mystery of the past" by Captain Ralph Bonehill in Golden Hours, Feb. 11-April 15, 1899 (044M).

289P.23X Boys of the fort; or, True courage wins. No. 120. Sept. 20, 1920; Sept. 1932.

First published by Mershon in 1901 as <u>Boys</u> <u>of</u> <u>the</u> <u>fort</u>; <u>or</u>, <u>A</u> <u>young</u>
<u>captain's</u> <u>pluck</u> by Captain Ralph Bonehill, vol. 5 of the FLAG OF
FREEDOM series (056S.5).

289P.24X On fortune's trail; or, The heroes of the Black Hills. No. 121.
Oct. 4, 1920; Sept. 1932.

First published by Mershon in 1902 as <u>With</u> <u>Custer</u> <u>in</u> <u>the</u> <u>Black</u> <u>Hills</u>;
<u>or</u>, <u>A</u> <u>young</u> <u>scout</u> <u>among</u> <u>the</u> <u>Indians</u> by Captain Ralph Bonehill, vol. 6
of the FLAG OF FREEDOM series (056S.6).

289P.25X Lost in the land of ice; or, Under the northern lights. No. 122.
Oct. 18, 1920; Oct. 1932.

First published as "Lost in the land of ice; or, Bob Baxter at the South
Pole" by Roy Rockwood in <u>Golden</u> <u>Hours</u>, Dec. 1, 1900-Jan. 26, 1901 (219M).

289P.26X Bob the photographer; or, Strictly on the job. No. 123. Nov.
1, 1920; Oct. 1932.

First published as "Camera Bob; or, The thrilling adventures of a
travelling photographer" in <u>Good</u> <u>News</u>, Oct. 7, 1893-Jan. 20, 1894
(262M).

290S   AMERICAN BOYS' BIOGRAPHICAL SERIES

Volumes: 2
Printed: 1901-1904
Publisher: Lee and Shepard
Reprint publisher: Lothrop, Lee & Shepard Co., vols. 1-2
Illustrator: A. Burnham Shute, vol. 1
             Charles Copeland, vol. 2
Source of annotations: Lothrop, Lee & Shepard Co. advertisements [L,L&S]
Additional information: Books were published without subtitles. Both edi-
    tions had the same illustrations and were also illustrated with photo-
    graphs.

290S.1   American boys' life of William McKinley. (Lee & Shepard, 1901;
Lothrop, Lee & Shepard).

[L,L&S]: "Here is told the whole story of McKinley's boyhood days, his
life at school and at college, his work as a school teacher, his glorious career in the army, his struggles to obtain a footing as a lawyer,
his efforts as a Congressman and a Governor, and lastly his prosperous
career as our President, all told in a style particularly adapted to
boys and young men. The book is full of interesting anecdotes, all
taken from life, showing fully the sincere, honest, painstaking efforts
of a life cut all too short. This volume will prove an inspiration to
all boys and young men, and should be in every library."

290S.2   American boys' life of Theodore Roosevelt. (Lee & Shepard, 1904;
Lothrop, Lee & Shepard).

Lothrop, Lee & Shepard edition listed as a "new and extended edition."
    [L,L&S]: "This excellent work for young people covers the whole
life of our strenuous executive, as schoolboy, college student, traveler,
author, hunter, and ranchman, as assemblyman, as civil service commis-
sioner, as Assistant Secretary of the Navy, as a daring rough rider, as
Governor of New York, and lastly as President. Full of stories taken
from real life and told in a manner to interest both young and old."

291S   BOUND TO SUCCEED

Volumes: 3
Printed: 1894-1899
Publisher: Merriam Co., vols. 1-2
            Lee and Shepard, vol. 3
Reprint publisher: Lee and Shepard, vols. 1-2
Illustrator: Charles E. Boutwood, vols. 1-2
              A. Burnham Shute, vol. 3
Source of annotations: Lothrop, Lee & Shepard Co. advertisements [L,L&S]
Additional information: This was Edward Stratemeyer's first series; volume
1 was his first published book.
    Some Merriam advertisements show Larry the wanderer; or, The pol-
ishing of a rolling stone as volume 3 of this series; however, Merriam
did not complete the series. When Lee & Shepard reprinted the series,
To Alaska for gold became the third volume; Larry the wanderer was published as a non-series title in 1904.

291S.1   Richard Dare's venture; or, Striking out for himself. (Merriam,
1894; Lee & Shepard, 1899).

    1899 edition revised. First published in Argosy, Jan. 10-March 21,
    1891 (278M).
    [L,L&S]: "'Richard Dare's Venture' relates the experiences of a
    country youth who comes to New York to seek his fortune. He finds life
    in the metropolis no bed of roses, and it is only by the hardest work
    that he gains a footing at all. He enters the stationery business, and
    the plot against the boy is one that youthful readers will doubtless
    follow with keen interest."

291S.2   Oliver Bright's search; or, The mystery of a mine. (Merriam,
1895; Lee & Shepard, 1899).

    1899 edition revised. First published as "One boy in a thousand; or,
    The mystery of the Aurora Mine" by Arthur M. Winfield in Argosy, Nov.
    12, 1892-Feb. 4, 1893 (327M).
    [L,L&S]: "In this story we have the adventures of a manly American
    youth, who goes West to locate a mine in which his invalid father owns
    a large interest. He is accompanied by his school chum, who has run
    away from home, and the trip is made by way of the Isthmus of Panama.
    Arriving at San Francisco, the boys, accompanied by an elderly friend
    and a guide, set out for the interior on horseback. The story gives
    many interesting sketches of mining life in the remote portions of
    California."

291S.3   To Alaska for gold; or, The fortune hunters of the Yukon. (Lee
& Shepard, 1899).

[L,L&S]: "A boy's book, but one anybody might read with interest. The hero, out of work and left alone in the world, strikes up an acquaintanceship with another young fellow, who is experienced as an auctioneer. The two form a partnership, purchase a horse and wagon, stock the turnout with goods, and take to the road. The numerous adventures of the partners are told in a graphic way."

292S.4X   Fighting for his own; or, The fortunes of a young artist. (Allison, 1897).

First published in Argosy, May 21-July 23, 1892, with the same title, but with Arthur M. Winfield as author (324M).
[L,L&S]: "Lester Fleming's one ambition was to become an artist, but being nothing but a poor country lad, he seemed at first far from realizing that ambition. But Lester was a wide-awake fellow, and when his foster-father was drowned, the boy took the care of the household on his shoulders, and worked his way along in spite of many obstacles."

293S   COLONIAL

Volumes: 6
Printed: 1901-1906
Publisher: Lee and Shepard, vols. 1-5
            Lothrop, Lee & Shepard Co., vol. 6
Reprint publisher: Lothrop, Lee & Shepard Co., vols. 1-5
Illustrator: A. Burnham Shute, vols. 1-5
              J. W. Kennedy, vol. 6
Source of annotations: Lothrop, Lee & Shepard Co. advertisements [L,L&S]
Additional information: Lee & Shepard became Lothrop, Lee & Shepard in 1904, but some books in 1905 still appeared under the Lee & Shepard imprint.

293S.1   With Washington in the West; or, A soldier boy's battles in the wilderness. (Lee & Shepard, 1901, 1904; Lothrop, Lee & Shepard).

[L,L&S]: "Mr. Stratemeyer has woven into an excellent story something of Washington's youthful experience as a surveyor, leading on to the always thrilling Braddock's defeat. The hero, David Morris, is several years younger than Washington, with whom he becomes intimately associated. Pictures of pioneer life are given; scenes with friendly Indians; and old time games."

293S.2   Marching on Niagara; or, The soldier boys of the old frontier. (Lee & Shepard, 1902; Lothrop, Lee & Shepard).

[L,L&S]: "The story relates the doings of two young soldiers who join the Colonial forces in a march on Fort Niagara, during the time of the war with France, when the whole territory between the Blue Ridge and the Great Lakes was in a state of unrest. Many side lights are thrown into the colonial homes, and much useful information is given of the pioneers who helped to make our country what it is today."

293S.3   At the fall of Montreal; or, A soldier boy's final victory. (Lee & Shepard, 1903; Lothrop, Lee & Shepard).

[L,L&S]: "This volume relates the adventures of Dave Morris and his cousin Henry during the two last campaigns against the French for the possession of Canada and the territory below the great lakes. The scaling of the heights of Quebec under General Wolfe, and the memorable battle on the Plains of Abraham, are given in detail. There are many stirring scenes of battle, and there are also adventures while fishing and hunting, and with the Indians."

293S.4   On the trail of Pontiac; or, The pioneer boys of the Ohio. (Lee & Shepard, 1904; Lothrop, Lee & Shepard).

[L,L&S]: "This volume tells of times in our country immediately after the war with France for the possession of Canada. A fight with the Indians and the French in a snowstorm is especially realistic, and the entire book carries with it the atmosphere of colonial times."

293S.5   The fort in the wilderness; or, The soldier boys of the Indian trails. (Lee & Shepard, 1905; Lothrop, Lee & Shepard).

[L,L&S]: "This story is one of the best tales of Colonial days penned by this favorite author for young people. A central figure is the noted Indian warrior, Pontiac, and the particulars are given of the rise and fall of that awful conspiracy against the whites, which will never be forgotten, and vivid pen pictures are given of fights in and around the forts and at a trading-post on the Ohio."

293S.6   Trail and trading post; or, The young hunters of the Ohio. (Lothrop, Lee & Shepard, 1906).

[L,L&S]: "A fine closing volume to this deservedly popular series. Here we again meet the Morris boys, and many other friends. The plot centres [sic] about the possession of a certain trading-post on the Ohio River at a time just previous to the Revolution, and there are some encounters with some Frenchmen who wished to claim the post as their own."

294S   DAVE PORTER

Volumes: 15
Printed: 1905-1919
Publisher: Lee and Shepard, vol. 1
            Lothrop, Lee & Shepard Co., vols. 2-15
Reprint publisher: Lothrop, Lee & Shepard Co., vol. 1
Illustrator: Harold Matthews Brett, vol. 1
              I. B. Hazelton, vol. 2
              F. Gilbert Edge, vol. 3
              Charles Nuttall, vols. 4-5
              Lyle T. Hammond, vol. 6
              John Goss, vol. 7
              H. Richard Boehm, vols. 8-9
              Walter S. Rogers, vols. 10-13
              R. Emmett Owen, vols. 14-15
Source of annotations: Lothrop, Lee & Shepard Co. advertisments [L,L&S]
Additional information: Volume 1 was actually published by Lothrop, Lee & Shepard, but was still issued under the Lee & Shepard imprint.
        Lothrop, Lee & Shepard reissued volumes 1-8 in "popular editions"

in 1916 and 1917 and reprinted the other volumes in "popular editions" in succeeding years.

294S.1   Dave Porter at Oak Hall; or, The schooldays of an American boy. (Lee & Shepard, 1905; Lothrop, Lee & Shepard, ca1905, ca1916).

[L,L&S]: "Never was there a brighter, more manly, thoroughly up-to-date boy than Dave Porter, and all boys who read about him, and girls too, for the matter of that, will be sure to love him from the start. How, as a green country boy, he went to Oak Hall, how he was hazed, and how he had to fight his way through is told with a naturalness that is true to life."

294S.2   Dave Porter in the South Seas; or, The strange cruise of the Stormy Petrel. (Lothop, Lee & Shepard, 1906, ca1916).

[L,L&S]: "Dave is the same bright, wide-awake youth he was at school, and his adventures on shipboard and among the unexplored islands of the South Seas will render him dearer to the hearts of the boys than ever. Dave is trying to solve the mystery of his parentage, and several of his school chums are with him during his wanderings, some sharing his perils. A great tidal wave sends the ship into a strange harbor and there follows a mutiny which places a number on board in great peril."

294S.3   Dave Porter's return to school; or, Winning the medal of honor. (Lothrop, Lee & Shepard, 1907, ca1916).

[L,L&S]: "In this volume the scene is shifted back to Oak Hall, and once again Dave becomes the centre [sic] of as interesting a group of schoolboys as it is possible to imagine. There is a strong plot, with plenty of fun, and not a few rivalries on the athletic field, and the whole volume has a swing and a dash that are irresistible."

294S.4   Dave Porter in the far North; or, The pluck of an American school-boy. (Lothrop, Lee & Shepard, 1908, ca1916).

[L,L&S]: "In this book Dave is still at his well-liked boarding-school, Oak Hall, with his lively but manly comrades, who rejoice with him that he not only has discovered his parentage, but has a father and sister living, though unaware of his existence. Dave cannot rest until he finds those of his own family, and having secured leave of absence from school and accompanied by his chum, the son of a United States Senator, he goes to England only to find that his father has left on an expedition to the upper part of Norway. The boys follow in a most exciting pursuit which is replete with adventure."

294S.5   Dave Porter and his classmates; or, For the honor of Oak Hall. (Lothrop, Lee & Shepard, 1909, ca1916).

[L,L&S]: "In this volume Dave is back at Oak Hall and he brings about the complete reformation of a former bully, who was rapidly going to the bad. Athletic events and jolly fun are constantly mingled, and as evidence that the boys are not at school entirely for that, many take high honors at the close of the year, Dave being prize essayist, to the great delight of his friends."

294S.6   Dave Porter at Star Ranch; or, The cowboy's secret. (Lothrop, Lee & Shepard, 1910, ca1916).

[L,L&S]: "From his home, Dave, in company with his sister and some chums, journeys to the boundless west. At the Ranch the lads fall in with both good and bad cowboys, and the hero has a thrilling time of it riding a 'busting bronco.' Some horses disappear in a mysterious manner, and while trying to get back to the ranch on foot two of the lads are caught in a furious storm, that blows down a big tree on top of them. There are many scenes of hunting and rounding-up of cattle, and once a stampede adds to the excitement. Mr. Stratemeyer has traveled through the country he describes and gives a picture as accurate as it is entertaining."

294S.7   Dave Porter and his rivals; or, The chums and foes of Oak Hall. (Lothrop, Lee & Shepard, 1911, ca1916).

294S.8   Dave Porter on Cave Island; or, A schoolboy's mysterious mission. (Lothrop, Lee & Shepard, 1912, ca1916).

294S.9   Dave Porter and the runaways; or, Last days at Oak Hall. (Lothrop, Lee & Shepard, 1913, 1918).

294S.10   Dave Porter in the gold fields; or, The search for the Landslide Mine. (Lothrop, Lee & Shepard, 1914, 1918).

294S.11   Dave Porter at Bear Camp; or, The wild man of Mirror Lake. (Lothrop, Lee & Shepard, 1915, 1919).

294S.12   Dave Porter and his double; or, The disappearance of the Basswood fortune. (Lothrop, Lee & Shepard, 1916).

294S.13   Dave Porter's great search; or, The perils of a young civil engineer. (Lothrop, Lee & Shepard, 1917).

294S.14   Dave Porter under fire; or, A young army engineer in France.* (Lothrop, Lee & Shepard, 1918).

294S.15   Dave Porter's war honors; or, At the front with the flying engineers. (Lothrop, Lee & Shepard, 1919).

295S   GREAT AMERICAN INDUSTRIES

Volumes: 1
Printed: 1903
Publisher: Lee and Shepard
Illustrator: A. Burnham Shute, vol. 1
Source of annotations: Lothrop, Lee & Shepard advertisements [L,L&S]

295S.1   Two young lumbermen; or, From Maine to Oregon for fortune. (Lee & Shepard, 1903).

---

*   Volume 13 lists the title of volume 14 as Dave Porter on the Atlantic; or, The castaways of the menagerie ship. This title was not published.

Reprinted by Lothrop, Lee & Shepard as part of the STRATEMEYER POPULAR SERIES (303S.14), and by Grosset & Dunlap as a non-series title. Also published by Street & Smith as The young lumberman; or, Out for fortune, no. 111 in the ALGER SERIES, in 1920 (289P.14X).

[L,L&S]: "A splendid story, the scene shifting from Maine to Michigan and the Great Lakes, and then to the Columbia and the Great Northwest. The heroes are two sturdy youths who have been brought up among the lumbermen of their native State, and who strike out in an honest endeavor to better their condition. An ideal volume for every wide-awake American who wishes to know what our great lumber industry is to-day."

296S   LAKEPORT

Volumes: 6
Printed: 1908-1912
Publisher: Lothrop, Lee & Shepard Co.
Illustrator: Charles Nuttall, vols. 1-3
             Max Klepper, vol. 4
             John Goss, vol. 5
             H. Richard Boehm, vol. 6
Source of annotations: Lothrop, Lee & Shepard Co. advertisements [L,L&S]
Additional information: Volumes 1 and 2 had previously appeared in book
    form as the OUTDOOR series by Captain Ralph Bonehill (061S).

296S.1   The gun club boys of Lakeport; or, The island camp. (Lothrop, Lee & Shepard, 1908).

First published as "Snow Lodge" in The Popular Magazine, Dec. 1903-Jan. 1904 (280M).
[L,L&S]: "A bright, breezy outdoor story, telling how several lads organized a gun club and went camping in the winter time. They had with them a trusty old hunter who revealed to them many of the secrets of Nature as found in the woods. A volume any boy who loves a gun will appreciate."

296S.2   The baseball boys of Lakeport; or, The winning run. (Lothrop, Lee & Shepard, 1908).

First published by A. S. Barnes in 1905 as The winning run, or, The baseball boys of Lakeport by Captain Ralph Bonehill vol. 2 of the OUTDOOR series (061S.2).
[L,L&S]: "With the coming of summer the boys turned their attention to baseball and organized a club, and played many thrilling games. The rivalry was of the keenest, and the particulars are given of a plot to injure the Lakeport nine and make them lose the most important game of all."

296S.3   The boat club boys of Lakeport; or, The water champions. (Lothrop, Lee & Shepard, 1908).

[L,L&S]: "This time the scene is shifted to the lake. The boys all know how to row and sail a boat, and they organize a club and have fun galore. During a squall on the lake something of great value is lost overboard. The abduction of a little girl adds to the interest of the volume. Every lad who loves the water will read this with pleasure."

296S.4   The football boys of Lakeport; or, More goals than one. (Lothrop, Lee & Shepard, 1909).

   [L,L&S]: "Football is one of the most popular sports of this country, and in this tale Mr. Stratemeyer has shown what the jolly and dauntless boys of Lakeport did when the football season came around. Their heroes of the baseball field were not long in organizing an eleven and getting into practice, and there followed a series of exciting contests for the Lake Pennant. The boys had a college man to coach them, and made a number of brilliant plays, some of which are described by the author in detail."

296S.5   The automobile boys of Lakeport; or, A run for fun and fame. (Lothrop, Lee & Shepard, 1910).

   [L,L&S]: "How the lads of Lakeport got their big touring car, how they went on a long trip through the hills, and how they won a peculiar race, is told in a manner to please both young and old. Once the machine was almost consumed in a fire, and again it was stolen by some rivals who carried it away on a flatboat to an island. Mr. Stratemeyer is a motorist himself and therefore understands his subject thoroughly."

296S.6   The aircraft boys of Lakeport; or, Rivals of the clouds. (Lothrop, Lee & Shepard, 1912).

297S   MEXICAN WAR

Volumes: 3
Printed: 1909
Publisher: Lothrop, Lee & Shepard Co.
Illustrator: Louis Meynelle, vol. 1
                J. W. Kennedy, vol. 2
                J. J. Mora, vol. 3
Source of annotations: Lothrop, Lee & Shepard Co. advertisements [L,L&S]
Additional information: The MEXICAN WAR series was first published by Dana Estes & Co. from 1900 to 1902, with Captain Ralph Bonehill as author (060S). Only the author's name and the publisher were changed for the reprint editions. Books were published without subtitles.

297S.1   For the liberty of Texas. (Lothrop, Lee & Shepard, 1909, 1917, 1930).

   First published by Dana Estes & Co. in 1900 with Captain Ralph Bonehill as author (060S.1).
      [L,L&S]: "Much is told here of Sam Houston, Davy Crockett, Colonel Bowie, and other Texan heroes in connection with the entertaining story of the fortunes of two brothers, Dan and Ralph Radbury. The fall of the Alamo is introduced, and other famous incidents."

297S.2   With Taylor on the Rio Grande. (Lothrop, Lee & Shepard, 1909, 1917, 1930).

   First published by Dana Estes & Co. in 1901 with Captain Ralph Bonehill as author (060S.2).

[L,L&S]: "As with each of the series, this is a complete story, but continues the adventures of the patriotic young Radbury brothers. They serve under General Taylor at Palo Alto, Monterey, and Buena Vista and share in the glory of 'Old Rough and Ready.'"

297S.3   Under Scott in Mexico. (Lothrop, Lee & Shepard, 1909, 1917, 1930?).

First published by Dana Estes & Co. in 1902 with Captain Ralph Bonehill as author (060S.3).
[L,L&S]: "In the concluding volume of this valuable historical series Dan and Ralph come under the command of Gen. Winfield Scott and finally bear their part in the triumphant entry of the proud city of Mexico."

298S   MINUTE BOYS

Volumes: 2*
Printed: 1898-1899*
Publisher: Estes & Lauriat
Reprint publisher: Dana Estes & Co., vols. 1-2*
                    L. C. Page & Co., vols. 1-2*
Illustrator: A. Burnham Shute, vol. 1
              J. W. Kennedy, vol. 2
Source of annotations: L. C. Page & Co. advertisements [LCP]
Additional information: Edward Stratemeyer wrote the first two volumes in this eleven-volume series; James Otis Kaier (under the name James Otis) wrote the other nine. By the time the third volume was published, Estes & Lauriat had become Dana Estes & Co.; the first two volumes were reissued.
    L. C. Page later reprinted the series, changing the series order, so that the Stratemeyer titles became volumes 9 and 10. The nine Otis titles are listed below, with the Estes & Co. series order; copyright dates and L. C. Page series order are in parenthesis.

3. The minute boys of the Green Mountains	(1904)	(8)
4. The minute boys of the Mohawk Valley	(1905)	(7)
5. The minute boys of the Wyoming Valley	(1906)	(6)
6. The minute boys of South Carolina	(1907)	(5)
7. The minute boys of Long Island	(1908)	(4)
8. The minute boys of New York City	(1909)	(3)
9. The minute boys of Boston	(1910)	(2)
10. The minute boys of Philadelphia	(1911)	(1)
11. The minute boys of Yorktown	(1912)	(11)

Books were published without subtitles.
Series description [LCP]: "These books, as shown by their titles, deal with periods in the history of the development of our great country which are of exceeding interest to every patriotic American boy--and girl. Places and personages of historical interest are here presented to the young reader in story form, and a great deal of information is unconsciously gathered."

---

* Number of volumes and years published apply only to volumes written by Edward Stratemeyer.

298S.1   The minute boys of Lexington. (Estes & Lauriat, 1898; Estes; Page).

Page edition published as vol. 10.

298S.2   The minute boys of Bunker Hill. (Estes & Lauriat, 1899; Estes; Page).

Page edition published as vol. 9.

299S   OLD GLORY

Volumes: 6
Printed: 1898-1901
Publisher; Lee and Shepard
Reprint publisher: Lothrop, Lee & Shepard Co., vols. 1-6
Illustrator: A. Burnham Shute, vols. 1-6
Source of annotations: Lothrop, Lee & Shepard Co. advertisements [L,L&S]

299S.1   Under Dewey at Manila; or, The war fortunes of a castaway. (Lee & Shepard, 1898; Lothrop, Lee & Shepard).

   [L,L&S]: "This book, published in September, 1898, at once sprang to the front as the greatest success among books for boys since the famous Army and Navy series by 'Oliver Optic,' and its popularity has steadily increased as the succeeding volumes of the series have appeared."

299S.2   A young volunteer in Cuba; or, Fighting for the single star. (Lee & Shepard, 1898; Lothrop, Lee & Shepard).

   [L,L&S]: "The career of Larry Russell, as recorded in 'Under Dewey at Manila,' was the hit of the season among juveniles. The fortunes of Larry are equalled in interest by the adventures of Ben, his older brother, and his friend, Gilbert Pennington, and the many exciting scenes through which they passed during their service in the army. Ben enlisted in a New York volunteer regiment, while Gilbert joined Colonel Roosevelt's famous Rough Riders. Their life in camp, the capture of El Caney, the charge at San Juan hill, are all vividly described."

299S.3   Fighting in Cuban waters; or, Under Schley on the Brooklyn, (Lee & Shepard, 1899; Lothrop, Lee & Shepard).

   [L,L&S]: "In this book Walter Russell, brother to Larry and Ben, the respective heroes of the two preceding volumes of the series, finds his way to Boston, secures employment, enlists in the navy, and is assigned to the 'Brooklyn.' Then follow intensely interesting chapters, telling of Commodore Schley, the routine life of the 'Jackies,' and blockade and discovery of Cervera's fleet, followed by the memorable conflict of July 3."

299S.4   Under Otis in the Philippines; or, A young officer in the Tropics. (Lee & Shepard, 1899; Lothrop, Lee & Shepard).

[L,L&S]: "The 'Young Officer in the Tropics' is none other than our old friend Ben Russell, who upon reenlisting for service in the Philippines is given the same position, that of second lieutenant, to which he had been promoted for gallantry while 'A Young Volunteer in Cuba.'"

299S.5   The campaign of the jungle; or, Under Lawton through Luzon. (Lee & Shepard, 1900; Lothrop, Lee & Shepard).

[L,L&S]: "Ben and Larry figure in the 'Campaign of the Jungle,' which has a truthful and graphic historical setting in two expeditions of the noble General Lawton, whose portrait adorns the cover, the first being that directed against Santa Cruz on the Laguna de Bay, and the second from Manila to San Isidro, through one hundred and fifty miles of jungle. The same sterling qualities that have made these brothers so well liked carry them through perilous scenes with true American fortitude.'

299S.6   Under MacArthur in Luzon; or, Last battles in the Philippines. (Lee & Shepard, 1901; Lothrop, Lee & Shepard).

[L,L&S]: "We have here a thoroughly up-to-date, clean, and entertainin boys' story, complete in itself, but forming the sixth and last volume of the 'Old Glory' Series. The boys in all parts of the country have been anxiously waiting to learn the final fortunes of the three Russel: brothers, Larry, Walter, and Ben, with scarcely less interest in Gilbe: Pennington, hero of 'On to Pekin,' and not forgetting other old friend on land and sea. All are here, doing their duty in the same straight-forward way as ever; and the final battles in the Philippines are followed with that accuracy of statement which Mr. Stratemeyer always employs, thereby giving general value to his books without in the least impairing the interest of the story."

300S   PAN-AMERICAN

Volumes: 6
Printed: 1902-1911
Publisher: Lee and Shepard, vols. 1-4
            Lothrop, Lee & Shepard Co., vols. 5-6
Reprint publisher: Lothrop, Lee & Shepard Co., vols. 1-4
Illustrator: A. Burnham Shute, vols. 1-4
              Charles Nuttall, vol. 5
              John Goss, vol. 6
Source of annotations: Lothrop, Lee & Shepard Co. advertisements [L,L&S]
Additional information: All editions had the same illustrators, but late editions reduced the number of illustrations.

300S.1   Lost on the Orinoco; or, American boys in Venezuela. (Lee & Shepard, 1902; Lothrop, Lee & Shepard, ca1905; 1930).

[L,L&S]: "This volume tells of five American youths, who, with their tutor, sail from New York to La Guayra, touching at Curacao on the wa They visit Caracas, go westward to the Gulf of Maracaibo and lake of the same name, and at last find themselves in the region of the might Orinoco, and of course they have some exciting experiences, one of wh gives name to the book."

300S.2   The young volcano explorers; or, American boys in the West Indies.
(Lee & Shepard, 1902; Lothrop, Lee & Shepard).

[L,L&S]: "The boys, with their tutor, sail from Venezuela to the West
Indies, stopping at Jamaica, Cuba, Hayti [sic], and Porto Rico. They
have numerous adventures on the way, and then set out for St. Pierre,
Martinique, where they encounter the effects of the eruption of Mt.
Pelee, and two of the boys are left on a raft to shift for themselves.
Life in the West Indies is well portrayed."

300S.3   Young explorers of the Isthmus; or, American boys in Central
America. (Lee & Shepard, 1903; Lothrop, Lee & Shepard).

[L,L&S]: "Relates adventures in a tour covering Nicaragua, Costa Rica,
and the Isthmus of Panama. The party travel the various canal routes,
and have a number of highly interesting experiences. The volume contains a vast amount of timely information, and will be read with interest by young men as well as boys."

300S.4   Young explorers of the Amazon; or, American boys in Brazil. (Lee
& Shepard, 1904; Lothrop, Lee & Shepard).

[L,L&S]: "An absorbing tale of sight-seeing and adventures in Brazil.
The five boys and their tutor travel the whole seacoast from Rio de
Janeiro to Para, and then move up the Amazon into rubber country and
beyond. The volume is filled with pen-pictures of life as it exists in
Brazil to-day, and will be heartily enjoyed by all young people."

300S.5   Treasure seekers of the Andes; or, American boys in Peru.
(Lothrop, Lee & Shepard, 1907).

[L,L&S]: "This volume takes the young explorers from the head of the
Amazon River to the coast of Peru and then into the mighty snow-topped
mountains. One of the boys obtains possession of a secret regarding a
Spanish treasure and, with a companion, goes in quest of the same, and
both get lost in a series of caves. The volume is up-to-date and will
please both young and old."

300S.6   Chased across the Pampas; or, American boys in Argentina and homeward bound. (Lothrop, Lee & Shepard, 1911).

301S   SHIP AND SHORE

Volumes: 3
Printed: 1894-1900
Publisher: Merriam Co., vols. 1-2
            Lee and Shepard, vol. 3
Reprint publisher: Lee & Shepard, vols. 1-2
Illustrator: anonymous, vol. 1
              Charles E. Boutwood, vol. 2
              A. Burnham Shute, vol. 3
Source of annotations: Lothrop, Lee & Shepard Co. advertisements [L,L&S]
Additional information: Merriam advertisements sometimes list True to
    himself, volume 3, as "in press," but Merriam did not publish this
    volume.

The Lee & Shepard editions had unsigned illustrations for the first two volumes.

301S.1   The last cruise of the Spitfire; or, Luke Foster's strange voyage. (Merriam, 1894; Lee & Shepard, 1900).

First published as "Luke Foster's grit; or, The last cruise of the Spitfire" in Argosy, Jan. 23-April 2, 1892 (274M).
[L,L&S]: "'The Last Cruise of the Spitfire' relates the adventures of a youth who ran away from his guardian's house because he could no longer stand the cruel treatment received. He had never before been to sea, and when he is unexpectedly carried off on the 'Spitfire' he encounters many adventures of which he had never before dreamed."

301S.2   Reuben Stone's discovery; or, The young miller of Torrent Bend. (Merriam, 1895; Lee & Shepard, 1900).

First published in Argosy, July 23-Oct. 15, 1892 (277M).
[L,L&S]: "'Reuben Stone's Discovery' tells, in a matter-of-fact way, the exploits of a young miller who is left in charge of his father's property while the parent goes West to seek a more promising field for business. A story which girls as well as boys will enjoy reading."

301S.3   True to himself; or, Roger Strong's struggle for place. (Lee & Shepard, 1900).

First published in Argosy, Oct. 17, 1891-Jan. 9, 1892 (283M).
[L,L&S]: "In this story we are introduced to Roger Strong, a typical American country lad and his sister Kate, who, by an unhappy combination of events are thrown upon their own resources and compelled to make their own way in the world. Roger tells his own story in a modest, manly way that will charm both boys and girls, and that their parents will equally admire."

302S   SOLDIERS OF FORTUNE

Volumes: 4
Printed: 1900-1906
Publisher: Lee and Shepard, vols. 1-2
            Lothrop, Lee & Shepard Co., vols. 3-4
Reprint publisher: Lothrop, Lee & Shepard Co., vols. 1-2
Illustrator: A. Burnham Shute, vols. 1-4
Source of annotations: Lothrop, Lee & Shepard Co. advertisements [L,L&S]
Additional information: Both editions had the same illustrations.

302S.1   On to Pekin; or, Old glory in China. (Lee & Shepard, 1900; Lothrop, Lee & Shepard).

[L,L&S]: "The hero, Gilbert Pennington, goes from the Philippines with the Ninth Regiment to take part in the rescue of the beleaguered British Embassy at Pekin by the international forces. Mr. Stratemeyer has risen to the occasion by giving, in addition to one of his very best stories, a store of information concerning China and the Chinese, conveyed in a natural and entertaining manner."

302S.2   Under the Mikado's flag; or, Young soldiers of fortune. (Lee & Shepard, 1904; Lothrop, Lee & Shepard).

[L,L&S]: "'Under the Mikado's Flag' relates the adventures of two young Americans in Korea and Manchuria during the outbreak of the great war between Russia and Japan, one of the leading characters being Gilbert Pennington, the hero of 'On to Pekin,' and the other, Ben Russell, who with his brothers, Larry and Walter, is so well known to the thousands of readers of the famous 'Old Glory Series.' It closes with the great Battle of Liao-Yang, and is as valuable for the information conveyed as it is interesting as a story."

302S.3   At the fall of Port Arthur; or, A young American in the Japanese Navy. (Lothrop, Lee & Shepard, 1905).

[L,L&S]: "This story relates, primarily, the adventures of Larry Russell, who is on board his old ship, the Columbia, which is carrying a cargo for the Japanese government. The young sailor joins the Japanese navy, and under Admiral Togo assists at the bombardment of Port Arthur. Life in the Japanese navy is described in detail, and also life in Port Arthur during the siege and bombardment, which has few parallels in history."

302S.4   Under Togo for Japan; or, Three young Americans on land and sea. (Lothrop, Lee & Shepard, 1906).

[L,L&S]: "The 'Soldiers of Fortune Series' is a continuation of the famous 'Old Glory Series,' and enjoys equal popularity. The principal characters are Ben and Larry Russell, Gilbert Pennington, and the fine old gunner, Luke Striker, all of whom are well known to thousands of readers. The climax of the book naturally deals with the Battle of the Sea of Japan and Admiral Togo's wonderful victory, in which Larry and Luke Striker bear an honorable part. The fortunes of Ben and Gilbert Pennington on land also furnish much that is of interest."

303S   STRATEMEYER POPULAR SERIES

Volumes: 15
Publisher: Lothrop, Lee & Shepard Co.
Illustrator: Charles E. Boutwood, vols. 1-2, 4-5
              A. Burnham Shute, vols. 3, 6-7, 12-14
              M. W. Bridges and G. B. Dupont, vols. 8, 11
              M. W. Bridges and H. Puente, vol. 9
              G. B. Dupont, vol. 10
              Charles Nuttall, vol. 15
Source of annotations: Lothrop, Lee & Shepard Co. advertisements [L,L&S]
Additional information: This series consisted of books from several of Edward Stratemeyer's series, reissued under the title STRATEMEYER POPULAR SERIES. Originally, the series had twelve volumes; it was later expanded to fifteen titles.
    There is a slight discrepancy in the series order between some advertisements. Joe the surveyor is alternately listed as volume 6 or volume 11, thus changing the volume numbers for the succeeding volumes.
    The series order below places Joe the surveyor as volume 11 and is identical to the order of Street & Smith's ALGER SERIES (289P).

Series description [L,L&S]: "Since the passing of Henty, Edward Stratemeyer is the most widely read of all living writers for the young, and each year extends the vast and enthusiastic throng. In obedience to the popular demand we have established this Popular Series comprising twelve representative books by this great writer, on which special prices can be made. The stories are bright and breezy, moral in tone, and while full of adventure, are not sensational."

303S.1   The last cruise of the Spitfire; or, Luke Foster's strange voyage. (Lothrop, Lee & Shepard).

First published as "Luke Foster's grit; or, The last cruise of the Spitfire" in Argosy, Jan. 23-April 2, 1892 (274M).
    [L,L&S]: "'The Last Cruise of the Spitfire' relates the adventures of a youth who ran away from his guardian's house because he could no longer stand the cruel treatment received. He had never before been to sea, and when he is unexpectedly carried off on the 'Spitfire' he encounters many adventures of which he had never before dreamed."

303S.2   Reuben Stone's discovery; or, The young miller of Torrent Bend. (Lothrop, Lee & Shepard).

First published in Argosy, July 23-Oct. 15, 1892 (277M).
    [L,L&S]: "'Reuben Stone's Discovery' tells, in a matter-of-fact way, the exploits of a young miller who is left in charge of his father's property while the parent goes West to seek a more promising field for business. A story which girls as well as boys will enjoy reading."

303S.3   True to himself; or, Roger Strong's struggle for place. (Lothrop, Lee & Shepard).

First published in Argosy, Oct. 17, 1891-Jan. 9, 1892 (283M).
    [L,L&S]: "In this story we are introduced to Roger Strong, a typical American country lad and his sister Kate, who, by an unhappy combination of events are thrown upon their own resources and compelled to make their own way in the world. Roger tells his own story in a modest, manly way that will charm both boys and girls, and that their parents will equally admire."

303S.4   Richard Dare's venture; or, Striking out for himself. (Lothrop, Lee & Shepard).

First published in Argosy, Jan. 10-March 21, 1891 (278M).
    [L,L&S]: "'Richard Dare's Venture' relates the experiences of a country youth who comes to New York to seek his fortune. He finds life in the metropolis no bed of roses, and it is only by the hardest work that he gains a footing at all. He enters the stationery business, and the plot against the boy is one that youthful readers will doubtless follow with keen interest."

303S.5   Oliver Bright's search; or, The mystery of a mine. (Lothrop, Lee & Shepard).

First published as "One boy in a thousand; or, The mystery of the Aurora Mine," by Arthur M. Winfield in Argosy, Nov. 12, 1892-Feb. 4, 1893 (327M).

[L,L&S]: "In this story we have the adventures of a manly American youth, who goes West to locate a mine in which his invalid father owns a large interest. He is accompanied by his school chum, who has run away from home, and the trip is made by way of the Isthmus of Panama. Arriving at San Francisco, the boys, accompanied by an elderly friend and a guide, set out for the interior on horseback. The story gives many interesting sketches of mining life in the remote portions of California."

303S.6X   To Alaska for gold; or, The fortune hunters of the Yukon. (Lothrop, Lee & Shepard).

First published by Lee & Shepard in 1899 as vol. 3 of the BOUND TO SUCCEED series (291S.3).
[L,L&S]: "This tale tells of the adventures of two Maine boys who grow tired of trying to make a living in the lumber district of that State. An uncle, who is an experienced miner, offers to take them on a trip to the famous Klondike gold region, and the boys start out, first for the West, where they join their relative and several other fortune hunters, and then for the heart of Alaska. The gold regions are gained at last, and a summer and winter are spent there, hunting for the precious yellow nuggets and fighting off starvation and other perils."

303S.7X   The young auctioneer; or, The polishing of a rolling stone. (Lothrop, Lee & Shepard).

First published in Good News, Dec. 15, 1894-March 9, 1895 (286M).
[L,L&S]: "A boy's book, but one anybody might read with interest. The hero, out of work and left alone in the world, strikes up an acquaintanceship with another young fellow, who is experienced as an auctioneer. The two form a partnership, purchase a horse and wagon, stock the turnout with goods, and take to the road. The numerous adventures of the partners are told in a graphic way."

303S.8X   Bound to be an electrician; or, Franklin Bell's success. (Lothrop, Lee & Shepard).

First published as "Bound to be an electrician; or, A clear head and a stout heart" by Arthur M. Winfield in Bright Days, April-Aug., 1896 (323M).
[L,L&S]: "Franklin Bell starts out under many difficulties. He is poor and has no friends to assist him in advancing himself. But a showing of what pluck can do at a most perilous moment gains for him the opening he seeks, and from that time on his advancement is steady. From the East he is sent to Chicago by his employer, where he clears up a business complication involving a large sum of money."

303S.9X   Shorthand Tom, the reporter; or, The exploits of a bright boy. (Lothrop, Lee & Shepard).

First published as "Shorthand Tom; or, The exploits of a young reporter" in Good News, Feb. 3-April 21, 1894 (279M).
[L,L&S]: "Tom Swift was a shorthand writer. Losing his position in the office of a rascally lawyer, he fell in with a newspaper editor and became a reporter on one of the leading New York dailies. His duties took him to several strange places and brought him in contact

with dangerous men who were trying to do Tom and his sister Susie out of some property which had been left to them. Poor Susie was kidnapped, and it was Tom who set out on a long and perilous search for her."

303S.10X Fighting for his own; or, The fortunes of a young artist. (Lothrop, Lee & Shepard).

First published with the same title, but with Arthur M. Winfield as author, in Argosy, May 21–July 23, 1892 (324M).
[L,L&S]: "Lester Fleming's one ambition was to become an artist, but being nothing but a poor country lad, he seemed at first far from realizing that ambition. But Lester was a wide-awake fellow, and when his foster-father was drowned, the boy took the care of the household on his shoulders, and worked his way along in spite of many obstacles."

303S.11X Joe the surveyor; or, The value of a lost claim. (Lothrop, Lee & Shepard).

First published in Good News, May 5–July 28, 1894 (270M).
[L,L&S]: "This story relates the trials and triumphs of a sturdy country youth, who is compelled, by the force of circumstances, to go forth into the world and earn, not alone his own living, but also support for his twin sister and his invalid father."

303S.12 Larry the wanderer; or, The rise of a nobody. (Lothrop, Lee & Shepard).

First published as "Larry, the wanderer; or, The ups and downs of a knockabout" in Good News, Aug. 11–Nov. 3, 1894 (273M).
[L,L&S]: "Larry is a youth who has been knocked around from pillar to post for a number of years. The unravelling of the curious mystery which surrounds the lad's identity makes good reading."

303S.13 Between Boer and Briton; or, Two boys' adventures in South Africa. (Lothrop, Lee & Shepard).

First published in book form by Lee & Shepard in 1900 (305N).
[L,L&S]: "Relates the experiences of two boys, cousins to each other, one American and the other English, whose fathers are engaged in the Transvaal, one in farming and the other in mining operations. While the two boys are off on a hunting trip after big game the war between the Boers and the Britons suddenly breaks out, and while endeavoring to rejoin their parents the boys find themselves placed between hostile armies."

303S.14 Two young lumbermen; or, From Maine to Oregon for fortune. (Lothrop, Lee & Shepard).

First published by Lee & Shepard in 1903 as vol. 1 in the GREAT AMERICAN INDUSTRIES series (295S.1).
[L,L&S]: "A splendid story, the scene shifting from Maine to Michigan and the Great Lakes, and then to the Columbia and the Great Northwest. The heroes are two sturdy youths who have been brought up among the lumbermen of their native State, and who strike out in an honest endeavor to better their condition. An ideal volume for every wide-awake American who wishes to know what our great lumber industry is to-day."

303S.15   First at the North Pole; or, Two boys in the Arctic Circle.
(Lothrop, Lee & Shepard).

> First published by Lothrop, Lee & Shepard in 1909, as a non-series
> title (307N).

304S   WORKING UPWARD

Volumes: 6
Printed: ca1898-1903
Publisher: W. L. Allison Company, vols. 1-4
             Lee and Shepard, vols. 5X-6X
Reprint publisher: Lee and Shepard, vols. 1-4
                     M. A. Donohue & Co., vols. 1-4
Illustrator: M. B. Bridges and G. B. DuPont, vols. 1, 4
               M. B. Bridges and Puente, vol. 2
               G. B. DuPont, vol. 3
Additional information: Allison first issued volumes 1 through 4 in the
   BOUND TO WIN series, then, sometime between 1897 and 1900, reprinted
   them as the WORKING UPWARD series. The Donohue editions were issued
   between 1900, when Donohue Bros. became M. A. Donohue & Co., and 1903,
   when the Lee & Shepard editions were published. Lee & Shepard added
   an additional two volumes from the BOUND TO SUCCEED series.
      All editions had the same illustrations.
      See Edward Stratemeyer, BOUND TO WIN (292S) for annotations for
   volumes 1 through 4; BOUND TO SUCCEED (291S) for annotations for volumes
   5 and 6.

304S.1   The young auctioneer; or, The polishing of a rolling stone.   (Allison, Donohue; Lee & Shepard, 1903).

> First published in Good News, Dec. 15, 1894-March 9, 1895 (286M).

304S.2   Bound to be an electrician; or, Franklin Bell's success.   (Allison; Donohue; Lee & Shepard, 1903).

> First published as "Bound to be an electrician; or, A clear head and a
> stout heart" by Arthur M. Winfield in Bright Days, April-Aug. 1896
> (323M).

304S.3   Shorthand Tom, the reporter; or, The exploits of a bright boy.
(Allison; Donohue; Lee & Shepard, 1903).

> First published as "Shorthand Tom; or, The exploits of a young reporter"
> in Good News, Feb. 3-April 21, 1894 (279M).

304S.4   Fighting for his own; or, The fortunes of a young artist.   (Allison; Donohue; Lee & Shepard, 1903).

> First published with the same title, but with Arthur M. Winfield as
> author, in Argosy, May 21-July 23, 1892 (324M).

304S.5X   Oliver Bright's search; or, The mystery of a mine.   (Lee & Shepard,
1903).

First published as "One boy in a thousand; or, The mystery of the Aurora Mine" by Arthur M. Winfield in Argosy, Nov. 12, 1892–Feb. 4, 1893 (327M).

304S.6X   Richard Dare's venture; or, Striking out for himself. (Lee & Shepard, 1903).

First published in Argosy, Jan. 10–March 21, 1891 (278M).

OTHER PUBLICATIONS

305N   Between Boer and Briton; or, Two boys' adventures in South Africa (Lee & Shepard, 1900; Grosset & Dunlap).

Illustrated by A. Burnham Shute. Reprinted as vol. 13 of Lothrop, Lee & Shepard's STRATEMEYER POPULAR SERIES (303S.13), as a non-series title by Grosset & Dunlap, and, in 1920, as no. 110 in Street & Smith's ALGER SERIES (289P.13X). Street & Smith edition titled The young ranch man; or, Between Boer and Briton.
[L,L&S]:* "Relates the experiences of two boys, cousins to each other, one American and the other English, whose fathers are engaged in the Transvaal, one in farming and the other in mining operations. While the two boys are off on a hunting trip after big game the war between the Boers and Britons suddenly breaks out, and while endeavoring to rejoin their parents the boys find themselves placed between hostile armies."

306N   Defending his flag; or, A boy in blue and a boy in gray. (Lothrop, Lee & Shepard, 1907).

Illustrated by Griswold Tyng. First published as "In defense of his flag" in The American boy, May 1906–June 1907 (266M).
[L,L&S]:* "This tale relates the adventures of two boys, or rather young men, during the first campaign of our great Civil War. One enlists in the infantry of the North, while the other throws in his fortunes with the cavalry of the South. Of the story Mr. Stratemeyer himself says:
"'In writing this work I have had but one object in view, and that was to give a faithful picture of a part of the Civil War as seen from both sides of that never-to-be-forgotten conflict. During the war, and for years afterward, grown folk and young people were treated to innumerable books on the subject, all written from either the Northern or the Southern point of view, thoroughly biased, and calculated to do more harm than good.
"'I think the time has come when the truth, and the whole truth at that, can be told, and when it will do positive good. Since the Spanish American War, when some of the gallant Southern officers and men made such records for themselves under Old Glory, the old lines have been practically wiped out. The reconstructed South is as firm a part of our nation as was the old South during the first half of the last century, and it has a perfect right to honor the memories of those who, while wearing the gray and marching under the stars and bars, fought gallantly for what they considered was right and true.'"

_____
* Source of annotations: Lothrop, Lee & Shepard Co. advertisements [L,L&

307N   First at the North Pole; or, Two boys in the Arctic Circle.
(Lothrop, Lee & Shepard, 1909; Grosset & Dunlap).

   Illustrated by Charles Nuttall. Reprinted by Lothrop, Lee & Shepard
   as vol. 15 in the STRATEMEYER POPULAR SERIES (303S.15), by Grosset &
   Dunlap as a non-series title, and by Street & Smith, in 1920, as no.
   112 in the ALGER SERIES (289P.15X). Street & Smith edition titled The
   young explorers; or, Adventures above the Arctic Circle.

308N   Joe the surveyor; or, The value of a lost claim. (Lee & Shepard,
1903; Grosset & Dunlap).

   Illustrated by A. Burnham Shute. First published in Good News, May 5-
   July 28, 1894 (270M).
      [L,L&S]:* "This story relates the trials and triumphs of a sturdy
   country youth, who is compelled, by the force of circumstances, to go
   forth into the world and earn, not alone his own living, but also support for his twin sister and invalid father."

309N   Larry the wanderer; or, The rise of a nobody. (Lee & Shepard,
1904; Grosset & Dunlap).

   Illustrated by A. Burnham Shute. First published as "Larry the wanderer; or, The ups and downs of a knockabout" in Good News, Aug. 11-
   Nov. 3, 1894 (273M).
      [L,L&S]:* "Larry is a youth who has been knocked around from pillar
   to post for a number of years. The unravelling of the curious mystery
   which surrounds the lad's identity makes good reading."

E. Ward Strayer

E. Ward Strayer is one of the few Stratemeyer or Stratemeyer Syndicate
pseudonyms that closely resembles Edward Stratemeyer's name. It was used
for only one book, published in 1918.

OTHER PUBLICATIONS

310N   Making good with Margaret.** (G. Sully & Co., 1918).

   Illustrated by A. O. Scott.

---

* Source of annotations: Lothrop, Lee & Shepard Co. advertisements [L,L&S].
** No subtitle.

Helen Louise Thorndyke

Helen Louise Thorndyke was the Stratemeyer Syndicate pseudonym responsible for the two HONEY BUNCH series: HONEY BUNCH (1923-1955; 34 vols.) and HONEY BUNCH AND NORMAN (1957-1963; 12 vols.). Although the two series totalled 46 volumes, five titles were originally published in the HONEY BUNCH series and reprinted in the HONEY BUNCH AND NORMAN series. Harriet Adams and Andrew Svenson both worked under this pseudonym.

SERIES PUBLICATIONS

311S   HONEY BUNCH

Volumes: 34
Printed: 1923-1955
Publisher: Grosset & Dunlap
Reprint publisher: McLoughlin Bros., Clover Books, vols. 9-10, 12-14,
                    16-19, 22-23, 25
Illustrator: Walter S. Rogers, vols. 1-12
              Marie Schubert, vols. 13-23, 28
              anonymous, vols. 24, 27, 29-31
Source of annotations: Grosset & Dunlap advertisements [G&D]
Additional information: The HONEY BUNCH books originally followed the
    adventures of HONEY BUNCH, with occasional appearances by the mis-
    chievous Norman. As the series progressed, Norman became a more ac-
    tive participant, possibly in an attempt to reach younger boys as well
    as girls.
        The last two volumes in the HONEY BUNCH series were actually the
    unofficial start of the HONEY BUNCH AND NORMAN series, as they marked
    the first use of HONEY BUNCH AND NORMAN in the title; indeed, they were
    later reprinted as volumes 5 and 6 in the HONEY BUNCH AND NORMAN series.
    Three other HONEY BUNCH books were retitled and reissued in the HONEY
    BUNCH AND NORMAN series: volumes 28, 30, and 32.
        Harriet Adams wrote at least seven volumes in the HONEY BUNCH se-
    ries from 1945 to 1955.
        Books were published without subtitles.
Series description [G&D]: "A pleasing series of stories for little girls
    from four to eight years old. Honey Bunch is a dainty, thoughtful lit-
    tle girl who keeps one wondering what she is going to do next."

311S.1   Honey Bunch: Just a little girl. (Grosset & Dunlap, 1923).

    [G&D]: "Happy days at home, helping mamma and the washerlady. And
    Honey Bunch helped the house painters too--or thought she did."

311S.2   Honey Bunch: Her first visit to the city. (Grosset & Dunlap,
1923).

    [G&D]: "What wonderful sights Honey Bunch saw when she went to visit
    her cousins in New York! And she got lost in a big hotel and wandered
    into a men's convention!"

311S.3   Honey Bunch: Her first days on the farm. (Grosset & Dunlap, 1923)

   [G&D]: "Can you remember how the farm looked the first time you visited it? How big the cows and horses were, and what a roomy place to play in the barn proved to be?"

311S.4   Honey Bunch: Her first visit to the seashore. (Grosset & Dunlap, 1924).

   [G&D]: "Honey Bunch soon got used to the big waves and thought playing in the sand great fun. And she visited a merry-go-round, and took part in a seaside pageant."

311S.5   Honey Bunch: Her first little garden. (Grosset & Dunlap, 1924).

   [G&D]: "It was great sport to dig and plant with one's own little garden tools. But best of all was when Honey Bunch won a prize at the flower show."

311S.6   Honey Bunch: Her first days in camp. (Grosset & Dunlap, 1925).

   [G&D]: "It was a great adventure for Honey Bunch when she journeyed to Camp Snapdragon. It was wonderful to watch the men erect the tent, and more wonderful to live in it and have good times on the shore and in the water."

311S.7   Honey Bunch: Her first auto tour. (Grosset & Dunlap, 1926).

   [G&D]: "This time Honey Bunch goes on a long auto tour with Mother and Daddy and many very interesting things happen."

311S.8   Honey Bunch: Her first trip on the ocean. (Grosset & Dunlap, 1927).

   [G&D]: "Honey Bunch sails to Bermuda. And while in Bermuda she has the best times ever."

311S.9   Honey Bunch: Her first trip west. (Grosset & Dunlap, 1928; McLoughlin).

311S.10   Honey Bunch: Her first summer on an island. (Grosset & Dunlap, 1929; McLoughlin).

311S.11   Honey Bunch: Her first trip on the Great Lakes. (Grosset & Dunlap, 1930).

311S.12   Honey Bunch: Her first trip in an airplane. (Grosset & Dunlap, 1931; McLoughlin).

311S.13   Honey Bunch: Her first visit to the zoo. (Grosset & Dunlap, 1932; McLoughlin).

311S.14   Honey Bunch: Her first big adventure. (Grosset & Dunlap, 1933; McLoughlin).

311S.15   Honey Bunch: Her first big parade. (Grosset & Dunlap, 1934).

311S.16   Honey Bunch: Her first little mystery. (Grosset & Dunlap, 1935; McLoughlin).

311S.17   Honey Bunch: Her first little circus. (Grosset & Dunlap, 1936; McLoughlin).

311S.18   Honey Bunch: Her first little treasure hunt. (Grosset & Dunlap, 1937; McLoughlin).

311S.19   Honey Bunch: Her first little club. (Grosset & Dunlap, 1938; McLoughlin).

311S.20   Honey Bunch: Her first trip in a trailer. (Grosset & Dunlap, 1939).

311S.21   Honey Bunch: Her first trip to a big fair. (Grosset & Dunlap, 1940).

311S.22   Honey Bunch: Her first twin playmates. (Grosset & Dunlap, 1941; McLoughlin).

311S.23   Honey Bunch: Her first costume party. (Grosset & Dunlap, 1943; McLoughlin).

311S.24   Honey Bunch: Her first trip on a houseboat. (Grosset & Dunlap, 1945).

311S.25   Honey Bunch: Her first winter at Snowtop. (Grosset & Dunlap, 1946; McLoughlin).

311S.26   Honey Bunch: Her first trip to the big woods. (Grosset & Dunlap, 1947).

311S.27   Honey Bunch: Her first little pet show. (Grosset & Dunlap, 1948).

311S.28   Honey Bunch: Her first trip to a lighthouse. (Grosset & Dunlap, 1949).*

   Reprinted in 1957 as Honey Bunch and Norman on Lighthouse Island, vol. 2 of the HONEY BUNCH AND NORMAN series (312S.2).

311S.29   Honey Bunch: Her first visit to a pony ranch. (Grosset & Dunlap, 1950).

311S.30   Honey Bunch: Her first tour of Toy Town. (Grosset & Dunlap, 1951).

   Reprinted in 1957 as Honey Bunch and Norman tour Toy Town, vol. 3 of the HONEY BUNCH AND NORMAN series (312S.3).

311S.31   Honey Bunch: Her first visit to Puppyland. (Grosset & Dunlap, 1952).

* Written by Harriet Adams

311S.32   Honey Bunch: Her first trip to Reindeer Farm. (Grosset & Dunlap, 1953).*

Reprinted in 1958 as Honey Bunch and Norman visit Reindeer Farm, vol. 7 of the HONEY BUNCH AND NORMAN series (312S.7).

311S.33   Honey Bunch and Norman ride with the sky mailman. (Grosset & Dunlap, 1954).

Reprinted in 1958 as vol. 5 of the HONEY BUNCH AND NORMAN series (312S.5).

311S.34   Honey Bunch and Norman visit Beaver Lodge. (Grosset & Dunlap, 1955).

Reprinted in 1958 as vol. 6 of the HONEY BUNCH AND NORMAN series (312S.6).

312S   HONEY BUNCH AND NORMAN

Volumes: 12
Printed: 1957-1963
Publisher: Grosset & Dunlap
Illustrator: Corinne B. Dillon, vol. 1**
            anonymous, vols. 2, 5-6
Source of annotations: Grosset & Dunlap advertisements [G&D]
Additional information: Volumes 2, 3, 5, 6, and 7 were originally published in the HONEY BUNCH series (311S); Harriet Adams wrote volumes 2 and 7. Andrew Svenson also worked on some titles in this series.
    Volume six advertises the next volume as Honey Bunch and Norman visit Cocoa Land; apparently this title was never published.
    Books were published without subtitles.
Series description [G&D]: "Irresistible little Honey Bunch Morton, the heroine of over thirty delightful stories, has long been a favorite among younger readers. Now, here are Honey Bunch and her mischievous little playmate, Norman Clark, in a group of hilariously entertaining books, fully illustrated, that provide hours of enjoyment for younger boys and girls."

312S.1   Honey Bunch and Norman. (Grosset & Dunlap, 1957)

312S.2   Honey Bunch and Norman on Lighthouse Island. (Grosset & Dunlap, 1957).

First published in 1949 as Honey Bunch: Her first trip to a lighthouse, vol. 28 of the HONEY BUNCH series (311S.28).

312S.3   Honey Bunch and Norman tour Toy Town. (Grosset & Dunlap, 1957).

First published in 1951 as Honey Bunch: Her first tour of Toy Town, vol. 30 of the HONEY BUNCH series (311S.30).

* Written by Harriet Adams.
** Illustrations unsigned; information from dust jacket.

312S.4   Honey Bunch and Norman play detective at Niagara Falls. (Grosset & Dunlap, 1957).

312S.5   Honey Bunch and Norman ride with the sky mailman. (Grosset & Dunlap, 1958).

First published in 1954 as vol. 33 of the HONEY BUNCH series (311S.33).

312S.6   Honey Bunch and Norman visit Beaver Lodge. (Grosset & Dunlap, 1958).

First published in 1955 as vol. 34 of the HONEY BUNCH series (311S.34).

312S.7   Honey Bunch and Norman visit Reindeer Farm. (Grosset & Dunlap, 1958).

First published in 1953 as Honey Bunch: Her first trip to Reindeer Farm, vol. 32 of the HONEY BUNCH series (311S.32).

312S.8   Honey Bunch and Norman in the castle of magic. (Grosset & Dunlap, 1959).

312S.9   Honey Bunch and Norman solve the pine cone mystery. (Grosset & Dunlap, 1960).

312S.10   Honey Bunch and Norman and the paper lantern mystery. (Grosset & Dunlap, 1961).

312S.11   Honey Bunch and Norman and the painted pony. (Grosset & Dunlap, 1962).

312S.12   Honey Bunch and Norman and the walnut tree mystery. (Grosset & Dunlap, 1963).

Burbank L. Todd

The Stratemeyer Syndicate used the pen name Burbank L. Todd for one short series, the BACK TO THE SOIL series, published from 1914 to 1920.

SERIES PUBLICATIONS

313S   BACK TO THE SOIL (HIRAM)

Volumes: 2
Printed: 1914-1915
Publisher: Sully & Kleinteich
Reprint publisher: George Sully & Company, vols. 1-2

Illustrator: H. Richard Boehm, vols. 1-2

313S.1   Hiram, the young farmer; or, Making the soil pay. (Sully & Kleinteich, 1914; Sully, 1918).

313S.2   Hiram in the Middle West; or, A young farmer's upward struggle.
(Sully & Kleinteich, 1915; Sully, 1920).

Ed Ward

Ed Ward appeared on one story by Edward Stratemeyer: a reprint of a short
tale which had been published under Stratemeyer's own name the year before.

MAGAZINE PUBLICATIONS

314M   "On Sam's point." Young Sports of America, no. 4, June 22, 1895.

    First published with the same title, but with Edward Stratemeyer as
    author, in Good News, Nov. 24, 1894 (275M).

Tom Ward

Edward Stratemeyer's only story under the pseudonym Tom Ward was published
in the NEW YORK FIVE CENT LIBRARY in 1892.

SERIES PUBLICATIONS

315P   NEW YORK FIVE CENT LIBRARY

Volumes: 1*
Printed: 1892*
Publisher: Street & Smith
Additional information: See Jim Bowie, NEW YORK FIVE CENT LIBRARY (071P).

315P.1X   The stable gang's last battle; or, Killed for revenge. No. 13.
Nov. 5, 1892.

---

* Number of volumes and years published apply only to titles written by
   Edward Stratemeyer under the pen name Tom Ward.

Frank A. Warner

The Stratemeyer pseudonym Frank Warner was credited with two boys' adventure series published by Barse & Hopkins and Barse & Co. Both series featured main characters with the name Bob: BOB CHASE (1929-1930; 4 vols.) and BOBBY BLAKE (1915-1926; 12 vols.).

SERIES PUBLICATIONS

316S   BOB CHASE BIG GAME

Volumes: 4
Printed: 1929-1930
Publisher: Barse & Company
Reprint publisher: Grosset & Dunlap, vols. 1-4
Illustrator: David Randolph, vols. 1-4
Source of annotations: Barse & Company advertisements [B&C]
Additional information: The reprint editions had the same illustrator, but
    reduced the number of illustrations. The books had no subtitles.
Series description [B&C]: "The average boy of to-day is keenly interested
    in adventures in out-of-the-way places and especially interested in the
    hunting of big game.
        "In this line of books the hero is a young lumberjack who is a crack
    rifle shot. While tracking game in the wilds of Maine he does some rich
    hunters a great service and they become interested in Bob and take him
    on various hunting expeditions in this country and abroad. Bob learns
    what it is to face not only wildcats, foxes and deer, but also bull
    moose, Rocky Mountain grizzly bears, and many other species of big game.
        "Stories that are absorbing from start to finish, and with much valuable data on animal life as lived in the wilderness."

316S.1   Bob Chase with the big moose hunters. (Barse, 1929; Grosset &
Dunlap).

316S.2   Bob Chase after grizzly bears. (Barse, 1929; Grosset & Dunlap).

316S.3   Bob Chase in the tiger's lair. (Barse, 1929; Grosset & Dunlap).

316S.4   Bob Chase with the lion hunters. (Barse, 1930; Grosset & Dunlap).

317S   BOBBY BLAKE

Volumes: 12
Printed: 1915-1926
Publisher: Barse & Hopkins
Reprint publisher: Barse & Company, vols. 1-12
                    Grosset & Dunlap, vols. 1-12
                    Whitman Publishing Company, vols. 1-2

```
Illustrator:   R. Emmett Owen, vols. 1-7
               Charles L. Wrenn, vol. 8
               E. J. Dinsmore, vol. 9
               Walter S. Rogers, vols. 10-11
               Oriet Williams, vol. 12
```
Source of annotations: Barse & Hopkins advertisements [B&H]
Additional information: The Barse & Company and Grosset & Dunlap editions
    had the same illustrators, but reduced the number of illustrations.
    The Whitman editions were not illustrated.
Series description [B&H]: "Books for boys from eight to twelve years old.
        "True stories of life at a modern American boarding school. Bobby
    attends this institution of learning with his particular chum and the
    boys have no end of good times. The tales of outdoor life, especially
    the exciting times they have when engaged in sports against rival
    schools, are written in a manner so true, so realistic, that the reader,
    too, is bound to share with these boys their thrills and pleasures."

317S.1   Bobby Blake at Rockledge School; or, Winning the medal of honor.
(Barse & Hopkins, 1915; Barse; Grosset & Dunlap; Whitman).

317S.2   Bobby Blake at Bass Cove; or, The hunt for the motor boat Gem.
(Barse & Hopkins, 1915; Barse; Grosset & Dunlap; Whitman).

317S.3   Bobby Blake on a cruise; or, The castaways of Volcano Island.
(Barse & Hopkins, 1915; Barse; Grosset & Dunlap).

317S.4   Bobby Blake and his school chums; or, The rivals of Rockledge.
(Barse & Hopkins, 1916; Barse; Grosset & Dunlap).

317S.5   Bobby Blake at Snowtop Camp; or, Winter holidays in the big woods.
(Barse & Hopkins, 1916; Barse; Grosset & Dunlap).

317S.6   Bobby Blake on the school nine; or, The champions of Monotook
Lake League. (Barse & Hopkins, 1917; Barse; Grosset & Dunlap).

317S.7   Bobby Blake on a ranch; or, The secret of the mountain cave.
(Barse & Hopkins, 1918; Barse; Grosset & Dunlap).

317S.8   Bobby Blake on an auto tour; or, The mystery of the deserted
house. (Barse & Hopkins, 1920; Barse; Grosset & Dunlap).

317S.9   Bobby Blake on the school eleven; or, Winning the banner of blue
and gold. (Barse & Hopkins, 1921; Barse; Grosset & Dunlap).

317S.10   Bobby Blake on a plantation; or, Lost in the great swamp. (Barse
& Hopkins, 1922; Barse; Grosset & Dunlap).

317S.11   Bobby Blake in the frozen north; or, The old eskimo's last message. (Barse & Hopkins, 1923; Barse; Grosset & Dunlap).

317S.12   Bobby Blake on Mystery Mountain.* (Barse & Hopkins, 1926; Barse;
Grosset & Dunlap).

---

* Subtitle missing; it may have been The ghost of the crags.

Frank V. Webster

Frank V. Webster was the Stratemeyer Syndicate pseudonym used for one series, the WEBSTER SERIES, containing twenty-five volumes printed from 1909 to 1915 by Cupples & Leon.

SERIES PUBLICATIONS

318S   THE WEBSTER SERIES

Volumes: 25
Printed: 1909-1915
Publisher: Cupples & Leon Company
Reprint publisher: Saalfield Publishing Co., vols. 4-6, 9-13, 16, 19, 23, 25
Illustrator: Charles Nuttall, vols. 1-12
              Richards, vols. 13-15
              H. Richard Boehm, vols. 16-17
              Walter S. Rogers, vols. 18-25
Source of annotations: Cupples & Leon Company advertisements [C&L]
Additional information: THE WEBSTER SERIES was composed of boys' adventure
    and success stories. The books did not share the same characters,
    settings, or themes.
Series description [G&D]: "Mr. WEBSTER'S style is very much like that of
    the boys' favorite author, the late lamented Horatio Alger, Jr., but
    his tales are thoroughly up-to-date. The stories are as clean as they
    are clever, and will prove of absorbing interest to boys everywhere."

318S.1   Only a farm boy; or, Dan Hardy's rise in life. (Cupples & Leon, 1909).

318S.2   Tom the telephone boy; or, The mystery of a message. (Cupples & Leon, 1909).

318S.3   The boy from the ranch; or, Roy Bradner's city experiences. (Cupples & Leon, 1909).

318S.4   The young treasure hunter; or, Fred Stanley's trip to Alaska. (Cupples & Leon, 1909; Saalfield, 1938).

318S.5   Bob the castaway; or, The wreck of the Eagle. (Cupples & Leon, 1909; Saalfield, 1938).

318S.6   The young firemen of Lakeville; or, Herbert Dare's pluck. (Cupples & Leon, 1909; Saalfield, 1938).

318S.7   The newsboy partners; or, Who was Dick Box? (Cupples & Leon, 1909)

318S.8   The boy pilot of the lakes; or, Nat Morton's perils. (Cupples & Leon, 1909).

318S.9   Two boy gold miners; or, Lost in the mountains. (Cupples & Leon, 1909; Saalfield, 1938).

318S.10   Jack the runaway; or, On the road with a circus. (Cupples & Leon, 1909; Saalfield, 1938).

318S.11   Comrades of the saddle; or, The young rough riders of the plains. (Cupples & Leon, 1910; Saalfield, 1938).

318S.12   The boys of Bellwood School; or, Frank Jordan's triumph. (Cupples & Leon, 1910; Saalfield, 1938).

318S.13   Bob Chester's grit; or, From ranch to riches. (Cupples & Leon, 1911; Saalfield, 1938).

318S.14   Airship Andy; or, The luck of a brave boy. (Cupples & Leon, 1911).

318S.15   The high school rivals; or, Fred Markham's struggles. (Cupples & Leon, 1911).

318S.16   Darry the life saver; or, The heroes of the coast. (Cupples & Leon, 1911; Saalfield, 1938).

318S.17   Dick the bank boy; or, The missing fortune. (Cupples & Leon, 1911).

318S.18   Ben Hardy's flying machine; or, Making a record for himself. (Cupples & Leon, 1911).

318S.19   The boys of the wireless; or, A stirring rescue from the deep. (Cupples & Leon, 1912; Saalfield, 1938).

318S.20   Harry Watson's high school days; or, The rivals of Rivertown. (Cupples & Leon, 1912).

318S.21   The boy scouts of Lenox; or, Hiking over Big Bear Mountain. (Cupples & Leon, 1915).

318S.22   Tom Taylor at West Point; or, The old army officer's secret. (Cupples & Leon, 1915).

318S.23   Cowboy Dave; or, The round up at Rolling River. (Cupples & Leon, 1915; Saalfield, 1938).

318S.24   Two boys of the battleship; or, For the honor of Uncle Sam. (Cupples & Leon, 1915).

318S.25   Jack of the pony express; or, The young rider of the mountain trails. (Cupples & Leon, 1915; Saalfield, 1938).

Jerry West

The HAPPY HOLLISTER series, originally published from 1953 to 1970, was written by Andrew Svenson, a Stratemeyer Syndicate partner, under the pseudonym Jerry West. It was the only series published under this pseudonym.

SERIES PUBLICATIONS

319S   HAPPY HOLLISTERS

Volumes: 33
Printed: 1953-1970
Publisher: Garden City Books, vols. 1-19
            Doubleday & Company, Inc., vols. 20-33
Reprint publisher: Doubleday & Company, Inc., vols. 1-19
            Grosset & Dunlap, vols. 1-3, 16
Illustrator: Helen S. Hamilton, vols. 1-33
Source of annotations: Doubleday & Company, Inc. advertisements [Dd]
Additional information: Andrew Svenson wrote this series. The books were
    published without subtitles, and the Helen S. Hamilton illustrations
    appeared in the Garden City, Doubleday, and Grosset & Dunlap editions.
Series description [Dd]: "From the day the five Hollister children move
    into the mysterious house on Pine Lake in Shoreham, adventures begin
    to come their way. What fun and excitement they have. PETE, the oldest
    is a sturdy boy of twelve, with sparkling blue eyes and blond, crew cut
    hair. His love for sports is shared by his sister Pam, who is ten.
        "PAM, whose real name is Pamela, has brown eyes and fluffy golden
    hair. She is kind to everyone and loves animals, especially their peppy
    collie dog, ZIP, whom she adopted. This faithful pet is on the go al-
    most as much as Ricky Hollister, a seven-year-old package of perpetual
    motion.
        "Lanky RICKY has reddish hair, which is usually mussed, and a turned
    up nose splattered with freckles. He is full of fun and sometimes teases
    his six-year-old sister, HOLLY.
        "But Holly, with her tomboy ways, can take it! In fact she looks a
    lot like Ricky, except that she has dancing brown eyes and dark hair,
    which she wears in pigtails. Holly's chief delight is her cat, White
    Nose, which she carries under her arm like a fluffy purse.
        "WHITE NOSE and her five kittens are cute too. Little Sue Hollister
    the baby of the family, likes to cuddle them. Although dark-haired SUE
    is only four, she romps in all the fun which the Hollister family enjoy
    day in and day out.
        "All their friends say that this is because Mother and Daddy share
    in the play and in the mysteries the children always solve.
        "Mrs. Hollister is always ready to meet any sudden need--for a sur-
    prise picnic or a helping hand. Mr. Hollister owns the Trading Post, a
    combination hardware, sports and toy shop. He is never too busy to play
    ball. And best of all, he likes to take his family on exciting adven-
    tures."

319S.1   The happy Hollisters. (Garden City, 1953; Doubleday; Grosset & Dunlap, 1979).

319S.2   The happy Hollisters on a river trip. (Garden City, 1953; Double-day; Grosset & Dunlap, 1979).

319S.3   The happy Hollisters at Sea Gull Beach. (Garden City, 1953; Doubleday; Grosset & Dunlap, 1979).

319S.4   The happy Hollisters and the Indian treasure. (Garden City, 1953; Doubleday).

319S.5   The happy Hollisters at Mystery Mountain. (Garden City, 1954; Doubleday).

319S.6   The happy Hollisters at Snowflake Camp. (Garden City, 1954; Doubleday).

319S.7   The happy Hollisters and the trading post mystery. (Garden City, 1954; Doubleday).

319S.8   The happy Hollisters at Circus Island. (Garden City, 1955; Double-day).

319S.9   The happy Hollisters and the secret fort. (Garden City, 1955; Doubleday).

319S.10   The happy Hollisters and the merry-go-round mystery. (Garden City, 1955; Doubleday).

319S.11   The happy Hollisters at Pony Hill Farm. (Garden City, 1956; Doubleday).

319S.12   The happy Hollisters and the old clipper ship. (Garden City, 1956; Doubleday).

319S.13   The happy Hollisters at Lizard Cove. (Garden City, 1957; Double-day).

319S.14   The happy Hollisters and the scarecrow mystery. (Garden City, 1957; Doubleday).

319S.15   The happy Hollisters and the mystery of the totem faces. (Garden City, 1958; Doubleday).

319S.16   The happy Hollisters and the ice carnival mystery. (Garden City, 1958; Doubleday; Grosset & Dunlap, 1979).

   Grosset & Dunlap edition published as vol. 4.

319S.17   The happy Hollisters and the mystery in skyscraper city. (Garden City, 1959; Doubleday).

319S.18   The happy Hollisters and the mystery of the little mermaid. (Garden City, 1960; Doubleday).

319S.19   The happy Hollisters and the mystery at Missile Town.   (Garden City, 1961; Doubleday).

319S.20   The happy Hollisters and the cowboy mystery. (Doubleday, 1961).

319S.21   The happy Hollisters and the haunted house mystery. (Doubleday, 1962).

319S.22   The happy Hollisters and the secret of the lucky coins. (Doubleday, 1962).

319S.23   The happy Hollisters and the Castle Rock mystery. (Doubleday, 1963).

319S.24   The happy Hollisters and the cuckoo clock mystery. (Doubleday, 1963).

319S.25   The happy Hollisters and the Swiss echo mystery. (Doubleday, 1963).

319S.26   The happy Hollisters and the sea turtle mystery. (Doubleday, 1964).

319S.27   The happy Hollisters and the Punch and Judy mystery. (Doubleday, 1964).

319S.28   The happy Hollisters and the whistle-pig mystery. (Doubleday, 1964).

319S.29   The happy Hollisters and the ghost horse mystery. (Doubleday, 1965).

319S.30   The happy Hollisters and the mystery of the golden witch. (Doubleday, 1966).

319S.31   The happy Hollisters and the mystery of the Mexican Idol. (Doubleday, 1967).

319S.32   The happy Hollisters and the monster mystery. (Doubleday, 1969).

319S.33   The happy Hollisters and the mystery of the midnight trolls. (Doubleday, 1970).

Janet D. Wheeler

Janet D. Wheeler was the Stratemeyer Syndicate pseudonym used for the nine-volume BILLIE BRADLEY girls' adventure series, published between 1920 and 1932.

SERIES PUBLICATIONS

320S   BILLIE BRADLEY

Volumes: 9
Printed: 1920-1932
Publisher: George Sully & Company, vols. 1-5
            Cupples & Leon Company, vols. 6-9
Reprint publisher: Cupples & Leon, vols. 1-5
Illustrator: Howard L. Hastings, vol. 2
              anonymous, vols. 4, 6
              Walter S. Rogers, vol. 5
Source of annotations [C&L]: Cupples & Leon Company advertisements [C&L]
Series description [C&L]: "A delightful series for girls who enjoy adven-
    ture and humor. The wholesome spirit and joyous youthfulness of Miss
    Wheeler's stories make of each new reader a new friend, and the reading
    of each succeeding volume further cements the friendship for the char-
    acters of Billie Bradley and her chums."

320S.1   Billie Bradley and her inheritance; or, The queer homestead at
Cherry Corners. (Sully, 1920; Cupples & Leon).

    Reprinted in Popular stories for girls, a four-in-one reprint, published
    by Cupples & Leon ca1934 (321N).
        [C&L]: "Billie Bradley fell heir to an old homestead that was un-
    occupied and located far away in a lonely section of the country. How
    Billie went there, accompanied by some of her chums, and what queer
    things happened, go to make up a story no girl will want to miss."

320S.2   Billie Bradley at Three-Towers Hall; or, Leading a needed rebellion. (Sully, 1920; Cupples & Leon).

    [C&L]: "Three-Towers Hall was a boarding school for girls. For a short
    time after Billie arrived there all went well. But then the head of the
    school had to go on a long journey and she left the girls in charge of
    two teachers, sisters, who believed in severe discipline and in very,
    very plain food and little of it--and then there was a row! The girls
    wired for the head to come back and all ended happily."

320S.3   Billie Bradley on Lighthouse Island; or, The mystery of the wreck.
(Sully, 1920; Cupples & Leon).

    [C&L]: "One of Billie's friends owned a summer bungalow on Lighthouse
    Island, near the coast. The school girls made up a party and visited
    the Island. There was a storm and a wreck, and three little children
    were washed ashore. They could tell nothing of themselves, and Billie
    and her chums set to work to solve the mystery of their identity."

320S.4   Billie Bradley and her classmates; or, The secret of the locked
tower. (Sully, 1921; Cupples & Leon).

    [C&L]: "Billie and her chums come to the rescue of several little chil-
    dren who have broken through the ice. There is the mystery of a lost
    invention and also the dreaded mystery of the locked school tower."

320S.5   Billie Bradley at Twin Lakes; or, Jolly schoolgirls afloat and ashore. (Sully, 1922; Cupples & Leon).

[C&L]: "A tale of outdoor adventure in which Billie and her chums have a great variety of adventures. They visit an artists' colony and there fall in with a strange girl living with an old boatman who abuses her constantly. Billie befriended Hulda and the mystery surrounding the girl was finally cleared up."

320S.6   Billie Bradley at Treasure Cove; or, The old sailor's secret. (Cupples & Leon, 1928).

[C&L]: "A lively story of school girl doings. How Billie heard of the treasure and how she and her chums went in quest of the same is told in a peculiarly absorbing manner."

320S.7   Billie Bradley at Sun Dial Lodge; or, School chums solving a mystery. (Cupples & Leon, 1929).

[C&L]: "The recovery of a stolen treasure forms the groundwork of an exciting story, that reveals Billie's ability at unraveling a mystery."

320S.8   Billie Bradley and the school mystery; or, The girl from Oklahoma. (Cupples & Leon, 1930).

[C&L]: "How Billie clears up a mystery in which she is apparently implicated makes delightful reading."

320S.9   Billie Bradley winning the trophy; or, Scoring against big odds. (Cupples & Leon, 1932).

[C&L]: "Billie deciphers the mysterious message and after an exciting time wins the trophy."

OTHER PUBLICATIONS

321N   Popular stories for girls. (Cupples & Leon, ca1934).

Contains Ruth Fielding of the red mill by Alice B. Emerson, published in 1913 (145S.1); Peggy and Michael of the coffee plantation by Anna Andrews, published in 1931; The Linger-nots and the mystery house by Agnes Miller, published in 1923; Billie Bradley and her inheritance* by Janet D. Wheeler, published in 1920 by G. Sully & Co., and ca1928 by Cupples & Leon (320S.1). Printed from the original plates.

---

* Title page of Popular stories for girls lists this as Billy Bradley and her inheritance.

Ramy Allison White

The Stratemeyer Syndicate pseudonym Ramy Allison White appeared on only one series, SUNNY BOY. This fourteen-volume children's series was published from 1920 to 1931.

SERIES PUBLICATIONS

322S   SUNNY BOY

Volumes: 14
Printed: 1920-1931
Publisher: Barse & Hopkins, vols. 1-10
            Barse & Company, vols. 11-13
            Grosset & Dunlap, vol. 14
Reprint publisher: Barse & Company, vols. 1-10
                    Grosset & Dunlap, vols. 1-13
Illustrator: Charles L. Wrenn, vols. 1-3
              Howard L. Hastings, vols. 4-9
              John M. Foster, vols. 10-13
Source of annotations: Barse & Hopkins advertisements [B&H]
Additional information: The books were published without subtitles.
Series description [B&H]: "Children meet Sunny Boy, a little fellow with
    big eyes and an inquiring disposition, who finds the world a large and
    wonderful thing indeed. And somehow there is lots going on when Sunny
    Boy is around. Perhaps he helps push! In the first book of this new
    series he has the finest time ever, with his Grandpa out in the country.
    He learns a lot and he helps a lot, in his small way. Then he has a
    glorious visit to the seashore, but this is in the next story. And
    there are still more adventures in the other books. You will like Sunny
    Boy."

322S.1   Sunny Boy in the country. (Barse & Hopkins, 1920; Barse; Grosset
& Dunlap).

322S.2   Sunny Boy at the seashore. (Barse & Hopkins, 1920; Barse; Grosset
& Dunlap).

322S.3   Sunny Boy in the big city. (Barse & Hopkins, 1920; Barse; Grosset
& Dunlap).

322S.4   Sunny Boy in school and out. (Barse & Hopkins, 1921; Barse; Grosset & Dunlap).

322S.5   Sunny Boy and his playmates. (Barse & Hopkins, 1922; Barse; Grosset & Dunlap).

    Grosset & Dunlap edition may have been titled Sunny Boy and his school-
    mates.

322S.6   Sunny Boy and his games. (Barse & Hopkins, 1923; Barse; Grosset & Dunlap).

322S.7   Sunny Boy in the far West. (Barse & Hopkins, 1924; Barse; Grosset & Dunlap).

322S.8   Sunny Boy on the ocean. (Barse & Hopkins, 1925; Barse; Grosset & Dunlap).

322S.9   Sunny Boy with the circus. (Barse & Hopkins, 1926; Barse; Grosset & Dunlap).

322S.10   Sunny Boy and his big dog. (Barse & Hopkins, 1927; Barse; Grosset & Dunlap).

322S.11   Sunny Boy in the snow. (Barse, 1929; Grosset & Dunlap).

322S.12   Sunny Boy at Willow Farm. (Barse, 1929; Grosset & Dunlap).

322S.13   Sunny Boy and his cave. (Barse, 1930; Grosset & Dunlap).

322S.14   Sunny Boy at Rainbow Lake. (Grosset & Dunlap, 1931).

Arthur M. Winfield

Edward Stratemeyer used the pseudonym Arthur M. Winfield for seven magazine stories (including one reprint), serialized between 1892 and 1896, and for forty-six different books,* published from 1897 to 1926. In addition, four of the eleven Horatio Alger, Jr., titles attributed to Edward Stratemeyer were listed as "completed by Arthur M. Winfield." (See Horatio Alger, Jr., RISE IN LIFE [011S].)

All but three of the Arthur M. Winfield books were incorporated into one of five series for their first appearance in book form: BOUND TO WIN (1897; 4 vols.), ROVER BOYS (1899-1926; 30 vols.), PUTNAM HALL (1901-1911; 6 vols.), BOYS' OWN LIBRARY (1902; 3 vols.),** SILVER LAKE (1902; 1 vol.).*** The remaining three books were published as non-series titles, but later reprinted in one or more series, such as the WINFIELD series, or the ENTER-PRISE books. The early Winfield titles were handled by a variety of publishers, including W. L. Allison, Street & Smith, Mershon, Saalfield, and Stitt; later works (after 1907) were published by Grosset & Dunlap.

Edward Stratemeyer's mother is thought to have suggested the pseudonym Arthur M. Winfield: "Arthur" was for "author"; "M" stood for a million (either a million dollars from book sales, or a million copies sold); "Winfield" showed she hoped he would "win" in his "field"--writing.

---

*   Some of the books first appeared as magazine stories. The count does not include the Alger completions.
**   Published by Street & Smith. This was the second appearance in book form for one title.
*** Alger completions not included.

MAGAZINE PUBLICATIONS

323M   "Bound to be an electrician; or, A clear head and a stout heart."
Bright Days, nos. 1-5, April-Aug. 1896.

   Reprinted in book form as Bound to be an electrician; or, Franklin Bell's
   success by Edward Stratemeyer for all editions. Published in 1897 as
   vol. 1 of W. L. Allison's BOUND TO WIN series (292S.1); reprinted as vol.
   2 of the WORKING UPWARD series by Allison, Donohue, and Lee & Shepard
   (304S.2). Also published by Lothrop, Lee & Shepard in the STRATEMEYER
   POPULAR SERIES (303S.8X), and by Grosset & Dunlap as a non-series title.
   Reprinted in paperback in 1920 as no. 105 in Street & Smith's ALGER SE-
   RIES (289P.8X).

324M   "Fighting for his own; or, The fortunes of a young artist."
Argosy, vol. 14, nos. 494-503, May 21-July 23, 1892.

   Reprinted with the same author, but with the title "Lester Fleming's
   struggles; or, The fortunes of an artist," in Young People of America,
   Nov. 9, 1895-Jan. 18, 1896 (325M). Published in book form with the
   original title, but with Edward Stratemeyer as author, for all editions.
   Issued in 1897 as vol. 12 of W. L. Allison's BOUND TO WIN series
   (292S.4X); reprinted as vol. 4 of the WORKING UPWARD series by Allison,
   Donohue, and Lee & Shepard (304S.4). Also published by Lothrop, Lee &
   Shepard in the STRATEMEYER POPULAR SERIES (303S.10X), and by Grosset &
   Dunlap as a non-series title. Reprinted in paperback in 1920 as no.
   107 in Street & Smith's ALGER SERIES (289P.10X).

325M   "Lester Fleming's struggles; or, The fortunes of an artist."
Young People of America, nos. 24-34, Nov. 9, 1895-Jan. 18, 1896.

   First published as "Fighting for his own; or, The fortunes of a young
   artist" in Argosy, May 21-July 23, 1892 (324M).

326M   "Missing money; or, The young bank messenger's discovery." Good
News, vol. 8, nos. 183-195, Nov. 4, 1893-Jan. 27, 1894.

   Reprinted in book form with the same author, but with the title The
   young bank clerk; or, Mark Vincent's strange discovery, for all editions.
   Published in 1902 by Street & Smith in the BOYS' OWN LIBRARY series
   (333P.2X) and by McKay in its BOYS' OWN LIBRARY series (332P.2X). Also
   published by Street & Smith in 1904 as no. 269 in the MEDAL LIBRARY
   (337P.2X), and in 1905 by Caldwell as part of the FAMOUS BOOKS FOR BOYS
   series* (336P.1X).

327M   "One boy in a thousand; or, The mystery of the Aurora Mine."
Argosy, vol. 15, nos. 519-531, Nov. 12, 1892-Feb. 4, 1893.

   Reprinted in book form as Oliver Bright's search; or, The mystery of a
   mine by Edward Stratemeyer for all editions. Published in 1895 as vol.
   2 of Merriam's BOUND TO SUCCEED series (291S.2). Revised edition published in 1899 by Lee & Shepard as vol. 2 of the BOUND TO SUCCEED series
   (291S.2). Reprinted by Lee & Shepard in 1903 as part of the WORKING

---

* Subtitle missing.

UPWARD series (304S.5X); later published by Lothrop, Lee & Shepard as part of the STRATEMEYER POPULAR SERIES (303S.5), and by Grosset & Dunlap as a non-series title. Reprinted as no. 102 in Street & Smith's paperback ALGER SERIES in 1920 (289P.5X).

328M   "The schooldays of Fred Harley; or, Rivals for all honors." Good News, vol. 9, nos. 229-241, Sept. 22-Dec. 15, 1894.

Published in book form in 1897 as vol. 2 of W. L. Allison's BOUND TO WIN series (330S.1X); reprinted as vol. 2 of the BRIGHT AND BOLD series by Allison and later by Donohue (334S.2). Also published as vol. 10 of Donohue's BOYS' LIBERTY series* (331S.2X).

329M   "Stolen gold; or, The brightest messenger in Boston." Good News, vol. 8, nos. 198-211, Feb. 17-May 19, 1894.

SERIES PUBLICATIONS

330S   BOUND TO WIN

Volumes: 4**
Printed: 1897
Publisher: W. L. Allison Company
Illustrator: G. B. DuPont, vols. 1X-4X
Additional information: See Captain Ralph Bonehill, BOUND TO WIN (047S).

330S.1X   School days of Fred Harley; or, Rivals for all honors. (Allison, 1897).

Title is also listed as Schooldays of Fred Harley. Published as vol. 2. First published in Good News, Sept. 22-Dec. 15, 1894 (328M).

330S.2X   The missing tin box; or, The stolen railroad bonds. (Allison, 1897).

Published as vol. 5. First published as "The tin box mystery; or, The stolen railroad bonds" by Edward Stratemeyer in Good News, April 15-June 24, 1893 (282M).

330S.3X   Poor but plucky; or, The mystery of a flood. (Allison, 1897).

Published as vol. 8. First published with the same title, but with Albert Lee Ford as author, in Young People of America, Nov. 3-Dec. 21, 1895 (153M).

330S.4X   By pluck, not luck; or, Dan Granbury's struggle to rise. (Allison, 1897).

Published as vol. 11. First published as "Quarterback Dan, the football

---

*   Subtitle missing.
**   Number of volumes applies only to titles published under the pseudonym Arthur M. Winfield.

champion; or, Kicking for fame and fortune: by Captain Young of Yale (first two installments) (350M) and Clarence Young (last five install-ments) (352M) in Young Sports of America (first installment) and Young People of America (remaining installments) from Oct. 26-Dec. 7, 1895. (The title of the magazine changed in Nov. 1895.)

331P   BOYS' LIBERTY

Volumes: 2*
Publisher: M. A. Donohue & Company
Additional information: This was an eighteen-volume reprint series. Three of the volumes were by Edward Stratemeyer, as Captain Ralph Bonehill (049P) and Arthur M. Winfield.

331P.1X   The missing tin box.**   (Donohue).

Published as vol. 10. First published as "The tin box mystery; or, The stolen railroad bonds" by Edward Stratemeyer in Good News, April 15-June 24, 1893 (282M).

331P.2X   School days of Fred Harley.**   (Donohue).

Published as vol. 15. First published in Good News, Sept. 22-Dec. 15, 1894 (328M).

332P   BOYS' OWN LIBRARY (MCKAY)

Volumes: 3*
Printed: 1902*
Publisher: David McKay
Additional information: See Captain Ralph Bonehill, BOYS' OWN LIBRARY (MCKAY) (050P).

332P.1X   Mark Dale's stage adventure; or, Bound to be an actor. (McKay, 1902).

First published as "A footlight favorite; or, Born to be an actor" by Manager Henry Abbott in Good News, April 6-June 29, 1895 (001M).

332P.2X   The young bank clerk; or, Mark Vincent's strange discovery. (McKay, 1902).

First published with the same author, but with the title "Missing money; or, The young bank messenger's discovery" in Good News, Nov. 4, 1893-Jan. 27, 1894 (326M).

332P.3X   The young bridge-tender; or, Ralph Nelson's upward struggle. (McKay, 1902).

---

*   Number of volumes and years published apply only to titles published under the pseudonym Arthur M. Winfield.
**   Subtitle missing.

First published as "By pluck alone; or, Ralph Nelson's upward struggle" by Harvey Hicks in Good News, Aug. 24-Nov. 16, 1895 (177M).

333P   BOYS' OWN LIBRARY (STREET & SMITH)

Volumes: 3*
Printed: 1902*
Publisher: Street & Smith
Additional information: See Captain Ralph Bonehill, BOYS' OWN LIBRARY
    (MCKAY) (050P).

333P.1X   Mark Dale's stage venture: or, Bound to be an actor. (Street & Smith, 1902).

    First published as "A footlight favorite; or, Born to be an actor" by Manager Henry Abbott in Good News, April 6-June 29, 1895 (001M).

333P.2X   The young bank clerk; or, Mark Vincent's strange discovery. (Street & Smith, 1902).

    First published with the same author, but with the title "Missing money; or, The young bank messenger's discovery" in Good News, Nov. 4, 1893-Jan. 27, 1894 (326M).

333P.3X   The young bridge-tender; or, Ralph Nelson's upward struggle. (Street & Smith, 1902).

    First published as "By pluck alone; or, Ralph Nelson's upward struggle" by Harvey Hicks in Good News, Aug. 24-Nov. 16, 1895 (177M).

334S   BRIGHT AND BOLD

Volumes: 4
Publisher: W. L. Allison Company
Reprint publisher: M. A. Donohue & Company, vols. 1-4
Illustrator: G. B. Dupont, vols. 1-4
Additional information: W. L. Allison originally published all four volumes
    as part of its BOUND TO WIN series (330S), then, between 1897 and 1900,
    reprinted them as the BRIGHT AND BOLD series. Donohue reissued the
    titles ca1905. Earlier Donohue editions had Dupont illustrations; later
    editions were not illustrated.

334S.1   Poor but plucky; or, The mystery of a flood. (Allison; Donohue, ca1905).

    First published with Albert Lee Ford as author in Young People of America, Nov. 3-Dec. 21, 1895 (153M).

---

* Number of volumes and years published apply only to titles published
   under the pseudonym Arthur M. Winfield.

334S.2   School days of Fred Harley; or, Rivals for all honors. (Allison; Donohue, ca1905).

First published in Good News, Sept. 22–Dec. 15, 1894 (328M).

334S.3   By pluck, not luck; or, Dan Granbury's struggle to rise. (Allison; Donohue, 1905).

First published as "Quarterback Dan, the football champion; or, Kicking for fame and fortune" by Captain Young of Yale (first two installments) (350M) and Clarence Young (last five installments) (352M) in Young Sports of America (first installment) and Young People of America (remaining installments) from Oct. 26 to Dec. 7, 1895. (The magazine title changed in Nov. 1895.)

334S.4   The missing tin box; or, The stolen railroad bonds. (Allison; Donohue, ca1905).

First published as "The tin box mystery; or, The stolen railroad bonds" by Edward Stratemeyer in Good News, April 15–June 24, 1893 (282M).

335P   ENTERPRISE BOOKS

Volumes: 1*
Publisher: Grosset & Dunlap
Source of annotations: Grosset & Dunlap advertisements [G&D]
Additional information: See Captain Ralph Bonehill, ENTERPRISE BOOKS (053P).

335P.1X   Bob the photographer; or, A hero in spite of himself. (Grosset & Dunlap).

Published as vol. 6. First published as "Camera Bob; or, The thrilling adventures of a travelling photographer" by Edward Stratemeyer in Good News, Oct. 7, 1893–Jan. 20, 1894 (262M).
    [G&D]: "Relates the experiences of a poor boy who falls in with a 'camera fiend' and develops a liking for photography. After a number of stirring adventures Bob becomes photographer for a railroad; thwarts the plan of those who would injure the railroad corporation and incidently [sic] clears a mystery surrounding his parentage."

336P   FAMOUS BOOKS FOR BOYS

Volumes: 2*
Printed: 1905*
Publisher: H. M. Caldwell Company
Additional information: This reprint series included four titles by Edward Stratemeyer: two as by Captain Ralph Bonehill (054P), and two as by Arthur M. Winfield.

---

* Number of volumes and years published apply only to titles published under the pseudonym Arthur M. Winfield.

336P.1X   The young bank clerk.* (Caldwell, 1905).

First published as "Missing money; or, The young bank messenger's discovery" in Good News, Nov. 4, 1893-Jan. 27, 1894 (326M).

336P.2X   The young bridge-tender.* (Caldwell, 1905).

First published as "By pluck alone; or, Ralph Nelson's upward struggle"
by Harvey Hicks in Good News, Aug. 24-Nov. 16, 1895 (177M).

337P   MEDAL LIBRARY

Volumes: 3**
Printed: 1904**
Publisher: Street & Smith
Additional information: See Captain Ralph Bonehill, MEDAL LIBRARY (059P).

337P.1X   The young bridge-tender; or, Ralph Nelson's upward struggle.
No. 249. March 12, 1904.

First published as "By pluck alone; or, Ralph Nelson's upward struggle"
by Harvey Hicks in Good News, Aug. 24-Nov. 16, 1895 (177M).

337P.2X   The young bank clerk; or, Mark Vincent's strange discovery. No.
269. July 30, 1904.

First published as "Missing money; or, The young bank messenger's discovery" in Good News, Nov. 4, 1893-Jan. 27, 1894 (326M).

337P.3X   Mark Dale's stage venture; or, Bound to be an actor. No. 279.
Oct. 8, 1904.

First published as "A footlight favorite; or, Born to be an actor" by
Manager Henry Abbott in Good News, April 6-June 29, 1895 (001M).

338S   PUTNAM HALL

Volumes: 6
Printed: 1901-1911
Publisher: The Mershon Company, vols. 1-2
            Grosset & Dunlap, vols. 3-6
Reprint publisher: Grosset & Dunlap, vols. 1-2
                    Stitt Publishing Company, vols. 1-2
                    Chatterton-Peck Company, vols. 1-2
Illustrator: A. Burnham Shute, vol. 1
              Clare Angell, vol. 2
              Charles Nuttall, vols. 3-6
Source of annotations: Grosset & Dunlap advertisements [G&D]

---

*   Subtitle missing.
**   Number of volumes and years published apply only to titles published
      under the pseudonym Arthur M. Winfield.

Additional information: All editions had the same illustrations.
        Grosset & Dunlap published the series from about 1908 until 1911,
then reissued the books, with altered titles and a different series
order, in 1921.
Series description [G&D]: "Being the adventures of lively young fellows at
a Military Academy. Open air sports have always been popular with boys
and these stories that mingle adventure with fact will appeal to every
manly boy."

338S.1   The Putnam Hall cadets; or, Good times in school and out. (Mershon, 1901; Stitt, 1905; Chatterton-Peck, ca1907; Grosset & Dunlap, ca1908,
1921).

    1921 edition titled The cadets of Putnam Hall; or, Good times in school
    and out and published as vol. 5.
        [G&D]: "The cadets are lively, flesh-and-blood fellows, bound to
    make friends from the start. There are some keen rivalries, in school
    and out, and something is told of a remarkable midnight feast and a
    hazing that had an unlooked for ending."

338S.2   The Putnam Hall rivals; or, Fun and sport afloat and ashore.
(Mershon, 1906; Stitt, ca1906; Chatterton-Peck, 1907; Grosset & Dunlap,
ca1908, 1921).

    1921 edition titled The rivals of Putnam Hall; or, Fun and sport afloat
    and ashore and published as vol. 6.
        [G&D]: "It is a lively, rattling breezy story of school life in
    this country written by one who knows all about its pleasures and its
    perplexities, its glorious excitements, and its chilling disappointments."

338S.3   The Putnam Hall champions; or, Bound to win out. (Grosset & Dunlap, 1908, 1921).

    1921 edition titled The champions of Putnam Hall; or, Bound to win out
    and published as vol. 4.
        [G&D]: "In this volume the Putnam Hall Cadets show what they can do
    in various keen rivalries on the athletic field and elsewhere. There is
    one victory which leads to a most unlooked-for-discovery."

338S.4   The Putnam Hall rebellion; or, The rival runaways. (Grosset &
Dunlap, 1909, 1921).

    1921 edition titled The rebellion at Putnam Hall; or, The rival runaways
    and published as vol. 3.
        [G&D]: "The boys had good reasons for running away during Captain
    Putnam's absence. They had plenty of fun, and several queer adventures."

338S.5   The Putnam Hall encampment; or, The secret of the old mill.
(Grosset & Dunlap, 1910, 1921).

    1921 edition titled Camping out days at Putnam Hall; or, The secret of
    the old mill and published as vol. 2.
        [G&D]: "A story full of vim and vigor, telling what the cadets did
    during the summer encampment, including a visit to a mysterious old mill,
    said to be haunted. The book has a wealth of fun in it."

338S.6   The Putnam Hall mystery; or, The school chums' strange discovery.
(Grosset & Dunlap, 1911, 1921).

> 1921 edition titled The mystery at Putnam Hall; or, The school chums'
> strange discovery and published as vol. 1.
>   [G&D]: "The particulars of the mystery and the solution of it are
> very interesting reading."

339S   ROVER BOYS

Volumes: 30
Printed: 1899-1926
Publisher: The Mershon Company, vols. 1-8, 10-11
            Stitt Publishing Company, vol. 9
            Grosset & Dunlap, vols. 12-30
Reprint publisher: The Mershon Company, vol. 9
                    Stitt Publishing Company, vols. 1-8, 10-11
                    Grosset & Dunlap, vols. 1-11
                    Chatterton-Peck Company, vols. 1-11
                    Whitman Publishing Company, vols. 1-2, 7-8, 10-11, 13-14
Illustrator: W. B. Bridge, vols. 1-6, frontispiece only
              Stacy Burch, vols. 1-6, interior illustrations
              anonymous, vols. 7-8
              A. Burnham Shute, vols. 9-10
              Charles Nuttall, vols. 11-14
              Walter S. Rogers, vols. 15-17, 19-30
              Dick Richards, vol. 18
Source of annotations: The Mershon Company advertisements [M], vols. 1-4
                        Grosset & Dunlap advertisements [G&D], series de-
                        scription, vols. 5-15
Additional information: The ROVER BOYS was published by Mershon, Stitt,
    and Chatterton-Peck, then involved in litigation between Edward Strate-
    meyer and the three publishers. In 1908, Grosset & Dunlap acquired the
    series, reprinted it, and began to add new titles. All four publishers
    used the same illustrations. Whitman later reprinted eight volumes in
    the series; the books were not illustrated.
        The first twenty volumes of the ROVER BOYS series chronicled the
    adventures of the three ROVER BOYS from childhood and their days at
    Putnam Hall* through college and marriage; the last ten volumes, called
    the "Second ROVER BOYS Series" or "Second Series," centered on the es-
    capades of the ROVER BOYS' sons. The ROVER BOYS was said to have been
    Edward Stratemeyer's favorite series.
Series description [G&D]: "No stories for boys ever published have attained
    the tremendous popularity of this famous series. Since the publication
    of the first volume, The Rover Boys at School, some years ago, over
    three million copies of these books have been sold. They are well writ-
    ten stories dealing with the Rover boys in a great many different kinds
    of activities and adventures. Each volume holds something of interest
    to every adventure loving boy."

339S.1   The Rover boys at school; or, The cadets of Putnam Hall. (Mershon,
1899; Stitt, 1905; Chatterton Peck, ca1907; Grosset & Dunlap, ca1908; Whitman).

---

* Putnam Hall was later used as the setting for the PUTNAM HALL series (338

[M]: "Arthur M. Winfield has written many tales for boys, but he has penned nothing better than this story of life and adventure at an American military school, introducing as he does all sorts and conditions of boys, as well as several girls, and a plot that is bound to hold the reader's attention from start to finish."

339S.2   The Rover boys on the ocean; or, A chase for fortune. (Mershon, 1899; Stitt, ca1905; Chatterton-Peck, ca1907; Grosset & Dunlap, ca1908; Whitman).

[M]: "During a vacation at the school a fortune is stolen and carried off to sea, and Sam, Tom, and Dick lose no time in following up the missing treasure. On the ocean they fall in with numerous adventures, as thrilling as they are absorbing."

339S.3   The Rover boys in the jungle; or, Stirring adventures in Africa. (Mershon, 1899; Stitt, ca1905; Chatterton-Peck, ca1907; Grosset & Dunlap, ca1908).

[M]: "The father of the Rover boys had gone to Africa and had not been heard of for a long time. At last, unable to stand the suspense, the boys, accompanied by some older heads, start on a search for the missing parent. The hunt leads them into the very heart of the Dark Continent, where they become lost and fall in with many strange and savage natives. How all escape makes reading that nobody would care to miss."

339S.4   The Rover boys out west; or, The search for a lost mine. (Mershon, 1900; Stitt, ca1905; Chatterton-Peck, ca1907; Grosset & Dunlap, ca1908).

[M]: "In this tale the Rover boys are first taken back to dear old Putnam Hall school and then transported to the mountainous districts of Colorado. A valuable mining property cannot be located, and the missing mine is claimed by both the Rovers and their enemies. Many adventures are encountered, including one with a landslide which is realistic in the extreme."

339S.5   The Rover boys on the Great Lakes; or, The secret of the island cave. (Mershon, 1901; Stitt, ca1905; Chatterton-Peck, ca1907; Grosset & Dunlap, ca1908).

[G&D]: "A story of a remarkable Summer outing; full of fun."

339S.6   The Rover boys in the mountains; or, A hunt for fun and fortune. (Mershon, 1902; Stitt, ca1905; Chatterton-Peck, ca1907; Grosset & Dunlap, ca1908).

[G&D]: "The boys in the Adirondacks at a Winter camp."

339S.7   The Rover boys on land and sea; or, The Crusoes of seven islands. (Mershon, 1903; Stitt, ca1905; Chatterton-Peck, ca1907; Grosset & Dunlap, ca1908; Whitman).

[G&D]: "Full of strange and surprising adventures."

339S.8   The Rover boys in camp; or, The rivals of Pine Island. (Mershon, 1904; Stitt, ca1905; Chatterton-Peck, ca1907; Grosset & Dunlap, ca1908; Whitman).

[G&D]: "At the annual school encampment."

339S.9   The Rover boys on the river; or, The search for the missing house-boat. (Stitt, 1905; Mershon, ca1906; Chatterton-Peck, ca1907; Grosset & Dunlap, ca1908).

[G&D]: "The Ohio River is the theme of this spirited story."

339S.10   The Rover boys on the plains; or, The mystery of Red Rock. (Mershon, 1906; Stitt, ca1906; Chatterton-Peck, 1907; Grosset & Dunlap, ca1908; Whitman).

[G&D]: "Relates adventures on the mighty Mississippi River."

339S.11   The Rover boys in southern waters; or, The deserted steam yacht. (Mershon, 1907; Stitt; Chatterton-Peck, 1907; Grosset & Dunlap, ca1908; Whitman).

[G&D]: "A trip to the coast of Florida."

339S.12   The Rover boys on the farm; or, Last days at Putnam Hall. (Grosset & Dunlap, 1908).

[G&D]: "The boys find a mysterious cave used by freight thieves."

339S.13   The Rover boys on Treasure Isle; or, The strange cruise of the steam yacht. (Grosset & Dunlap, 1909; Whitman).

[G&D]: "A search for treasure; a particularly fascinating volume."

339S.14   The Rover boys at college; or, The right road and the wrong. (Grosset & Dunlap, 1910; Whitman).

[G&D]: "Brimming over with good nature and excitement."

339S.15   The Rover boys down east; or, The struggle for the Stanhope fortune. (Grosset & Dunlap, 1911).

[G&D]: "Old enemies try again to injure our friends."

339S.16   The Rover boys in the air; or, From college campus to clouds. (Grosset & Dunlap, 1912).

339S.17   The Rover boys in New York; or, Saving their father's honor. (Grosset & Dunlap, 1913).

339S.18   The Rover boys in Alaska; or, Lost in the fields of ice. (Grosset & Dunlap, 1914).

339S.19   The Rover boys in business; or, The search for the missing bonds. (Grosset & Dunlap, 1915).

339S.20   The Rover boys on a tour; or, Last days at Brill College. (Grosset & Dunlap, 1916).

339S.21   The Rover boys at Colby Hall; or, The struggles of the young cadets. (Grosset & Dunlap, 1917).

339S.22   The Rover boys on Snowshoe Island; or, The old lumberman's treasure box. (Grosset & Dunlap, 1918).

339S.23   The Rover boys under canvas; or, The mystery of the wrecked submarine. (Grosset & Dunlap, 1919).

339S.24   The Rover boys on a hunt; or, The mysterious house in the woods.
(Grosset & Dunlap, 1920).

339S.25   The Rover boys in the land of luck; or, Stirring adventures in
the oilfields. (Grosset & Dunlap, 1921).

339S.26   The Rover boys at Big Horn Ranch; or, The cowboys' double round-
up. (Grosset & Dunlap, 1922).

339S.27   The Rover boys at Big Bear Lake; or, The camps of the rival cadets. (Grosset & Dunlap, 1923).

339S.28   The Rover boys shipwrecked; or, A thrilling hunt for pirates'
gold. (Grosset & Dunlap, 1924).

339S.29   The Rover boys on Sunset Trail; or, The old miner's mysterious
message. (Grosset & Dunlap, 1925).

339S.30   The Rover boys winning a fortune; or, Strenuous days afloat and
ashore. (Grosset & Dunlap, 1926).

340S   SILVER LAKE

Volumes: 1
Printed: 1902
Publisher: Street & Smith
Additional information: This was a one-volume series.

340S.1   The young bridge-tender; or, Ralph Nelson's upward struggle.
(Street & Smith, 1902).

    First published as "By pluck alone; or, Ralph Nelson's upward struggle"
    by Harvey Hicks in Good News, Aug. 24-Nov. 16, 1895 (177M).

341S   WINFIELD

Volumes: 2
Publisher: Saalfield Publishing Co.
Additional information: Saalfield also published a two-volume BONEHILL
    series (046S). Both series were reprint series.

341S.1   Larry Barlow's ambition; or, The adventures of a young fireman.
(Saalfield).

    First published as "Brave Larry Barlow; or, The fire fighters of New
    York" by Roy Rockwood in Golden Hours, May 11-July 13, 1901 (216M).

341S.2   A young inventor's pluck; or, The mystery of the Wellington legacy. (Saalfield).

   First published as "Jack the inventor; or, The trials and triumphs of
   a young machinist" by Edward Stratemeyer in The Holiday, April 25-June
   3, 1891 (268M).

OTHER PUBLICATIONS

342N   Bob the photographer; or, A hero in spite of himself.   (A. Wessels,
1902; Stitt, 1905; Chatterton-Peck, ca1907).

   First published as "Camera Bob; or, The thrilling adventures of a travelling photographer" by Edward Stratemeyer in Good News, Oct. 7, 1893-
   Jan. 20, 1894 (262M).

343N   Larry Barlow's ambition; or, The adventures of a young fireman.
(Saalfield, 1902; Caldwell).

   Saalfield edition illustrated by W. H. Fry. First published as "Brave
   Larry Barlow; or, The fire fighters of New York" by Roy Rockwood in
   Golden Hours, May 11-July 13, 1901 (216M).

344N   A young inventor's pluck; or, The mystery of the Wellington legacy. (Saalfield, 1901; Caldwell).

   First published as "Jack the inventor; or, The trials and triumphs of
   a young machinist" by Edward Stratemeyer in The Holiday, April 25-June
   3, 1891 (268M).

Edna Winfield

Like Julia Edwards, Edna Winfield was a Stratemeyer pseudonym used for wom-
en's romances published in weekly story papers and paperback libraries.
One Edna Winfield story was serialized in the New York Weekly in 1896; several others may have been printed in the Chicago Ledger about that time.*
In 1899 six Edna Winfield stories were published in Mershon's paperback
HOLLY LIBRARY and later reprinted as the EDNA WINFIELD series. A seventh
tale was published in Street & Smith's EAGLE LIBRARY in 1898.

MAGAZINE PUBLICATIONS

345M   "Estella, the little Cuban rebel; or, A war correspondent's sweetheart." New York Weekly, vol. 51, nos. 17-28, Feb. 15-May 2, 1896.

---

* Information on the contents of the Chicago Ledger, a weekly story paper,
   is still missing.

Reprinted as The little Cuban rebel; or, A war correspondent's sweetheart, no. 68 in Street & Smith's EAGLE LIBRARY, in 1898 (346P.1X).

346P   EAGLE LIBRARY

Volumes: 1*
Printed: 1898*
Publisher: Street & Smith
Additional information: See Julia Edwards, EAGLE LIBRARY (142PQ).

346P.1X   The little Cuban rebel; or, A war correspondent's sweetheart.
No. 68.   June 13, 1898.

   First published as "Estella, the little Cuban rebel; or, A war correspondent's sweetheart" in the New York Weekly, Feb. 15-May 2, 1896
   (345M).

347S   EDNA WINFIELD

Volumes: 6
Publisher: The Mershon Company
Source of annotations: The Mershon Company advertisements [M]
Additional information: This paperback library reprinted the Edna Winfield
   tities that had appeared in Mershon's paperback HOLLY LIBRARY (348P).
   Although the series description suggests that many Edna Winfield stories
   appeared in the New York Weekly and the Chicago Ledger, only one Edna
   Winfield romance was ever serialized in the Weekly; several stories may
   have been issued in the Ledger.**
Series description [M]: "EDNA WINFIELD is rapidly becoming one of America's
   leading writers of attractive love stories. For years she has contributed series to the New York Weekly, Chicago Ledger, and other household
   journals. This series embraces her best stories, which are all copyrighted and which cannot be had in any other form."

347S.1   The temptations of a great city.*** (Mershon).

   First published as The temptations of a great city; or, The love that
   lived through all, no. 154 in Mershon's HOLLY LIBRARY, in 1899 (348P.1X).
      [M]: "In 'The Temptations of a Great City' Miss Winfield is at her
   best--depicting the haps and mishaps of a poor girl suddenly thrown upon
   her own resources. . . . Its true-to-life scenes are not easily forgotten."

347S.2   The girl from the ranch.*** (Mershon).

   First published as The girl from the ranch; or, The Western girl's rival
   lovers, no. 155 in Mershon's HOLLY LIBRARY, in 1899 (348P.2X).

---

*   Number of volumes and years published apply only to titles published
     under the pseudonym Edna Winfield.
**   Information about the contents of the Chicago Ledger is still missing.
*** Subtitle missing.

[M]: "'The Girl from the Ranch' comes to Chicago to find her fathe
who has been missing for some time. At the time of his disappearance t
parent had with him a large sum of money, and it is naturally supposed
that he has met with foul play. How the mystery is cleared up, and wha
important parts the rivals play, make a story of the deepest interest."

347S.3   An actress' crime.* (Mershon).

First published as An actress' crime; or, All for name and gold, no.
156 in Mershon's HOLLY LIBRARY, in 1899 (348P.3X).
[M]: "'An Actress' Crime' takes the reader behind the footlights
on the stage, among actors, actresses, playwrights, and those who cling
to the skirts of theatrical life. A most unusual crime furnished a plc
as fascinating as it is strong."

347S.4   A struggle for honor.* (Mershon).

First published as A struggle for honor; or, The world against her,
no. 157 in Mershon's HOLLY LIBRARY, in 1899 (348P.4X).
[M]: "Photographs from real life fill the pages of 'A Struggle
for Honor,' pictures of both city and country life. How, for honor's
sake, a woman must suffer and yet be silent, is told in a pathetic man
ner that is sure to touch even the most callous heart."

347S.5   Because of her love for him.* (Mershon).

First published as Because of her love for him; or, The mystery of a
spell, no. 158 in Mershon's HOLLY LIBRARY, in 1899 (348P.5X).
[M]: "'Because of Her Love for Him' is another of Miss Winfield's
inimitable stories of the stage. But here the heroine is a conjurer's
daughter, and we are shown what hypnotism can accomplish, wrecking a
life that seemed destined to be filled with nothing but sunshine. The
a sturdy man from the West proves he has a power superior to that of
the hypnotist, and all ends happily."

347S.6   Lured from home.* (Mershon).

First published as Lured from home; or, Alone in a great city, no. 15¢
in Mershon's HOLLY LIBRARY, in 1899 (348P.6X).
[M]: It is said that 'Lured from Home' is based upon the actual e
periences of a New England girl who drifted to one of our large citie
in search of a fortune. Be that as it may, the tale certainly reads
like a page from real life, with tragedy and comedy intermixed."

348P   HOLLY LIBRARY

Volumes: 6**
Printed: 1899**
Publisher: The Mershon Company
Additional information: The HOLLY LIBRARY was a paperback series which
    began about November, 1898, and was issued weekly for about two month

---

*   Subtitle missing.
**   Number of volumes and years published apply only to titles published
     under the pseudonym Edna Winfield.

then, in early 1899, was published daily for about six months.   In
July 1899, the schedule changed to semi-monthly. The series lasted for
at least 196 numbers; the six Edna Winfield titles were published from
July to September, 1899.
     Except for the cover artwork, the books were published without il-
lustrations.

348P.1X   Temptations of a great city; or, The love that lived through all.
No. 154.   July 3, 1899.

     Reprinted as vol. 1 of the EDNA WINFIELD series* (347S.1).

348P.2X   The girl from the ranch; or, The Western girl's rival lovers.
No. 155.   July 18, 1899.

     Reprinted as vol. 2 of the EDNA WINFIELD series* (347S.2).

348P.3X   An actress' crime; or, All for name and gold. No. 156. Aug. 3,
1899.

     Reprinted as vol. 3 of the EDNA WINFIELD series* (347S.3).

348P.4X   A struggle for honor; or, The world against her. No. 157. Aug.
18, 1899.

     Reprinted as vol. 4 of the EDNA WINFIELD series* (347S.4).

348P.5X   Because of her love for him; or, The mystery of a spell. No.
158. Sept. 3, 1899.

     Reprinted as vol. 5 of the EDNA WINFIELD series* (347S.5).

348P.6X   Lured from home; or, Alone in a great city. No. 159. Sept. 18,
1899.

     Reprinted as vol. 6 of the EDNA WINFIELD series* (347S.6).

Nat Woods

Edward Stratemeyer's first story in the NEW YORK FIVE CENT LIBRARY appeared
in 1892 as by the "author of 'Nat Woods.'" A little more than a year later,
a story by Edward Stratemeyer's brother Louis was published under the same
by-line; stories by other writers were also advertised as by the "author of
'Nat Woods.'"

---

* Subtitle missing.

SERIES PUBLICATIONS

349P   NEW YORK FIVE CENT LIBRARY

Volumes: 1*
Printed: 1892*
Publisher: Street & Smith
Additional information: See Jim Bowie, NEW YORK FIVE CENT LIBRARY (071P).

349P.1X   O'Brien the bunco king; or, Nat Woods' capture of an all-around
crook. No. 2. Aug. 20, 1892.

Captain Young of Yale

Captain Young of Yale was the only Stratemeyer pseudonym credited with only
half a story--or two-sevenths of a story, to be exact. (The pseudonym appeared on the first two installments of a seven part magazine story; the
last five parts were credited to Clarence Young.) Indeed, the oddities in
Captain Young's publishing career did not end there. Although he only appeared for two issues, the magazine's title was changed during that time,
so the first installment was in Young Sports of America, while the second
was in Young People of America.

MAGAZINE PUBLICATIONS

350M   "Quarterback Dan, the football champion; or, Kicking for fame and
fortune." Young Sports of America,** nos. 22-23, Oct. 26-Nov. 3, 1895.

    Story continued under the name Clarence Young in Young People of America
    Nov. 10-Dec. 7, 1895 (352M). Reprinted as "Football Dan; or, Pluck and
    luck" by Clarence Young in Bright Days, Nov. 21, 1896-Jan. 16, 1897
    (351M). Published in book form as By pluck, not luck; or, Dan Granbury'
    struggle to rise by Arthur M. Winfield, for all editions. Published in
    1897 as vol. 11 of W. L. Allison's BOUND TO WIN series (330S.4X); re-
    printed by Allison and later by Donohue as vol. 3 in the BRIGHT AND
    BOLD series (334S.3).

---

*   Number of volumes and years published apply only to titles written by
     Edward Stratemeyer under the pseudonym Nat Woods.
**   Magazine title changed from Young Sports of America to Young People of
     America with the publication of no. 23, Nov. 3, 1895.

Clarence Young

Clarence Young was used as a Stratemeyer pseudonym from 1895 to 1897, and as a Stratemeyer Syndicate house name from 1906 to 1924. The pseudonym made its debut in the last five installments of a story in Young People of America in 1895, as a replacement for Captain Young of Yale. When the story was reprinted in Bright Days in 1896 and 1897, Clarence Young was again listed as author.

The pseudonym did not reappear until 1906, when Cupples & Leon published the MOTOR BOYS, a Stratemeyer Syndicate series. In the next eighteen years, thirty-four books in three Stratemeyer Syndicate series were issued as by Clarence Young: the MOTOR BOYS (1906-1924; 22 vols.), JACK RANGER (1907-1911; 6 vols.), and the RACER BOYS (1912-1914; 6 vols.). Cupples & Leon was the original publisher for all three series; Whitman later reprinted three of the RACER BOYS books (with new titles) as the FRANK AND ANDY series by Vance Barnum (029S).

Howard Garis worked with Edward Stratemeyer on some of the MOTOR BOYS books published under this pseudonym.

MAGAZINE PUBLICATIONS

351M   "Football Dan; or, Pluck, not luck." Bright Days, nos. 17-25, Nov. 21, 1896-Jan. 16, 1897.

First published as "Quarterback Dan, the football champion; or, Kicking for fame and fortune" by Captain Young of Yale (first two installments) (350M) and Clarence Young (last five installments) (352M) in Young Sports of America (first installment) and Young People of America (remaining installments), from Oct. 26-Dec. 7, 1895.*

352M   "Quarterback Dan, the football champion; or, Kicking for fame and fortune." Young People of America, nos. 24-28, Nov. 10-Dec. 7, 1895.*

Last five installments. The first two parts appeared in Young Sports of America (first installment) and Young People of America (second installment), from Oct. 26-Nov. 3, 1895,* with Captain Young of Yale as author (350M). Reprinted as "Football Dan; or, Pluck and luck" by Clarence Young in Bright Days, Nov. 21, 1896-Jan. 16, 1897 (351M). Published in book form as By pluck, not luck; or, Dan Granbury's struggle to rise by Arthur M. Winfield, for all editions. Published in 1897 as vol. 11 of W. L. Allison's BOUND TO WIN series (330S.4X); reprinted by Allison and later by Donohue as vol. 3 in the BRIGHT AND BOLD series (334S.3).

---

* Magazine title changed from Young Sports of America to Young People of America with the publication of no. 23, Nov. 3, 1895.

SERIES PUBLICATIONS

353S   JACK RANGER

Volumes: 6
Printed: 1907-1911
Publisher: Cupples & Leon Company
Illustrator: Charles Nuttall, vols. 1-6
Source of annotations: Cupples & Leon Company advertisements [C&L]

353S.1   Jack Ranger's schooldays; or, The rivals of Washington Hall.
(Cupples & Leon, 1907).

    [C&L]: "You will love Jack Ranger--you simply can't help it. He is
so bright and cheery, so full of fun, so earnest in all he does, so up-
right and honest, so clever in getting the best of his enemies, so
willing to help those who are down, and so real and lifelike. A typical boarding school tale without a dull line in it."

353S.2   Jack Ranger's western trip; or, From boarding school to ranch and
range. (Cupples & Leon, 1908).

    [C&L]: "This volume takes the hero and several of his chums to the
great West. Jack is anxious to clear up the mystery surrounding his
father's disappearance. At the ranch and on the range adventures of
the strenuous sort befall him."

353S.3   Jack Ranger's school victories; or, Track, gridiron and diamond.
(Cupples & Leon, 1908).

    [C&L]: "In this tale Jack gets back to Washington Hall and goes in for
all sorts of school games. There are numerous contests on the athletic
field, and also a great baseball game and a football game, all dear to
a boy's heart. The rivalry is bitter at times, and enemies try to put
Jack 'in a hole' more than once."

353S.4   Jack Ranger's ocean cruise; or, The wreck of the Polly Ann.
(Cupples & Leon, 1909).

    [C&L]: "Here is a tale of the bounding sea, with many stirring adven-
tures. How the ship was wrecked, and Jack was cast away, is told in a
style all boys and girls will find exceedingly interesting."

353S.5   Jack Ranger's gun club; or, From schoolroom to camp and trail.
(Cupples & Leon, 1910).

    [C&L]: "Jack, with his chums, goes in quest of big game. The boys
fall in with a mysterious body of men, and have a terrific slide down
a mountain side."

353S.6   Jack Ranger's treasure box; or, The outing of the schoolboy
yachtsmen. (Cupples & Leon, 1911).

    [C&L]: "This story opens at school, but the scene is quickly shifted to the ocean. The schoolboy yachtsmen visit Porto Rico and other places, and have a long series of adventures, including some on a lonely island of the West Indies. A yachting story all lovers of the sea will wish to peruse."

354S   MOTOR BOYS

Volumes: 22
Printed: 1906-1924
Publisher: Cupples & Leon Company
Illustrator: Charles Nuttall, vols. 1-9
              R. Richards, vols. 10-15
              Walter S. Rogers, vols. 16-17, 22
              R. Emmett Owen, vols. 18-21
Source of annotations: Cupples & Leon advertisements [C&L]
Additional information: Volumes 17 through 22 were advertised as "The MOTOR BOYS--Second Series."   Four of these books (volumes 17 through 21) were first published with titles beginning with the words "Ned, Bob, and Jerry" instead of the traditional "The MOTOR BOYS;" they were later reissued with standard titles.
      The MOTOR BOYS series marked the beginning of Howard Garis's work with the Stratemeyer Syndicate; he contributed to some of the volumes in this series. (His wife, Lillian Garis, assisted with some of the titles in the MOTOR GIRLS series [211S].)
Series description [C&L]: "In 'The Motor Boys Series' Mr. Clarence Young has, at a single bound, placed himself in the front rank of writers for boys and young men. This line of stories is clean, bright, up-to-date, and full of adventure."
      [Advertisement for "Second Series"] [C&L]: "This, the Second Series of the now world famed Motor Boys virtually starts a new series, but retains all the favorite characters introduced in the previous books. The Motor Boys series is the biggest and best selling series of books for boys ever published."

354S.1   The motor boys; or, Chums through thick and thin. (Cupples & Leon, 1906).

      [C&L]: "In this volume is related how the three boys got together and planned to obtain a touring car and make a trip lasting through the summer."

354S.2   The motor boys overland; or, A long trip for fun and fortune. (Cupples & Leon, 1906).

      [C&L]: "With the money won at the great motor cycle race the three boys purchase their touring car and commence their travels. When in the West they hear of the opening up of a new gold diggings and resolve to visit the locality in their car."

354S.3   The motor boys in Mexico; or, The secret of the buried city. (Cupples & Leon, 1906).

      [C&L]: "From our own country the scene is shifted to Mexico, where the motor boys journey in quest of a city said to have been buried centuries ago by an earthquake."

354S.4   The motor boys across the plains; or, The hermit of Lost Lake. (Cupples & Leon, 1907).

    [C&L]: "This is the latest volume in this highly successful series and takes the boys through a variety of adventures. How they found Lost Lake, unraveled the mystery surrounding the lonely hermit who dwelt there, and saved their precious gold mine from falling into the hands of a band of sharpers."

354S.5   The motor boys afloat; or, The stirring cruise of the Dartaway.* (Cupples & Leon, 1908).

    [C&L]: "In this volume the boys take to a motorboat, and have many adventures."

354S.6   The motor boys on the Atlantic; or, The mystery of the lighthouse. (Cupples & Leon, 1908).

    [C&L]: "How the lads foiled the bad men who wanted to wreck a steamer by means of false lights is dramatically related."

354S.7   The motor boys in strange waters; or, Lost in a floating forest. (Cupples & Leon, 1909).

    [C&L]: "Telling of many adventures in the mysterious Everglades of Florida."

354S.8   The motor boys on the Pacific; or, The young derelict hunters. (Cupples & Leon, 1909).

    [C&L]: "The derelict was of great value, and the hunt for it proved full of perils."

354S.9   The motor boys in the clouds; or, A trip for fame and fortune. (Cupples & Leon, 1910).

    [C&L]: "The boys fall in with an inventor and invest in a flying machine. After a number of stirring adventures in the clouds they enter a big race."

354S.10   The motor boys over the Rockies; or, A mystery of the air. (Cupples & Leon, 1911).

    [C&L]: "Here is a story of airship adventures quite out of the ordinary."

354S.11   The motor boys over the ocean; or, A marvelous rescue in mid-air. (Cupples & Leon, 1911).

    [C&L]: "From the mountains the scene is shifted to the broad Atlantic. Once again the dauntless Motor Boys are to the front, in a series of happenings as interesting as they are exciting."

354S.12   The motor boys on the wing; or, Seeking the airship treasure. (Cupples & Leon, 1912).

---

* Subtitle sometimes listed as The cruise of the Dartaway.

354S.13   The motor boys after a fortune; or, The hut on Snake Island. (Cupples & Leon, 1912).

> [C&L]: "Enthusiastic over their success in locating the stolen bank treasure, the Motor Boys hearing of a fortune in radium supposed to be located in the Grand Canyon, start out to seek it, using first an auto, then a motor boat and then in an airship. A truly remarkable story, full of new interest and adventure."

354S.14   The motor boys on the border; or, Sixty nuggets of gold. (Cupples & Leon, 1913).

354S.15   The motor boys under the sea; or, From airship to submarine. (Cupples & Leon, 1914).

354S.16   The motor boys on road and river; or, Racing to save a life. (Cupples & Leon, 1915).

354S.17   Ned, Bob and Jerry at Boxwood Hall; or, The motor boys as freshmen. (Cupples & Leon, 1916).

> Reprinted as The motor boys at Boxwood Hall; or, Ned, Bob and Jerry as freshmen.
> [C&L]: "Fresh from their adventures in their automobile, their motor boat and their airship, the youths are sent to college to complete their interrupted education. Some boys at the institution of learning have heard much about our heroes, and so conclude that the Motor Boys will try to run everything to suit themselves.
> "A plot is formed to keep our heroes entirely in the background and not let them participate in athletics and other contests. How the Motor Boys forged to the front and made warm friends of their rivals makes unusually interesting reading."

354S.18   Ned, Bob and Jerry on a ranch; or, The motor boys among the cowboys. (Cupples & Leon, 1917).

> Reprinted as The motor boys on a ranch; or, Ned, Bob and Jerry among the cowboys.

354S.19   Ned, Bob and Jerry in the army; or, The motor boys as volunteers. (Cupples & Leon, 1918).

> Reprinted as The motor boys in the army; or, Ned, Bob and Jerry as volunteers.

354S.20   Ned, Bob and Jerry on the firing line; or, The motor boys fighting for Uncle Sam. (Cupples & Leon, 1919).

> Reprinted as The motor boys on the firing line; or, Ned, Bob and Jerry fighting for Uncle Sam.

354S.21   Ned, Bob and Jerry bound for home; or, The motor boys on the wrecked troopship. (Cupples & Leon, 1920).

> Reprinted as The motor boys bound for home; or, Ned, Bob and Jerry on the wrecked troopship.

354S.22   The motor boys on Thunder mountain; or, The treasure chest of Blue Rock.* (Cupples & Leon, 1924).

355S   RACER BOYS

Volumes: 6
Printed: 1912-1914
Publisher: Cupples & Leon Company
Illustrator: Walter S. Rogers, vols. 1-6
Source of annotations: Cupples & Leon Company advertisements [C&L]
Additional information: The main characters' names were Frank and Andy
    Racer; the first three volumes were reprinted by G. Sully & Co. and by
    Whitman as the FRANK AND ANDY series by Vance Barnum (029S).
Series description [C&L]: "The announcement of a new series of stories by
    Mr. Clarence Young is always hailed with delight by boys and girls
    throughout the country, and we predict an even greater success for
    these new books, than that now enjoyed by the 'Motor Boys.' The stories
    are in Mr. Young's best vein, full of vim and vigor from start to fin-
    ish, and of a high moral order. They are in the same style that has
    made 'The Motor Boys Series' the most popular young people's line on
    the market."

355S.1   The Racer boys; or, The mystery of the wreck. (Cupples & Leon,
1912).

    Reprinted by G. Sully & Co. in 1921 and later by Whitman, both times
    as Frank and Andy afloat; or, The cave on the island by Vance Barnum,
    vol. 1 of the FRANK AND ANDY series (029S.1).
       [C&L]: "This, the first volume of the new series, tells who the
    Racer Boys were and how they chanced to be out on the ocean in a great
    storm. They rescue another in a wrecked motor-boat and take him to thei
    home only to discover later that the stranger has lost his mind and can-
    not remember who he is or where he comes from. Adventures follow each
    other in rapid succession, and the Racer boys finally solve the mystery
    in a manner that only our author, Mr. Young, can describe."

355S.2   The Racer boys at boarding school; or, Striving for the championship. (Cupples & Leon, 1912).

    Reprinted by G. Sully & Co in 1921 and later by Whitman, both times
    as Frank and Andy at boarding school; or, Rivals for many honors by
    Vance Barnum (029S.2).
       [C&L]: "When the Racer Boys arrived at the school they found every-
    thing at a standstill. The school was going down rapidly and the stu-
    dents lacked ambition and leadership. The lacked even the heart to
    take part in any athletic contests. The Racers took hold with a will,
    and got their father to aid the head of the school financially, and ther
    reorganized the football team. Much to the astonishment of everybody,
    the school won the championship of the league."

355S.3   The Racer boys to the rescue; or, Stirring days in a winter camp.**
(Cupples & Leon, 1912).

---

*   Subtitle sometimes listed as The treasure box of Blue Rock.
**   Subtitle sometimes listed as Stirring adventures in a winter camp.

Reprinted by G. Sully & Co. in 1921 and later by Whitman, both times
as Frank and Andy in a winter camp; or, The young hunters' strange discovery by Vance Barnum, vol. 3 in the FRANK AND ANDY series (029S.3).
    [C&L]: "Here is a story filled with the spirit of good times in
winter--skating, ice-boating and hunting. How the lads went out after
big game, how they stumbled upon a queer trail and made a great discovery, and how they came to the rescue of a crippled boy who was vir-
tually held a prisoner in a wilderness cabin, are related in a manner
to chain the attention of the reader from beginning to end."

355S.4   The Racer boys on the prairies; or, The treasure of Golden Peak.
(Cupples & Leon, 1913).

    [C&L]: "From their boarding school the Racer Boys accept an invitation
to visit a ranch in the West."

355S.5   The Racer boys on guard; or, The rebellion at Riverview Hall.
(Cupples & Leon, 1913).

    [C&L]: "Once more the boys are back at boarding school, where they
have many frolics, and enter more than one athletic contest."

355S.6   The Racer boys forging ahead; or, The rivals of the school league.
(Cupples & Leon, 1914).

    [C&L]: "Once more the Racer Boys go back to Riverview hall, to meet
their many chums as well as several enemies. Athletics play an important part in this volume, and the rivalry is keen from start to finish.
The Racer Boys show what they can do under the most trying circumstances."

Zimmy

Edward Stratemeyer's pseudonyms really did run from A to Z--from Abbott to
Zimmy, to be exact. The pen name Zimmy was used on four "Jack and Jerry"
stories printed in the NEW YORK FIVE CENT LIBRARY in 1893.

SERIES PUBLICATIONS

356P   NEW YORK FIVE CENT LIBRARY

Volumes: 4*
Printed: 1893*
Publisher: Street & Smith
Additional information: See Jim Bowie, NEW YORK FIVE CENT LIBRARY (071P).

---

* Number of volumes and years published apply only to titles written by
   Edward Stratemeyer under the pseudonym Zimmy.

356P.1X   Jack and Jerry, the bicycle wonders; or, Lively times on the wheel. No. 52. Aug. 5, 1893.

356P.2X   Jack and Jerry's spurt; or, The bicycle wonders' ride for life. No. 56. Sept. 2, 1893.

356P.3X   Jack and Jerry's scratch race; or, The bicycle wonders' strange discovery. No. 60. Sept. 30, 1893.

356P.4X   Jack and Jerry's tight squeeze; or, The bicycle wonders' remarkable pluck. No. 64. Nov. 4, 1893.

ADDENDA

Victor Appleton II

023S   TOM SWIFT, JR.

023S.37X   Tom Swift: The war in outer space. (Wanderer, 1981).

Julia Edwards

143aPQ SELECT SERIES

Volumes: 1*
Printed: 1891*
Publisher: Street & Smith
Additional information: The SELECT SERIES was a paperback series which was
    published monthly from August 1889 to February 1890, and weekly from
    March 12, 1890 until at least September 2, 1891 (no. 109). Much of
    its material originally appeared in the New York Weekly.
        Six Julia Edwards stories were published in this series; five
    are thought to be John Coryell's work.

143aPQ.1X Stella Sterling.** No. 91. April 29, 1891.

    Also published as "Stella Sterling; or, A beautiful girl's struggles
    with fate. The most thrilling and pathetic love story ever written,"
    in the New York Weekly, March 21-June 6, 1891 (134MQ).

Harvey Hicks

177aMQ   "Ned Purcell, the boy engineer; or, The hero of the Valley Central."
Good News, vol. 13, nos. 319-331, June 13-Sept. 5, 1896.

---

* Number of volumes and years published apply only to Julia Edwards titles
    originally published in the New York Weekly from 1890 to 1900.
** Subtitle missing.

Roy Eliot Stokes

255aP   OUTDOOR

Volumes: 1*
Publisher: World Syndicate Publishing Co.
Additional information: See Roy Rockwood, OUTDOOR series (233P).

255aP.1X   Andy at Yale.**   (World).

  First published by Sully & Kleinteich in 1914 as <u>Andy</u> <u>at</u> <u>Yale</u>; <u>or</u>, <u>The</u>
  <u>great</u> <u>quadrangle</u> <u>mystery</u>, vol. 1 of the UNIVERSITY series (256S.1).

* Number of volumes applies only to titles written by Edward Stratemeyer
   under the pseudonym Roy Eliot Stokes.
** Subtitle missing.

APPENDIX A

Stratemeyer and Stratemeyer Syndicate Pseudonyms

Pseudonym	Dates used*	Pseudonym	Dates used*
Abbott, Manager Henry	(1895-1896)	Dawson, Elmer A.	(1926-1932)
Adams, Harrison	(1912-1928)	Dixon, Franklin W.	(1927-1981)
Alger, Horatio, Jr.	(1901-1919)	Duncan, Julia K.	(1931-1932)
Allen, Captain Quincy	(1911-1916)		
Alyer, Philip A.	(1895-1896)	Edwards, Julia	(1890-1932)
Appleton, Victor	(1910-1941)	Edison, Theodore	(1895)
Appleton, Victor, II	(1954-1981)	Emerson, Alice B.	(1913-1934)
		Endicott, Ruth Belmore	(1918-1920)
Barnes, Elmer Tracey	(1917)		
Barnum, P. T., Jr.	(1895)	Ferris, James Cody	(1926-1942)
Barnum, Richard	(1915-1922)	Forbes, Graham B.	(1912-1927)
Barnum, Theodore	(1896)	Ford, Albert Lee	(1895-1896)
Barnum, Vance	(1916-1921)		
Bartlett, Philip A.	(1929-1934)	Gordon, Frederick	(1912-1917)
Barton, May Hollis	(1926-1937)		
Beach, Charles Amory	(1918-1920)	Hamilton, Ralph	(1890-1904)
Bell, Emerson	(1893-1906)	Hamilton, Robert W.	(1917-1918)
Bonehill, Captain Ralph	(1895-1912)	Hardy, Alice Dale	(1924-1929)
Bowie, Jim	(1892-1893)	Harkaway, Hal	(1900-1901)
		Harrington, Ralph	(1896-1899)
Carr, Annie Roe	(1916-1937)	Hawley, Mabel C.	(1920-1930)
Carson, Captain James	(1913-1915)	Henderley, Brooks	(1916-1917)
Carter, Nick	(1892-1927)	Henty, D. T.	(1896-1901)
Chadwick, Lester	(1910-1928)	Hicks, Harvey	(1894-1895)
Chapman, Allen	(1896-1933)	Hill, Grace Brooks	(1915-1926)
Charles, Louis	(1896-1900)	Holmes, Thomas K.	(1919-1923)
Cooper, James A.	(1917-1933)	Hope, Laura Lee	(1904-1981)
Cooper, John R.	(1947-1953)	Hunt, Francis	(1935-1937)
Daly, Jim	(1892-1893)	James, Captain Lew	(1892-1893)
Davenport, Spencer	(1916-1918)	Judd, Frances K.	(1934-1980)

---

* From first publication to date of most recent publication, including reprints.

Pseudonym	Dates used*	Pseudonym	Dates used*
Keene, Carolyn	(1930-1981)	Sperry, Raymond, Jr.	(1915-1916)
		Steele, Chester K.	(1911-1930)
Lancer, Jack	(1967-1969)	Stokes, Roy Eliot	(1914-1918)
Locke, Clinton W.	(1931-1934)	Stone, Alan	(1967)
Long, Helen Beecher	(1914-1919)	Stone, Raymond	(1912-1917)
		Stone, Richard H.	(1930-1936)
Mackenzie, Dr. Willard	(1903-1904)	Strayer, E. Ward	(1918)
Marlowe, Amy Bell	(1914-1933)		
Martin, Eugene	(1931-1933)	Thorndyke, Helen Louise	(1923-1963)
Moore, Fenworth	(1931-1937)	Todd, Burbank L.	(1914-1920)
Morrison, Gertrude W.	(1914-1919)		
		Ward, Ed	(1895)
Optic, Oliver	(1899)	Ward, Tom	(1892)
		Warner, Frank A.	(1915-1926)
Pad, Peter	(1893)	Webster, Frank V.	(1909-1938)
Penrose, Margaret	(1908-1930)	West, Jerry	(1953-1979)
Peter	(1895-1896)	Wheeler, Janet D.	(1920-1932)
		White, Ramy Allison	(1920-1931)
Ridley, Nat, Jr.	(1926-1927)	Winfield, Arthur M.	(1892-1926)
Rockwood, Roy	(1895-1978)	Winfield, Edna	(1896-1899)
Roe, Harry Mason	(1929-1930)	Woods, Nat	(1892)
St. Meyer, Ned	(1890-1903)	Young, Captain, of Yale	(1895)
Scott, Dan	(1960-1964)	Young, Clarence	(1895-1924)
Sharpe, Walden F.	(1895)		
Sheldon, Ann	(1962-1981)	Zimmy	(1893)
Speed, Eric	(1975-1978)		

* From first publication to date of most recent publication, including reprints.

APPENDIX B

Chronological List of Stratemeyer and Stratemeyer Syndicate Series Excluding Publishers' Series and Undated Reprint Series

1894

Bound to succeed, 1894–1899 (291S)
Ship and shore, 1894–1900 (301S)

1897

Bound to win, 1897 (047S, 292S, 330S)
Young sportsman's,* 1897?–1902? (065S)

1898

Minute boys, 1898–1899 (298S)
Old Glory, 1898–1901 (299S)
Working upward,* 1898?–1903 (304S)

1899

Flag of freedom, 1899–1902 (056S)
Rover boys, 1899–1926 (339S)

1900

Mexican War, 1900–1902 (060S)
Rise in life, 1900–1912 (011S)
Soldiers of fortune, 1900–1906 (302S)
Young hunters, 1900? (064S)

1901

American boys' biographical series, 1901–1904 (290S)
Colonial, 1901–1906 (293S)
Putnam Hall, 1901–1911 (338S)

1902

Pan-American, 1902–1911 (300S)
Silver Lake, 1902 (340S)
Zero Club, 1902 (066S)

1903

Frontier, 1903–1906 (057S)
Great American industries, 1903 (295S)

1904

Bobbsey twins, 1904–   (183S)
Outdoor, 1904–1905 (061S)

1905

Dave Porter, 1905–1919 (294S)
Deep sea, 1905–1908 (229S)

---

* Contains volumes previously published in other series.

1906

Boy hunters, 1906-1910   (048S)
Boys of business, 1906-1908   (082S)
Boys of pluck,* 1906-1911   (083S)
Great marvel, 1906-1935   (231S)
Motor boys, 1906-1924   (354S)
Railroad (Ralph of the railroad),
   1906-1933**   (088S)

1907

Jack Ranger, 1907-1911   (353S)

1908

Darewell chums, 1908-1911   (085S)
Dorothy Dale, 1908-1924   (210S)
Lakeport,* 1908-1912   (296S)

1909

Mexican War,*** 1909   (297S)
The Webster series, 1909-1915
   (318S)

1910

College sports, 1910-1913   (079S)
Motor girls, 1910-1917   (211S)
Tom Swift, 1910-1941   (021S)

1911

Outdoor chums, 1911-1916   (014S)

1912

Baseball Joe, 1912-1928   (078S)
Boys of Columbia High, 1912-1920
   (150S)
Flag and frontier,* 1912   (055S)
Pioneer boys, 1912-1928   (005SQ)
Racer boys, 1912-1914   (355S)
Tommy Tiptop, 1912-1917   (258S)
Up and doing, 1912   (156S)

1913

Dave Dashaway, 1913-1915   (227S)

1913 (continued)

Fred Fenton athletic series, 1913-
   1915   (086S)
Motion picture chums, 1913-1916
   (018S)
Moving picture boys,* 1913-1922
   (020S)
Outdoor girls, 1913-1933 (187S)
Ruth Fielding, 1913-1934 (145S)
Saddle boys, 1913-1915   (073S)
Speedwell boys, 1913-1915   (235S)
Tom Fairfield, 1913-1915   (090S)

1914

Amy Bell Marlowe's books for girls,
   1914-1933**   (201S)
Back to the soil (Hiram), 1914-1915
   (313S)
Do something (Janice Day), 1914-
   1919   (198S)
Fairview boys,* 1914?-1917   (155S)
Girls of Central High, 1914-1919
   (206S)
Moving picture girls, 1914-1916
   (186S)
University, 1914   (256S)

1915

Bobby Blake, 1915-1926   (317S)
Corner house girls, 1915-1926   (179S)
Kneetime animal stories, 1915-1922
   (026S)
White ribbon boys, 1915-1916   (248S)

1916

Bunny Brown and his sister Sue,
   1916-1931   (184S)
Joe Strong, 1916   (030S)
Nan Sherwood, 1916-1937   (072S)
Rushton boys, 1916   (103S)
Y.M.C.A. boys, 1916-1917   (174S)

1917

Boys' pocket library,* 1917   (084S)
Motion picture comrades, 1917   (024S)

---

*   Contains volumes previously published in other series.
**   Dates include four-in-one reprint volume.
*** Reissued series--previously published with the same series title, but
     with a different publisher.

1918

Air service boys, 1918-1920   (034S)
Carolyn, 1918-1919   (148S)
Dave Fearless,* 1918   (228S)
Six little Bunkers, 1918-1933**
  (188S)

1920

Betty Gordon, 1920-1932   (144S)
Billie Bradley, 1920-1932   (320S)
Four little Blossoms, 1920-1930
  (173S)
Make-believe stories, 1920-1923
  (185S)
Oriole, 1920-1933**   (202S)
Sunny Boy, 1920-1931   (322S)

1921

Frank and Andy,* 1921   (029S)

1922

Radio boys, 1922-1930   (087S)
Radio girls, 1922-1924   (212S)

1923

Honey Bunch, 1923-1955   (311S)

1924

Riddle Club, 1924-1929   (165S)

1925

Blythe girls, 1925-1932   (182S)
Don Sturdy, 1925-1935   (017S)
Flyaways, 1925   (164S)

1926

Barton books for girls, 1926-1937**
Bomba the jungle boy, 1926-1938
  (226S)
Dave Fearless,*** 1926-1927   (228S)
Frank Allen,*** 1926-1927   (151S)
Garry Grayson football stories,
  1926-1932 (105S)

1926

Movie boys,* 1926-1927   (019S)
Nat Ridley rapid fire detective
  stories, 1926-1927   (215S)
X bar X boys, 1926-1942   (149S)

1927

Hardy boys, 1927-   (106S)
Ted Scott flying series, 1927-1943
  (107S)

1929

Bob Chase big game, 1929-1930
  (316S)
Lanky Lawson, 1929-1930   (241S)
Roy Stover, 1929-1934   (031S)

1930

Buck and Larry baseball stories,
  1930-1932   (104S)
Campfire girls,* 1930   (209S)
Nancy Drew mystery stories, 1930-
  (193S)
Slim Tyler air stories, 1930-1936**
  (259S)

1931

Doris Force, 1931-1932   (109S)
Jerry Ford wonder stories, 1931-
  1937**   (204S)
Perry Pierce mystery stories, 1931-
  1934   (197S)
Sky flyers (Randy Starr), 1931-
  1933?   (203S)

1934

Dana girls, 1934-   (192S)
Kay Tracey mystery stories, 1934-
  1942   (191S)

1935

Mary and Jerry mystery stories,
  1935-1937   (189S)

*   Contains volumes previously published in other series.
**   Dates include four-in-one reprint volumes.
*** Contains some volumes previously published in other series, but the
     majority of the volumes are new titles.

1947

Mel Martin baseball stories, 1947–
1953 (101S)

1951

Kay Tracey mystery stories,* 1951–
1953 (191S)

1953

Bomba the jungle boy,* 1953 (226S)
Happy Hollisters, 1953–1970 (319S)

1954

Tom Swift, Jr. 1954–   (023S)

1957

Honey Bunch and Norman,** 1957–1963
(312S)

1960

Bret King mystery stories, 1960–1964
(244S)

1961

Kay Tracey mystery stories,* 1961?–
1964 (191S)

1962

Linda Craig, 1962–1964 (246S)

1967

Christopher Cool/TEEN agent, 1967–
1969 (196S)
Tolliver adventure series, 1967
(257S)

1975

Wynn and Lonny, 1975–1978 (247S)

1977

Nancy Drew picture books, 1977
(194S)

1978

Bomba the jungle boy,* 1978 (226S)
Kay Tracey mystery stories,* 1978
(191S)

1979

Happy Hollisters,* 1979 (319S)

1980

Kay Tracey mystery stories,* 1980
(191S)

1981

Linda Craig,* 1981 (246S)

---

*   Reissued series--previously published with the same series title, but
     with a different publisher.
**   Contains some volumes previously published in other series, but the
     majority of the volumes are new titles.

APPENDIX C

Series Publishers

W. L. ALLISON COMPANY
(Plates acquired by DONOHUE
BROTHERS in 1900)

Bound to win (047S, 292S, 330S)
Bright and bold (334S)
Working upward (304S)
Young hunters (064S)
Young sportsman's (065S)

HENRY ALTEMUS COMPANY

Doris Force (109S)
Perry Pierce mystery stories
(197S)
Sky flyers (Randy Starr) (203S)

AMERICAN NEWS COMPANY

Favorite library (143PQ)

BANTAM BOOKS

Kay Tracey mystery stories (191S)

A. S. BARNES & CO.

Outdoor (061S)

BARSE & HOPKINS
(BREWER, BARSE & HOPKINS to 1910;
BARSE & COMPANY from 1928 to 1931
or 1932)

BARSE & HOPKINS (continued)

Bob Chase big game (316S)
Bobby Blake (317S)
Corner house girls (179S)
Kneetime animal stories (026S)
Lanky Lawson (241S)
Roy Stover (031S)
Sunny Boy (322S)

BEADLE & ADAMS

Half-dime library (232PQ)

BERKLEY PUBLISHING CORPORATION

Kay Tracey mystery stories (191S)

BOOKS, INC.

Kay Tracey mystery stories (191S)
Mel Martin baseball stories (101S)

H. M. CALDWELL COMPANY

Famous books for boys (054P, 336P)

CHATTERTON-PECK COMPANY
(A. L. CHATTERTON COMPANY from
1909; see also THE MERSHON COM-
PANY)

Bobbsey twins (183S)
Flag of freedom (056S)

CHATTERTON-PECK COMPANY (continued)

  Frontier (057S)
  Putnam Hall (338S)
  Railroad (Ralph of the railroad)
    (088S)
  Rise in life (011S)
  Rover boys (339S)

THE CHRISTIAN HERALD

  Do something (Janice Day) (198S)

CUPPLES & LEON

  Barton books for girls (032S)
  Baseball Joe (078S)
  Betty Gordon (144S)
  Billie Bradley (320S)
  Bomba the jungle boy (226S)
  Boy hunters (048S)
  Boys of business (082S)
  Boys of pluck (083S)
  Boys' pocket library (084S)
  College sports (079S)
  Darewell chums (085S)
  Dave Dashaway (227S)
  Dorothy Dale (210S)
  Four little Blossoms (173S)
  Fred Fenton athletic series
    (086S)
  Great marvel (231S)
  Jack Ranger (353S)
  Jerry Ford wonder stories (204S)
  Kay Tracey mystery stories (191S)
  Mel Martin baseball stories
    (101S)
  Motor boys (354S)
  Motor girls (211S)
  Racer boys (355S)
  Radio girls (212S)
  Ruth Fielding (145S)
  Saddle boys (073S)
  Slim Tyler air stories (259S)
  Speedwell boys (235S)
  Tom Fairfield (090S)
  The Webster series (318S)
  White ribbon boys (248S)
  YMCA boys (174S)

DODD, MEAD & CO.

  Carolyn (148S)

DONOHUE BROTHERS
(M. A. DONOHUE & COMPANY from
1901; see also W. L. ALLISON)

  Bobbsey twins (183S)
  Boys' liberty (049P, 331P)
  Boys' prize library (052P)
  Bright and bold (334S)
  Doris Force (109S)
  Land and sea (058P)
  Perry Pierce mystery stories
    (197S)
  Success (089S)
  Working upward (304S)
  Young hunters (064S)
  Young sportsman's (065S)

DOUBLEDAY & COMPANY, INC.
(See also GARDEN CITY BOOKS, GAR-
DEN CITY PUBLISHING COMPANY)

  Happy Hollisters (319S)
  Linda Craig (246S)

ESTES & LAURIAT
(DANA ESTES & CO. from 1898 to
1914; acquired by L. C. PAGE &
CO. in 1914)

  Mexican War (060S)
  Minute boys (298S)

GARDEN CITY BOOKS
(A subsidiary of DOUBLEDAY &
COMPANY, INC.)

  Happy Hollisters (319S)
  Kay Tracey mystery stories (191S)
  Mel Martin baseball stories
    (101S)

GARDEN CITY PUBLISHING COMPANY
(Organized in 1920 as a subsidiary of DOUBLEDAY & COMPANY, INC.)

  Dave Fearless (228S)
  Frank Allen (151S)
  Movie boys (019S)
  Nat Ridley rapid fire detective
    stories (215S)

GOLDSMITH PUBLISHING CO.

  Air service boys (034S)
  Allen Chapman (081S)
  Bobbsey twins (183S)

GOLDSMITH PUBLISHING CO. (continued)

Campfire girls (209S)
Darewell chums (085S)
Do something (Janice Day) (198S)
Doris Force (109S)
Girls of Central High (206S)
Motor girls (211S)
Moving picture girls (186S)
Nan Sherwood (072S)
Outdoor chums (014S)
Perry Pierce mystery stories
  (197S)

GRAHAM & MATLACK
  (C. E. GRAHAM CO. from 1917)

Fairview boys (155S)
Tommy Tiptop (258S)
Up and doing (156S)

GROSSET & DUNLAP

Amy Bell Marlowe's books for
  girls (201S)
Blythe girls (182S)
Bob Chase big game (316S)
Bobbsey twins (183S)
Bobby Blake (317S)
Bomba the jungle boy (226S)
Boys of Columbia High (150S)
Bret King mystery stories (244S)
Buck and Larry baseball stories
  (104S)
Bunny Brown and his sister Sue
  (184S)
Carolyn (148S)
Christopher Cool/TEEN agent
  (196S)
Corner house girls (179S)
Dana girls (192S)
Deep sea (229S)
Do something (Janice Day) (198S)
Don Sturdy (017S)
Enterprise (053P, 230P, 335P)
Flag and frontier (055S)
Flag of freedom (056S)
Flyaways (164S)
Frontier (057S)
Garry Grayson football stories
  (105S)
Girls of Central High (206S)
Happy Hollisters (319S)
Hardy boys (106S)
Honey Bunch (311S)
Honey Bunch and Norman (312S)

GROSSET & DUNLAP (continued)

Make-believe stories (185S)
Mary and Jerry mystery stories
  (189S)
Motion picture chums (018S)
Moving picture boys (020S)
Moving picture girls (186S)
Nancy Drew mystery stories (193S)
Nancy Drew picture books (194S)
Oriole (202S)
Outdoor chums (014S)
Outdoor girls (187S)
Putnam Hall (338S)
Radio boys (087S)
Railroad (Ralph of the railroad)
  (088S)
Riddle Club (165S)
Rise in life (011S)
Rover boys (339S)
Roy Stover (031S)
Sea treasure (234S)
Six little Bunkers (188S)
Sunny Boy (322S)
Ted Scott flying series (107S)
Tom Swift (021S)
Tom Swift, Jr. (023S)
Wynn and Lonny (247S)
X bar X boys (149S)

HEARST'S INTERNATIONAL LIBRARY CO.
  (Organized in 1914; juveniles
  acquired by GEORGE SULLY & COM-
  PANY circa 1918)

Joe Strong (030S)
Rushton boys (103S)

LAMPLIGHT PUBLISHING, INC.

Kay Tracey mystery stories (191S)

LEE AND SHEPARD
  (LOTHROP, LEE & SHEPARD CO. from
  1904, although some titles were
  issued as by LEE AND SHEPARD in
  1905)

American boys' biographical se-
  ries (290S)
The blue and the gray series--
  on land (207S)
Bound to succeed (291S)
Colonial (293S)
Dave Porter (294S)
Great American industries (295S)

LEE AND SHEPARD (continued)

Lakeport (296S)
Mexican War (297S)
Old Glory (299S)
Pan-American (300S)
Ship and shore (301S)
Soldiers of fortune (302S)
Stratemeyer popular series (303S)
Working upward (304S)

DAVID MCKAY

Boys' own library (050P, 332P)

MCLOUGHLIN BROS. (CLOVER BOOKS)

Bomba the jungle boy (226S)
Honey Bunch (311S)

MERRIAM CO.

Bound to succeed (291S)
Ship and shore (301S)

THE MERSHON COMPANY
(Founded from CASWELL PUBLISHING
CO. in 1899; STITT PUBLISHING COM-
PANY handled most series from 1905
to 1906; publications acquired by
CHATTERTON-PECK COMPANY in 1906)

Bobbsey twins (183S)
Edna Winfield (347S)
Flag of freedom (056S)
Frontier (057S)
Holly library (348P)
Putnam Hall (338S)
Railroad (Ralph of the railroad)
  (088S)
Rise in life (011S)
Rover boys (339S)

NEW YORK BOOK CO.

Motion picture comrades (024S)

L. C. PAGE & CO.
(See also ESTES & LAURIAT)

Minute boys (298S)
Pioneer boys (Young pioneers)
  (005SQ)

SAALFIELD PUBLISHING CO.

Adventure (045S)
Air service boys (034S)
Bobbsey twins (183S)
Bonehill (046S)
Do something (Janice Day) (198S)
Four little Blossoms (173S)
Girls of Central High (206S)
Motion picture comrades (024S)
Nan Sherwood (072S)
Popular authors (062P)
Sky flyers (Randy Starr) (203S)
The Webster series (318S)
Winfield (341S)

SIMON & SCHUSTER (WANDERER BOOKS)

Bobbsey twins (183S)
Hardy boys (106S)
Linda Craig (246S)
Nancy Drew mystery stories (193S)
Tom Swift, Jr. (023S)

STITT PUBLISHING COMPANY
(founded 1905; published books
until 1906 or, possibly, 1907;
see also THE MERSHON COMPANY)

Deep sea (229S)
Frontier (057S)
Putnam Hall (338S)
Rise in life (011S)
Rover boys (339S)

STREET & SMITH

Alger series (010P, 289P)
Boys' own library (051P, 333P)
Brave and bold (004PQ, 037P)
Clover series (141PQ)
Eagle library (142PQ, 346P)
Eagle series (142PQ)
Log cabin library (190P)
Magnet library (074P)
Medal library (059P, 337P)
New eagle series (142PQ)
New magnet library (075P)
New York five cent library (071P,
  102P, 208P, 315P, 349P, 356P)
Nick Carter library (076P)
Nick Carter weekly (077P)
Nugget library (243PQ)
Round the world library (063P)
Silver Lake (340S)
Zero Club (066S)

SULLY & KLEINTEICH
(Founded 1913; GEORGE SULLY &
COMPANY from 1918 to 1932; plates
acquired by A. L. BURT COMPANY;
see also HEARST'S INTERNATIONAL
LIBRARY CO.)

Air service boys (034S)
Back to the soil (Hiram) (313S)
Billie Bradley (320S)
Dave Fearless (228S)
Do something (Janice Day) (198S)
Four little Blossoms (173S)
Frank and Andy (029S)
Joe Strong (030S)
Nan Sherwood (072S)
Rushton boys (103S)
University (256S)

WHITMAN PUBLISHING COMPANY

Blythe girls (182S)
Bobbsey twins (183S)
Bobby Blake (317S)
Frank and Andy (029S)
Garry Grayson football stories
  (105S)

WHITMAN PUBLISHING COMPANY (continued)

Great marvel (231S)
Joe Strong (030S)
Outdoor girls (187S)
Rover boys (339S)
Rushton boys (103S)
Tom Swift (021S)

WONDER BOOKS

Bobbsey twins (183S)

WORLD PUBLISHING COMPANY

Tolliver adventure series (257S)

WORLD SYNDICATE PUBLISHING CO.

Air service boys (034S)
Detective library (249P)
Girls of Central High (206S)
Heroine (096P)
Moving picture girls (186S)
Nan Sherwood (072S)
Outdoor (233P)

APPENDIX D

Series Contributors

Note: Information on writers behind the series is scarce, and the list below is incomplete: several writers mentioned probably assisted with Syndicate series other than those listed, while many other writers still remain anonymous.

It should be stressed that except for the Syndicate partners the writers listed below assisted with some titles in the series, but neither plotted nor edited the books. Edward Stratemeyer, and later his daughter and other members of the Stratemeyer Syndicate, created and developed all the series and the individual plots and characters in the books. In addition, Edward Stratemeyer wrote all magazine stories and books published before 1906, as well as all titles published after 1905 under his own name and the pseudonyms Captain Ralph Bonehill and Arthur M. Winfield.

ADAMS, HARRIET*

    Barton books for girls (032S)
    Bobbsey twins (183S)
    Dana girls (all) (192S)
    Hardy boys (106S)
    Honey Bunch (311S)
    Honey Bunch and Norman (312S)
    Linda Craig (246S)
    Nancy Drew (all) (193S)
    Nancy Drew picture books (all) (194S)
    Tom Swift (021S)
    Tom Swift, Jr. (023S)

ALMQUIST, JOHN

    Tom Swift, Jr. (023S)

AXELRAD, NANCY*

    Bobbsey twins (183S)

DOUGHERTY, WILLIAM

    Tom Swift, Jr. (023S)

FOSTER, W. BERT

    Betty Gordon (144S)
    Ruth Fielding (145S)

GARIS, HOWARD

    Baseball Joe (078S)
    Bunny Brown and his sister Sue (184S)
    Great Marvel (231S)
    Motor boys (354S)

---

* Stratemeyer Syndicate partner.

GARIS, HOWARD (continued)

Six little Bunkers (188S)
Tom Swift (021S)

GARIS, LILLIAN

Bobbsey twins (183S)
Dorothy Dale (210S)
Motor girls (211S)
Outdoor girls (187S)

GARIS, ROGER

X bar X boys (149S)

KARIG, WALTER

Doris Force (109S)
X bar X boys (149S)

LAWRENCE, D. L.

Tom Swift, Jr. (023S)

MCFARLANE, LESLIE

Dave Fearless (228S)
Hardy boys (106S)
X bar X boys (149S)

MCKENNA, RICHARD

Tom Swift, Jr. (023S)

MULVEY, THOMAS

Tom Swift, Jr. (023S)

RATHBORNE, ST. GEORGE

Boys of Columbia High (150S)
Frank Allen (151S)
Outdoor chums (014S)
Pioneer boys (005SQ)

SKLAR, RICHARD

Tom Swift, Jr. (023S)

STRATEMEYER, LOUIS CHARLES

Land of fire (095N)

SVENSON, ANDREW*

Bret King mystery stories (244S)
Happy Hollisters (all) (319S)
Hardy boys (106S)
Honey Bunch and Norman (312S)
Tolliver adventure series (257S)
Wynn and Lonny (247S)

---

* Stratemeyer Syndicate partner.

APPENDIX E

Secondary Bibliography

Articles and Books Containing
Information about Edward Stratemeyer
and the Stratemeyer Syndicate

Abbott, Deborah. "Drew and the Hardys: Sleuths for a new age." Sun-Times Book Week [Chicago, Ill.], 8 June 1980, p. 13.

Adams, Harriet [Carolyn Keene]. "Nancy Drew." In The great detectives. Ed. Otto Penzler. Boston: Little, Brown and Company, 1978, pp. 79-86.

Adams, Harriet. "Their success is no mystery." TV Guide, 25 June 1977, pp. 13-14.

"Adams, Harriet S(tratemeyer)." Contemporary authors. Ed. Clare D. Kinsman. 1st revision. Vols. XVII-XX. Detroit: Gale Research Co., 1976.

"Adams, Harriet Stratemeyer." Who's who in America. 40th ed. Vol. I. Chicago: Marquis Who's Who, 1978.

"Age does not dim the glory of the Rover Boys." Literary Digest, 21 April 1928, p. 38.

Allison, Gordon. "Tom Swift quit inventing in '41; His future secret." New York Herald Tribune, 14 April 1946, sec. 2, pp. 1-2.

"Bayport's famous sleuths." The Mystery and Adventure Series Review, No. 4 (Spring, 1981), n.p.

Beckman, Margaret. "Why not the Bobbsey twins?" Library Journal, 15 Nov. 1963, pp. 4612-4613.

Cantwell, Robert. "A sneering laugh with the bases loaded." Sports Illustrated, 23 April, 1962, pp. 66-76.

Cheney, O. A. Letter dated Nov. 11, 1901. Reprinted in Newsboy, 19 (Aug. 1980), 6.

Chenu, Julius R. "The boys of Columbia High." Boys' Book Buff, no. 5, n.p.

_____. "Juvenalia." Yellowback Library, 1, no. 2 (March/April 1981), 12.

_____. "Juvenalia." Yellowback Library, 1, no. 3 (May/June 1981), 16-17.

_____. "The Racer boys series: A Stratemeyer product." Mimeographed paper.

_____. "Winning World War I." Dime Novel Round-Up, 49 (June 1980), 50-51.

Cohen, Sol. "Minority stereotypes in children's literature: The Bobbsey twins 1904-1968." Educational Forum, Nov. 1969, pp. 119-125.

Crandall, Rick. "Early juvenile aviation fiction." Dime Novel Round-Up, 49 (Oct. 1980), 82-86.

"Dates of originals [Hardy boys books] and rewrites." The Mystery and Adventure Series Review, no. 4 (Spring 1981), n.p.

Deane, Paul C. "The persistence of Uncle Tom: An examination of the image of the negro in children's fiction series." Journal of Negro Education, Spring 1968, pp. 140-145.

Deems, Paul. "Tom Swift and the great nostalgia." Boys' Book Collector, 4, no. 1 (1973), 386-392. Reprinted from Air Force Magazine, Aug. 1963.

Dikty, Alan S. The American boys' book series bibliography 1895-1935. Naperville, Ill.: BBC Publications, 1977.

_____. "Boys' books and the times." Two parts. Boys' Book Collector, 1, no. 1 (1969), 11-12; 1, no. 2 (1969), 50-51.

Dizer, John T., Jr. "Boys' books and the American dream." Two parts. Boys' Book Collector, 1, no. 1 (1969), 3-8; 1, no. 2 (1969), 52-55. Reprinted from Dime Novel Round-Up.

_____. "Chronological listing of boys' books by Edward Stratemeyer first published as serials." Dime Novel Round-Up, 44 (Oct. 1975), 118-119.

_____. "Early Stratemeyer writings." Dime Novel Round-Up, 50 (June 1981), 50-60.

_____. "Fortune and the Syndicate." Two parts. Boys' Book Collector, 2, no. 1 (1970), 146-153; 2, no. 2 (1971), 178-186.

_____. "Serials and boys' books by Edward Stratemeyer." Dime Novel Round-Up, 44 (Dec. 1975), 126-148.

_____. "Shopton, home of the Swifts." Two parts. The Tutter Bugle, 1, no. 3 (1 Oct. 1973), 11-12; 1, no. 4 (1 Jan. 1974), 8.

_____. "Stratemeyer and science fiction." Two parts. Dime Novel Round-Up, 44 (15 July 1975), 66-82; 45 (Aug. 1976), 74-90.

_____. "Stratemeyer and the blacks." Dime Novel Round-Up, 44 (Oct. 1975), 90-117.

_____. "Street & Smith Box M58." Dime Novel Round-Up, 46 (Aug. 1977), 78-84.

_____. Tom Swift & company. Jefferson, N. C.: McFarland & Co., 1981.

Dizer, William D., and John T. Dizer, Jr. "Series books: Their influence on children." Two parts. Boys' Book Collector, 1, no. 3 (1970), 68-70; 1, no. 4 (1970), 98-103.

Donelson, Ken. "Censorship and early adolescent literature: Stratemeyer, Mathiews, and Comstock." Dime Novel Round-Up, 47 (Dec. 1978), 119-121.

_____. "Nancy, Tom and assorted friends in the Stratemeyer Syndicate then and now." Children's Literature, 7 (1978), 17-44.

Dunlap, George Terry. The fleeting years: A memoir. New York. Privately printed, 1937.

Enright, John M. "The dust-jacket era, 1927-1961." The Mystery and Adventure Series Review, no. 4 (Spring 1981), n.p.

_____. "Hardy boys tie-ins." The Mystery and Adventure Series Review, no. 4 (Spring 1981), n.p.

Erickson, Byron. "Order of revision [of Hardy boys books]." The Mystery and Adventure Series Review, no. 4 (Spring 1981), n.p.

Fields, Sidney. "Whatever happened to. . . ?" Boys' Book Collector, 4, no. 1 (1973), 393-394. Reprinted from the Daily News, 4 April 1968.

"For it was indeed he." Fortune, April 1934, 86-89.

Foreman, Judy. "The saga of a mysterious author." Newsboy, 19, no. 4 (Nov. 1980), 18-19. Reprinted from The Boston Globe, 3 July 1980.

"Funeral tonight for E. Stratemeyer." New York Times, 12 May 1930, p. 21.

Gardner, Ralph D. Horatio Alger; or, The American hero era. New York: Arco Publishing Co., 1978.

Garis, Roger. "My father was Uncle Wiggily." Saturday Evening Post, 19 Dec. 1964, pp. 64-66.

_____. My father was Uncle Wiggily. New York: McGraw-Hill Book Co., 1966.

Girls series books: A checklist of hardback books published 1900-1975. Minneapolis: Children's Literature Research Collections, Univ. of Minn. Libraries, 1978.

"Grosset sues Simon & Schuster and Stratemeyer for $50-million." Publishers' Weekly, 7 May 1979, p. 25.

Haitch, Richard. "At 83, her pen is far from dry." New York Times, 27 March 1977, sec. 11, p. 19.

"Hardy boys illustrators: Paul Laune." The Mystery and Adventure Series Review, no. 4 (Spring 1981), n.p.

"Harriet Stratemeyer Adams." American women writers from colonial times to the present: A critical reference guide. Ed. Lina Mainiero. Vol. I. New York: Ungar Publishing Co., 1979.

Herz, Peggy. Nancy Drew and the Hardy boys. New York: Scholastic Book Services, 1977.

"Howard Garis, author, is dead; Created 'Uncle Wiggily' series." New York Times, 6 Nov. 1962, p. 33.

Hudson, Harry K. "Biblio addendum/errata." Boys' Book Buff, no. 6, n.p.

_____. "Biblio addendum/errata." Boys' Book Buff, no. 7, n.p.

_____. A bibliography of hard-cover boys' books. Tampa, Fla.: Data Print, 1977.

_____. "Boys' book oddities." Two parts. Boys' Book Collector, 1, no. 2 (1970), 43; 1, no. 4 (1970), 112-113.

_____. "Phantom titles." Boys' Book Buff, no. 3, n.p.

Jennings, Robert. "Bomba the jungle boy." Boys' Book Buff, no. 5, n.p.

_____. "The boys go to war." Boys' Book Buff, no. 2, n.p.

_____. "The Great Marvel series." Boys' Book Buff, no. 7, n.p.

Johnannsen, Albert. The House of Beadle & Adams and its dime and nickel novels: The story of a vanished literature. 3 vols. Norman: University of Oklahoma Press, 1950-1962.

Johnson, Mary Ellen, and Bernadine Chapman. "Nancy Drew collectibles." The Antiques Journal, July 1975, pp. 46-48.

Jones, James P. "Nancy Drew, WASP super girl of the 1930's." Journal of Popular Culture. Spring 1973, pp. 707-717.

_____. "Negro stereotypes in children's literature: The case of Nancy Drew." Journal of Negro Education, Spring 1971, 121-125.

Jordan, Charles J. "So who wrote Poppy Ott and the Pedigreed Pickle?" Yankee, May 1971, 140-145.

Kilgour, Raymond L. Lee and Shepard: Publishers for the people. N.p.: The Shoe String Press, Inc., 1965.

Klemesrud, Judy. "100 books--and not a hippie in them." New York Times, 4 April 1968, p. 52.

Kuskin, Karla. "Nancy Drew and friends." New York Times Book Review, 4 May 1975, pp. 20-21.

Leithead, J. Edward. "Now they're collector's items." Boys' Book Collector, 2, no. 1 (1970), 154-160.

Lindskoog, John and Kay. How to grow a young reader. Elgin, Ill.: David C. Cook Publishing Co., 1978.

Louis, Robert. "Tom loved Mary. . . Remember that?" Boys' Book Collector, 4, no. 1 (1973), 402-403.

MacDonald, J. Frederick. "'The foreigner' in juvenile series fiction." Journal of Popular Culture, Winter 1974, pp. 534-547.

McFarlane, Leslie. Ghost of the Hardy boys. New York: Two Continents, 1976.

Maryles, Daisy. "Venerable young sleuths find new home." Publishers' Weekly, 5 March 1979, p. 18.

Mason, Bobbie Ann. The girl sleuth: A feminist guide. Old Westbury, N.Y., 1975.

Mathiews, Franklin K. "Blowing out the boy's brains." Boys' Book Collector, 1, no. 4 (1970), 106-109. Reprinted from Outlook, 18 Nov. 1914.

May, Roger B. "Durable heroes: Nancy Drew and kin still surmount scrapes--and critics' slurs." Wall Street Journal, 15 Jan. 1975, p. 1.

"Meet Carolyn Keene." Nancy Drew/Hardy Boys Mystery Reporter. [Newsletter of the Official Nancy Drew/Hardy Boys fan club.] 1980.

"The mystery of Nancy Drew." In Murder Ink. Ed. Dilys Winn. New York: Workman Publishing, 1977. Reprinted from Children's Express.

National NOW Times. March 1978, p. 2.

Nye, Russell. The unembarrassed muse: The popular arts in America. New York: The Dial Press, 1970.

Patten, Gilbert. Frank Merriwell's "father:" An autobiography by Gilbert Patten. Ed. Harriet Hinsdale. Norman: University of Oklahoma Press, 1964.

"People." Time, 28 April 1980, p. 85.

Prager, Arthur. "Edward Stratemeyer and his book machine." Saturday Review, 10 Oct. 1971, pp. 15-17.

_____. Rascals at large; or, The clue in the old nostalgia. Garden City: Doubleday & Co., Inc., 1971.

_____. "The secret of Nancy Drew--Pushing forty and going strong. Saturday Review, 25 Jan. 1969, 18-19.

Pother, Dick. "Nancy Drew's back!" Detroit Free Press, 10 Oct. 1975, sec. C, p. 1.

Quinby, Brie. "Nancy Drew, at 50, is still the top bubble gumshoe." Family Weekly, 3 Aug. 1980, p. 15.

Reynolds, Quentin. The fiction factory; or, From pulp row to quality street. New York: Random House, 1955.

Schorr, Jack R. "What makes a juvenile book valuable." Boys' Book Collector, 1, no. 1 (1969), 10.

Science fiction encyclopedia. Ed. Peter Nicholls. Garden City: Doubleday & Co., 1979.

Soderbergh, Peter A. "The Stratemeyer strain: Educators and the juvenile series book, 1900-1973." Journal of Popular Culture, Spring 1974, 864-872.

Sojka, Gregory S. "Going 'From rags to riches' with Baseball Joe; or, A pitcher's progress." Journal of American Culture, 2, no. 1 (1979), 113-121.

Something about the author. Ed. Ann Commire. Vol. I. Detroit: Gale Research, 1971.

Steinbrunner, Chris, and Otto Penzler, eds. Encyclopedia of mystery and detection. New York: McGraw-Hill Book Co., 1976.

"Stratemeyer and S & S call Grosset suit frivolous." Publishers' Weekly, 14 May 1979, p. 124.

"Stratemeyer, author, is dead." Publishers' Weekly, 24 May 1930, p. 2627.

"Stratemeyer, Edward." American authors and books, 1640 to the present day. W. J. Burke and William D. Howett. Rev. by Irving Weiss and Anne Weiss. 3rd rev. ed. New York: Crown Publishers, Inc., 1972.

"Stratemeyer, Edward L." Contemporary authors. Ed. James M. Ethridge Barbara Kopola, and Carolyn Riley. Vols. XIX-XX. Detroit: Gale Research 1968. Also in Contemporary authors--Permanent series.

"Stratemeyer, Edward." Dictionary of American biography. Ed. Dumas Malone. Vol. XVIII. New York: Charles Scribner's Sons, 1936.

"Stratemeyer, Edward." _National cyclopedia of American biography_.
Vol. XVI. New York: James T. White & Company, 1918.

"Stratemeyer, Edward." _National cyclopedia of American biography_.
Vol. XXXII. New York: James T. White & Company, 1945.

"Stratemeyer, Edward." _The readers' encyclopedia of American literature_.
Max J. Herzberg. New York: Thomas Y. Crowell Co., 1962.

"Stratemeyer, Edward." _Who's who in America_. Ed. Albert Nelson Marquis.
Vol. XV. Chicago: The A. N. Marquis Company, 1928.

"Stratemeyer Syndicate properties written by Edward Stratemeyer and
others." _Boys' Book Collector_, 3, no. 4 (1973), 377-378.

Svenson, Andrew E. "Bless you, Tom Swift." _Boys' Book Collector_, 2,
no. 1 (1970), 130-133.

"Swift justice." _Time_, 30 June 1980, p. 71.

Tebbel, John. _A history of book publishing in the United States_. Vols.
II-III. New York: R. R. Bowker, 1975-1978.

"Tom, Jr." _New Yorker_, 20 March 1954, pp. 26-27.

Treloar, Jim. "Jim Treloar and the great search for the lost books of
childhood." _Detroit_ [magazine] in _Detroit Free Press_, 1 May 1966, pp. 28-
32.

Van Devier, Roy B. "Edward Stratemeyer." Two parts. _Dime Novel Round-
Up_, 26 (15 Feb. 1958), 10-12; 26 (15 March 1958), 20-21. Reprinted in
Boys' Book Collector, 1, no. 1 (1969), 21-25.

Walther, Peter C. "Evidence of another Edward Stratemeyer pseudonym."
Dime Novel Round-Up, 49 (April 1980), 41-42.

White, Jane See. "The mystery of Carolyn Keene." _Ann Arbor News_,
19 Feb. 1980.

_____. "Nancy Drew is ageless." _Newsboy_, 18 (April 1980), 13-14.
Reprinted from an Associated Press release 17 Feb. 1980.

Winslow, Kent. "A laughing ghost." _The Mystery and Adventure Series
Review_, no. 4 (Spring 1981), n.p.

Woolworth, Fred. "Capwell Wyckoff--A Hardy author." _The Mystery and
Adventure Series Review_, no. 4 (Spring 1981), n.p.

Ybarra, I. R. "The Hardy boys: A few criticisms of the series and its
background." _The Mystery and Adventure Series Review_, no. 4 (Spring 1981),
n.p.

Yost, Edna. "The fifty cent juveniles." _Publishers' Weekly_, 18 June
1932, pp. 2405-2408.

_____. "Who writes the fifty-cent juveniles?" Publishers' Weekly, 20 May 1933, pp. 1595-1598.

Zbiciak, Randall. "The hows, whys, ifs, ands, buts, of collecting Big Little Books." Boys' Book Buff, no. 4, n.p.

Zuckerman, Ed. "The great Hardy boys whodunit." Rolling Stone, 9 Sept. 1976, 36-40.

Sources Containing Background or Additional Information

The American catalogue [1890-1910]. New York: Office of the Publishers Weekly, 1895-1911.

The American catalogue 1900-1904: Full title entries. New York: Offic of the Publishers' Weekly, 1905.

The annual American catalogue [1894-1897]. New York: Office of the Publishers' Weekly, 1895-1898.

Books in print [1978-1980]. New York: R. R. Bowker Co., 1978-1980.

Bragin Charles. Dime novels bibliography 1860-1928. Brooklyn. Privately printed, 1938.

_____. Dime novels bibliography 1860-1964. Brooklyn. Privately printed, 1964.

"Business notes." Publishers' Weekly, 10 Feb. 1906, p. 672.

Comstock, Anthony. Traps for the young. Ed. Robert Brenner. Cambridge Harvard University Press, Belknap Press, 1967.

Cox, J. Randolph. Bibliographic listing: New Nick Carter Weekly. Supplement to Dime Novel Round-Up, 44 (Dec. 1975).

_____. Bibliographic listing: Nick Carter Library. Supplement Supplement to Dime Novel Round-Up, 43 (15 July 1974).

Cumulative book index: A world list of books in the English language [1928-1972]. New York: H. W. Wilson Co., 1933-1973.

Harvey, Charles M. "The dime novel in American life." Atlantic Monthl July 1907, 37-45.

"The house for juveniles." [Chatterton-Peck advertisement/notice]. Publishers' Weekly, 4 Jan. 1908, p. 34

"The house for juveniles." [Chatterton-Peck announcement]. Publishers Weekly, 7 March 1908, p. 1102.

"Important announcement to the trade." [Grosset & Dunlap advertisement notice]. Publishers' Weekly, 7 March 1908, p. 1108.

LeBlanc, Edward T. Bibliographic listings for the Clover series, Eagle library, Eagle and New Eagle series, Far and Near series, Favorite library, Medal and New Medal library, New York five cent library, New York Weekly, and Select series. Unpublished.

Library of Congress and National Union Catalogue author lists, 1942–1962: A master cumulation. Detroit: Gale Research, 1969.

Library of Congress catalogues: National Union Catalogue [1973–1978]. Washington D. C.: Library of Congress, 1979.

"Lothrop, Lee & Shepard Company may use the name Lothrop." Publishers' Weekly, 14 April 1906, pp. 1172–1173.

"Lothrop, Lee & Shepard's right to the name Lothrop." Publishers' Weekly, 21 April 1906, p. 1219.

Mayo, Chester G. Bibliographic listing: Good News, with further listings of Army and Navy Weekly, Half Holiday, The Boys' Holiday, The Holiday. Dime Novel Round-Up supplement no. 4. Sept. 1960.

The National Union Catalogue: Pre-1956 imprints. London: Mansell, 1968– .

National Union Catalogue: 1956–1967 imprints. Totowa, N. J.: Rowman and Littlefield, 1970–1972.

National Union Catalogue: 1968–1972 imprints. Ann Arbor, Mich.: J. W. Edwards, 1973.

Noel, Mary. Villains Galore. . . The heyday of the popular story weekly. New York: Macmillan Co., 1954.

Pearson, Edmund. Dime novels; or, Following an old trail in popular literature. 1929; rpt. Port Washington, N. Y.: Kennikat Press, 1968.

Rogers, Denis R. "The Edward S. Ellis stories published by the Mershon complex." Three parts. Dime Novel Round-Up, 42 (15 July 1973), 70–76; 42 (15 Aug. 1973), 86–92; 42 (15 Sept. 1973), 104–110.

Steinhauer, Donald L. Bibliographic listing: Golden Days. Supplement to Dime Novel Round-Up, n.d.

"The Stitt Publishing Company." Publishers' Weekly, 28 Jan. 1905, p. 114.

The United States Catalogue: Books in print [1902, 1912, 1928]. Minneapolis: H. W. Wilson Co., 1903–1912; New York: H. W. Wilson Co., 1928.

The United States Catalogue supplement [1902–1905]. Minneapolis: H. W. Wilson Company, 1906.

The United States Catalogue supplement [1912–1924]. New York: H. W. Wilson Company, 1918–1924.

APPENDIX F

Partial List of Libraries with Stratemeyer or
Stratemeyer Syndicate Holdings

Children's Literature Research Collection
University of Minnesota
Minneapolis, Minnesota

   Extensive series book holdings (primarily older series); dime novels
   also.

Cooperative Children's Book Center
Madison, Wisconsin

   Small collection, but representative titles from roughly forty series.

Library of Congress
Washington, D. C.

Margaret Clapp Library
Wellesley College
Wellesley, Massachusetts

   Extensive Stratemeyer and Stratemeyer Syndicate series holdings (most
   series represented, including recent ones).

Russell B. Nye Popular Culture Collection
Michigan State University
East Lansing, Michigan

   Representative titles from twenty-seven pseudonyms; some dime novels.

University of Delaware
Newark, Delaware

   Some boys' series (primarily older series).

University of Missouri
Columbia, Missouri

   Small collection, but representative titles from roughly forty-five
   series.

University of South Florida
Tampa, Florida

   Extensive series book holdings (primarily older series); dime novels
   also.

University of Wyoming
Laramie, Wyoming

   Manuscripts, galleys, and outlines from Andrew Svenson (primarily Happy
   Hollisters and Hardy boys).

ILLUSTRATOR INDEX

MAGAZINE, SERIES, AND SHORT-TITLE INDEX

References are to entry numbers, not page numbers. Magazine titles
are underlined; series titles are in capitals.

Campaign of the jungle, 299S.5

Camping out days at Putnam Hall, 338S.5

Cap'n Abe, storekeeper, 097N

Cap'n Jonah's fortune, 096P.2X, 098N

Captain Bob's secret, 263M-264M

Carl, the juggler and magician, 027M

CAROLYN, 148S

Carolyn
  of the corners, 148S.1
  of the sunny heart, 148S.2
  the factory girl, 115MQ

Cast away in the land of snow, 204S.3

Castaways of the stratosphere, 107S.18

Champions of Putnam Hall, 338S.3

Charlotte Cross and Aunt Deb, 032S.14

CHASE, BOB. See BOB CHASE BIG GAME

Chased across the Pampas, 300S.6

Chet at Harvard, 256S.2

CHRISTOPHER COOL/TEEN AGENT, 196S

Chunky, the happy hippo, 026S.11

Circle of footprints, 192S.6

City beyond the clouds, 231S.7

Clearing his name, 159M, 265M

Cliff Island mystery, 031S.3

Cloak of guilt, 074P.8X, 075P.6X

CLOVER SERIES, 141PQ

Clue in the cobweb, 192S.8

Clue in the crossword cipher, 193S.44

Clue in the crumbling wall, 193S.22

Clue in the diary, 193S.7

Clue in the embers, 106S.35

Clue in the ivy, 192S.14

Clue in the jewel box, 193S.20

Clue in the old album, 193S.24

Clue in the old stagecoach, 193S.37

Clue of the black flower, 192S.18

Clue of the black keys, 193S.28

Clue of the broken blade, 106S.21

Clue of the broken locket, 193S.11

Clue of the dancing puppet, 193S.39

Clue of the hissing serpent, 106S.53

Clue of the leaning chimney, 193S.26

Clue of the rusty key, 192S.11

Clue of the screeching owl, 106S.41

Clue of the tapping heels, 193S.16

Clue of the velvet mask, 193S.30

Clue of the whistling bagpipes, 193S.41

College league mystery, 101S.5

COLLEGE SPORTS, 079S

Collis express robbers, 190P.4X

COLONIAL, 293S

Comfort Magazine, 006M

Comrades in peril, 289P.20X

Comrades of the saddle, 318S.11

Concealed booty, 076P.8X

Confession by mistake, 076P.20X, 077P.10X

COOL, CHRISTOPHER. See CHRISTOPHER COOL/TEEN AGENT

Cool Dan, the sport, 190P.1X

Cool Dan the sport's contest, 190P.5X

Cool Dan the sport's wonderful nerve, 190P.3X

CORNER HOUSE GIRLS, 179S

Corner house girls, 179S.1
  among the gypsies, 179S.10
  at school, 179S.2
  facing the world, 179S.13
  growing up, 179S.7
  in a play, 179S.4
  odd find, 179S.5
  on a houseboat, 179S.9
  on a tour, 179S.6
  on Palm Island, 179S.11
  snowbound, 179S.8
  solve a mystery, 179S.12
  under canvas, 179S.3

Cowboy Dave, 318S.23

CRAIG, LINDA. See LINDA CRAIG

Crazy Bob, the terror of Creede, 190P.2X

Crime at Red Towers, 250N

Crime on the limited, 215S.4

Crimson brier bush, 191S.8

Crisscross shadow, 106S.32

Crooked banister, 193S.48

Cruise of the treasure ship, 229S.2 234S.2, 236N

Curious coronation, 192S.31X

DALE, DOROTHY. See DOROTHY DALE

Dalton gang wiped out, 076P.5X

DANA GIRLS, 192S

Danger on Vampire Trail, 106S.50

Danger trails of the sky, 107S.14

DAREWELL CHUMS, 085S

Darewell chums, 085S.1
  in a winter camp, 085S.5
  in the city, 085S.2, 089S.4
  in the woods, 085S.3
  on a cruise, 085S.4

Daring abduction, 215S.5

Darry the life saver, 318S.16

DASHAWAY, DAVE. See DAVE DASHAWAY

STOVER, ROY. See ROY STOVER
Straight-flush Lou, the man from
    Denver, 190P.8X
Strange echo, 191S.2
Strange message in the parchment,
    193S.54
STRATEMEYER POPULAR SERIES, 303S
Strike for freedom, 075P.2X,
    075P.16X
STRONG, JOE. See JOE STRONG
Struck down at midnight, 215S.16
Struggle for honor, 347S.4, 348P.4X
STURDY, DON. See DON STURDY
SUCCESS, 089S
SUNNY BOY, 322S
Sunny Boy
    and his big dog, 322S.10
    and his cave, 322S.13
    and his games, 322S.6
    and his playmates, 322S.5
    and his schoolmates, 322S.5
    at Rainbow Lake, 322S.14
    at the seashore, 322S.2
    at Willow Farm, 322S.12
    in school and out, 322S.4
    in the big city, 322S.3
    in the country, 322S.1
    in the far West, 322S.7
    in the snow, 322S.11
    on the ocean, 322S.8
    with the circus, 322S.9
Sunset ranch, 201S.8X
Sunshine for Youth, 009M
Superboy, supergirl anthology, 022N,
    108N, 195N
SWIFT, TOM. See TOM SWIFT
SWIFT, TOM, JR. See TOM SWIFT, JR.

Tamba, the tame tiger, 026S.14
Tangled case, 074P.13X, 075P.14X
TED SCOTT FLYING SERIES, 107S
Temptations of a great city, 347S.1,
    348P.1X
Tempted to leave her lover, 135MQ
Testing of Janice Day, 198S.2
That coon Rastus, 214M
They fell in love at the sea-shore,
    136MQ
Thirteenth pearl, 193S.56
$35,000 swindle, 076P.9X
Three girl chums at Laurel Hall,
    032S.2
Three on a vacation, 182S.5
Three ranch boys, 281M
Three young ranchmen, 045S.1X,
    046S.2, 069N

Three-cornered mystery, 192S.4
Thrilling stories for boys, 204S.5X
Through space to Mars, 231S.4
Through the air to Alaska, 107S.12
Through the air to the North Pole,
    231S.1
Tin box mystery, 282M
Tinkle, the trick pony, 026S.9
TIPTOP, TOMMY. See TOMMY TIPTOP
To Alaska for gold, 289P.6X,
    291S.3, 303S.6X
Tobias o' the light, 096P.1X, 100N
TOLLIVER ADVENTURE SERIES, 257S
Tollivers
    and the mystery of Pirate Island,
        257S.2
    and the mystery of the lost pony,
        257S.1
    and the mystery of the old jalopy,
        257S.3
TOM FAIRFIELD, 090S
Tom Fairfield
    at sea, 090S.2
    in camp, 090S.3
Tom Fairfield's
    hunting trip, 090S.5
    pluck and luck, 090S.4
    school days, 090S.1
Tom Fairwood's schooldays, 225M
TOM SWIFT, 021S
Tom Swift
    among the diamond makers, 021S.7
    among the fire fighters, 021S.24
    and his aerial warship, 021S.18
    and his air glider, 021S.12
    and his air scout, 021S.22
    and his airline express, 021S.29
    and his airship, 021S.3
    and his aquatomic tracker, 023S.23
    and his atomic earth blaster,
        023S.5
    and his big dirigible, 021S.33
    and his big tunnel. 021S.19
    and his chest of secrets, 021S.28
    and his cosmotron express,
        023S.32
    and his deep-sea hydrodome,
        023S.11
    and his diving seacopter, 023S.7
    and his Dyna-4 capsule, 023S.31
    and his electric locomotive,
        021S.25
    and his electric rifle, 021S.10
    and his electric runabout,
        021S.5
    and his electronic retroscope,
        023S.14

ABOUT THE COMPILER-EDITOR

DEIDRE A. JOHNSON is a Teaching Associate in the English Department of the University of Minnesota, where she is working toward her doctorate in American Studies.

.